The Cultural History of Goa

From 10000 B.C. to 1352 A.D.

Anant Ramkrishna Sinai Dhume

The Cultural History of Goa
From 10000 BC to 1352 AD

First Edition (1986)
published by Dr. R. A. Dhume

Second Edition (2009)
© Revised by Dr. R. A. Dhume

Edited by:
Dr. Nandakumar Kamat, M.Sc., Ph.D.
Dept. of Botany, Goa University
Taleigao, Goa 403 206
&
Dr. Ramesh Anant S. Dhume, M.D., F.A.M.S.
Kamala-Niwas, Santa Inez
Panaji, Goa 403 001

© Published by

BROADWAY BOOK CENTRE
1st Floor, Ashirwad Bldg., Next to Rizvi Towers,
Near Caculo Island, 18th June Road, Panjim, Goa
Tel: 6647037/38
Website: www.bbcbooks.net
Email: bbcbooks@rediffmail.com

ISBN: 978-81-905716-7-8

Price: Rs. 795/-
$ 25
£ 15

Printed by : Rama Harmalkar 9326102225

TO THE MEMORY OF
MY BELOVED
MOTHER

Anant Ramkrishna Sinai Dhume

(07.09.1911 - 24.05.1997)

C O N T E N T S

PREFACE TO SECOND EDITION

I published the first edition of this book in the year 1986 on the eve of the author's platinum jubilee year. The book was released on November 3, 1986 by Prof. Henry Sholberg, renowned Historian and Librarian of Minnesota University, USA and the function was presided over by Dr. B. Sheik Ali, noted Historian and Vice Chancellor of Goa University. At the same function the author handed over stone carved archeological artifacts described in this book to Dr. P.P. Shirodkar, then Director, Directorate of Archeology and Archeological Museum to be preserved under his custody.

This book was a product of exhaustive work carried out by the author for almost nine consecutive years despite his growing age and deteriorating eye-sight. He was not a professional historian and hence the publishers were reluctant to publish the book. Therefore, I ventured to publish it facing all the hurdles, financial and others, that are ordinarily faced by a naïve person without previous experience in the field. At this juncture, I feel obliged to express my gratitude to Dr. Nandkumar Kamat, who like a shadow, religiously followed the manuscript of the author.

It was our misfortune that the printer with his office in Goa entrusted the printing work to a party in Mumbai, and who, without checking the exhaustive galley proofs prepared by Dr. Nandkumar Kamat printed the book at his own discretion and dumped the copies at my residence.

As expected the book was full of typographical, grammatical and overall printing mistakes, which were quite naturally deplored by experts in the field. My father was downcast. But Dr.Nandkumar Kamat, who had assumed the responsibility of editing the book, once again undertook the arduous task of preparing the corrigendum to rectify the typographical mistakes. The books were by then put on sale but the post-factum efforts were not as fruitful as expected.

There is a saying in Marathi "*neendakache ghar asave shezari*" meaning the critic's house should be in your neighborhood. As such this book was extensively criticized and well scrutinized at different levels by experts in the field of the history of Goa.

To quote Dr. Teotonio R.D. Souza S.J., the then Director, Xavier Centre of Historical Research, in bitter comments published by him in a newsletter of the International Seminar on Indo-Portuguese history, Vol. 8 No. 2, December 1986, pointed out the presence of a large number of misprints, and also criticized the organization of the bibliography and called for a serious debate amongst more knowledgeable scholars in the field to scrutinize the data published in the book.

B.D. Satoskar published his views in the 'Gomantak' newspaper's Diwali issue of 1987 challenging the Sumerian connections with Goa because the evidence provided by the author was too slender to draw the inferences made in the book. However, he opined in the same article that if in future concrete and corroborative evidence comes to light to confirm the facts expressed in this book, the credit should go to the author as being the first person to discover the Sumerian connections with Goa.

On other hand, Dr. H.D. Sankalia, a renowned historian in the ancient history of Mesopotamia that includes Sumer (present Iraq) and a scholar of Paleography (Cuneiform Script), while reviewing the book in his article "Once Upon a Goa" published in "Sunday Review" of November 15, 1987 remarked on the issue raised by the author on the connection of the Indus valley civilization to Goa and that this work was an important pointer for scholars in this field to do further research in this direction.

Further, Dr. Sankalia during his inaugural speech given at the Indian Congress History held in Goa made laudable references to this book that covers a span from the genesis of the land of Goa till the medieval period and the cultural impact on contemporary Goan society through the ages.

Among other comments that appeared in different publications, I quote the views of Mr. Carmo D'souza on "Dhume's Goa" published in 'The Gomatak Times' of August 19, 1990. He says, "Dhume has decided to deal with the book not as a mere piece of history, though history too it is. Rather the book is like a route of discovery to the cultural Goa... History is often controversial, several historians approaching the same evidence and reaching to different conclusions. History does make mistakes and accepts their rectification too. It is the approach and methodology used that one should appreciate in the writing of history which Dhume certainly has".

At this juncture, I draw the attention of readers to the news item published in the local daily 'The Navhind times' dated September 29, 1986 titled 'Pre-historic Temple Discovered'. It reported: "A pre-historic temple and rock paintings have been discovered during excavation work by the State Department of Archaeology and Museum at the place named Edithannaru in Medak district of Andhra Pradesh. The Director of department Dr. V.V. Krishnasastry told PTI that a 6-inch idol found in the temple resembled the figure of "Gudea" a deity of the people of the ancient Assyrian civilization in the Middle East. The interesting parallel could well explain the origin of the word "Gudi" meaning temple in Telugu from "Gudea" of the Assyrian Culture, Dr. Krishnasastry said.

I request the readers of this book to go through the pages of the fourth chapter, 'Advent of Sumerians in Goa' where one finds the description of maritime traffic of the Sumerians on the East coast of India during the reign of king Sargon I and his successor Gudea. The latter was worshiped as God and had temples constructed at different places at Sumer as well as at the places that he visited. Obviously one of the ports of entry was Gowba, the contemporary Goa put forward by the author of this book.

While analyzing these events one should be cautious of the fact that history was often distorted by the rulers or embellished by religious bodies for their own ulterior motives. Further, there is a saying in Portuguese "*Quem Conta acrescenta*" meaning "the one who narrates adds to it (his own)".

With this in mind, I put before you an episode, rather a discovery, made by the author. He was carefully scrutinizing a photograph published on the front page of the daily newspaper 'Gomantak' depicting the 'Bhavani talwar' (sword) of Shivaji, the founder and king of the Maratha Empire. The sword was brought from the British museum back to Mumbai after special efforts made by the then chief Minister of Maharashtra, Mr. A.R. Antulay. It was believed that the sword was offered to Shivaji by his deity Bhavani.

My father, while scrutinizing the picture of the sword noticed some engraved letters in Roman Script. He requested me to examine carefully whether indeed there were Roman letters engraved on the sword. I could see some scattered letters in the Roman script partially effaced. I could read the first word "CONDE" and then another one "XYVAJY". The other letters were fuzzy. The author immediately contacted Gajanan Ghantkar, then archivist of the Historical Archives of Goa. He confirmed the wording and read the sentence as "CONDE TAVARES OFFERECE XYVAJY"... The last word was indistinct but likely to be "ESPADA" (sword), he said. The meaning of the sentence was "Count Tavares offers (the Sword) to Shivaji". My father immediately contacted Dr. V.T, Gune then Director of Archeology in Goa, who reluctantly received this information from my father. We do not know what further developments took place. But the fact is that a grand function organized to celebrate the return of the "Bhavani talwar" was abruptly announced as cancelled without any plausible explanation.

The details of this event were reported by me in the daily 'Gomantak' dated January 19, 2006. In this issue I made reference with appreciation to the statement made by Babasaheb (Balwantrao) Purandare, a renowned historian of the period and Shivaji's biographer, during the closing ceremony of the function held in December 2002 in honour of Shivaji at Farmagudi, Goa. He said, "The relationship between Maharashtra and Goa is very old dating back to centuries. The sword that Shivaji got with the blessing of Deity Bhavani was in fact manufactured in Goa! The caliber of an efficient Historian reflects on his ability and readiness to accept new evidence that might come to the surface and rectify the previous historical data after carefully scrutinizing the new evidence.

The author had a huge collection of multidisciplinary books not only on ancient, medieval and contemporary history but also on mathematics, trigonometry, archeology, astrology, astronomy, geology, ancient and modern world maps, law, sociology, Indian mythology, dictionaries related to various Indian regional languages as well as foreign languages. He donated his entire collection of about 730 books to Goa University in the year 1992. These books are available to scholars for their ready reference at the University Library.

The author of the book Anant Ramkrishna Sinai Dhume, passed away on May 24,

1997 at the age of 85 years. He desired to publish the second edition of the book and for that purpose he made alternations and corrections with the help of his adept pupil Dr. Nandkumar Kamat.

The first edition of the book went out of print within five years or so. The book was considered as a reference book for school going children, graduates, as well as for post-graduate studies approved by the Goa Education Board and Goa University. I am glad to mention here that the paleographic data such as the one found at Usgalimol and archeological findings mentioned in this book have served as an important clue to many scholars to move further and study details of rock carvings and engravings found around the places indicated in this book.

This book was extensively referred to by various scholars in the field. To quote a few, Romesh Bhandari, former Governor of Goa, in his book "Goa" (1999) made references to the author's work on the tribes of pre-historic Goa as also on the impact of the Sumerian influence on Goan cultural traditions. Manohar Malgonkar, the well-known writer, in his book "Inside Goa" (2004) made laudable reference to the then 24 year old author who discovered the Mahadev temple in the deep forests of Tambde Surla, till then a monument unknown to Goan historians.

Recently Luis de Assis Correia covered Goa's History in his book "Goa Through the Mists of History from 10000 BC–AD 1958" (2006). In the first part of his book (10000 BC-AD 1510) he meticulously followed chapter wise the evolution of settlements and their cultural impact as described in the first edition of this book and presented the data in a"nutshell" in a fluent and enjoyable style.

In the first edition, the author had intentionally omitted the last mute letter "m" (e.g. "Sangue" in place of "Sanguem") because the English educated reader pronounces it in a different way. For example Sanguem is read as "San-gu-e-am" and Pernem as "Per-ne-am". Further, the original Konkani village name "Diuchal" was changed in Marathi to "Di-cho-lee" written in Portuguese as Bicholim ("li" nasal, "m" mute). This was read by English educated non–Konkani readers as "By-kho-lee-am"). Therefore in this edition, care has been taken to print in italics the names of the places pronounced in the local dialect along with the original cartographic village names in regular roman.

Now the main task was to rectify the mistakes detected in the previous edition taking into consideration alterations suggested by the author to me so many years ago which I did without altering the basic content of the book. I am glad that once again Dr. Nandkumar Kamat accepted the job of correcting and giving the final touch to this book.

I am thankful to Prajal Sakhardande, Lecturer at Dhempe College of Arts and Science and a promising historian of Goa for going through the corrections made by me. I am also thankful to Prof. Dr. Dilip Loundo, Brazilian Chair of Goa University,

X

who has gladly accepted the task of checking and putting in order as per the standard norms the references quoted by the author in this book.

If readers find that this second edition adequately presented, the credit goes to these three experts who have helped me in this venture, more so to pay homage to the memory of my father. The faults, if any, are entirely mine. But I am aware that the soul of my father will certainly condone me, conscious of my limitations in this field.

I have to express here my gratitude to Manohar Shetty for giving his "finishing touch" in editing and proof reading this manuscript.

I am deeply indebted to Ajit M. Gude for rendering all the help to prepare this final computerized manuscript and making it ready for publication.

Ramesh Anant Sinai Dhume

June 23, 2008

ACKNOWLEDGEMENT

A book of this kind causes a great strain on the goodwill, time and material of several friends and relatives who have ungrudgingly obliged me in accomplishing this work.

I am deeply indebted to the late Sarvashree Sadassiva S. Bhatikar and late Shri Padmakar Bhatt Savaikar who got me interested in the cultural history of Goa. I am also grateful to Shri Vidhyadhar G. Shilkar and Shri Sadanand P. Savaikar who helped me in site searching at Savai-Verem.

I wish to express my gratitude to Dr. Vishwanath G. Dhume, Professor of Goa Medical College, for taking keen interest and devoting his time in correcting the manuscript.

I also wish to record my thanks to Dr. P. P. Shirodkar, Director, Shri V. R. Mitragotri, Assistant Superintending Archaeologist, Shri V. M. Naik, Technical Officer and Nayan V. Nailk, photographer of the Directorate of Archives and Archaeological Museum, for having visited the sites indicated by me and shooting the relevant pictures.

I am grateful to Shri Nandakumar M. Kamat, the young researcher of Goa's history, for his help in correcting the manuscript and galley proofs of this book.

I am indebted to Mrs. Archana Kakodkar, Assistant Librarian, Centre of Post Graduate Instruction and Research (University of Bombay), Panaji, Goa for compiling the index.

I would also like to thank Shri Arvind P. Nadkarni, who helped in the printing of this book.

Author

Kamala Niwas
Santa Inez, Panaji-Goa 403 001
Anantchaturdashi, September 27, 1985

PREFACE TO FIRST EDITION

The history of Goa is a fascinating subject. It touches the realm of ideas at more points than almost any other study. It relates to all periods of Goa's past, whether ancient, medieval or modern. Whereas the medieval and modern periods have attracted the sufficient notice of scholars, the ancient and, in particular, the pre-historic and proto-historic period has remained practically unexplored. This is because of the paucity of relevant material. It needs great intellectual skill to piece together the scanty archaeological, anthropological, epigraphical and literary evidence to reconstruct the growth of man's mind during this period. It requires planned effort, great ingenuity and sustained interest together with psychological insight to weave an intelligent account from the confused and hazy happenings of the distant past. More than the discovery of new facts, the problem of interpretation of these facts offer a challenging job. To grasp the relationships at work beneath conflicting forces and unearth the real issues that helped society evolve a pattern of its own is more difficult for a historian of ancient period than one of the medieval or modern period, who depicts a scene, narrates a war or delineates the picturesque character of a group or people. Realising the importance of any historical writing on ancient Goa, I readily agreed to contribute a short preface to this creative piece of work.

I am not competent to assess or comment upon the veracity of the massive new information brought out in this work. What I am most impressed is the zeal with which the scholar has dedicated his whole life to the pursuit of historical knowledge, the honesty and ingenuity with which he has handled his complex material, the vast span of time he has covered and the emphasis he has laid on geographical, sociological, political, cultural and economic aspects of the life of the people. He has traced the events from the murky coast of the Neolithic Age to the brighter period of the Middle Ages when a civilized and centralised authority in the form of the Vijayanagar Empire took control of the situation. The life and conditions of the numerous pastoral groups, their struggle to survive in the midst of hash surroundings, the cyclones and the oppressively hostile elements of nature, the migration of tribes to safer places, the emergence of a rudimentary type of agriculture, the advent of the Aryans, the formation of kingdoms in Goa, the rise and fall of the several dynasties whether Satavahana or Chalukya or Rashtrakuta or Kadamba, have all been delineated in an exhaustive way. But political history is not the soul and essence of man's life, and the author has done well to delve deep into the cultural ethos of the people. The nerve-racking drama of man's struggle and march across the centuries from the stage when he was ignorant of fire to an orderly state of society, which we call civilization, is the main thrust of this work, as applied to the conditions that existed in Goa For this reason the scholar deserves the highest approbation, as this study is the life-work of a dedicated soul who believes in history as saints believe in God. I am particularly thankful to him for the privilege and the honour he has done to me in asking me to write a preface to his magnum opus.

B. Sheik Ali
(Vice-Chancellor)

Goa University
May 26, 1986

XIV

INTRODUCTION

This book is proof of how a person is impelled by destiny to produce a work covering twelve thousand years of life of a land and its people. Some people may be sceptical of my view which advocates determinism, but there is no other way to justify my finds which completely alter what has been told by eminent German as well as English geologists about the formation of the land of Goa. The advent of the Sumerians around 2,000 B.C. and their settlement in Goa has also not been discovered so far by any writers on the history of Goa. "Against facts, no arguments" is a Portuguese saying. The following narration about my wanderings may convince the sceptical reader.

In the year 1932 (I was then 20 years old), I was invited to accompany my youngest sister, just married, to her village Bhati at Sanguem taluka. Bhati is a forest village of Astagrahar division of Sanguem taluka. When I visited it, it was like entering a new world as all the other villages I had visited were well populated. My native place, Cumbharjuvem village in Tiswadi taluka, had about 5,000 souls, and the people were bound together not by mutual love, but only by business interests. Here in Bhati, I noticed mutual love. There were twelve hamlets but the population was sparse. A hamlet at that time had about 70 souls, and each hamlet comprised two houses or more but never more than 25 houses. The people were somewhat lethargic perhaps due to the climate and the spread of malaria, but always lived in peace.

Under the direction of Shri Sadashiv (alias Namibab) Bhatikar, father-in-law of my sister, and with the help of a guide and servants, I visited many places such as the tomb (samadhi) of Karana Siddha, a place named "*Killyant*" of the Having Brahmins where two tombs and a well were situated. I also visited the temples of Curdi and Naiquinim villages. When he was free from his work, Namibab took me to a place named "*Holiemola*" situated in Talauli village. This place was plain land with a water-spring flowing even in the month of April, irrigating a small sugarcane field. At a short distance from the spring, he showed me four remnants of the huts of tribes known as Shabaras. The Holiemola is about one kilometre long and about four hundred metres wide. Bordering it at one side there is a huge mountain with a plain plateau on top named "*Ranamandala*". Namibab told me that according to traditional history, it was the place where the battle between Shri Krishna and Jarasandha took place, and that it is said that near that place there is a cave where Kalayavana was killed by Muchukunda. Namibab informed me that it was not known for how many centuries the remnants of those four huts existed, but he said, nobody touches the stones found there, because of a belief that tragedy will befall such a person. He told me about the history of different settlements of all the areas of Astagrahar and it was he who aroused in me my curiosity over the history of settlements in Goa. He taught me to take note of ancient relics of all kinds. Thus a new field of history opened before me.

In June 1932, I was appointed as professor of the Science Section of the Lyceum in Almeida College at Ponda town. There I visited the place known as Mardangad. On the road, near Vadi village, I saw a big idol which is now named "Naga-Devata" and is kept in Panaji Museum. I also climbed the Siddhanath mountain, visited the temple of Siddhanath, and all other temples situated around Ponda, attended the festivals and observed the special rites and rituals.

In 1933, I joined the Directorate of Land Survey which gave me the unique opportunity to wander around and collect what I wanted to expand my knowledge of the cultural history of Goa. In 1933, I was appointed as Ancillary Technician of the Brigade for construction of roads. I drew the layout of the road connecting Molem to the boundary of Sattari taluka. It was necessary to construct a bridge on the river 'Ragado' and for this purpose, I had to select a suitable place. And so, I crossed the river and came to Surla village where I was told that a temple constructed entirely of black stone existed there. I visited it with the help of a guide and while returning, the guide showed me a stone inscription with characteristics of the Kanadi style. I visited the temple again for the second time in about 1955, while preparing the plan of a mining lease. But I had no time to revisit the site of the inscription. In 1976, I had the opportunity to go to Surla again, but this time nobody in the village could show me the stone inscription.

From 1942 to 1944, I was appointed the head of a cadastral survey batch of Sattari taluka. There, in 1943, a surveyor named Ganaba Kantak was appointed by me to prepare a cadastral survey map of Surla village. In the month of March, 1943, he found a fossilized marine conch by chance. When I visited the place, he pointed out the place from where it had been recovered. I calculated its altitude to be about 600 metres. This was clear proof that the area had emerged along with the Sahyadri Range due to the upheaval caused by tectonic movement. This was the first find in respect of the history of the formation of the land of Goa.

In 1950, I went to Savoi-Verem of Ponda taluka to prepare a plan for the partition of a paddy field. Shri Padmakar Bhatt Savaikar who was in charge of the field as one of the parties, took me to the slope of a hill situated in the same village and showed me a carved rock-cave. The speciality of this cave was that the inner chamber had an entrance in the form of a square hole of one metre dimension. It was a rare carving—like the mouth of a womb, a genuine "garbhakuda". It was a representative form of Sumerian type carving. While in search of the carved rock-cave, I visited by sheer chance a place named "Barazan" in the village where I found two signs carved on black rock—two parallel lines on top, and a cross parallelogram at one side, both being Sumerian signs and meaning "Dwadasha Gana" or say "Barazan" in the local language.

In 1959, I had occasion to visit a place named Silvado, situated in the same village (Savoi-Verem) as an expert appointed by one of the party opponent of Shri Padmakar

Bhatt, Savaikar. There was also another expert with us, namely Shri Shripad R. S. Adwalpalkar. On the way to the property, Shri Savoikar showed me an idol which he had discovered of whitish black stone of exquisite style. It was in the form of a human figure except the legs which were like those of an eagle, and there was a fish in three pieces. The idol had no hair, moustache or beard, the forehead was small, the eyes broad and round, nose straight, ears relatively large but natural in form and the mouth showing four teeth in each jaw in a closed position. The arms were folded with the fingers resting on the chest. The legs were folded in the knees as usual and spread to lend stability and necessary form for the terminal of the fish. The idol was about 70 cms in height. The three of us could not identify it with any Hindu diety, but while going through some literature in the year 1972, I identified it with God Anu of Sumer! Shri Savaikar had found it in a tank situated in the same property named "Sil-cum-Inam". On the way, he pointed out a niche named "*Mhatari*", meaning "an old woman". I noticed there a black rock with a small linga, with a carved line at the top symbolizing a "vulva". From that time my thoughts were focussed on Sumerian history and also on the settlement of the pastoral tribe in the land of Goa.

In 1968, I retired from service, and intensified my study on the cultural history of Goa. I revisited the earlier sites. I visited the rock-cave temples of Surla of Bicholim taluka, the house of Desai of Priol, the temple of Shri Parashurama at Poiguinim in Canacona taluka, and many other places in Goa.

Around 1971, while resurveying a boundary at Rivem village of Sattari taluka, I found a piece of mud with the petrified roots of a tree.

In 1976, while excavating an area at Naneli of Sattari taluka, some idols and a Viragal (hero-stone) were found. An oblong flat stone planted vertically and named "*Sati*" was found on the bank of a rivulet. I picked up all these finds for my study.

At the same time, Shri Anant Purushottam Khadilker, a primary teacher, while digging ditches for an areca garden, found in Brahma-Karmali of Sattari taluka, three pieces of mud with petrified roots of trees at a depth of approximately one metre. Similarly, Sou. Nalinidevi Baburau Desai of Thane of Sattari taluka found at a depth of about one metre, a scimitar—a long Turkish type dagger—the core of basaltic schist, while digging a ditch for another areca garden. These specimens are at present with me.

During my 35 years of service in Land Survey, I visited about three-fourths of the area of Goa, and half of it on foot. So, I had many opportunities to see objects of antiquity. I found in Zarmem village, Sattari taluka, stones like the menhir in Cornwall and an oval slab of basalt schist with a carving of a female figure—an image of Brahmadeva in worship—at Karambolim-Brahma village of Sattari taluka, the Mahamaya temple of Nundem village in Astagrahar division of Sanguem taluka, Mallicarjun at Shristhal at Canacona (*Kankon*) village with many other images of

Purushas around that temple, and many more in the New Conquest talukas. All this material was stored in the depths of my mind over the years. With this material and more collected from books on geology and histories on the antiquity of India, Sumer, South-East Asia and South America, some brought from abroad, and photographs obtained from the Archaeological Museum of Iraq, I have tried my best to identify, classify and collect my finds and write the following chapters. It may be said that I had cinematized the history on the screen of my mind from 1932 to 1982, a period of 50 years, like a satellite revolving round the earth and taking long-distance photographs. If readers discover in this book something new and are convinced by my views, I would feel that my efforts have been rewarded.

Anant Ramkrishna Sinai Dhume

MAP
OF
GOA

showing location
of villages referred
to in this book.

SCALE 1:375.000

Legend
Road
Taluka boundary
District ,,
Railway line

Chapter - 1
GENESIS OF THE LAND OF GOA

In this study I shall consider the land of Goa as defined politically. However, this does not mean that the geology, ethnography, natural resources, cultural and even socio-economic evolution in general, and ancient ruling dynasties are exclusive to of the land of Goa. On the contrary, the land of Goa, in all aspects, is more or less similar to the adjacent coastal land of India, generally known as the Malabar Coast, and sometimes divided into two zones, namely Konkan and the Malabar Coast proper.

GOA : A BRIEF GEOGRAPHICAL DESCRIPTION

Goa Territory lies between 15º 48' 00" N and 15º 53' 54" N latitude and 74º 20' 13" E Gr. and 73º 40' 33" E. Gr. longitude with an area of about 3701 square kilometres. In the North, Goa shares its boundary with the Sawantwadi taluka of Sindhudurg district and Kolhapur district of Maharashtra State. The mouth of the Tiracol, alias *Terekhol,* river lies within Goa and includes the Tiracol Fort across the mouth. The riverside boundary of the Tiracol river stretches eastwards to a distance of 26.6 kilometres and is shared by the Sindhudurg district. Onwards, the land boundary extends continuously to a length of 136.3 kilometres to the East and South and is shared by the Kolhapur district of Maharashtra State and Belgaum, Dharwad and North Kanara districts of Karnataka state. Here several stretches are in accord with the natural features of the Sahyadrian watershade. On the West, the Arabian Sea boundary extends to 132.9 kilometres from the Tiracol Fort to the southern extremity of the peak, 111.8 metres in height, just West of Polem on the Goa-Sadasivgad road. In the sea-waters float the islands of St. George, Morcego and Anjediva.

The population census of Goa Territory furnishes the following figures (in Lakhs): Year 1921:4.65; 1961:5.90; 1971:7.95; and 1981:10.02. So, the population has doubled over a period of sixty years-1921 to 81. Comparing the two consecutive periods of ten years (i.e. 1961-71 and 1971-81), the ratio of the increase of population in Portuguese times is lower than that of the later periods.

GEOHISTORICAL PANORAMA

The legend of Parashurama

The sacred Hindu Sanskrit poetic composition 'Skanda Purana' (Sahyadri khanda, sub-division) and 'Keralotpatti', as well as the epics Ramayana, Mahabharata and the Bhagavatapurana refer to the Shree Parshurama episode. Summarizing the episode, the first two Puranas narrate that "After conquering lands from the Kshatriyas, Shree Parashurama celebrated his victory by performing Ashvamedh Yajna. The sage Kashapa was his high-priest, and after ending the rituals, Shree Parashurama gifted all the conquered land to the high-priest Kashyapa.

"Kashyapa, the high-priest, was of the opinion that the land, for maintenance of peace and order, needed to be governed by the Kshatriyas. Despite 21 raids of Shree Parashurama, some Kshatriyas had succeeded in escaping the raids, living in forests and hills, and they would not come back unless they had total reassurance that Shree Parashurama would leave the land forever and never set foot in the area again. Therefore, Kashyapa made the observation to Shree Parashurama that since the latter had gifted the land, he had lost the right to reside there and so he should go away forthwith. Shree Parashurama let fly seven arrows over the waters and ordered the sea to roll back and release that much land. After him, this strip of land (extending from the Vaitarana river to the south up to Kanya Kumari) was named 'Parashurama Kshetra' in the Puranas."

There are many places in this area bounded on the East by the Sahyadri dedicated to the worship of Shree Parashurama. In Goa, there is a shrine dedicated to him in Poinguinim (*Paingin*) village, Canacona (*Kankon*) taluka. In the northernmost zone of this strip there is again a shrine of Shree Parshurama on a hill named Sallher and at the North of this shrine and about 100 cubits there are two foot-marks carved in a rock to commemorate His position when He ordered the sea to roll back and release the land. In the southern-most zone of the strip, there is a place on the top of a mountain named Mahendragiri (Trivendrum district, Kerala State) which is considered by the people to be the permanent residence of Shree Parashurama, as He is supposed to be immortal. Outside this strip also there are many places throughout India linked with the name of Shree Parashurama as far North as the eastern boundary of Assam and the mountain Mahendraparvata in Orissa on the East.

The Indologist Dr. Pargiter says that behind every Hindu legend there is a truth. What is the truth hidden in the legend of Shree Parashurama? The reply will also verify whether or not the legend is linked directly or indirectly to the subject of this chapter.

To find a reply to the question proposed, we will have to examine the events and the religion as well as political and social concepts of the people of South India over a long period of time — starting from the sixteenth century A.D. and going backwards up to the end of the Rigvedic age.

Geohistorical demystification of the legend

In the last quarter of the fifteenth and the first quarter of the sixteenth centuries A.D., there were many rulers in South India, not always on good terms with one another, on grounds such as that the Raja who was of the Kshatriya caste had no right to use the royal umbrella and other insignia of sovereignty. The right, as per social customs, belonged exclusively to the king of the Brahmin caste or the offspring of that caste. Zamorin who was of the Nair caste, a matrilineal one and probably an offspring of a Nambudri Brahmin, used those insignia. This has been referred to, to highlight the concept for the people of that area, which is part of present Kerala state on the western coast of South India. The concept envisages that only Brahmins had the right to sovereign insignia.

As against this concept, it is worthwhile to note that in the case of the coronation of Shivajiraje Bhonsle of the Maratha caste, he had to prove that his family was of the Kshatriya caste. He sought help from Gagabhatt, an eminent Shastri from Benaras who, after consulting the genealogy trees from different places, pronounced his verdict that the Bhonsle family was a branch of the Sisodia clan of the Rajput caste. So, Shivajiraje could be coronated as "Chhatrapati" with rights to the insignia of sovereignty.

Now let us enter the medieval period. One of the ancient dynasties in South India is of the Cheras; but their history during the pre-Christian times is, however, still in darkness. [1] pg. 2. There were many chieftains even in the area of the present day Kerala state, but there is no evidence that the Cheras, Cholas and Pandyas existing in the first three centuries of the Christian era had claims to sovereignty.

During the same period, or say, from c 230. B.C. to c 230 A.D. a dynasty of the "Satavahanas" or "Andhras" ruled over a large area of South India. Some kings of that dynasty were entitled to the epithet "Rao-Rao" i.e. king of kings, a sovereign. And it is most curious that one of them, Goutamiputra Satakarni (106-130 A.D.), in the rock-inscription of Nashik, is mentioned with the epithet "Ekabrahmana" i.e. matchless Brahmin [2]. According to historians, the Satavahanas were not of the Brahmin caste. More about this later.

Now let us examine the subsequent ruling families of South India, and then, we shall be able to make up our minds. The next dynasty is of the Kadambas of Banavasi. They were declared to be of the Brahmin caste, Manavya gotra. There are many legends in respect of the progenitor of that dynasty. One of these legends included in a Kannada work named "Grama-Paddhati" says: "When Shiva and Parvati were re-joicing on the land created by Parashurama, a child was born to Parvati under the Kadamba tree. He was named Kadamba and was placed in charge of the Western Ghat region. Mayur Sharma who had made Banavasi his capital was born subse-quently in his dynasty". [3] pg. 42.

The other sovereign dynasty in South India, after the Kadambas, was of the Chalukyas of Badami. In respect of the origin of the progenitor of this dynasty there are some legends, but two of them deserve mention here to show how divine origin was connected to the post-vedic Aryan deities who gained reverence from the people. In fact, some kings of that dynasty had taken the title "Prithivi-Vallabha" (Lord of the Earth), denoting sovereignty.

According to one legend, the Kings of the Chalukya dynasty claimed descendence from Lord Narayana Himself. The Chalukyas, like the Kadambas, belonged to the Manavya gotra and they were also the descendants of the original ancestor Hariti. Again like the Kadambas, the Chalukyas were worshippers of Kartikeya and being Brahmins of a kingly race, they performed vedic sacrifices. These similarities natu-rally suggest that they were Brahmins who, like the Kadambas, took to arms when the situation demanded it. The Hyderabad granth of Pulakeshin II (612 A.D.) states: "The family of the Chalukyas who are haritaputras of the Manavya gotra which is praised throughout the world, who have been nourished by the seven mothers who are the mothers of the seven worlds; who have acquired an uninterrupted continuity of prosperity through the protection of Kartikeya, who have had all kings made sub-ject to them at the sight of the boar crest which they acquired through the favour of the divine Narayana." This statement is very significant and symbolic. This crest was adopted to indicate the nature of their work, that of protecting the earth from devastation by bad rulers. It implies a comparison with the task achieved by Lord Narayana in his boar incarnation.

When the Kadamba rule fell to bad days the feudatories began to assert their independence. In the resultant confusion that followed, the Chalukyas seized power and stepped into the shoes of their erstwhile masters.

According to the other legend, the Chalukyas are linked with God Brahmaveda. It is noteworthy that at the time of Pulakeshi II, a temple was consecrated to the image of God Brahmadeva, while according to the Puranas, the God Shiva had prohibited his worship due to his sinful conduct. This temple was situated in Aihole village, Bijapur district, the original home of the Chalukyas. It is necessary to emphasize here that Vantuvallabha Senanandraja, maternal uncle and feudatory of Pulakeshi II, governing Goa and the adjacent area, constructed five temples in the area of Goa dedicated to God Brahmadeva, the history of which will be referred to at the proper chronological stage. Thus, the worship of Brahmadeva, otherwise banned by the Puranic legend, is in favour of the legend linking the origin of the progeny of the Chalukyas with that God.

This legend also appears in the period of another dynasty of the same family of Chalukyas of Kalyani in the time of Tribhuvanmalla Vikramaditya (1076-1126 A.D.) Vidyapati Bilhana, his court poet, in his work Vikramankadevacharita, says: "On one occasion when Brahmadeva was engaged in the morning sandhya devotions, God Indra came up to him and complained of the ever-increasing sinfulness of the world in which no man performed the Brahmanical sacrifices and rites or offered ablutions to God. He prayed to God Brahma to create a hero powerful enough to destroy the wicked people and put an end to the profane state of affairs. The appeals of Indra moved Brahmadeva to action, who, thereupon, looked at his chulika, i.e. the hollow of his palm where he held water in the course of devotional exercise for the purpose of pouring out libation, and from it sprang a mighty warrior capable of protecting the three worlds. He became the eponymous ancestor of the line."

Another ruling dynasty of South India was the Pallavas of Kanchi (275-550 A.D.), who are considered in epigraphical records as Brahmins of the Bharadwaja gotra, and their origin is mentioned in a legend: "Tondai is the name of a creeper. The eponymous ancestor of Pallava, a son of Ashvatthama and a nymph, was so called because at his birth he was cradled in a litter of sprouts. There is an epigraphic reference to the marriage of Ashvatthama, a descendant of Maharishi (Bharadwaja) with the apsara Madani. But the Velur palayam inscription avers that an early member of the dynasty named Viracurcha, obtained the insignia of royalty along with the hand of a Naga princess. Though these are legends, they point to the north Indian Brahmanical origin of the Pallavas. The Pallavas may have been originally provincial rulers under the Later Satavahana and risen to power in the Kanchi region at the expense of the Nagas, who, according to Ptolemy, were ruling there about the second quarter of the second century A.D." [4] Pg. 201.

To summarize, all these five dynasties namely Satvahanas, Kadambas, Chalukyas (Badami & Kalyani), Chutus and Pallavas which governed in South India and gained sovereignty declared themselves to be of the Brahmin caste and claimed divine origin to post-vedic Aryan deities. However, they took pains to link their origin to an eminent personage of the Brahmin caste of North India like Ashvatthama.

Conditions of Sovereignty

What might have been the reason for claiming this kind of origin? According to the Indo-Aryan post-vedic social order, the Kshatriyas had the right to sovereignty and later on at the time of the rise of the Satavahanas, in Southern India, there was no religious rule declaring that only a person of the Brahmin caste might be the sovereign.

There is no ground in the Dharmashastras which can be interpreted to mean that only a person of the Brahmin caste had the right to sovereignty. But the fact is that the people's concept in South India up to the time of the Zamorin in the sixteenth century A.D. continued from the third century A.D. What was the reason for this concept which was deeply rooted in the minds of the people? We cannot find a reply from political history but must try elsewhere. It is to be emphasized that in the same area the Nambudri (alias Namputiri) Brahmins, in the twelfth century A.D. were rule-makers and providers of administration and the constitution and later on they held hegemony in the sixteenth century directly through their offspring, the Nayars. Megasthenes, ambassador of the Greek Seleucus, in the court of Chandragupta Maurya (320 B.C.), in his book "Indica", says: "It is not permitted to contact marriage with a person of another caste, nor to change one profession or trade to another, nor to the same person to undertake more than one, except he is of the Caste of philosophers." The statement of Megasthenes brings two of the most salient features of the institution to the forefront, but fails to give a complete idea of the system. [5] p. 2. The caste of philosophers obviously was the Brahmin one.

On the other hand, it is worth noting that before Chandragupta Maurya, the Nanda dynasty was in power with their sway up to Kuntala of Karnataka in the South. Some relatively late inscription in Karnataka recall traditions of Nanda rule in the area. But the founder of the dynasty Mahapadmananda was not of Kshatriya nor of the Brahmin caste, but was the son of a courtesan and a barber, according to the Jain account, who ruled from c. 403 B.C. However, he is described in the Puranas as "a second Parashurama or Bhargava", also as the exterminator of all Kshatriyas and as the whole sovereign (Ekacchatra). [4] p. 80 and [6] p. 82. Was the genealogy of the founder of the Nanda dynasty unknown to the Brahmins (Pandits) of the time of the Satavahanas, especially at the time of Goutamiputra Satakarni who prepared the draft of the rock inscription mentioning him as 'Eka-Brahman'? Probably not.

According to the genealogy of the founder of the dynasty of Nandas and Chandragupta Maurya being a Kshatriya, as history suggests, it can be inferred that in Northern India there was no condition that the sovereign (Eka-cehatra) should be only of the Brahmin caste.

The worship of Parashurama

Dr. Mirashi from the word 'Ekabrahmanasa' in the inscription, concluded that the Satavahanas were of the Brahmin caste, while some other declare their caste to be obscure. In fact, the reason given by him is insufficient to draw that conclusion. [2] p. 109 11, pp. 43-44. In the same inscription it is mentioned that he (Gautamiputra Satakarni) subdued the Kshatriyas, but this does not help to indicate that he was of the Brahmin caste, as there are identical phrases in respect of the Shakas, Yavanas and Pallavas. So, this type of description does not point to caste. Here it is pertinent to quote the phrase from the inscription as well as its translation made by Dr. Mirashi and further, to scrutinize it. In the 7th and 8th lines of the inscription a phrase runs as follows: 'ekadusasa ekadhanurdharasa eka surasa ekabrahmanasa rama-kesava-arjuna-bhimasenatulaparakramasa' (pp. 43-44 of the second part of the book) and translated as follows: 'matchless ruler, matchless archer, matchless warrior (and) matchless Brahmin, and valiant like Rama, Krishna, Arjuna and Bhimasena'. If we consider, like Dr. Mirasi, the word 'Ekabrahmanasa' as simply 'matchless-Brahman', then its place in the phrase is improper because the preceding words and subsequent line with reference to that word 'Ekabrahmana are exclusive to the person of the Kshatriya, except Shree Parashurama. Moreover, Shree Parashurama is known in Goa, Maharashtra and Karnataka as 'Eka-Vir' (matchless-Hero), corresponding to the eulogy mentioned above with the prefixed work 'Eka'. I think that in carving the word "Ekabrahmanasama" the last letter "ma" was omitted.

Renuka, mother of Shree Parashurama, is worshipped in Maharashtra and Karnataka under the name of 'Eka vira', meaning mother of 'Eka vir'. The records existing in the Goa archives, in Panaji, provide accounts of demolished Hindu temples and shrines. [7]. There you can find the names of the deities existing in the villages of Tiswadi, Salcete and Bardez talukas at the time when temples were demolished by the Portuguese at the peak of religious fervour in the sixteenth and seventeenth centuries. Names of such deities were recorded simply as 'Vir'. From those talukawise and villagewise lists, I selected the names which I considered to be connected to Shree Parashurama. I found one that had been incompletely recorded: a deity from village Cortalim (alias *Kutthal*), Salcete taluka was mentioned as 'Vir' while in fact the name of the deity is 'Virabhadra'. Ignoring those that had no link to Shree Parashurama, I found three places dedicated to the worship of Shree Parashurama: *'Torno-Vir'* ('Youthful-Hero' in Cujira village, Tiswadi taluka, 'Quello-

Vir' (alias *Eklo-Vir*) meaning 'Matchless-Hero' in Betalbatim (*Betalbhati*) village and 'Eklo-Vir' in Utorda village, the latter two in Salcete Taluka. As such in Goa, there were places dedicated to the worship of Shree Parashurama. Besides these three places, as of today there is a shrine of Parashurama at Poinguinim (*Paingin*) village of Canacona Taluka (*ill. 1a*). Here there is no idol of black stone like of the other deities nor is it in

ill. 1a : Rear wall of the Temple of Shree Parashurama at Paiguini Village, Kankon Taluka.

the 'linga' form. The place under worship is a flat rock with a small irregular elevation in the middle of that stone, natural and so not carved. After the morning-worship on the rock is over, an image of alloyed metal is placed (*ill. 1b*).

To the North of Goa at Chiplon village, Ratnagiri district (now Raigad district, its subdivision) there is also a place of worship of the same type. In the year 1500 A.D. a Begum (Muslim wife) of Adilshahi Sultan constructed this temple in fulfilment of the vow made by her to the un-iconic Shree Parashurama. Very recently a person of the Purchure family has installed there three idols, namely Kama (Cupid), Shree Parashurama and Kala (Time). It is noticeable, moreover, that when in the 7th century A.D., Goa territory was ruled by Vantuvallabha-Senanandaraja of the Sendraka (Sinda) family, the maternal uncle and feudatory of Chalukya Pulakesin II, he provided the impetus to change the idols of Puranic types but without putting any pressure on the people to effect the change. But no idol of Shree Parashurama was established by him. The reason might be that traditionally Shree Parashurama was considered a human being, an ancestor of Brahmins settled in the place and who, as an ancestor, must be worshipped in the spirit form. And so, the Hindu people who migrated elsewhere at the time of forced conversion to the Catholic religion, replaced all the village deities in their new settlements except "Eka-Vira" since at the time the worship of his iconic form was not yet established. (It is remarkable that, like in Poinguinim village, in Banavasi there is a temple exclusively dedicated to Shri Parashurama) *(ill. 2)*.

The image of Shree Parashurama is vivid in the mind of all the people of the Malabar coast. This is more intense in the southernmost areas. The Kollam era established there in 825 A. D. is also named as 'Parshurama Sanvat'. I remember, ten or twelve years ago Trivandrum Radio broadcasting a speech during the Onam festival. The orator explained that Mahabali in whose memory the festival was celebrated was the name of Shree Parashurama. Evidently his affirmation is correct as the word 'Mahabali' is identical to the 'Eka-Vira'.

ill. 1b: Shrine of Shree Parashurama at Paiguini Village, Kankon Taluka.

He is considered to be the first who established peace and law and order in that region. He is worshipped without any iconic form from the Himalayas to Kanyakumari by all castes, including the Kshatriyas. The puranas mention that Shree Parashurama had taken help from Gadhi and other kings to kill the Heihayas and other ignoble rulers of the Kshatriya caste and restituting peace, law and order. He had no ambition of governing either by himself or by his clan-followers. The puranas talk about him in relation to Balarama and his brother Krishna.

All the facts mentioned above leads us to conclude that Shree Parashurama was

ill. 2 : Temple of Shree Parashurama at Banavasi, Karnataka.

not simply a legendary and mythical figure but lived as a human being in blood and flesh. I felt it necessary to give such a lengthy account because there are many scholars who consider him as a mythical personage. Further, the legend of Shree Parashurama has strongly influenced not only the various dynasties of South India but also in the territory of Goa.

Dating of the Shree Parashurama legend

This is a very important factor in understanding the geo-history of the Malabar Coast in general and of Goa (included in it) in particular. For this purpose it is necessary to find the date from the Rigvedic Age. The Rigveda Samhita includes the hymns composed by Jamadagni Bhargava, father of Shree Parashurama (III, 62; VII, 101; IX, 62; IX, 65; IX, 67; X, 110; X, 137. And X, 167). This is an important clue towards the dating of Shree Parashurama. According to scholars the first and last (10th) Mandalas are relatively modern; but they admit also that some hymns of these two Mandalas were more ancient than those of the remaining Mandalas. The first Mandala, hymn 179, is a dialogue between Agastya and his wife Lopamudra, daughter of a king of Vidarbha. This shows that at the end of the Rigvedic Age if not a little earlier, the Aryans had crossed the Vindya Range. Atharvaveda Samhita, which constitutes an appendix to the Rigveda Samhita, makes in the 5th chapter (Kanada) hymns 18 and 19, reference to the conflict between Heihaya-Kshatriya on one side and Angirasas and other Brahmins, probably including the Bhargavas, on the other. Haihayas slaughtered the father of Shree Parashurama.

The fourth song (richa) of the 18th hymn (sucta) is very important for dating its composition: it refers to a serpent named 'Teimata' which word is of non-Aryan language, according to some scholars, including the late Lokamanya B.G. Tilak, who declared that the names of the serpents mentioned in that veda were of non-Aryan languages, probably from those of the Middle East. At that time, archeological studies of that area were in their infancy, and almost nothing was done in that respect in India. Now it is known that 'Timat' was the name of a serpent in the legends of the peoples of the Semitic race about two-and-a half centuries B.C. The 'Timat' serpent is shown in an Akkadian seal dated c. 2360-2180 B.C., depicting a seven-headed dragon being attacked by two gods and their attendants. The conflict of Baal and Anat is mentioned in the tablets found at Ras-Sharma (Sumer, Present Iraq) with Seven Heads, Primeval chaos, the drought [8 and9]. This is to be equated with drought, named Vritra, and described as a serpent in the Rigveda-Samitha.

The seal is probably of the time of Sargon, king of Akkad and Sumer. And both the

Sumeriologists and Indologists admit that at his time there was commercial contact between his domain and north-western coastal India which is named as '**Meluha**' in his inscriptions. History says that around 2400 - 2171 B.C., the quarelling overlords of Sumer bowed to the rule of the great king, the Akkadian Sargon [10]. However, long before Sargon, there was such commercial contact. Some scholars place Sargon in c.2500 [11] and about 2750 B.C. [12]

In the light of the above, the conflict between the Heihayas and the Brahmins (Angirasas, Bharvagas and their allies) took place not later than 2400 B.C. The Puranas described this conflict as between Kartavirya Heihaya and Shree Parashurama Bhargava. **Dr. Pusalkar has placed Shree Parashurama rightly between 2550 and 2350 B.C.** [12].

However, the Heihayas started their vendetta very soon, noting the total absence of awe of Shree Parashurama, either because he was far away or had passed away. Soon they had conquered all the area to the North of the Narmada river. The Brahmins crossed the river and went to the South of the Narmada. This happened around 2300 B.C.

It is likely that before they settled, the area was occupied in scattered form here and there by people who had migrated from neighbouring areas crossing the Range. Their ancestors also must have migrated much earlier but must have experienced the earthquake and fled. This traditional history was vivid in the minds of the aborigines, and was transmitted to the new-comers who recorded it in the form of a legend. This is the first written lesson in respect of geo-history of the region named by the newcomers as 'Parashurama Kshetra'.

Now let me turn from traditional and historical evidence to scientific ones to prove that the land of Goa from about 600 mts. altitude close to the Sahyadri Range to the sea-shore was a part of the bottom of the sea raised by violent tectonic movements c. 12,000 years ago.

PALEONTOLOGICAL FINDINGS

1. Fossilized marine conches

In the year 1943, I was the head of a batch engaged in the cadastral survey of Satari taluka and so I had appointed Mr. G. S. Kantak to prepare the plan for Surla village. One day he appeared at my headquarters at Dongurli village (*Bocal* hamlet) and showed me a conch (*shankh*) with its surface completely degraded but the shape absolutely intact. The outer and inner surfaces were opaque, of ashed colour and except for a small hole of one millimeter diameter near the apex exposing the translucid inner layer at about half mm depth, the conch was without any perforation. If I remember well the thickness of the conch was about two mm and length ten cm. It could not possibly have belonged to a Jogi, as it was too small and not perforated.

Mr. Kantak informed me that while he was opening a traverse for measuring the land at mid-day, he noted a shining point not very far from the line. Out of curiosity he removed the earth around that scintillating point with the shoe of the surveyor's rod and noted that it was a *shankh.*

I visited the site. It was at about 600 mts altitude and situated in a low-lying area surrounded on the North, South and West by a basaltic dyke in the form of the Roman letter 'U' with a large opening obviously on the East. The dyke was a branch of the main Deccan trap with a height of about three mts. At the curve of the 'U' form, and being almost perpendicular, its visible face was on the side of that low-lying area. The topographic position of that low lying area was such that not a drop of rain water flow could reach that area. So, the erosion might have been caused only by direct rain water. The spot where the conch was found was situated about three mts. south of the dyke and about ten mts. east of the apex of the 'U' form near a shrub. Mr Kantak was skilled in wood carving, and with his patient and meticulous work removed the deteriorated layer. The conch was of a milky a colour, lustrous, but with a diminished shape. I wanted to keep it with me since it was discovered at high altitude, but Mr Kantak's wife was somewhat superstitious and would not part with it.

About 80 years before me, Antonio Lopes Mendes, a Portuguese surveyor, was in charge a villagewise cadastral survey and record of rights of that area, besides the study of its geology, hydrography, agriculture, forest and census of population as well as of cattle.

This work was taken up in the year 1865 by the Portuguese Government on the recommendations of a commission. The reports were published in the Government Gazette, and later in booklet form [13]. Mr. Mendes, inter alia, prepared in 1866 the plans and reports concerning Surla and its adjoining Ambeacho-Gor village. In the report on Ambeacho-Gor village he mentions that at the bottom of the precipice of the Ghats, at the boundary of the village, he found fossilized marine conches. He also found branches of trees close to the bottom of the basaltic face and, further, he says that the area including the village, shows by its physical panorama the effects of a turbulent tectonic movement.

I had no opportunity to visit the site mentioned by Mr. Mendes where he found the fossils but I presume that the type of conches cannot be different from the one that I had seen in 1943 in Surla village and also the one existing in the shrine (math) of 'Askinsidh', as mentioned earlier. Even today one can find conches of the same type on the shores of Dona Paula, near Panaji. Four years ago, one of my friends, Mr Narendra Shah, a merchant of Panaji offered me one collected from that site. This proves that the land of Goa rose upto 600 m. altitude close to the Sahyadri range in the period relatively recent in the geological scale of India.

2. Petrified roots

I retired in 1968 and very soon I started my professional work as a degree holder chartered surveyor. In December 1971, I had gone to check the boundary between two properties already demarcated by me in 1943, in Rivem village, Sattari taluka to draw up the plan of a piece of land to be sold. The labourers were cleaning the line passing through a narrow valley between two hillocks. No direction was needed for my part for clearance. So, while wandering in the nearby area, inspecting the huge blocks of basalt existing on the other side of the line, I came across two pieces with uncommon features: one was very small, about four cms. length and width, in the form of a net and the other was bigger with mud pressed on a face. I collected only the latter to study at leisure. This I found was a specimen of petrified roots of a tree similar to what is described by Mr. Mendes *(ill. 3)*. At around 800 mts. eastwards from the spot where I found the specimens, stand two huge basaltic natural pillars, 30 mts. from each other and named 'Darvazo' by the local people. These pillars are witnesses of volcanic eruption. Both these lie about four kilometres South-West of the place where the conch was discovered in 1943.

The evidence provided by the conch (Shankh) at Surla village, the fossilized marine conches discovered by Mr. Mendes in 1863 at Ambeacho-Gor village adjacent to Surla village and the two huge basaltic natural pillars discovered by me at Rivem village, together are in favour of the argument that the land of Goa had risen up from the sea bed as a result of violent tectonic movement. We have to consider further other findings and scrutinize them.

ill. 3 : Fossilized roots along with petrified mud found at the hill of Rivem Village, Sattari taluka, dated c. 9,000 B.C.

3. Deskeletonized fossil cavity

In the year 1975, a Marathi newspaper published that a cave was found at Altinho, Panaji, at a site where digging operations were on to lay the foundations for the construction of Government quarters. Accompanied by the executive engineer, I visited the site. By then, the upper laterite cap of the cave had already been removed, but the engineer informed me that the inner face of the cap was inclined in a dome form like the upper part of the shell of a tortoise. What still remained there of interest was the oblong tunnel, a continuation of the cave of about 1.10 m. in diameter vertically and 0.80 m. horizontally at its mouth. Continuing almost horizontally further, simultaneously narrowing down, so that a person could enter the tunnel on his knees first and afterwards could advance on his belly upto 8 mts. in a straight line. Later on, the tunnel narrowed stepwise and it was difficult to measure the total length. The main cave was more or less oblong, the maximum diameter being 3.40 m. and height 2.2 m. near the tunnel end. No fossil remains were discovered. This site is on a flank of slope but nearer the top of the hill, at an altitude of about 60 m. At the bottom of the same slope, when digging before for the foundations of the Bhatlem Government Colony some similar hollow spots were found but not much notice was taken of them as they were relatively small. The information gathered and my personal inspection led me to conclude that, due to the tectonic movement a part of the bottom of the sea was raised and at that time a *Raia-fish* (Skate fish) was caught in the laterite silt deposited on the sea-bed. While the main oblong cave represents its body, the tunnel was caused by the tail. Probably by the pressure of silt, the lard of the fish spread over its body in such a way that the wet slime mixed with silt did not interfere with the integrity of the body of the fish. The climate at that time was rainy, not heavy rains but sufficient to expurgate the salinity of the deposits. Probably after some centuries, the climate suddenly changed and became completely arid. This started the cohesion between the particles of deposits which gave room for the formation of sedimentary laterite rocks of a soft structure locally named *Mirio*, in opposition to the massive one, of metamorphic origin, named *Khadpo*.

After the arid period, started seasonal rains and then animals, especially ants, migrated from the firm land of the Western Ghats and devoured completely the remains of the body of the fish. However, by then the laterite rock had gained sufficient stability, so that the space originally occupied by the body of the fish continued intact as a hollow oblong cavity upto the time of digging. Even at present we find that species of fish named *Vagolem* on the shores of Goa but of a very small size and rarely is a big one found. However, on the shores of Kumbhakonam, in the southernmost area of India there are big varieties with a 3.5 m. long tail which can even overturn small canoes. On the shores of Angola, West Africa, the skate-fish, named locally as Nemata, is so big and strong that it overturns a canoe 6 m. long and fully loaded with cargo.

The existence at present of the species of conch (*Shankha*) and of skate-fish in the waters of Arabian Sea on the coast of South India and their continuous existence from the time when the land of Goa rose up out of the sea-waters as explained before lead to the conclusion that both species existed at the same time when the upheaval of the land occurred. Now we are left with the remaining question of dating them as well as the dating of the subsequent changes of climate, that is, the period of dry climate and the starting of seasonal rains. Let us search for answers in the evidence given below.

4. The Oceanographic evidence

In 1978, 'Gavesani', the ship of the National Institute of Oceanography, Dona Paula, Goa, discovered a bank of living corals about 100 km. west of *Malpem* (in South Kanara) near an island named Netrana. The Institute calculated that its formation must have started c. 11,000 years ago, or say probably in the Pleistocene period, when the sea-level was low. During the late Pleistocene (Holocene) period, when the sea-level started rising, the coral growth continued. In other words, as the sea became progressively deeper, coral growth continued, but maintaining more or less a constant depth below the surface of the sea and resulting ultimately in a coral bank. The maximum height of this bank is about 70 mts. and the depth of water over the back ranges from 38 to 60 metres.

During this period 1979-1981, 'Gavesani' further discovered living coral reefs at Malvan and Mormugao Harbour. While the corals at Malvan are essentially intertidal i.e. exposed to atmosphere during low waters, those of Mormugao are subtidal or fully submerged and are at a depth of 8 to 12 metres. [14] and [15].

Taking into consideration the natural conditions which the zoologists consider necessary for starting growth of the coral formations, the discovery of living coral formation at the three sites mentioned above is of very great importance from the point of view of the geo-history of the Malabar Coast in general and of the land of Goa, in particular.

Mr. E. L. Jordan in his book "Invertebrate Zoology" [16] states that "coral colonies are most abundant in tropical seas, though some occur in Arctic and temperate seas, but most of them flourish at a temperature of about 22 C. In a vertical plane the sea coral reefs are limited to a depth of 50 m at most. Light and the amount of sediment also limit the corals. They fail to grow in dark shaded areas and where the sediment is more than their cilia can remove. Below 50 m there are no reefs though solitary forms exist upto a depth of 8,000 m..."

"...The coral reefs have great vertical thickness though reef-building corals live only upto depth of 50 mts, and those of past geological ages also lived in shallow litoral waters. How the great thickness of the coral reefs has been made is explained by several theories of which two may be considered: (1) Darwin's Subsidence Theory states that coral reefs were first formed as fringing reefs on sloping shores, they became reefs when the shores sank with water channel between them and the land. If the land is an island which sinks completely, then an atoll is formed. Thus sinking of subsidence has caused the thickness of the reefs. (2) Daly's Glacial-control Theory states that during the last glacial period the formation of ice caps lowered the ocean level by 60 to 70 m. below the present surface. Waves cut the shores to make flat platforms suitable for growth of corals. As the ice caps melted and temperature rose, corals began to grow on these platforms and rose upwards with rising ocean level, and all types of reefs were formed on the pre-existing platforms, but many reefs were formed according to Darwin's subsidence theory."

"Observation of living corals show, that their rate of growth is from 5 mm to 20 cm per year, thus a **5 m. deep reef could be formed in less than 8,000 years**, and all the known reefs could have been built in under 30,000 years."

In short, the existence of a coral reef denotes that the region at the time of formation of the coral reef was covered by sea-water but the depth was not much (only around 50 m.). The water was limpid, airy, temperature was more than 20ºC and there was access to sunlight. The coral reefs continue to grow as long as such conditions last.

The evidence provided by the coral reefs is important because the National Institute of Oceanography has fixed the date of their commencement of formation to around 11,000 years ago (9,000 B.C.) i.e. in the Holocene period. Secondly, based on the above evidence the piece of the petrified root found by me at Rivem village also dates back to around the same period. And the same is true also of the fossilised branches of trees found by Mr. Mendes at Ambeacho-Gor village in 1863. Let me now turn over the records of the works of geologists and of experts in antiquity.

5. Other supporting evidence

The Portuguese Government had sent a commission consisting of some mining engineers and a geologist to study the mineral occurrences and the geology of the territory of Goa. Dr. Gerhard Oertel, a German citizen and professor of Geology at Pomona College, Claramount, California (U.S.A.) was entrusted with the study of Geology. He worked in Goa from December 1953 to September 1957 and studied all the areas of Goa except the northern portion of Sattari taluka and the north-easterned portion of Pednem taluka. The portion of Sattari taluka, not visited by Dr. Oertel, lies at the north of the line Morlem-Valpoi-Gavanem and is of great importance as it covers the area furnishing evidence of the occurrence of tectonic movements. He had begun his visits to those talukas in October 1955 when the national movement was growing and those zones were the most affected by it, so he was advised not to visit those areas. This is why he ignored the ring in the north-eastern part of Sattari taluka, well exposed between Ivrem-Curdi and Vainguinim villages and which was discovered after Liberation by Indian geologists. Because of the same limitations he had no opportunity to check the existence of fossils referred to by Mr Antonio Lopes Mendes and found in Ambeacho-Gor village. That's why, Dr. Oertel in his book "Geologia de Goa" [17] (p.55) says that he did not find fossils, even of a recent period.

Dr. Oertel, in respect of stratigraphy, observes (p. 22): "In the Goa District only sediments of the most ancient and of the most recent geological periods are found. The ancient strata belonging exclusively to the pre-Cambrian and the recent ones do not reach Tertiary era. The latter are of aluvial type and belong to the recent and the Sub-recent periods." Dr. Oertel, citing the book of Dr. Krishnan, observes: "In the western Ghats the rivers still show an early development probably because there may have been an upward tilt as well as an uplift of the Western part of the Peninsula in the tertiary era, as indicated by the presence of the Upper Tertiary rocks along the western coast which were laid down when the western coast was faulted down in early Miocene". (pp. 15-16) On the other hand the Goa Gazetteer [18] (p. 17) gives the stratigraphic succession of the rocks in Goa as follows: Recent, Sub-recent, Lower Eocene, Upper Cretaceous and Pre-Cambrian.

Admitting even the scale from the Goa Gazetteer, it is evident that in the land of Goa there are no rocks of the period between the Upper Eocene and the Holocene (Sub-recent) periods or say of the period from 60 million to 10 thousand years ago. [18] So, this evidence proves that the land of Goa during this period was under sea-waters, probably interspersed here and there with basaltic islands over the sea-surface. These islands were obviously subject to weather conditions giving rise to formation of the massive laterite on the faces exposed to the atmosphere and named locally as *khodpo*. The same phenomenon probably occurred in the area of the Western Ghats in the area adjacent to the sea.

The elevation of Sahyadri range from the sea-bed

The northern and the north-eastern boundary of Goa passes more or less through the Sahyadri Range which is an integral part of the Deccan trap.

Dr. Wadia in his book "Geology of India" [19] says: "Towards the close of the Creaceous system a large part of Peninsula was affected by a stupendous outburst of volcanic energy, resulting in the eruption of a thick series of lava and associated pyroclastic materials. This series of eruptions proceded from fissures and cracks in the surface of the earth from which highly liquid lava welled out intermittently, till a thickness of some thousands of metres of horizontally bedded sheets of basalts had resulted"... "The term 'trap' is used in its Swedish meaning of 'stairs', of 'steps' in allusion to the usual step-like aspect of the weathered flat-topped hills of basalt which are so common a feature in the scenery of the Deccan." (p. 275).

"Peninsular India is a segment of ancient complex of rock-beds that stand upon a firm and immovable foundation that have, for an immense number of ages, remained so impassive amid all the revolution that have again and again changed the face of the earth. Lateral thrusts and mountain-building forces have had but little effect in folding or displacing its original basement. Deccan is, however, subject to the kind of structural disturbances, viz., fracturing of the crust into blocks, and their radial or vertical movement due to tension or compression." (p. 2).

"In the Peninsula, the mountains are mostly of the 'relict' type i.e. they are not mountains in the true sense of the term, but are mere outstanding portions of the old plateau of the Peninsula that have escaped, for one reason or another, the weathering of ages that has cut out all the surrounding parts of the land; they are, so to say, huge 'tors' or blocks of the old plateau." (p. 2).

"The Koyna earthquake of December 11, 1967 with the epicentre about 320 km. South of Bombay, was the first recorded major tectonic earthquake in the Deccan Peninsula shield (peripheral area). The epicentre (17° 22' N, 73° 44' E.) lies about 55 km east of the Malabar coast line, the site of the giant Malabar fault, from Kutch of Cape Kamorin, of Mio-Pliocene age, which disrupted this coastline, throwing down a large slice and the Koyna earthquake may be ascribed to a slippage along this fault-plane. Pending collection of data by detailed geological mapping, the depth of the focus is provisionally regarded at about 8 km." (p. 42).

"Local alteration of level elevation of the peninsular table and few hypogene disturbances have interfered with the stability of the Peninsular continental land-mass for an immense length of geological time, but there have been a few minor movements of secular upheaval and depression along the coasts within past as well as recent times. Of these, the most important is that connected with the slight but appreciable elevation of the Peninsula, exposing portions of the plain of marine denudation as a shelf or platform round its coasts, by west as well as the east. Raised beaches are found at altitudes varying from 30 to 45 m at many places round the coasts of India; a common type of raised beach is the littoral concrete, composed of an agglutinated mass of gravel and sand with shells and coral fragments; while marine shells are found at several places some distance inland, and at a height far above the level of the tides. The steep face of the Sahyadri mountains, looking like a lime of sea-cliffs and their approximate parallelism to the coast leads to the inference that the escarpment is a result of elevation of the Ghats from the sea and subsequent sea-action modified by subaerial denudation. Marine and estuarine deposits of post-Tertiary age are met with on a large scale towards the southern extremity of the Peninsula. (pp. 42-43). From the note made by Dr. Wadia it is seen that the recent elevation of the Ghats mentioned by him refers to the Pleistocene movement in Peninsula."

From these findings it is evident that the elevation of the Sahyadri Range along with the adjacent land of Goa, occurred most probably at the time of the end of the Pleistocene period. Now remains the problem of the petrified roots discovered at Rivem village. For resolving it as well as the fixing of its date even tentatively, we have to examine the climatic conditions from the end of the Pleistocene period or say during the next Sub-recent period.

The glaciation period and the great drought

1. Dr. Wadia in the chapter on the Pleistocene system, says: "The great Ice Age of northern world was experienced in the southernly latitude of India as a succession of cold pluvial epochs. The Pluvio-glacial deposits of the Potwar, described on p. 385, and the boulder bed referred to in p. 343 as within the Upper Shivaliks of the Sheikbudin hills in the Trans-Indus Saly-Range, are the only instance of actual glacial deposits recorded in India in latitude so far south as 33° N". (p. 354).

2. Dr. Wadia accepted glacial stages during the Pleistocene period for the Upper Shivalies of NW India which were established by the geologist de Terra who admitted four glaciations with three inter glacial periods, like the American and the English geologists. So they refer in context to North-western Europe and North America. However, Dr Wadia, while subdividing the Pleistocene period employs nomenclature like a Russian geologist, namely Lower, Middle and Upper Pleistocene.

Dr. Wadia doest not mention absolute dating of the systems and their subdivisions. However, we can rightly consider that the last Pleistocene corresponds to the fourth glaciation period of the English geologists, designated as the "Wurm" period.

An expert says:

"The Wurm glaciation, however, had four distinct maxima with slightly warmer conditions intervening. In many regions, as will appear, evidence for the earliest, Gunz glaciation is exiguous or still lacking, but in general there is no doubt that four fold glaciation was a worldwide phenomenon affecting both northern and southern hemispheres and causing a shift in the rain belts that brought corresponding wet phases to lower latitudes. Thus wherever there were living men who were building up their Palaeolithic cultures during the Pleistocene Age were affected by this periodic freezing of their planet, often being forced into slow migrations and sometimes finding wide areas habitable which under warmer conditions would be dry or desert...

"While in the northern hemisphere the continents were weighted down by many million square miles of ice, in the northern the drops of temperature which we have attributed to the lessening of solar heat must have led to a considerable speed of sea ice, but the glacial history of this ocean hemisphere passed with little trace and is of almost no concern in the development of man. There was a growth of the glaciers in the Andes and in the mountains of New Zealand and Australia."

"What are of great significance for this development are the changes of climate which were the counterpart of the Ice Age in regions of lower latitude not directly affected by glaciation. The existence of ice-fields caused a shift, the belt of rain bearing eastwards the cyclonic storms of some fifteen degrees towards the south in the northern hemisphere and towards the north in the southern hemisphere. So it was that Africa, the Mediterranean, Asia Minor, Central Asia and North China, South-West of United States and southern south America experienced 'pluvial' periods corresponding to the glaciations of higher latitudes. The reality of these shifts in rain belts is shown mainly in the swelling of rivers, in a rise in existing lake levels and the filling up of basins now dry, and in the spread of vegetation in many areas now desert. Thus the Caspian and Aral seas were united as were the Baltic sea and sea of Azov". [21] p. 24.

The above mentioned quotation is from a book published by UNESCO, but unfortunately not a single reference has been made to the Indian subcontinent or to the Malaya Peninsula. However, another writer, [22] indirectly makes such a reference: "The ice beings... A series of major swings to cold periods and back to warm again... Pushed by the cold and ice subartic zones moved down towards the equator; and in the tropics there were rainly phases which apparently matched the ice advances, followed by droughts when the climate once more warmed up." (p. 138).

"After its (of homo sapiens) first assault on Europe, known as the early Wurm or Wurm I, the Fourth Glacial phase, somewhat between 42,000 B.C. and 30,000 B.C. with the climax at about 35,000 B.C." (p. 205). The author in this way considers only two phases, Wurm I, already mentioned and consequently the remaining period 30,000 B.C. to 10,000 B.C. as Wurm II, the climax being 18,000 B.C."

All the Western writers cited above and many others not cited here, stress more on the situation in the northern hemisphere, especially in Europe, America, and Africa and only sporadically to southern areas. Hence we will concentrate on the situation in South India in the Pleistocene period.

An eminent writer (20) furnishes the following information concerning South-east Asia : "He (Pithecanthropus-Sinanthropus man of southern China) was able to reach Java from the mainland during the Ice Age, when the glaciation of so much water meant that the sea-level dropped about 300 feet (or 100 metres) and exposed land-bridges linking Indo-Chinese Peninsula with Sumatra, Java and Bali".(p. 21).

"The next human type to be revealed by fossil finds was also found in Java, in fact very near to where the first remains of Pithecantropus man were discovered. This Ngandong or Solo Man inhabited Java in the third interglacial period (we are now in the fourth, which in all likelyhood will end with another glaciation in about 40,000 years' time". (p.76).

"The glaciation of course only affected South-east Asia (at about latitude 10º S.) to the extent that it was slightly cooler and rainier than usual, and during the last one, that is from 80,000 to 15,000 years ago, yet another human type reached the Indonesian Archipelago: Wadjak Man..." (p.77).

These quotations furnish the dating of the end of the last glaciation/pluviation in South-East Asia, but does not refer to the next draught, which is verified elsewhere.

The fluctuating climate of the fluvial period

Two writers of a book [22] give us the following information: "From the evidence listed above it is clear that a major fluctuation in climate occurred close to 11,000 years ago. The primary observation that both surface ocean temperatures and deep sea sedimentation rates were abruptly altered at this time is supplemented by evidence from more local systems. The level of Great Basin lakes fell from the highest terraces to a position close to that observed at present. The silt and clay load of the Mississipi river was suddenly retained in the alluvial valley and delta. A rapid ice retreat opened the northern drainage systems of the Great Lakes and terrestrial temperatures rose to nearly interglacial levels in Europe. In each case the transition is the most obvious feature of the entire record." (p. 304).

"Evidence from a number of geographically isolated systems suggest that the warming which occurred at the close of Wisconsin (last glaciation) glacial times was extremely abrupt."

"It seems there must have been a rather abrupt warming of the climate in order for the glaciers to melt and the oceanic temperature to change as rapidly as the evidence indicates. This again argues for some sort of explanation outside the scope of doctrinate uniformitarianism. It is possible to speculate that some new tectonic activity, perhaps a sudden change in either continental or marine topography or possibly new vulcanic activity, or even perhaps extra-terrestrial encounters with cemetery bodies or the like may have been the trigger mechanism" (pp. 304-305).

"The effect of the Pleistocene conditions of the moisture in presently arid areas is second in importance only to the contemporaneous glaciation in higher latitudes, the major desert areas, which are today uninhabited barren wastes, although they occupy a very large part of the temperate zones, were formerly fertile, well watered lands. These areas, which were often covered by very large lakes, include the Sahara and Arabian deserts, the desert of Central Asian, the Australian Kalahari, the North American, the Atacama, and the Patagonian deserts." (p. 314).

This last quotation helps us to get the dating of the advent of the drought. But we need to have more details. Hence we shall search the early history of Iran, a country adjacent to the Indian sub-continent.

Mr. R. Grishman [23] observes: "Recent geological research has shown that at the time when the great part of Europe was covered by glaciers, the Iranian Plateau was passing through pluvial period, during which even the high valleys were under water. The central part of the Plateau, today a great salt desert was then an immense lake or inland sea into which many rivers ran from the high mountains. Fossil fish and shells, which have been found not only in the desert but also in the high valleys, illustrate the physical aspect of the country as it was many thousands of years before the Christian era."

"At a period which may be put as between 10,000 and 15,000 B.C. there was a gradual change of climate, the pluvial period being followed by the so-called dry period, which is still in progress. The decreased rainfall on the one hand, and the high altitude of the lakes and inland seas on the other, slowed down the current of the rivers and stream carrying off water from the mountains. Owing to the greater regularity of their flow, alluvial deposits accumulated at the river mouths and formed terraces which eventually rose above the water and formed a transitional zone between the future plain or valley and the mountain proper."

"At this period prehistoric man was already living on the Iranian Plateau, dwelling in holes which were roofed with branches of trees into the wooded mountains-sides, or more often, occupying one of the many caves or rock shelters, most of which are the underground channels of ancient rivers. In the spring of 1949 we identified traces of human remains of this age for the first time in Iran in our exploration of a cave at Tang-I-Pabda, in the Bahktari mountain, north-east of Shustar. Here man led the life of a hunter, seeking his food, and to this end employing cunning more often than force. He knew how to use a stone hammer, the hand-axe and axe tied to a cleft stick, all primitive tools fashioned by flaking. Implements, represented by awls made from tough animal bones, were far fewer than stone artifacts. But he already used a coarse, poorly baked pottery, which by the end of his occupation of the caves was deep black in colour owing to the increased use of smoke in firing. This type of pottery has also been found with the earliest human remains on the plain, and is therefore an important pointer in the connection between these two phases of settlement."

"In this primitive society a special task fell to the lot of the woman, guardian of the fire and perhaps inventor and maker of pottery. It was she who, armed with a stick, sought edible roots or gathered wild berries in the mountains. Knowledge of plants both of long and assidous observations, led her to experiment in cultivation. Her first attempt in agriculture were made on the alluvial terraces. Whereas man made but little progress, woman with her primitive agriculture introduced many innovations during the neolithic period, to which the cave settlements belong. As a result, a lack of balance must have arisen between the parts played by man and woman. This may perhaps be the origin of certain primitive societies in which the woman is predominant. In such matriarchies (and also, perhaps, in societies practising polyandry) the woman directs the affairs of the tribe and is raised to the priesthood while family succession is through the female line, the woman being considered as transmitting its purest form the life-blood of the tribe. We still see that this form of matriarchy was one of the peculiar practices of the original inhabitants of the Plateau and that later it passed into the customs of the conquering Aryans." (pp. 27-28).

The author of the book, however, considers that the Aryans invaded Iran in the first millennium B.C. (pp. 73-76). This dating occurs when he declares that the theory may be controversial (footnote at p. 73). In fact, in the present time, Orientalists admit that the Indian Great War (Bharatiya Yuddha) took place about 1400 B.C., if not earlier, so it is obviously evident that the Indo-Aryans settled in Iran long before this date. However, the author of 'Iran' mentions the change of climate between 10,000 and 15,000 B.C. in that area and this point deserves scrutiny. The sacred books of the Persians, the 'Avesta', and of the Indo-Aryans, the 'Rigveda', mention this change of climate, but only allegrically. In the eight chapter of the fourth division of 'Avesta' designated 'yatri' there is praise for a star named 'Tishatriya' who defeated the demon, producer of the drought named 'Veretraghana'. (23).

Similarly, in the Rigveda, Indra is named 'Vitraghna', meaning killer of Vitra, demon who produced the drought, and who is also mentioned with the name of Ahi meaning big cloud. (Rigveda I, 32; I, 52; II, 12, 3; VI, 72, 3; X, 99, 4; and X, 113, 3).

According to Orientalists, the compilation of the 'Vedas' took place C. 1400 B.C., and that of 'Avesta', according to some scholars, in the 4th or 6th century A.D., while according to others, in the time of the Achaemedian age (558 B.C. to 300 B.C.). (12) p. 318.

Whatever may be the date of the compilation of those books, the fact is that traditional historical events incorporated in these books were noticed by both Indo-Aryans and Iranians which proves that the drought and subsequent seasonal rains were experienced by their ancestors when living together or side by side at Baght in Iran. Now to arrive at the time of occurrence.

Lamberg-Karlovsky and Sabloff [24] p. 51 say: "The geographical area in which this process (of the Neolithic Revolution) took place extends from the Anatolian plateau in Turkey to the deserts of Central Asia, and from the uplands of Palestine to the Caucasian range in Russia. The time was during the millennia that followed the stabilization of our modern climate after the last Ice age - by 9,000 to 8,000 B.C. in the high land zones of near Bukhta."

It is comprehensible that while Western scholars are of the opinion that soon after the end of the last Pleistocene age, there was a sudden change of climate which became arid and hot producing cyclones and later on was responsible for the seasonal rains in the areas of pluviation of the Pleistocene age, the geologists of India do not make a single reference to that change. Dr. Wadia who compiled the opinions of experts in writing his book "Geology of India" and the essay "Geology" in 'Gazetteer of India', in respect of our subject-matter, has only this to say [19] p. 387: "In the foregoing account of the later geological deposits of India there is everywhere a gradual passage from Pleistocene to sub-recent and thence to the prehistoric recent. These periods overlap each other as do the periods of human history, and there is no general agreement among geologists as to the exact limits of each."

From this statement it is clear that geologists did not find fossils on the Malabar coasts at least, like the one found in 1866 at Ambeacho-Gor by Mr. Antonio Lopes Mendes and by me in 1971 at Rivem village, Sattari taluka.

However, Dr. Sankaliya is aware of this environmental change. He says [25] p. 151: "Microliths - the review shows that in a few areas in India the microliths claim a fairly good (geological) antiquity. This in Tinnevelly or at Birbhanpur or even at Langhmij and Admgarh might mean the last Pleistocene times or the beginning of Holocene. The exact age in years is difficult to guess, but may be placed between 10,000-4,000 B.C."

Environmental change

In all the regions, there were various environmental changes, differing in intensity and nature from region to region. But on the whole, a climate drier in the preceding phase may be generally postulated. This had, as in many parts of the world, created sand dunes. These, as well as raised, dry, lightly forested regions were preferred as habitations by the neolithic people. Except in Northern and Central Gujarat no conclusion can be made of the contemporary fauna or flora (though even in Gujarat the evidence for flora is almost nil).

Dr. Sankaliya writes: "So we may end with the observation that the microlithic industries have a wide distribution, excluding Assam, the Punjab plains and Kerala and are associated with an environmental change: that they do indicate a change in the mode of life of man in India, but it is not exactly clear whether the microliths developed out of the earlier industries or due to the influence of some eternal stimuli."

Dr. Sankaliya does not refer to any fossil, but his view is correct. And now that we have evidence before our eyes in the form of fossil or petrified roots along with consolidated mud of basaltic schist, his views become fortified.

SUMMARY

The land of Goa in all aspects is more or less similar to the adjacent coastal belt of India, generally known as Malabar Coast. Goa forms a part of South Konkan.

In this chapter, Location, Area, Boundaries and Census of population of Goa as defined politically are described.

The Legend of Parashurama: *The Parashurama Legend is referred to by many ancient texts like the 'Skanda Purana', 'Ramayana', 'Mahabharata' etc. The legend says that Parashurama ordered the sea to roll back and release that much land. The strip of land from Vaitarana river to Kanyakumari on the west coast was named as 'Parashurama Kshetra.'*

Parashurama was a historic figure: *The word 'Ekabrahmanas' occurring in the Satavahana inscription is discussed to unfold the legend of Parashurama. During the 7th century A.D. Vantu Vallabha Senandaraja of the Sendraka family gave impetus to a special style in the iconography of Puranic Gods.*

Shree Parashurama was not a legendary or mythical figure but a historical personality.

Dating of Shree Parashurama age: *The dating of the Shree Parashurama age is a very important factor in understanding the Geo-history of the Malabar Coast in general and of Goa in particular.*

The dating of the conflict between Heihayas and Brahmins is concluded to be not later than 2400 B.C. The origin of the legend of Parashurama is traced back to the aborigines who transmitted it to new-settlers.

The author supports Dr Pusalkar's dating of Parashurama Bhargava between 2550 to 2350 B.C.

Paleontological findings and their interpretation: *The scientific evidence: The evidence provided by the conch (shankh) at Surla village, fossilized marine conches discovered by Mr. Mendes at Ambeacho-Gor village adjacent to Surla village and the two huge basaltic natural pillars discovered by the author at Rivem village, together favour the argument that the land of Goa had risen up from the sea-bed as a result of* *violent tectonic movement. To consolidate this view, other paleontological findings have been scrutinized such as the fossilized cave found at Altinho-Panaji; this tunnel shaped oblong cavity was originally occupied by a body of trapped Rai-fish (Skate-fish).*

The existence of a coral reef at Malvan and off Mormugao harbour as discovered by 'M. V. Gavesani' denotes that the region at the time of the formation of the coral reef was covered very superficiallt by seawater. The National Institute of Oceanography (N.I.O.), Dona Paula, Goa, has fixed their date of commencement of formation to be around 9000 B.C. This evidence along with the piece of petrified root found by the author at Rivem settle the question of the dating of paleontological findings and sub-sequent changes of climate.

Other sources also support the author's views: *Dr Oertel and Dr. Wadia's viewpoints are discussed to throw more light on Goa. The various findings show that the elevation of the Sahyadri Range along with the adjacent land of Goa, occurred most probably at the time of the end of the Pleistocene period.*

The problem of dating of petrified roots settled: *The problem of dating of petrified roots found by the author at Rivem is settled by citing Indian and Western viewpoints. Western scholars are of the opinion that soon after the end of the last Pleistocene age, there was a sudden change in climate which became arid and hot producing cyclones and later seasonal rains in the area of pluviation. Dr. Sankaliya's views are correct as he takes note of environmental change which occurred between 10,000 - 4,000 B.C.*

Conclusive remarks on the land of Goa

Taking into consideration all the above mentioned findings and the dating of the coral reefs at Netrana island as a landmark, we can safely formulate the following conclusions:

1. *At the decline of the intensity of pluviation in the last Pleistocene age, c. 10,000 B.C. the bottom of the Arabian sea adjacent to the Deccan Plateau was lifted up and out of sea-waters by tectonic movement and now forms the Malabar coast, the land of Goa being a part of it.*

2. *The land of Goa with its adjacent northern and southern coastal areas, so elevated and defined on the west by the sea-shore Netrana island - Marmagoa, Malvan line, and on the east by the line at about 600 m altitude.*

3. *By the tectonic movement, massive laterite caps of the basaltic elevation were broken and thrown down sometimes even to a long distance. We find this at present on the marine coast and river-beds even at a depth of 15 mts in the rivers as well as in subarial land.*

4. *The subarial land continued to be washed by the pluviation-rains but gradually with decreasing intensity, c. 9,000 B.C. there was a change of climate. The atmosphere became dry and hot and very soon there were violent cyclones. These cyclones destroyed the vegetation at high altitude and uprooted trees in valleys and low lying areas. Loose sand and gravel carried by the cyclone poured over them. Wherever the uprooted trees were lying near the basaltic elevation, they got transformed into petrified pieces, like the ones Mr. Mendes found at Ambeacho-Gor village and I found at Rivem village.*

   At the same time the corals started their formations as discovered by Gavesani at Netrana island, Mormugao Harbour and Malvan.

5. *C. 8,500 B.C. possibly seasonal monsoon rains started which washed away the loose materials existing on the surface. In this way, the original hydrographic system gradually changed and the recent age of flora and fauna began.*

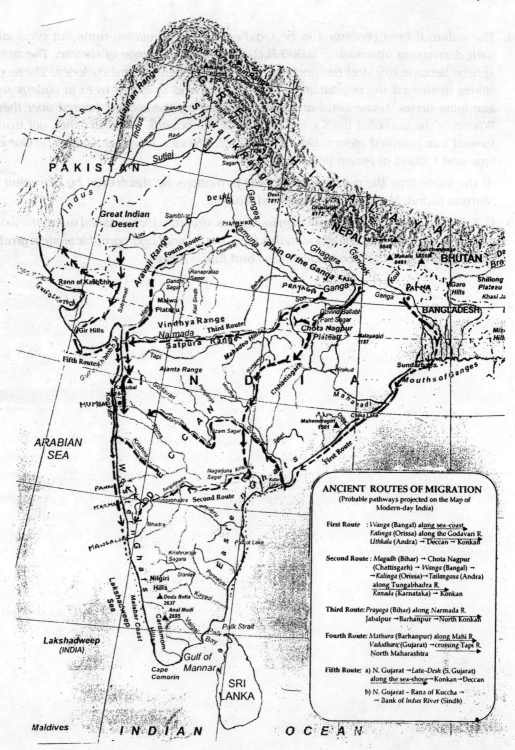

ANCIENT ROUTES OF MIGRATION
(Probable pathways projected on the Map of
Modern-day India)

First Route : *Wanga* (Bangal) along sea-coast
Kalinga (Orissa) along the Godavari R.
Uthkalu (Andra) → Deccan → Konkan

Second Route : *Magadh* (Bihar) → Chota Nagpur
(Chattisgarh) → *Wanga* (Bangal) →
→ *Kalinga* (Orissa)→*Tailangana* (Andra)
along Tungabhadra R.
Kanadu (Karnataka) → Konkan

Third Route: *Prayaga* (Bihar) along Narmada R.
Jabalpur→Barhanpur→North Konkan

Fourth Route: *Mathura* (Barhanpur) along Mahi R.
Vadodhara (Gujarat) →crossing Tapi R.
North Maharashtra

Fifth Route: a) N. Gujarat →*Lata–Desh* (S. Gujarat)
along the sea-shore→Konkan→Deccan

b) N. Gujarat – Rana of Kuccha →
→ Bank of *Indus* River (Sindh)

Chapter - 2
THE ORIGIN OF SETTLEMENTS IN GOA

In the preceding chapter, it has been postulated that at c. 8,500 B.C., the land of Goa was suitable for the settlement of mankind. Now let us move on to investigate into the tribal groups who established their settlements here and their cultural trends.

It is obvious that the primitive settlements in Goa originated from the migration of the people from adjacent parts of the land. So we need to consult the human history of India in that epoch before it, from the period corresponding to the last phase of the Pleistocene age.

This period corresponds to the Wurm II of Europe which started c. 30,000 B.C., climaxed around 18,000 B.C. and ended c. 10,000 B.C., as mentioned before. This corresponds to the Upper Pleistocene of Indian geologists. Our study will be limited to the minimum necessary to find the human type existing around 8,500 B.C.

THE PREHISTORIC TRIBES AND RACES OF INDIA

It is but natural that I focus my attention first on the work of Indian scholars, though I could not find satisfactory information from them about that period.

In the last edition of the Gazetteer of India, volume I, (26), chapter VI, 'The People', gives an account of the presence of tribes with their anthropometric measurements.

In volume two, part I, chapter I (27) referred to the pre-historic period, p. 7. The writer says, "we are still in the dark about the racial type or types of the makers of these tools who roamed practically all over India and whether they knew fire as in China or had temporary camps as in East Africa." This is told in respect of the Old Stone age, but the position is the same in the subsequent periods more or less upto the pre-Harappan culture, according to vol. I of the Gazetteer.

However, in chapter VII of the same Gazetteer (26) dealing with 'Language', the writer says that the primitive settlers were Negroids. He says: (p. 375) "A negroid people, originally from Africa, first established their language on the soil of India. The Negroids were in Neolithic stage of primitive culture, and they were food-gatherers rather than food-producers; their culture could not have been of a high order; they had, nevertheless, spread over considerable parts of India. Traces of Negroid physical characteristics are found in parts of Western India, at least upto the middle of the first millennium B.C. Negroid tribes are still found in parts of the Tamil country—the Irulas, Kadars, Paniyans and Kurumbas. Remnants of the ancient Indian Negroids, they have lost their language and speak forms of Tamil. There are a few hundred Negroids also in the Andaman Islands—they are probably descendants of the Negroids who came along the coastal lands through Bengal into Assam and then by canoes into Burma. Anthropologists have discovered traces of Negroid characteristics among the Mongloid or Tibeto-Burmese speaking hill people of Assam State, like Nagas. From Burma they probably crossed, in prehistoric times, the 230 km stretch of sea which separates the North Andaman Islands from Cape Negrais in South Burma. Other groups of Negroids passed down to Malaya, where we still have the Samangs, a Negroid people who now speak Indonesian".

The writer further says that the Negroids came from Africa, and in support of this theory he supplies the following evidence: (28) Recently one skeleton was unearthed from a late Paleolithic site near Bishwanath railway station situated at a distance of about 30 kilometres north of Allahabad in Uttar Pradesh. The skull is mesocranial, the index being 76.04. The face is broad and low. The nose is broad and the nasal root is deep. By radioactive carbon dating method its age has been estimated to be 10,500 years...

"Dr. Sankalia unearthed several skeletal remains from the microlithic beds in North Gujarat. The skulls suggest that the microlithic men of that area were dolichocephalic. According to the discovery they were proto-Egyptian because they show Hemitic Negroid characteristics". [25] (p. 192).

But in Southern India, skulls of the Negroid type have not been found so far. [28].

Sarkar examined the skeletal remains at Brahmagiri in Mysore. Though remains of about twenty individuals were collected, eleven were made available to Sarkar for study. Sarkar has identified two racial types. One the Australoid type and the other perhaps Irano-Scythian. The second type is of medium stature and is mesocephalic. A skull of a child of about twelve years was evidence of the Australoid type during that period.

Dr. Das, author of the book 'Outlines of Physical Anthropology', citing different writers concludes that the Negroid race did not exist in India and that, "Following Sarkar and Mujumdar we can say that there are more reasons than one to regard the Austric or Australoids as the original inhabitants of India." (pp. 194-200) [28]. So, the tribes of South India like the Kadars, Irulas etc. constitute a sub-race or variety of Australoids, and not of Negroids. Those are named as Negritos because their appearance is almost like Negroes.

The cave dwellers of Central India

Recently V. S. Wakankar published his article entitled 'Archaeology' in Madhya Pradesh [29] in which he says: "The political boundary of Madhya Pradesh touches almost all the important linguistic and cultural regions of India. Hence it is situated on the crossroads of cultural migrations that took place since the emergence of prehistoric man some 20 million years ago.

"During major paleoclimatic changes the Shivalic flora and fauna got a suitable refuge on the out-stretching Vindhya and Satpura hills covering nearly one-third of the total area of the province.

"Some two million years ago a race like the Australopithacus of Africa emerged on the plateaus of Malwa and Chindawara, on the hilly tracts of Mahakaushal, Chota-Nagpur, Chattishgarh and on the plains of Bundelkhand. The crude stone tools generally known to archaeologists as pebble tools are found scattered in the laterite fields of these above regions.

"Successive tribes left a rich heritage of stone axes and picks all over the River valleys, natural caves and shelters of the sandstone hills of the Arraulli, Vindhaya, Satpura and Mahendra hills. Their remains have been excavated at Bhimbetka and Hoshangabad.

"Some 30,000 years ago India witnessed an extreme dry climate and the luxuriant forests disappeared, grass lands and dry valleys attracted cactus and palms which still survive. The ostrich moved over these grass lands and fossilised ostrich egg shells have been discovered in the Ken valley. They have been discovered on Malwa plateau and the homo sapiens Bhimbetkian (ancestor of the modern Indian) used these eggs as bowls—decorating them ingeniously and engraving designs on them—made beads and amulets. These have been discovered at Bimbetka, Bhopal, Nagda, Runija, Dangawada, Pagaria, Kota, Badnagar and a few Ken River sites.

"These are the first and earliest records of art activities in India. Ostrich egg shells have been dated by C¹⁴ dating method of 25,000 years Before Present (BP).

"This was the time known to archaeologists as the Upper Palaeolithic age and during this period the prehistoric humans had abandoned heavy stone tools and discovered the art of preparing handy microlithic tools and invented archery to become masters of the living world. Their achievements, rituals, struggles and socio-religious conceptions have been recorded in the shelters and caverns discovered all over Madhya Pradesh by several archaeologists of different Universities and the State and Central Archaeological Departments.

"The famous caves and shelter sites of Bhimbetka, Jaora, Adamgarh, Pachmardhi, Sujanpura, Abchanda, Gwallior, Shivapuri, Modi-Gandhisagar, Bhopal and Raisen have rich heritage of painted records of the Upper Palaeolithic and Mesolithic man. Bhimbetka has proved to be the paradise of prehistoric rock art and has become an international centre for archaeologists and art critics as well as art historians. The sandstone belt between Raisen, Bhopal and Jaora had the richest concentration of painted caves and shelters in the world (more than 3,600 shelters).

"Rice production — From seven to five thousand years B.P. Neolithic tribes started rice production and developed small, settled community centres along the northern fringe of the Vindhya hills facing the Ganga valley. They spread towards Jashpur, Raigarh, Bastar and the Jabalpur area and often came in contact with the newly settled Chalcolithic communities of the Betwa, Chambal and Narmada valleys. The Chalcolithic communities had migrated from the banks of Ganga-Yamuna and occupied the Malwa plateau. They had developed their economy based on agriculture, a highly decorative ceramic industry and metallurgy.

"The Kayatha culture was the earliest of these cultures (4,200 B.P.) followed by the Ahar and Malwa Chalcolithic. They came in contact on the eastern side with neolithic and on the western side with the Harappan communities. The excavations at Nawada Toli by Deccan College and Baroda University, at Eran by Sagar University, at Vidisha by the Archaeological Survey, at Kayatha by Vikram University, at Indore, Mandasaur, Dangawada, Pipliya, Lorka and Runija by Vikram University and State Department of Archaeology and Museums have brought out important archaeological material to build up a fairly good picture of these agricultural settlements occupying the plateau of Malwa and the River valley of Narmada".

Dr. Wakankar gives an excellent account of the period that we are interested in, say the pluviation period of the last phase of the Pleistocene age, and this account in broad terms is more or less the same for other areas of the Indian continent starting from 33° N latitude upto the South. But he does not refer to the dry and hot climate with cyclones experienced in Goa, evidence of which is provided by the fossils of roots referred to in the previous chapter. This period corresponds to the time about 1,000 years after the end of the Pleistocene age. This omission may be due to two circumstances: first, because the archaeologists did not find the fossils. Second, the cyclones were derived from western winds. These might have lost their intensity progressively and since the area under study—Madhya Pradesh—is very far from the west coast, the cyclones were not experienced in Madhya Pradesh.

Dr. Wakankar also says that during major palaeoclimatic changes the Shivalic flora and fauna (at the footings of Himalayas) found a refuge on the out-stretching Vindhya and Satpura. Some of these Himalayan flora and fauna are seen even at the southernmost tip of India like the hilltops of the Nilgiri mountains.

Human migrations

What we observe in respect of flora and fauna, may also be seen in mankind. In the arid period before the pluviation started—named as the third inter-glacial/pluvial period—men migrated to the valleys in search of sweet water for drinking and when the pluviation began they shifted to the shelters and caverns. In the Deccan plateau there are very few caverns. So when pluviation gained its climax in c. 18,000 B.C., the people residing there fled helter-skelter in search of proper shelter. Due to the migration and sedentary life in the caverns for millenia, hybridization took place with anthropological differentiation as well as differentiation in ability to produce tools and weapons, religious rituals and customs. This type of change is universal during the period under study, that is from the third interglacial/pluvial to the post-fourth glacial/pluvial periods. It is well known that the main processes responsible for the formation of races, sub-races and the tribes are: mutation, natural selection, genetic drift, migration, isolation, hybridization, sexual selection and social selection. These processes continued later also, but let us dwell on this aspect for the moment.

H.G. Rawlinson in his book on India, summarizes Von Elickstedt's theory of Indian anthropology with the observation that 'it will, with due additions as knowledge advances, stand the test of future research'. It is therefore worth mentioning here his views.

Von Elickstedt holds the view that the terms Dravidian and Aryan refer to languages and should not be confused with ethnic types. Without involving the reader in the complexities of ethnology we may summarize the theory thus:

In the early post-glacial period, there lived in the Indian peninsula dark-skinned people akin to the early Negroid stock of Africa and Melanesia. These Indo-Negroids were of two major types, one of smaller stature and more primitive, living in the forest and the other of high stature and more progressive, living in the plains. Next after them came from the north another primitive stock akin to the Veddas of Ceylon and the Irula of the Nilgiris and gradually intermingled with the Indo-Negroids. These people were of short stature and had long hair and broad noses. They are called the Veddas who fall into two subtypes, Melanids and Gondids. The Veddas and the mixed stock stand in definite ethnic contrast to the other peoples and castes of India in face and physique.

The second ethnic stock termed Melanids have a high degree of variation in physical characteristics which can be seen in the people of northern Ceylon and the Tamils. In Von Eickstedt's view Tamil was not the original speech of the Melanids, but was forced upon them from the North.

Dr. Sankalia, in his exhaustive investigation observed that in the Deccan Plateau there existed between 40,000 and 20,000 years ago a mesolithic culture (p. 27) but the next finds are only of 1,500 B.C. onwards, representative of the Chalcolitic period (p. 29). Hence there is a gap of about 16,000 years between the finds, and this gap starts from C 18,000 B.C., the climax of the pluviation period. He says that (p. 31) the Chalcolithic agriculturist culture with permanent settlements found in different areas of the Deccan plateau dating between 1,500 B.C. to 8000 B.C. extended as far as the Narmada and Tapti River valleys in the North, and Krishna and Tungbhadra River valley in the South. In the Inamgaon excavation he found a mixture of both northern Malwa cultures with very clear evidence. However, the circumstances which led to this are not understandable, he says. In the later period c. 600 B.C. the influence of southern culture is more intensive. [25]

This is what he says in respect of the area of the Deccan plateau making reference to the change of climate but without dating it, which he does in his other work. Here he says that the last Pleistocene period ended and the Holocene period started between 10,000 and 4,000 B.C. Around the beginning of the Holocene period, he says, dry climate was experienced throughout the world with differing intensity and nature from region to region; Further, he adds that, "This had, as in many parts of the world, created sand-dunes."

For our purpose, to get a clear picture of the first settlements and their dating in pre-historic times, we need the account of finds of archaeological value from the area on the west of the Sahyadri range or say of the Malabar coast. Dr. Sankalia made investigations in Sasti island and in Bombay area but he did not find objects of archaeological value. However, he gives in fig. 60 pictures of microliths found in that area previously, investigated by Gordon and Todd, and among them picture No. 32-a mace-head—seems to be of a relatively modern time. This had a geometrical curved form and the central hole is also round with the boundary (bit) circular in form (25) p. 141. From this type of carving it's clear that the object, if it is genuine, cannot be contemporaneous with the other implements shown on the same page, which are prepared only by the method of flacking with the use of a chisel made of chalcedony. The picture does not furnish dimensions of the depth of the circular hole. These dimensions need to be known to find out if the chisel was of chalcedony or of a metal, probably iron, because only this metal is available in the nearest site of the locality. The dating of this find cannot therefore be determined.

ARCHAEOLOGICAL FINDINGS FROM GOA

Now, we will examine the findings from Goa.

After the liberation of Goa, the Archaeological Survey of India, deputed from South-Western Circle S. A. Sali in the year 1965. He submitted his report, under the title "Exploration in Goa". (30). The age-wise classification made by him of his finds is very doubtful because all the finds that he collected were lying on the surface of the soil. Often we find on the tops of forest mountains in Goa regular cut-back stone slabs and stone rollers taken from outside and placed there by the Kumeri cultivators to grind their condiments. Sometimes, to keep themselves busy and to pass the time in the long leisurely hours of rain, these cultivators even carved out stone tools like sickles and left them on the spot as they were not of any practical use. I had the opportunity to witness this while working in the Land Survey Department, preparing plans of mining claims. So, whenever the finds are from the surface, I do not consider them of archaeological value unless similar finds are also found underground. Dr. Sankalia also, on the same grounds, did not accept a collection from the surface at Kandivli (now part of Greater Bombay) as of archaeological value. (25) p. 128. All the same, I might have tried to study the finds collected by Sali, but could not do so as the whole collection was sent to the Aurangabad museum at the branch of Central Archaeology.

I harboured doubts concerning the report of S.A. Sali, not only because the finds were from the surface of the soil but also because of wrong classification of some of his finds. Sali classified the finds of Shigaon village (Hemadbarcem division of Sanguem taluka) as of Early Stone Age (Palaeolithic Age), those of Arali and Fatorpa (Quepem taluka) as of the Middle Stone Age, and those of villages of other talukas as of the Late Stone Age. According to his report, the finds from Fatorpa and Arali were of quartz in irregular cores, arrow treads, etc.

It is known that some of the families named *Walars* or *Kankancars* residing in Cuncolim village (Salcete taluka) made bangles from quartz, through generations, collecting pieces of quartz from Fatorpa and nearby Cuncolim village. So, the same families may have collected the quartz from Arali. The collection was probably abandoned when glass became available in the market. Hence the classification made by Sali in this respect is untenable and based on this defect, the classification of other finds also become doubtful.

There are some quartzite pieces in the collection of the museum of Central Archaeology at Old Goa. On the label it is mentioned that these pieces were found in beds of the Mandovi and the Zuari rivers, but without mention of the locality. These kind of finds do not characterize any type of implements, or determine their palaeological age.

Now, let me consider the finds observed by me and evaluate their archaeological value.

Prehistoric tools: hand-axes & stone scimitars

In 1980, Chakravarti, B.Ed. from Anantapur in Andhra Pradesh was travelling in Goa. Being a Jain, he was visiting sites considered as localities of Jain idols.

One day he came with a hand-axe (*ill. 4*). He had found it on a rock on the bank of a river adjacent to a property named 'Usgalimola' where sugarcane was planted by a

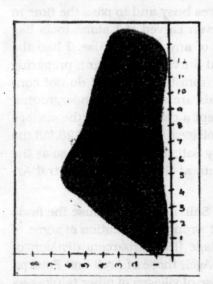

ill. 4 : Hand-Axe found at Cavorem village, Quepem Taluka, dated c. 6,000 B.C.

person of the Savoikar family of Savoi-Verem of Ponda taluka. The site, according to his description, I presume to be in Cavorem of Quepem taluka. The hand-axe is a prototype of an iron axe in use at present and its size and shape is similar to the iron axe customarily employed in cuttings of forest trees. The proportional and geometric carving denotes that an iron-chisel must have been used for this purpose. It is my opinion that a rumendatary iron tool like the scissor might have been used for carving this hand-axe. The hand-axe lacked a hole to insert a wooden stick (handle). Then what might be its proposed use? Was it a votive? But there is no deity in Goa which is worshipped with this type of votive. Paikadev, the deity of that area is offered a horse of clay, sometimes even of brass as a votive, as this idol is carved on horseback. So another alternative was that it might be the symbol of Shree Parashurama whose weapon was a battle-axe; but this idea could not be

taken into consideration, because firstly, in all the places venerated as of Shree Parashurama, there is no such symbol, and, secondly, except on the coastal area of

Goa, there is no site dedicated to him, nor is there any legend in that area connected to him. A remote possibility is that the axe might be a votive for Deuchar (a beneficent spirit), but I have never heard of an axe being offered to him. Let me also state that I was hesitant to consider that hand-axe of any archaeological value because it was found on the surface of a rock, but I was impressed by the information given by Shri Chakravarti that there were faint line carvings of an elephant and sun on the rock, this being of archaeological importance.

Later, in the month of July, 1981, an European came to my residence. He had gone through my articles published in the daily 'Navhind Times' on Oracle-plates discovered at Savoi-Verem (Ponda taluka). He was from London, a hippy residing on the beach of Anjuna (Bardez taluka). He informed me that he was an archaeologist and showed me a piece of black stone which was a hand-axe. I have seen figures of many stone hand-axes in different books of Indian Archaeology, but this hand-axe was so beautifully carved that I had some doubts regarding its authenticity. Firstly, because the piece was found, as he told me, on the top of a rock situated at the sea-shore at Anjuna. Secondly, the stone used for it was not basaltic schist, but a very finely grained dark black stone not obtainable on the Goan sea-shore. Thirdly, (see sketch, ill. 5) the hand-axe was made from the core of stone with clear cut edges on two opposing sides which I presume, might be cut only with an iron chisel. It was 15 cm long, 3 cms thick, 14 cms wide on the top and 10 cm on the bottom. On the top an excellent curve was cut so that this piece could be caught firmly in the fist. On the lower edge, in the opposite direction to the fist, the stone was maintained in a conical form—3 cm. long, but the apex of the cone was not sharp. It was 3 mm in diameter. The whole cone had a rough surface, the base being somewhat large in diameter (say about 5 cm), while the thickness of the upper portion was only around 3 cm. Both the faces measured about 15 cm in length and were geometrically parallel to one another. I thought that the person had visited me with the intention of selling it, but being suspicious about its genuineness, I did not ask him. Later I got a stone weapon which changed my view. I received from Nalinidevi Baburau Bhivam Rau Desai, wife of Baburau Bivan Rau

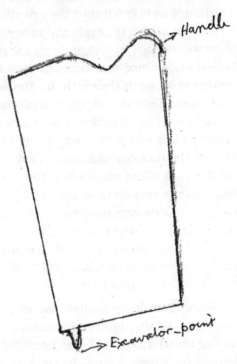

ill. 5 : Sketch of Hand-axe shown by a hippy as found on a rock on the sea-shore at Anjuna, Bardez Taluka.

Desai of Thane (Sattari taluka) a scimitar—a long dagger—of basalt schist similar to the one made from steel which was used as a weapon by the Arabs and Turks *(ill. 6)*. The lady was supervising the digging of trenches in the field for an areca-nut garden in the property named Mathacho-sard situated at Thanem in Dongurli village. The scimitar was discovered by a labourer while opening a trench. It was found at 90 cm. depth about 35 metres away from the bank of the rivulet. Before this discovery I had heard in 1943, from the villagers, that long ago a skirmish had taken place at that site between two villages. A person of the Naik family had told me that his ancestor was killed in that struggle and so a piece of land was granted to his family. The cause of the skirmish, according to his explanation, was that the symbol of Askin-Siddha existing at present in that area in a shrine, was taken from a distant village. I could not accept the explanation because there was no logic in bringing only the symbol—a linga since the samadhi of Askin-Siddha is beneath the earth. In the adjacent village, Golauli, there is a small shrine carved on a face of rock at about a height of two metres where the villagers offer worship in the memory of Siddha.

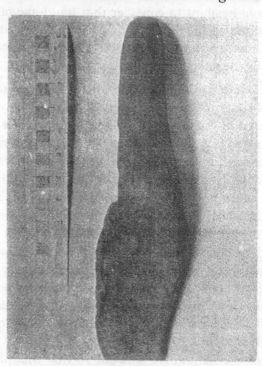

ill. 6 : Scimitar of Basalt schist found at a depth of one metre while opening a trench at Thane village, Sattari taluka, dated c. 1st Century A.D.

However, the pertinent fact is that in time past, skirmishes had taken place when the use of iron for weapons was unknown. Even then some points remain to be clarified: (1) how is it that the shape of this scimitar is like that of the weapons used by the Arabs and Turks; (2) which material was utilized for the making of the chisel employed in carving the shape of the scimitar. The rock material used for the scimitar is dolomite. But, the finding of the scimitar similar to the weapons used by Arabs and Turks does not mean that Arabs and Turks had contact with Goa at that time.

Remnants of residential round houses are found in different sites in India. In Inamgaon (Maharashtra) a remnant of a round house with pots and vessels of clay dating about 1,500 B.C. has been discovered. In Karnataka also remnants of round houses have been found. In 1932, I had the opportunity to visit the area of a property named 'Holiechem-mol' situated at Talaulim of Bhati in Sanguem taluka where there were remnants of four round houses. In 1935, I saw two remnants of such round houses at Surla village in Sanguem taluka. But what is more interesting is that thousands of kilometres away from those sites, round house constructions of mud-clay and wood and marked between 8,500 and 8,000 B.C. with radioactive carbon dating were unearthed in the site of Mureybit on the Middle Euphrates River, 80 kilometres east of Alippo, Syria (24) p. 56. This does not mean that there was contact between South India and Mureybit. I can cite another example: in respect of and combined arcs of circles with different radius noticed in the fabrication of implements (such as the scimitar) found in Goa, and cited by me, I have to point out that in the Boreal period or say before 8,000 B.C. the people of Europe made geometric points of arrows. [31] p. 35.

But despite the above justification, I could not accept those two finds as of ancient times, or say, of the neolithic-Chalcolithic period, because their styles and shapes are identical to those of the modern period. The hand-axe may be efficiently utilized for digging and getting edible roots for food; but for that purpose this type of beautiful carving was unnecessary. Here, another idea comes up. There are many geometrically proportional paintings of animals of the Pleistocene period found in natural caves in Madhya Pradesh and South India. Hence, we cannot rule out the possibility of that type of mankind with developed intelligence, when it migrated to this side of Goa might have produced some time after migration those implements — the hand-axe and the stone scimitar which are prototypes of modern implements. However, the axe is without a hole-socket and the scimitar is with a straight handle while the modern one is with undulations to enable firm handling in the fist.

The dilemma of a stone scimitar found at Thanem (Sattari)

I was caught on the horns of a dilemma as to whether these two implements were of historical value or not. At this juncture I was reminded of Sir John Marshall. He says, "Now we come to two small statuettes which are more surprising even than the masterly engraving of the bull stamped on the covers of these two volumes, these two sculptures, which are reproduced in pla. X and XI, were found in strate of the Chalcolithic Age at Harappa. When I first saw them I found it difficult to believe that they were prehistoric; they seemed so completely to upset all established ideas about early art. Modelling such as this was unknown in the ancient world upto the Hellenistic age of Greece, and I thought, therefore, that some mistake must surely have been made.

"We know definitely that the Indus engrave could anticipate the Greek in the delineation of animal forms: and if we compare the statuette of Pl. X, with, for example Seal 337 we must admit that there is a certain kinship between the two, both in the "monumental" treatment of the figures as a whole and in the perfection of their anatomical details. Experienced sculptors whom I have consulted on the subject take the view that an artist who could engrave the seal in question would have had little difficulty in carving the statuette; archaeologists will probably take another view and prefer to wait for further discoveries before committing themselves". [32].

Setting aside my doubts and accepting the view of Sir John Marshall, I considered those two implements as of antiquity, but another problem raised its head— the nature of material of the chisel used for making these implements. This problem is also relevant in respect of the cutting of the sides and cleaning of both the faces of the stone hand-axe shown to me by the hippy, as the quartzite chisel would be ineffective for this purpose. At this juncture, I have before my eyes the lines geometrically carved on a hard stone denoting genuine Sumerian script found at the locality named "Barazan" at Savoi-Verem, and the lines carved on two stones identified by me as oracle-plates discovered in the same village (which will be referred to at length in the next chapter). The major metal ore available in Goa is iron ore, so the metal tools from antiquity could be of iron only.

Primitive metallurgy

Now the point is to define the time when the people started using this material. According to the archaeological finds, the archaeologists define its use c. 1200 B.C. in Northern India and about 1,000 B.C. in the South. But some Indologists referring to a song from the Rigveda (in which is mentioned that Asvinikumars made a leg of iron and attached it to a person) and the profuse reference to iron, designated as "Shukla-Ayas", in the Atharva-Veda which includes hymns dating even to 2,700 B.C., indicates that iron was known to the Aryan people at that time, despite the fact that no object of iron was discovered in the Indus Valley culture.

On the other hand, Rev. Halffman in his Encyclopaedia Mundarika (33) narrates a folk-tale in great length, under the name "Asura Kahani". The gist of it is that the Asura tribes of Chota Nagpur were producing iron by heating the iron ore; this operation resulted in a huge smoke column which even reached heaven, annoying the God Sing-Bonga. He sent orders to stop the work but the tribes refused. Hence Sing-Bonga punished them. All the male elements of the tribe died—burnt in the furnace, and their wives abandoned. They were driven away by the other tribe occupying the areas developed by initiating regular agriculture with the use of iron tools, changing the primitive process of cultivation by the slash-and-burn system (*Cumeri* in the Konkani language). Thus it is most likely that the use of iron was known to the aborigines not only of the North but also of the South before the advent of the Aryans, as mentioned by Dr. Dixitar . According to V. R. Ramachandra Dixitar, the iron age in South India may be dated between 10,000 and 8,000 B.C. (34).

"According to metallurgy, the melting point of iron is 900 centigrade an . .o obtain this temperature it is necessary to utilize, besides a leather bellows, a furnace of a special type. However, iron oxides reduce at lower temperature, at about the same heat as those of copper, but owing to the much higher melting point, the experimenters were not rewarded with a flow of metal. The small lumps of metal were lost in the spongy mass of the 'bloom'. It is hardly surprising that millenia went by before men discovered the many processes needed to produce an iron that was superior to bronze, the heavy work of extracting the metal by much heating and hammering was not enough, for this wrought iron remained soft. It was more fit for ornaments than for tools or weapons".

"It was not until the second half of the second millennium B.C. that the essential process of carbonizing, or steeling, by repeated heating in the presence of charcoal, and hammering was fully mastered. It seems to have been accomplished by those famous metallurgists, the Chalybes, then subject to the Hittites. For some two centuries (1400-1200 B.C.) the Hittites held a near monopoly. Then with the collapse of their empire and the general ethnic upheaval of the time, the blacksmith's art was spread rapidly in all directions. Mesopotamia, however, was slow to adopt the new metal. Although it had been known and sparingly used centuries earlier, it can be said, that was not true Iron Age there before the ninth century." [35] (p. 140).

"About forty centuries ago, man learned how to win this metal from ore. This may have happened in Egypt or Mesopotamia. In any case, archaeologists have found fragments of tools made from this metal in the Great Pyramid of Cheops. Over 3,000 years ago this metal became known to the Greeks and the ancient peoples of the Caucasus. In China, the metal turned up some five hundred years later. The aborigines of America and Australia learned about it as late as a few hundred years ago".

"Wherever it came along, the new metal fully ousted stone as the material for tools and weapons. It was made into swords and axes, utensils and ornaments, ploughs and hammers. It also ousted bronze which had given its name to a whole age in man's history. Now the new metal gave its name to a new age". [35] pp. 65-66.

It is seen from the history of Sumer, the southernmost part of Mesopotamia, that Sir John Wooley discovered in excavation at Ur, city of Sumer, a furnace with some pieces of iron which when treated afterwards with C^{14}, were found to be of the time 2,200 B.C. In Sumer the meteoritic iron was employed for the making of weapons for the Patesi—rulers of the city states, and for manufacturing weapons for high officials. The Sumerians utilized the iron obtained from the ores situated in Northern Mesopotamia, like the Zogros mountains. [36].

There is no need to mention that from the beginning iron was obtained by heating the ore. It is also an admitted fact that in ancient times the iron produced by heating was through wood-fire or charcoal-fire, but it was in the solid form (open air process) and not in melted ones, as this last form can be attained only when the temperature of heating was more than 900 centigrades, which can be attained only with a special type of blast furnace.

Both the writers mentioned above, namely M. Vasilyev [35] and Sir John Wooley [36] are of the opinion that the iron obtained by heating in antiquity was spongy. However, they do not mention whether any type of flux, like limestone or dolomite was used to remove the impurities like sulphur, phosphorous, silica and alumina. The main point is that those writers do not make any reference to India, inspite of the fact that India is a country rich in iron ore, producing iron objects from 1,000 B.C., if not earlier. Bihar, Orissa, Goa, Hospet, Bellari in India have been famous for long for their hematite ore of high grade ranging between 60 and 68. So, I would like to concentrate on my own observations during my lifetime.

Metallurgy in Goa

In 1950, while working in the Land Survey Department, I noticed in the forest land at Sancordem (Sanguem taluka) a high laterite rock with a natural plain surface on the top. On this large surface there were five blocks of white colour, out of which two had the upper portion demolished. Each block (cube) was about 25 cms (each side), and at the bottom was an arched hole, and, if I remember well, a cup-type hollow part on the top about 7 cms in height and welled on all four sides. I wanted to extract one of the cubes which was wedged into the rough surface of the laterite rock and though I tried with a penknife to remove them one by one, my work was unfruitful. Soon after inserting the pen-knife in the bottom of the cube, the slight pressure made by me to remove it was sufficient to demolish the cube. I verified that the material used for manufacturing the cube was powder of lime-stone. When asked, the old man of the village informed me that these cubes had been made by the *Dhavads*—men of the blacksmith caste from the Western Ghats—and that, they had used the iron ore from surrounding areas as well as limestone and charcoal prepared from local wood. They did not know from where the limestone was obtained by the *Dhavads*; neither did they know the process used for the production of the metal. The cubes were without doubt a blast furnace.

A century ago, Antonio Lopes Mendes in his report in respect of Gavanem village of Sattari taluka mentioned that in that village there was excellent iron ore, mixed with chromium which the *Dhavads* were utilizing to get iron. As Head of Section of Mines and Industries in the Portuguese times, I had the opportunity to visit an iron ore mine in Gavanem village. I found that the average grade of ore was fluctuating between 64 and 65, and some lumps were even of 67 grade. The same was the position of another mine at Colem village of Sanguem taluka. But, unlike the observation of Lopes Mendes, there was no chromium found at Gavanem by the mine owners. Both these sites (Colem and Gavanem) are within 15 kms from the site where the said cubes of limestone were discovered. The limestone is available in Sattari taluka. As we know, charcoal and limestone are both very important elements in the production of good iron.

Even the villagers were not able to explain the process used by the *Dhavads*. I presume that they produced the metal by the solid process (open air method) and probably they were mixing a small quantity of manganese to add strength to the metal. In Goa, like iron ore, there are many locations with excellent manganese ore as well as ferro-manganese deposits. All this ore is being exported abroad, mainly to Japan.

I presume that the art of producing iron originated thousands of years ago. Here I remember the phrase previously quoted: "Man first came upon this metal (iron) in the Stone Age". In many sites of Goa, lumps of iron-oxide, mostly hematite of high grade quality encrustated in the laterite rock were visible even in 1955 on the surface of the soil. It is easy to understand that the men who occupied the land in the early settlements might have discovered its use by trial-and-error method, and the use of the ore might have spread very soon with the migration of people. The original settlers came to Goa with knowledge on the making of tools from iron ore—the knowledge which they had gained at their original homes. However, the point of dating the beginning of the use of iron remains open and so, at least the preliminary stage of tentative dating has to be gauged.

ETYMOLOGY OF LOCALITIES AND CASTE NAMES

I have already referred to the line-carvings noticed in Savoi-Verem. The carving of two words of the genuine Sumerian script on basalt rock and the carving of the lines of two oracle-plates on gneiss-Schist rocks is a evidence for the fact that iron scissors were used. Based on this, I put its dating at 1,500 B.C. and this dating will be explained further in chapter IV. Now comes the question: Did the use of iron start with the advent of the Sumerians, or was it in vogue before them? To answer this, we have to study the nomenclature of some localities, as well as caste names. For the time being we will set aside the knowledge of iron to the people of Aryan stock, in view of its mention as "Shukla-Ayas" in the Atharva-Veda.

There is a village in Pednem taluka named Kansarvorne and with the same name lies a property measuring about 3 hectares situated in Nanelim village (Sattari taluka). There is another village in Bicholim (*Dicholi*) taluka named Cansarpale and a place named "Vorne or Vorn" near Bali village (Quepem taluka). Now we have to analyse both the words, Cansar (Kansar) and Vorne or Vorn.

The word "Kansar" in Marathi means copper-smith, but in the Deccan plateau of Maharashtra and in the north of Goa, glass bangle-makers are also designated as

"Kansar". On the other hand, since in Goa there is no copper ore, there is no reason why a caste of this designation should exist in Goa. The word "Kansar" cannot denote exclusively the glass banglemaker as in Cansarpale village, which means village of 'Kansars', there are no workers engaged in glass bangle making neither is there any tradition of that type of work. Moreover, there is no quartz in that village or in the vicinity to account for the designation.

On the other hand, a carpenter is designated by the word "Thawai" (derived from the sanskrit word 'sthapati') or 'Chari' as the surname. The goldsmiths are named "Shet", the same word meaning merchant. A copper-plate designated in history as the copper-plate of Nagadeva, denotes the names of the donees as being Kansars (coppersmiths) or Sonars (goldsmiths). There is no proper word in the Konkani language for blacksmith. The blacksmith as well as the carpenter are uniformly designated as "Mesta", a corrupted version of the Portuguese word 'Mestre', meaning skilful. However, from Cuncolim village of Salcete taluka to the south of Goa the blacksmith is named 'Kammar', a word from Kannada.

The point I want to emphasize is that the Kansars (coppersmiths) settled in Goa before the advent of the Sumerians.

Now, let me analyse the other word 'Vorne' or 'Vorn' to get a clear picture of the words 'Kansar Vorne'. I think that 'Vorne' is of the Mundari language. The publication of the Encyclopaedia Mundarika which is valuable in obtaining the definition of words, stopped at the alphabet P. So, it can't offer a solution. We need to make an indirect approach. The furnace of a clay vessel utilized for soaking and parching of gram is named 'Khorn'. The furnace used for preparation of lime from marine shells is also named "Khorn" in Goa. However, I could not conclude that "Khorn" or "Khornem" was a corruption of the Mundari word 'Vorn'. So, it appears that in prehistoric and even in protohistoric times the word 'Kansar' was employed to denote a class of workers in minerals. It has been noticed in the history of the period before 2,000 B.C. that the work in copper, lead, gold and sporadically in iron was being done by the people of only one class of smiths. This will be explored in more detail in Chapter 3.

Now let me turn to the finds described earlier. One of those finds is a stone scimitar discovered in the excavation at Mathacho-sord at Thane of Sattari taluka. The property named 'Cansarvorne' situated in Naneli village lies about three kilometres from "Mathacho sord". So, the iron-chisel used for cutting must obviously have been moulded in the blast furnace established there. The site was suitable for the purpose. Good iron ore could be had from Codal or Gavanem village, the limestone selected from the path which passes through Rivem village and the charcoal easily prepared from the wood (especially trees imparting heat of great intensity such as the tamarind, gum-Arabic, myrobalan etc.) from the adjacent forest. I could not find any sign of the existence of such a furnace, except the name of the property, since a long time ago the whole area was tilled and occupied by medicinal bushes. I presume that the sites continued to be used for the making of iron objects like nails and other implements like horse shoes in the 7th century A.D., in the time of Vantudeva or Vantuvallabha, King of Goa, and the Chalukyas of Badami.

So, I can say with assurance that the stone axe found by Chakravarti and the stone scimitar found by Nalinidevi Desai may be dated c. first century A.D., and if the stone hand-axe shown to me by the hippy is genuine then this implement is to be placed at c. 3,000 B.C., all the implements being of the neolithic-chalcaeolithic period.

At this stage, the arrow point of basalt-schist discovered in the bed of the Kushavati river by V M Naik, Technical Officer for the local Archaeological Section of the Direc-torate of Archives and Museum should also be taken into account.

This point is an isolated find and we can take this object to be chronologically more ancient than the find previously referred to. The arrow head is geometrically cut so that the base may be inserted in a cut (crack) in the middle portion of a wooden stick upto 3.5 cm length so that the remaining portion of the arrow point is suitable for wounding by shooting it from a wooden bow. This implement of basalt-schist is likely to be classified as of the Late Stone period of the Palaeolithic Age. However, there is no way of ascertaining its date because there is no mention of such a regular size arrow-point in the archaeological works of the neighbouring area. The pictures of points given by Dr. Sankalia in his book are of different types and shapes and, moreover, in a curved form and even he does not date them [25].

Hence, we will attempt its dating tentatively by the indirect method. Dr. Wakankar in his quoted article says that rice-producing started in the area of Madhya Pradesh from seven to five thousand years before the present (B.P.). (29).

The probability of the advent of the first settlers in Goa is more likely from the coastal area from the South as well as from the North, with least probability from the East, or say, from the Deccan Plateau because it is obvious that the Plateau was occupied after the occupation of the coastal area.

The first chapter of the recent edition of 'History of Karnataka' furnishes the summary of Prehistoric cultures, but even tentative dating is not mentioned [3]. So also no racial or tribal names are given to compare with the finds and social struc-ture of Goa. The microliths found in the southern most area like Tinnevelly of South India are placed between 8,000 and 6,000 B.C. However, we have to reduce this time scale concerning Goa, if we consider that this culture which was on the east side spread to the west of the Peninsula, crossing the Sahyadri range through Karnataka. People move elsewhere when a calamity strikes forcing them to change the site, but they look for a similar environment, and so much movement takes place along the same latitude. In cases where people stayed on the banks of rivers, they move along the banks, but once they reach the sea-shore, they continue to spread along this shore, except in the case of attack from that side. In the human history of antiquity this fact stands verified.

We have already touched on this point before, but here the circumstances has been repeated to ascertain the dating of the first settlers. It is a very intricate problem. We get names of villages like Ivrem in Sattari taluka, where the Kols and Mundari tribes lived in ancient times (the proof for this will be referred to later) and interestingly, there is also a village with the same name in the area of Chota Nagpur. We have a village named 'Dhavaj' in Tiswadi taluka, and a hamlet with the same name in Kundai village, Ponda taluka, a small village named Ela of Tiswadi taluka, and the household of the matrilineal caste of this village is named "Sthawaj". The name Ela is a corruption of the Kanadi word 'Helle' meaning 'a clod of clay'. There are places named "Dhumak" in Cumbarjuvem (*Cumbarjua*) village of Tiswadi taluka and in Orgao and Volvoi villages of Ponda taluka. A similar designation "Dhumakari" is given in the Oraon tribe of Chota Nagpur for dormitories. Nearby, there are sites named "Manda" for dancing (in Goa named '*Dhalo*') during the month of "Poushha", but this type of festival is not observed in the South of Goa. In many villages of Goa, from Bardez taluka to Sanguem town of Cotarli village of Sanguem taluka, we find the tradition of worship of a "Khunti", like in Chota-Nagpur. Today we do not find this in the talukas of the Old Conquests (Tiswadi, Bardez and Salcete talukas), since it was wiped out during the fervour of propagation of Christianity. Yet the Portuguese records refer to it. However, the worship of "Khunti" continues in other talukas. It is strange that while the priest in charge of worship is named "Pahan" in Chota Nagpur, here the person is named "Jalmi". The worship is made by a person of Gavda (Satarkar and Velip castes) or of Naik caste except in the village of Cotombi of Quepem taluka where a person of the Mhar caste performs the rituals. It is noticeable that in Kerala state the headman of the village is named "Janmi", who obviously conducts such type of rituals but there is no "Khunti" worship. Probably the word "Jalmi" is a corruption of "Janmi", and it appears that this word has a Sanskrit derivation meaning 'born' or the 'original settler'. But how could this type of word be employed in a place with the Malyalam language? [1].

ANCIENT ROUTES OF HUMAN MIGRATIONS

I have furnished these examples to show how intricate the problem is of finding the original home of the different tribes which settled in Goa. Dr. Irawati Karve admits that the movement of the people from North to the South and vice-versa took place long ago and mentions (37) (pp. 54-56) the five ancient routes along which this movement occurred.

The first route, starting from Bengal runs along the sea-coast, enters Orissa and passes through Jaganathpuri, Konark and lake Chilka and further moves up to the mouth of the Godawari River. This is not of importance to Maharashtra because it runs to the South. However, from the mouth of the Godavari, it may turn to the West and thus pass Maharashtra.

The second route, from the plateau of Chhatisgarh runs to the junction of the Veinganga and the Warda Rivers. By this route from Magadha (Bihar), Wanga (Bengal) and Kalinga (Orissa) one may enter Maharashtra or from eastern Maharashtra one may pass to the North. This is the route through which the Santal, Munda, Ho, Korku and other tribes speaking Mon-Khmer language migrated, not only to other parts of India but also to Maharashtra. Perhaps, Agasthi might have travelled along this route to go to South India. This route goes further to the Tailangana (Andhra) crossing the Wardha River. The troops of Bhounsule of Nagpur passed to Katak and Puri by this route in the reverse direction.

The third route passes from the North to the South, crossing the Narmada River at Bhedaghat and consists of two branches, Jabalpur-Prayaga and Jabalpur-Barhanpur.

The fourth route, starting from Barhanpur, crosses the Tapti River. By this route many human groups came from the North to the South. The tribes Gujara, Parvar, Ahir, etc., came by this route to northern Maharashtra. In historic times, the Muslim travelled to the South by this route and the Marathas for their raids on Delhi also utilized this route for mobilizing their troops.

The fifth route passes along the sea-shore. This is also important for our study. Starting from northern Gujarat it runs through Lata-Desha (Southern Gujarat) and then through the northern Konkan, crosses the Western Ghat on the East and enters the Deccan Plateau. One of its branches running along the sea-shore goes to the South, the main route starting from northern Gujarat has two branches at its North, one moving to the West and crossing the Rana of Kaccha goes straight to the banks of the Indus River.

It is worthwhile to note that one of the most important deities of India—the Mother Hingulla—named in Kathewad and Gujarat as Hinglaj-Mata has its shrine situated almost on the boundary of Sind common to Baluchistan while the other shrine is situated at Ghaul in Konkar. According to Prof. D. D. Kosambi (38) the shrines and in some cases the famous temples in Maharashtra were resting places in the long routes of ancient times. In Goa also we have such ancient routes with shrines (now there is no population because of migration) like the temple of Shree Mahadev at Tamdi of Surla village (Sanguem taluka). The route from the Western Ghats passing near this temple was in use for commerce even in modern times. Improved by the queen of that area in c. 13th century A.D., this route might have been utilized in ancient historic times by the Maratha people for invasion against the aboriginal tribes.

The second batch on the same route passed from Rajasthan to the Punjab and from there to the Kheibar Pass. The wandering groups from the plateau of the Middle Asia, the Aryans from the Caspean sea, the merchants Panis and those from Armenia, Turkasthan and Iraq as well as the invaders, Shakas and Kshatrapas came by that route and imposed their sway upto Maharashtra.

By these five routes not only the tribes migrated from North to South, but some must also have passed from South to North. There is no clear evidence whether the Kolams and Gonds, among other jungle-tribes, were in the second category.

DATING THE FIRST GOAN SETTLEMENTS

I will now quote an observation referred to by K. A. Nilkanth Sastri: (39)

"At the south, in the valleys of the Krishna and the Tungabhadra River are found polished stone implements dating from 5 to 10 thousand years ago".

The observation quoted above is useful for our purpose in fixing the names of tribes which originally settled in Goa and their routes of migration. Nevertheless, the colonization of the land of Goa, a coastal land, must have probably been done before that of the Deccan Plateau which is at a high altitude, densely forested and, as such, at first sight could not be selected for settlement by the migrating human elements.

Dr. Irawati Karve, in the same book, [37] after giving an account of anthropometric measurements of the different castes of Maharashtra (chap. IV) says: (p. 43). "In all the present castes (cultivators, Brahmins, artisans etc.) there appears some mixture of forest tribal ones". What she says in respect of the present people of Maharashtra is applicable also to the people of Goa. So, as mentioned before, I shall refer only to the present caste names and whenever possible, I will trace and identify with those of the tribes of other Indian regions by the manner which will be seen in the next chapters.

However, the main point of dating of the first settlement in Goa remains open. Dr. Irawati Karve says nothing about it. Even if she presumes that the finds discovered in the Krishna and the Tungabhadra Rivers date between five to ten thousand years ago, this does not help in the dating of the primitive settlement in Maharashtra.

The exhaustive archaeological survey of Maharashtra also does not provide the dating of the first settlements there. Any find before 12,000 years ago has no application, and what they give of the later dating is of finds of the chalcaolithic period of about 2,000 B.C. It is seen that no implement of the period between 10,000 B.C. and 2,000 B.C. (approx.) is found not only in Maharashtra but also in other regions of northern India. (pp. 30-31). It is too far-fetched to admit that after the end of the Pleistocene Age, mankind which was out of the natural caves and shelters, had gained the knowledge of the art of cultivation as well as of domestication   settled directly in Maharashtra. Dr. Sankaliya thinks [25] that these people of chalcolithic culture probably came from outside (p. 30), but before them some social groups like the Bhills, Gonds, etc., whom Dr. Karve considers to have migrated from South to North might have occupied the land without any permanent settlements. With their inferior culture and scarcity of evidence, dating them is impossible. Moreover, we do not know which type of tribe settled in the round houses, remnants of which (dating about 1,500 B.C.) are found in Inamgaon and other sites.

Taking into view all the aspects of the case, I am inclined to postulate that the first man seen by the land of Goa cannot be dated earlier than 10,000 B.C.

Let us pause here, review and summarize what we have gathered in the preceding pages of this chapter.

SUMMARY

As the land of Goa along with the coastal land at North and South, emerged out of sea-waters c. 10,000 B.C., salinity was lost and vegetation sprang up and so the land became suitable for permanent settlement c. 8,500 B.C. However, soon after the upheaval of land, some people might have wandered through the foothills of the Western Ghats. It is obvious that the original settlers of Goa must have been immigrants from the adjacent area, most probably from the adjacent sea-shore land. So, we have investigated the position of human kind in those areas beginning from 8,000 B.C. onwards.

According to the historians the prevailing race in the middle and South India was Australoid, the Negri to being a variation of the same race. The noticeable variations in the race occurred due to isolation, environmental conditions, nature of food and natural selection, at least during the fourth glacial period, or say, from 30,000 B.C. to 10,000 B.C. and mixing of elements thus differentiated after that period, which gave birth to different tribal groups with different socio-religious conceptions and so on. Here we have not considered Mongoloid and other races because those are out of the region from which the migration to Goa took place.

During the fourth glacial/pluvial period, man had abandoned heavy stone tools and had shifted to producing microlithic implements, and had acquired the knowledge of archery.

Then we have scrutinized the archaeological value of the finds discovered in Goa, which are very few. It is postulated that the knowledge of use of iron was acquired by man in Goa c. 3,000 B.C., making it by heating in the solid process (open air process) and thus shaping tools like the chisel.

Next we have reviewed the position of settlement in the southern most area of South India and Maharashtra for dating of the first settlement in Goa. Despite finds of dubious age from adjoining areas, comparing them with the finds from Goa, it might be postulated that the first man seen by the land of Goa was not earlier than 10,000 B.C. Permanent settlements however started around 8,500 B.C.

Chapter - 3
CULTURAL TRENDS OF THE ORIGINAL
SETTLEMENTS IN GOA

From the preceding chapter it is seen that the land of Goa, being part of a strip of land designated in the Puranas as 'Parashurama Kshetra', was out of sea-waters about twelve thousand years ago (C: 10,000 B.C.), at the time the continued pluviation period was over. Man who had secluded himself in natural caves, was out in the plains, and changed his implements from big stone ones to small microliths which continued to be prepared from quartzite.

During the period of seclusion, the increase of population was very negligible owing to low fertility due to constant humidity, scarcity of substantial food and increase in mortality. Then the conditions completely changed. Population increased suddenly and man wandered in small groups in search of good food and sweet water. Even these groups did not try to settle permanently because they had to change their dwellings always in search of edible roots, wild fruits and live grams. Step by step, started permanent settlements, but when the population increased, some families changed their sites, establishing new settlements pari passu, and by natural instinct especially the women folk practised rudimentary agriculture, cultivating wild quality grain and fruit and making mud-vessels for storing the grain. This primordial phase of the Neolithic stage is noticed in all parts of the world, differing only in respect of time.

THE PIONEER SETTLERS OF PARASHURAMA KSHETRA

It is said that "...the Palaeolithic man in India knew the use of fire. Traces of fire having been used are found in Kurnul Caves". [40] (p. 24)

Obviously, the strip of land, Parashurama Kshetra, contained a high degree of salinity in the beginning, but from c. 10,000 to c. 9,000 B.C. the rains continued, though irregularly, and so the salinity of the surface area of the strip went on dwindling. The decrease of salinity upto a depth of two metres is sufficient for the growth of even a big tree; so after a lapse of one or two centuries, grass, bushes and even trees started to grow and spread throughout that strip of land. Subsequently, animals migrated to this zone.

The increase in population forced migration from South as well as from North zones of India, and as such, the land of Goa was occupied by people who came from both these directions. The route of migration was naturally along the river and brook-banks, crossing the mountain range through low-lying clefts and passes, generally near the source of the brooks. After staying at the bottom of the western slope of the Sahyadri and Nilgiri ranges, the emigrants found themselves mostly in the plain area by the sea-shore and spread out in the North-South direction more or less along the foothills of the mountains. Step by step, they migrated westwards upto the sea-shore. One point however remains to be resolved— whether this movement started from the South or from the North, especially in respect of the area of Goa. It is certain, though, that these primitive settlers did not come from the Deccan Plateau, which was colonized after Goa. Let us consult scholars on this point [42].

TRIBAL MIGRATION FROM THE SOUTH

The Uraons

In the introduction to his book Roy refers to E. A. Gait's view that "a tribe of Dravidian speakers migrated thither (Baluchisthan) from the South. It is unlikely that, at the time when Northern India was inhabited by speakers of Munda language, Baluchisthan, Sind and Bombay, like the South of India, were occupied by speakers of Dravidian languages".[41]

Further, Roy says on page 67: "A few centuries later, however, a Dravidian tribe, followed hard by pursuing enemies from the North, found their intrusive way into the jungle tracts which hitherto the Mundas had called all their own. These unwelcome intruders were the Kuruks, better known to us as the Uraons (Note: The name Kurukh was sometimes supposed to mean 'hill-men'). Colonel Dalton seems inclined to think that the name is derived from Konkan, the people of Konkan being supposedly identical with the Kamkanas who are included in the topographical list given in the Vishnu Purana. The form Kurukh is supposed to be due to the Uraon's partiality for gutturals and Konkan is supposed to have been the cradle of the race (vide Dalton's Ethnology [43], p. 245). More probable, however, appears to be the derivation of the name I have heard some Uraons give. According to them, the name Kurukh is a variant of Coorg where the Uraons formerly lived. M. Dhanmasi Panna of the Subordinate Executive Service, the first Uraon Graduate of the Calcutta University is one of the Uraons who gave me this derivation. Since writing the above I have come across a paper on the Uraons and Mundas contributed by Rev. Father F. A. Grignard, S.J. in the Anthrop edited by the great ethnologist Dr. Schmidt. Father Gregnard has sought to prove the identity of the Uraons or Kurukhs with the Kurushas of Sanskrit literature. He further maintains that the term Rakshasa as applied to the aborigines is nothing else than a wilful mispronunciation of the word Karusha."

The ancient history of the Uraons is enveloped in still deeper darkness than even that of the Mundas.

"Uraons claim their descent from Ravana, the legendary king of Lanka. Whatever may be the worth of this ambitious claim to renowned ancestry, it seems pretty certain that at some remote period in their history they had lived in Southern India. ...The Uraons' tongue is akin to the Canarese (Kannad) language". [41] p. 68.

These quotations lead us to the hypothesis that from Coorg (now part of Karnataka State) tribal waves migrated upto Baluchistan via Bombay - Sind - Baluchistan, and bifurcating at the North of Bombay, passed to Ranchi district, now in Chota Nagpur, under the name of Korukh or Uraon, in times immemorial. Now, it is necessary to verify whether this view of migration from South to Northern direction is a simple hypothesis or fact. For this purpose, I have prepared three comparative charts (see Appendix Pg. 352) of the names of villages and various places of Goa, Ratnagiri and Kolaba District with linguistic links. It is admitted by scholars that according to human instinctive tendency, the settlers almost invariably try to repeat the name of their original home in the new settlement. This has been true even in the sixteenth century A.D. leading to names such as New York, New Guinea, New Zealand etc. It is also admitted that the names of villages as well as places and/or rivers, hills, etc. include at least one root-word of any language, so these names cannot be considered meaningless. Sometimes we are not in a position to decipher the meaning of such designations either because we are not versatile in many languages and tongues, or because those words have disappeared from today's tongue or language.

From the above referred comparative charts prepared by me, it is seen that:

1. Names of about 167 villages of Goa including a dozen hamlets, one mountain and three properties are either identical with or similar to the names of villages of Ratnagiri and Kolaba districts.

2. Many of these names are repeated not only in Goa, but also in both the districts mentioned above.

3. A majority of such names have root words referable either to a tree or an animal or a topographical feature or the nature of soil. Some names are attributable as well to a tribal such as Kol. However there are some names such as Bhom, whose significance is unknown due to reasons already mentioned.

4. Generally, the names ending in -vali, -pal, and -de, are of the South Indian origin. For example, we have a village named Kandivali in Kolaba district, Candolim (Bardez taluka) and Khandolem (Ponda district) in Goa. Interestingly, a village of the same name is found in the south-eastern most part of India. It should be noted that microliths found in that village may be placed between 8,000 and 6,000 B.C. [40] p. 51.

The linguistic evidence

In South India, we have many names with such endings as mentioned above. Vasant S. Joshi [43] is of the opinion that the ending syllables of the place— names like patti, padi pada - vadi, vada-hatti, hat, hadi etc. are reflective of Dravidian culture. His opinion is correct. In addition, there is evidence to that effect in Goa.

There is a village named Pali in *Dicholi* (Bicholim) taluka, while an identically named 'Pali' appears as the capital of Nannan, a feudatory of the Chera kings of South India. In Goa there are two villages named Navelim, in Salcete and *Dicholi* (Bicholim) talukas, while there is a village with a similar name Nelveli in the area surrounding Madurai.

However, objections may be raised that in Sanskrit the word 'Palli' means a small village; and I go further in support of this view: in a copper plate of a king of the Bhoja dynasty ruling from Chandra-Ura (not Chandrapura as was designated afterwards as the present Chandor village of Salcete taluka) there is a word 'pallika', meaning small village in the Sanskrit language. But this objection is untenable, because in the earlier Sanskrit literature up to the time of writing of the epics Ramayana and Mahabharata, a small village is designated as 'Ghoshha', the village as 'Graama' and the village of commercial importance as a 'Nagara'. So, it is clear that the word 'Palli' was borrowed by the Sanskrit language in the later Sanskrit literature. It is admitted by scholars that many non-Aryan words were adopted in the

Sanskrit language.

So we can definitely conclude that the original settlements in Goa started from the South and the most ancient or say the primitive settlers were of Southern origin. Once they were in the plains by the sea-shore, successive generations, due to the rise in population spread to the remaining portion at the north of Goa, and afterwards migrated to Baluchistan as well as to the area of Chota Nagpur. Now comes the query as to why these tribes instead of remaining in the plains, migrated to the hilly areas of Chota Nagpur. Here is the answer.

THE NEOLITHIC CLIMATE

c. 9,000 B.C. the climatic conditions suddenly changed. There were violent western winds, arid and hot, which uprooted trees in the western coast of India. The historians of India have not taken cognizance of this change, except Dr. Sankalia who has noted its occurrence but did not ascribe much importance to it because he did not find clear archaeoligical proof about it, which I did, as already mentioned before. However, we also do not know if these dry and violent western winds attacked the entire western coastal zone with equal intensity and whether they reached from the sea shore all the way up to the western slope of the Sahyadri and Nilgiri ranges. We also do not know if these winds were in the form of cyclones throughout the whole area. Similarly, variations in intensity are seen in tectonic movements of the Earth. Be that as it may, the essential fact is that dry and violent winds attacked the western coastal zone and the people with permanent settlements in that zone abandoned their habitat in panic and frantically ran to places which they thought safe. Only very few families might have taken shelter here and there in the strip of Konkan land, obviously including Goa, where they found shelter from the winds and a perennial supply of sweet water.

We have also no account of the time when the seasonal rains started; tentatively I consider that at least five hundred years might have lapsed since then. However, it is an established fact that during that period of five centuries, the initial arid condition of the atmosphere changed in a short time, as the land was on the sea shore. Gradually, the atmosphere became more and more humid. Lastly, clouds formed in the sky but no precipitation took place up to the end of that period, when the monsoon winds started, with the result that very soon—but one cannot say exactly or even approximately when—vegetation appeared. The sequence of this may be first grass, then bushes and afterwards trees which grew only atmospheric humidity. The land was covered with vegetation, the surface became somewhat cool, the level of underground water rose, the original fountains and springs which had become dry due to the sudden change of climate again came to life, and perhaps some more springs might have originated anew in this period. Consequently, the land which was previously occupied by animals and people was again occupied by such beings, but in extremely scattered form. The settlers of this period were obviously the descendants of those of the primitive stock who were residing nearby. Tentatively, we may fix the time of this new colonization one century after the sudden rise of western winds.

This theory might be objected to the grounds that the springs which became dry due to the dense vegetation of the surface give water when trees are cut off, as can be seen in the cut-and-fire or say, *cumeri* system of cultivation. However, this objection is untenable because in this case the atmosphere was periodically humid, due to annual rains before and after cutting of the trees, while in the present case the atmosphere was completely dry. Scholars with knowledge of the science of agro-hydrostatics will accept my views, taking into consideration the relation between vertical movement of underground water and the local climatic variations of a certain duration.

These people and their descendants spread throughout the Konkan area, establishing new settlements and villages, and gave them the names. I have referred to these village names earlier mainly to show from where the primitive settlers were, as the present people are descendants of that stock, which today continues, under the designation of 'Mhar', as a caste. (Later in this study this caste will be referred to again, regarding their cultural trends).

Hitherto we have described the movement of southern people to prove how those people travelled to the northern zone of India upto Chota Nagpur, taking note of the settlement of the Konkan area. The same type of movement took place in that area upto 8,500 B.C. —not much influenced or only sporadically influenced by the cyclones. Sharad Chanda Roy in the previously cited book gives a good account of the tribes of Chota Nagpur, but all the tribes of that area as well as of Ranchi district are classified by him as Kolarian tribes [42]. The names of different tribes are given, except the Kurukh or Uraons who are considered as non-Kolarian tribes. However, while describing the customs and village and patti-group of villages—the administration—he always refers to the Mundaris. From this, it appears that the Munda tribe enjoyed the highest status among all the tribes such as Kols, Hos (Larka Kols), Santals, Bhumija, Korwars, Juang, Bir-hor, Asuras and so on. There are also many offshoots of the Mundas, one of them being the Kok-Pat Mundas in Chota Nagpur (presently in Bihar). The main difference between the Uraons and Kolarian tribe is that the Uraon's tongue is of Dravidian type and that they eat beef, like the Mhar of the same origin. There is evidence, like the southern Indian peoples, that the Kolarian went westward up to Sopara on the west coast. The identical name "Sopari" is that of a village in Chota Nagpur. I do not have in hand the list of villages of both sides to make a comparative study like the one I have done in the appendix attached. However, I feel that the movement/migration of the people of Northern India must have involved the zone up to the western coastal area at the time of the last Pleistocene Age which ended c. 10,000 B.C.

During the drought that occurred c. 9,000 B.C., the Kolarian people residing on the sea-shore must have left the occupied place, moving to the East and settling under safe conditions. It is also seen that these people had long before in the last Pleistocene Age occupied the hillside of Arauli and Vindhyan ranges, taking shelter in the caverns there. When the effects of the arid western winds ended, the Kolarian tribes, like the people from Southern India or say, Dravidians in Konkan might have occupied again the Gujarat area. This can be stated from the fact that besides the Sopari side there is a zone named Golvana in northern Gujarat which is a proof of the existence in antiquity of the settlements in that area of the Kol, other tribes like Munda or Mundari with the hegemony of the former, contrary to the Chota Nagpur region in the later period.

New settlements in the Konkan

Here, we must make an important observation:

The historian Nilkant Sastri says that mankind in India had known fire in the Palaeolithic age, and for proof they refer to the Kurmul (in South India) caves [39] p. 24. "It is not possible to fix the dates of the different ages in the history of India. However, it may be stated that the Palaeolithic Age lasted from about 35,000 to 10,000 B.C. and the Neolithic Age from about 10,000 B.C. to 5,000 B.C. The Copper Age probably started about 4,000 years ago. The view of Dr. V. A. Smith is that the earliest of the copper tools may be as old as 2,000 B.C. The discovery or introduction of iron in South India may have occurred much later and quite independently". (p. 27)

However, it seems that the people who had settled in the western zone of India might have witnessed the kindling of fire by friction of trees caused by the violent western winds c. 9,000 B.C. At that time the Asura tribe which was living in the present mining area of copper and iron-ore of good quality, of Chota Nagpur, observed that the ore on the surface of the soil, exposed to air had been melted by fire and pieces of such melted ore were useful to make ornaments. Perhaps they tried their best to make tools from this otherwise somewhat spongy metal for excavating soil to get edible roots for which they were using quartzite tools. The same might have taken place in Southern India. The discovery by human beings of kindling of fire throughout the world has its origin in witnessing the friction of trees due to violent winds. This resulted in a great revolution in their lives which has been described in many histories and so there is no need to repeat it here. The melting by fire of rocks containing metal in rich percentage was also witnessed at that time by settlers in different parts of the world. This observation too has been equally revolutionary. But the people in different parts of the world took more or less time according to their ability, and by the trial-and-error method, to get somewhat pure metal, and this happened wherever iron-ore existed. In the same way, the Asura tribe of Chota Nagpur might have continued the trial-and-error method for thousands of years, and might have discovered pure iron or say, wrought iron, which is referred to in the tale 'Asura Kahani' inserted in Encyclopedia Mundarika by Rev. Hoffman and by Roy in the book cited before. This tale in essence shows that the primitive settlers of a certain area of Chota Napgur—the Asuras—who had learnt the art of melting iron-ore and producing wrought iron had been displaced through a sanguineous struggle by the members of other Kolarian tribes, namely the Mundas and Hos (Larka Kols). Only a few families were kept back for their service as smiths and allied pursuits like weaving.

It is worth noting that according to the opinion of both the above mentioned writers, all those who belonged to the same ethnic groups had similar customs, religious concepts and language (but with a little variation in dialect). However, the Mundas and other tribes do not take food cooked by Asuras, and if they do then they take it without salt. This conduct does not represent any element of untouchability but arises from the generation-old rivalry between these groups, which persisted even when they separately migrated to Goa. It is to be noted that the Asuras were persecuted by the Kol, probably Hol, during the entire period of migration, forcing the Asuras to abandon their settlements. It appears that the Asuras were industrious people; they knew the art of working in metal, but failed in life because their knowledge in metals was limited to moulding small tools only for agriculture. They were not able to make weapons of war. For this purpose they used weapons only of stone and bows and arrows. The Kols, though they used the same type of weapons, were more versatile in the art of hunting and of battle. According to some historians the word 'Kol' is of Sanskrit origin meaning 'pig', and this name was given to them by the Aryans when they came in contact with them in the northern-most areas of India, because of their proficiency in hunting wild boars. The Asuras were mild, like the Jews and Greeks. The latter were versatile in the different sciences but had been subjugated by the Romans who were good fighters with the result that the Greeks lived the life of slaves, teaching the Roman children different arts, sciences and philosophy. The lesson we learn from this history is that all advancements are futile unless one also gets the most advanced technology in defence. The custom of the Mundas of not taking cooked food with salt from the hands of Mahali-Mundas is comparable to the identical custom of the Muslims in Goa. The Muslims do not take such meals in the house of Hindus, because if they did take such a meal, they would be obligated to be life-long friends. Otherwise they would be condemned as "namak-haram", which is a great sin according to their religion.

Some quasi-historical traditions of Asuras, Mundas and Kols

Roy, quoting from 'Philosophy of History' , says, "It is high time then that antiquarian investigators should turn their attention to the quasi-historical traditions of those interesting tribes and land, with the aid of their traditions, seek to trace back their early history so far as it is still possible". [41] (p. 2)

I am also guided by similar opinion, and so in respect of the episode of Shree Parashurama I fixed his dating from the Rigveda Samhita and the dating of the episode of Vritra from the same Samhita, noting that the later episode was recorded by Vyas, about 6,500 years after it took place. In future writing I will proceed in the same manner, when I find other facts and evidence corroborating such episodes as well as tales, irrespective of the time elapsed, even if it is 4,000 years. The custom and cultural trends when cited will be those which I had observed myself sixty years ago, from childhood. I shall also refer to those facts and events narrated by villagers of different parts of Goa while I travelled around during my official field-work. Many such old customs are gradually disappearing, and as such, deserve to be chronicled.

It is necessary to clarify some points referred to by B. D. Satoskar, in his Marathi book [44] "Gomantak - Physiography and Culture—Part I—Social architecture and Social life—Formation and Mode of Living of its People" (Gomantak Prakriti and Sanskriti- Khand: Samaj rachana wa Samaj Jiwan) published in 1979, wherein the author has made direct references to my work. The book was prepared, as the author says, by compiling matter from the works of different authors, and finally, the author has offered his own views.

Ethnological observations

Nagas in place names

B. D. Satoskar in his book points out that I did not refer to the Naga Tribe in my article published in "Gomantakachi Pratima" (Image of Goa). In fact I did mention it but in a condensed form, avoiding digressions purely of theoretical and academic value. I am convinced, that the word Naga was a Sanskrit one, meaning 'related to the mountain' (Naga) and as such the Nagas did not exist as a tribe but as a group of different tribes living in mountainous areas. The Puranas refer to Shabaras, Punindas, Nishadas, Yakshas, Kimnars, Gandharuvas and Nagas as aboriginal tribes; from their description it appears that the Nagas form a group of different tribes, excluding those specifically designated.

Satoskar gives an account of different opinions and concludes that "even today there exist evidences of ancient existence of the Naga people in Konkan and Karnataka on the sea-shore land. The place names and matriarchal system existing in some castes at some places are two of those signs. There is no doubt that long ago the Naga tribe existed in Goa, as this area is included within that already mentioned."

"The dating of the arrival of Naga people in India and Konkan has not yet been fixed. However these people might have intermingled with other people without maintaining their separate existence. Rajwade is of the opinion that these people passed as being Kshatriyas, and as proof, he cites some surnames of Marathas of the Konkan country". This is Satoskar's view. Now we will verify the correctness of this statement.

It is known that the Marathas enjoying hegemony in the country tried to link their genealogical origin with the mythical Nagas, like— the Yadavas. Balarama, the brother of Shree Krishna is considered to be an incarnation of Sheshha Naga, and his image in Gujarat is carved with a five-headed hood instead of a human face. There is a human idol with the lower part of a serpent made of stone found at Vadi village of Ponda taluka, now preserved in the local archaeological museum. It is probably of the 6th century A.D. There is also an image worshipped at a hillside of Ponda town named 'Shembro Dev', so called because his nose is cut, with each hand holding a serpent and the Naga's hood shading the head. It appears that both were installed simultaneously in the regime of Vantu-Vallabha-Senenandaraja of the Sendraka family in the 6th century A.D. He was the maternal uncle of Chalukya Pulakesi II of Badami and was then the ruler of Goa. Both of them are considered as Nagavamshi, at least the Chalukyas, through the legend which says that the progenitor of Chalukyas was of northern India and was fed by a Naga (king cobra). So Rajwade's opinion is not acceptable. Satoskar does not mention the names of places which in his opinion are related to the Naga settlements.

I tried my best to find place names from Goa and village-names of Ratnagiri and Kolaba districts constituting the Northern and Southern Konkan, except Karwar district, with 'Nagas' as a root-word.

In Goa, there are four villages named 'Nagvem' (in Bardez, Quepem, Salcete and Sattari talukas, and a place named 'Nagzar' in Pednem taluka).

In Ratnagiri district, there is Nagane village in Chiplun taluka and Nagavem village in Kankavali taluka.

In Kolaba district we find Nagaloi in Savantwadi taluka, five villages named Nagany in five different talukas, Nagazari in Poladpur taluka, two villages named 'Nagashe' in Murud and Sudhagad talukas, Nagaroli in Mangaon taluka, Nagasari in Alibag taluka and Nagothane in Roha taluka.

In the Kolarian tribe group (Kol, Munda, Ho, etc.) there was a belief that a Naga (king cobra) or his spirit 'Naga-bonga', always existed near springs and ponds. The name Nagzori or Nagzar ('zari' means spring) is derived from that belief; the same is the case with Nagashet ('shet' means rice field) because a spring or pond always exists in these ricefields. Other names of villages may be derived from 'Naga-Era', a deity of the same tribal group. So this kind of place-names cannot be identified as of Naga tribe origin unless other proofs of its existence are also given, and these are not present in Satoskar's postulation.

Moreover, Shree Nagesh of *Bandivadem* (Bandora) village, Ponda taluka is probably the sublimation of the Kolarian deity Naga-Era, as all their deities were symbolised by a black stone which in later times were designed as 'linga', though this word technically represents the phallus symbol of Shiva. As such the stone of Naga Era was sublimated as that symbol. The rituals performed in the great festival provide testimony to the Kolarian tribal origin.

There is another temple of Shree Naguesh (alias Nageswara) also in the form of a linga in Priol village, Ponda taluka. There is evidence that it was established by a Brahmin named Nagarya in the time of Tribhuvanamalla Kadamba, as can be seen from the copper plate dated 1099 A.D.

So going by the deities, there is no evidence of the settlement of the Naga people in Goa. That brings us to the last point—that of the matriarchal system. B.D. Satoskar says that the system is of Naga tribal origin and spread from Konkan to Karnataka. But in Kerala, adjacent to Karnataka, that system existed upto 1932 when by law, it was substituted by the patriarchal one, in use throughout India except Assam and in some tribes such as the Khansi. In Kerala, the matriarchal system was used among the Nayars, Thiya Menons and some other castes. So the point made by Satoskar is untenable. However, the point of origin of matriarchy and its existence in Goa remains open, and we will try to study this at the proper stage.

Yes, Indian history talks of a Naga as an ethnic stock of a historic period; but here it should be noted that the dynasty of Bharasivas which governed from about 185 A.D. to about 300 A.D. with their capital at Kantipura near Mirzapur in U.P. were Brahmins by caste, followers of the Shiva cult, and were described as "pleasing Shiva by carrying Shiva-Linga on their shoulders" [46] p. 24. There were also ruling families in Chota Nagpur and in adjacent areas calling themselves as "Nagabansi", supposedly of the Rajput caste. However, both these cases have no link to the above case of the Naga being an ancient tribe in Goa, and a matriarchal one. Here we have to note the other case: in Gujarat there is a caste designated as 'Naik' but that caste has no link with the Naik caste of Goa. The similarity of names of stocks or castes cannot define their links with one another.

Finally, Satoskar in his cited book (pp. 78-79), referring to the observations of Rajwade, says that "taking into view the said observation and existence of matriarchal system in some castes in Goa, there is no doubt that the Naga tribe settled in Konkan and consequently in Goa but they later on possibly mixed with other tribes". He cites also a chapter of Sahyadri Khanda as well as the opinion of Tarktirth Lakshaman

Shashtri Joshi who considers that in ancient times some tribes were known under the name of Naga, Garuda, Vanara, etc.

The opinion of Rajwade is untenable since the word Naga means nothing more than the people who lived in a mountainous area. Now turning to the Sahyadri-Khand in which is included "Nagavhya Mahatmya"—narration of the exhalted value of Nagvem village of Salcete taluka—there is an account [46] pp. 250-54, which, in summary, says that the Nagas (king-cobras) lodged in Nagave village by Shree Parushrama, were harassed by Garuda (the eagle). Shree Parashurama prayed to Shree Shankara, who, in response to his prayer settled with his wife Uma in that village, and in this way stopped the harassment by the eagle. In this legend those Nagas are referred as Naga-Dwija (twice born Naga), which means that this allegoric form of legend does not certainly refer to the Naga tribe. Perhaps and possibly it refers to the Padya Bhats (priest-class).

Kolgiro and Mundalgiro

The views of Lakshaman Shashtri Joshi also are not applicable here. I have doubts about the classification made by him. It is probable that some clan-totem may be of such type, but in Goa there are no tribes or class with such a totem.

Hence, there was no tribe in Goa which could be classified as Naga.

B. D. Satoskar in his book, besides making gross mistakes, arrives at contradictory conclusions. I will show such discrepancies only in reference to the above mentioned groups, because many readers who might have read that book may be confused when they go through this present work of mine. He says on page 23, that about five or six thousand years ago when mankind began settling in Goa, the village-panchayat system was introduced and that the sysem was introduced by Kol and Gavda (Gond) tribes. But soon after on page 33 he says that the Kol tribe mixed with other social groups and so at present there is no representative of the Kol tribe. He considers the Gavde tribe as Gond and does not say that the Kol tribe even partially mixed with that tribe. Then what characteristics and in which tribe or caste did Satoskar find these characteristics to say that the Kol tribe had settled here? If Satoskar has made such an affirmation based on the principle that all the waves of mankind which came to India must have passed Goa, why do we not find evidence in this regard? Thus, in the same way, it was necessary for him to make local observations of different castes existing here. But he did not take this trouble, and penned his history sitting in a room. Moreover, he intentionally ignored what I have said in my article cited by him. I have already said that the Kol tribe is now known as Satarkar Gavdo or simply Satarkar.

Now, to the subject of the settlement of the Mundari tribe in Goa. In this respect,

Satoskar says at pp. 48-50 that there are many words of Mundari origin in the Konkani language (for example, a word 'Munda', a form of 'Mundkar'). Inspite of this evidence, he does not think that this tribe ever migrated to Goa because in the Oraon tribe of the Mundari group there is a custom which is absent in Goa. If a girl reaches puberty before her marriage, first she is married to her grandfather and after that the proper marriage takes place. This reason is futile, because this kind of ritual may be exclusive to the Oraon tribe dwelling in a separate area, for example in Bengal, far from the borders of Ranchi district, and this custom may be of the modern period and may have a local reason as its basis. For comparison, I present here an example: 'The Illustrated Weekly' published an article on Saraswats and inserted it in its Annual 1972 issue, but one para of the original article is omitted. In that original article it was said that among the Saraswats there is a custom of marriage of the maternal uncle with his niece. I accept that even today there is a custom of marriage between cousins of kinship like the maternal uncle's daughter or son with their respective cousins but not directly with the maternal uncle. But after inquiries, I discovered that a century ago, when, due to lack of easy communication, the Saraswats lived in isolation in the Mangalore area, it was very difficult to get bridegrooms of different gotra,

ill. 7a : Frontal view of the idol Mundalgiro at Thane, Sattari taluka, dated c. 6th Century A.D. Please note the mask covering the head of the idol.

with the age higher than that of the girl; so that type of marriage was rarely adopted. Only because of that old custom we cannot hold that those Saraswats are different from Goan Saraswats despite the fact that their ancestors migrated from Goa. So the argument of Satoskar is baseless, and moreover that custom is referred to the Oraons who are considered to be of Dravidian origin while the Mundas are Proto-Australoids. Even more, in my article cited by him, I have clearly mentioned that in Thane hamlet of Dongurli village (Sattari taluka) are installed in a open place named 'Mundalgireachemmol' two idols named 'Kolgiro' and 'Mundalgiro' *(ill. 7a and 7b)*. In Konkni 'giro' means 'devourer', so those names mean 'devourer of Kols' and 'devourer of Mundari' respectively. The 'Kolgiro' is considered to be a king and 'Mundalgiro' his minister. Triennially a great festival named 'Ghodemanni' is celebrated at that place. These idols which are of black stone have

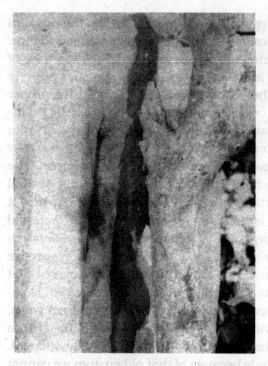

been re-installed at least twice because I found remnants of two earlier idols, which represent its very ancient antiquity. These were placed originally by the ancestors of the present Maratha Gaonkars of seven villages to commemorate the subjugating of both those tribes, which occurred possibly in the 3rd century A. D. The same victory is commemorated by a Hero-stone at Naneli village, adjacent to Thanem hamlet, probably installed at the time of the ruler Shree Vantuvalabha Senanandaraja of the Sendraka family, between the last half of the 6th and the first half of 7th century A.D. *(ill. 8).*

I had clearly mentioned in my

ill. 7b : Side view of the idol Mundalgiro at Thane, Sattari taluka, dated c. 6th Century A.D. Note the braid of hair ("veni" in Konkani language)

article cited by Satoskar, the existence of both of those idols and its significance and that the Mundaris in those villages were named 'Naik'.

All these facts are evident even today at those various sites; Satoskar ignored these facts because his mind was already made up based on certain deeply rooted presumptions. He tried to convert these presumptions into conclusions, with the result that one of the Gavda castes considered as the original settlers of Goa has been considered as the Gond tribe, while at present they worship the 'Kolpurush' at Curti village (Ponda taluka).

ill. 8 : Hero-stone at Rangachem-mol at Naneli Village, Sattari taluka, dated c. 6th Century A.D.

Demystifying Kulambis

Now let us refer to the Kulambi. Satoskar deals with this in pages 38 and 41 of his book and says that the Christian Kunbis of Salcete taluka may be originally of the

Gavda tribe or representatives of Kunbis of the Konkan. Among the Hindus of Goa, they are found in Sattari and Sanguem talukas, under the designation of Kunbi or Kulvadi who are of the Maratha caste. They are also named as Rayat in Sattari taluka because that taluka was under the *Mocasso* system of the Ranes and Desais.

Satoskar made a blunder in considering the designation Kunbi or Kulambi as an ethnic group. It, in fact, represents the professional status of different ethnic groups of lower status in Goan society whose main means of subsistence was agriculture. The word Kunbi is corruption of the word Kulambi; this word as well as Kulvadi have the same significance, and is derived from the word 'Kul'. In Kannad, Kul means a definite area of land and in Sanskrit it means the area which may be ploughed with a pair of bullocks. Derived from this word 'Kul', we have the name Kulkarni which was in use in Goa about two centuries ago, as also in Karnataka and Maharashtra, meaning the village-accountant who maintained various records in respect of village-lands.The record of granted lands was known in Goa as Kularog before the domination of the Portuguese.

The following castes in Goa are commonly designated as Kulambis: (a) the Christian Gavdes of Salcete taluka who even today consult oracles in the Hindu temples of Ponda taluka where their original village-deity is established, (b) the Christian Bharvankar Gavdes of Salcete and Quepem talukas, and (c) the Velips and Ganvkars of their kindship of Sanguem and *Kankon* (Canacona) talukas. Under the designation of Kulvadi are: (a) members of the Satarkar caste existing mainly in Ponda taluka and in Rivona village of Quepem taluka and (b) those of lower Maratha caste at Sanguem, Sattari, *Dicholi* (Bicholim) and Pednem talukas.

On the north side of Goa, in Ratnagiri district, the lower castes are of Gaudes, Kunbis and Marathas. In the south of Goa, in Karnataka, there is a caste named Konkni Kunbis. This caste formed the Konkni cultivating class of Goa, many of whom have migrated from the provice to Kanara. The Konkni Kunbis must be distinguished from the Arers of Are Marathas who speak a corrupt Marathi and are found in South Kanara. The Konkni Kunbis of Kanara maintain intimate relations with the Goa Kunbis. They eat fish and meat, except beef and domesticated birds like fowls. The Kunbi settlements have each their 'budvant', and are grouped into circles called Mahals, with its head called Mahal 'budvant' or 'gauda' who owe allegiance to the 'gauda' at Phonda (*Ponda*) in Goa.

From these observations one may easily verify how the significance of the word Kindbi characterizes different origins in those three adjacent areas. So the word Kunbi means only the cultivating class and not caste or tribe.

The antiquity of Gavdes

Now concerning the Gavdes. B.D. Satoskar in pp. 32-37 discusses the presence of a tribe under the designation of Gavde and considers those to be of the Gond sub-race. According to their description given in pp. 306-611, it appears that Satoskar ignores the existence of the Satarkar and Bharvankar Gavde in Goa, who have different customs and origins from those described by him who are commonly named as Kelsi-Kutthalkar Gavdes. Besides these three main groups of Gavdes, there are also others in the Maratha caste of Goa with Gavde as the surname, namely the Marathe Gaonkars of Zarmem, Poriem and Surla villages of Sattari taluka who with the Maratha Gaonkars of the adjacent nine villages, including Kankubi located in Belgaum and which constitute together a group of twelve villages, are considered as brothers and so do not intermarry. In Kankubi village there is a temple of Mavuli with a spring close by. Every twelve years there is a grand festival as the waters of the Bhagirathi River appear in that spring, and on the appointed day, the inhabitants of Kankubi village send messages and invitations to all the Gaonkars of the said villages to assemble in that village and conduct all the rites of celebrating the festival. Readers will remember that in about 1930, Shankarrau Gavde, Sardar of the Tukojirao Holkar, ruler of Indore State, was sentenced to death in the murder case of Baula-Bauli (Mumtaj Begum—a concubine of the Holkars), which denotes that the surname Gavde existed also in the higher Maratha caste. In Goa also we have in the Marathas of Quepem-Canacona 'Gavad' as surnames. In some Hindu temples, in Goa, we find among others, a stone named 'Gadvamsh': in Amona, in a hamlet named Khadpal Odauli and Kansarpal of Latambarcem, Mulgaon, Nanodem (originally from Calangute of Bardez taluka), Narvem, Poira—a hamlet of Maem village, *Dicholi* taluka hailing from Khorjuvem of Bardez taluka—the village of Dicholi (Bicholim) taluka; in the temples of Harmal (5th group), Halarn, Torshem, Tuem, villages of Pednem taluka; in the temples of Betki, Tivrem—villages of Ponda taluka; in the temple of Atbarcem of Sanguem taluka; and in the temples of Poriem and Pissurlem villages of Sattari taluka [47].

From this account, it is seen that Gad-vamsh temples existed in six villages of Dicholi (Bicholim) taluka, two in Bardez taluka, four in Pednem taluka, two in Ponda taluka, one in Sanguem taluka and two in Sattari taluka. They were established in the Hindu temples at least before the advent of the Portuguese in Goa. The statutes of Mazanias (Mahajanki) of the respective temples were being approved by the Government and published in the Government Gazette from the year 1881 onwards. It is seen from these statutes —one being of the Kelbai deity of Mulgaon village of Bicholim taluka (statute of 1950) and a deity from Calangute village of Bardez taluka transferred to Nanodem village of Bicholim taluka (statute of 1924) —that at the time of publication of the statutes, there were Mahajanas with the Gad surname, who are considered to be of the Maratha caste. The Christians of Calangute village (original place of that deity) call themselves of the Chardo (Chaddo) caste. The Mahajanas of the temples of Poriem and Pissurlem of Sattari taluka are considered to be of the Maratha caste. It is worth noting that in the temple of Poriem there is also 'Chardo' (Chaddo-purush) and the Gaonkars of Pissurlem in their prayer call themselves 'Chaddo-vounsh' and do not marry with the Maratha Gaonkars.

The construction of temples started four thousand years ago by the Paddye-bhats and Fattes of the Vani caste, who had come from Sumer (now part of Iraq) and their advent will be treated in another chapter. Step by step, this system was copied by others. In Sumer, the custom of installing the image of the person who has constructed the temple prevailed, and so, such custom was passed on to the Hindu temples, and later on in some cases the images of the ancestors of the presumed founders of the temple was placed, characterized generally by the name of their clan. The respective village society had its symbols established in the form of vounsh, purusha etc., and in proportion with the new settled tribes and castes, the number of these symbols grew, but this procedure probably was stopped—it seems—at c. 2,000 B.C.

Differing the point of mixing of the Maratha and Chaddo castes in Hindu society, we will focus now on the Gad-vounsh of the Maratha caste, the surname Gavad of a Maratha family, and the Gavde name of the Gaonkars of the Maratha caste, Zalmi of Pali and Surla villages of Ponda taluka. Since the last name is linked with the Gaonkars of nine villages of Belgaum district, it is beyond doubt that this word Gavde had its origin in the Kannad word Gavund, meaning originally Gaonkar in Goa. History says that the Belgaum district from the 3rd to 9th century A.D., if not earlier, was under the ruling powers of the chieftains of the Sendraka family and the Chalukyas of Badami from the 6th century A.D. onwards. In the Deccan we come across many references to the mahajanas of the villages who were in charge of local administration under the leadership of gamundas (headmen). Near the Tamil side in about the 11th century, we find references to gamundas as well as to gamunds-wamins. From this evidence it is seen that in the Deccan in the 6th century A.D., the word Gamunda was used to denote the Gaonkars. In Tamil country they came to be designated only as headman, and the leaders, otherwise named before the 6th century as gamundas, or better, gavundas, are designated in inscriptions as Mahajanas, a word of Sanskrit origin. It is clear that the usual Kannad name 'gavunda' was changed to 'gamunda', a partly Sankritized form derived from the Sanskrit word 'grama', meaning village.

Were Gavdes the original settlers?

From the discussion you may note that the word Gavda cannot mean original settler of the village. It means only the settler, or at most, one of the ancient settlers, as the Marathas appeared after the Kols and Mundaris, which is clearly proved by the fact verified at Thane of Sattari taluka, where the Kolgiro (devourer of Kols) and Mundalgiro (devourer of Mundari) idols are installed as representatives of the Maratha caste, otherwise, tribe, as mentioned before. As recorded earlier, Satoskar, while considering the Gavdas as the first settlers of Goa [44] (pp. 166 and 350), ignored completely not only the existence of Satarkar Gavdes and Bharvankar Gavdes but even of the Maratha Gavdes in Goa and refers only to the Gavdes generally known as Kelsi-Kuthalkars Gavdes, those who migrated to Ponda taluka and elsewhere due to the persecution of the Portuguese in the 16th and 17th centuries from the talukas of the Old Conquests (Bardez, Salcete, Ilhas now Tiswadi and Mormugao talukas). And he characterizes their womenfolk as dressing in a "dentli" system, i.e. the last fold of the garments covering only the abdomen and breasts, fixed by a knot made on a necklace, and so the back is bare. Another characteristic of theirs is that the women-folk used bangles made of tin or brass. But this description also is a half-truth, because the same characteristics are also found amongst the womenfolk of Velip and their allies of *Kankon* (Canacona) and Sanguem talukas, as well as of the Satarkar castes of Curti, Nirancal and Vadi villages of Ponda taluka. About the beginning of the 17th century some Saraswat Brahmin families with the surname 'Prabhu', accompanied by some Gavda families from Morgi and other villages of Pednem Taluka as also one family of the Vani caste named Moraskar, migrated to the Astagrahar division of Sanguem taluka. One of these Gavada families settled in Bhati village and so are named as "Bhatikars". The Gavdes of this family mixed with the former settlers, 'Velips' and 'Gaonkars', who cannot be distinguished now as they intermarry. Their women-folk dress in the 'dentli' style, using bangles of tin or brass, they do not eat the flesh of goat and fowl, eat only vegetables and fish and the meat of animals like wild boar, deer and the like, flesh of some birds like the partridge and do not drink liquor. Their custom of dressing, eating and drinking are similar to those of the Kelshi-Kutthalkar Gavdes. However, the Bhatikar clan (of the Gavdes) did not have the right to perform the rites of sacrifice which belonged exclusively to the Velips. Similarly the right of performing rituals at the beginning of sowing and reaping called 'Fudlik', belongs only to the Velips and Gaunkars, among whom the rice-fields are distributed.

The migration of the three families, namely Prabhu, Moraskar and Bhatikar (Gavda) is testified to by the existence of the Gavdo-vounsh in the temple of the principal village deity 'Morzai'. In the same temple the symbol of Prabhu-vounsh also exists. There are also two symbols named Sodan-Shet and Mala-shetti, probably of the said Moroskar family and in the respective catalogue of the Mahajans families with the surnames Kulkarni, Sansguiri and Moroskar are recorded.

Besides the symbol of Gavdo-vounsh at Morji, there are similar symbols under the same name in the temple of Torshem of Pednem taluka, and under the name of Gavdo-purush at Bandodem village of Ponda taluka. Though devoid of a specific symbol, the members of the Gavda caste are Mahajanas (among others) of the Shree Kamaleswar temple of Corgaon village of Pednem taluka.

It is worth noting that in Curti village of Ponda taluka there is a small temple of Kol-purush of the Gavdes of that village who call themselves as Satarkars. The Gavdes also of Nirancal and Vadi villages of the same taluka who call themselves Satarkars. They are all members of village societies (grama-samstha in Marathi and comunidade in Portuguese). They are also Mahajans of the village temple.

From the Portuguese records of descriptions of Hindu temples, prepared in the 16th century, it is found that in Carambolim village of Tiswadi taluka the symbol of the Kulambipurush (designated in the records as Curumbim-purus) existed, which certainly refers to the representation of ancestors of the group of Kelshi-Kathalkar Gavdes who were called by the Portuguese writers as Curumbins —a corruption of the word Kulambis.

The Kelashi-Kuthalkar Gavdes

I have no clear evidence to define whether these Kelshi-Kuthalkar Gavdes are Kols or Santals. Both tribes, whose branches expanded long ago upto the Ganges valley, have identical customs in religious and land-tenure systems. But the branch which exists in Chota Nagpur have a flat-nose characteristic which is not observed in these Gavdes, and so I am inclined to admit that those are Kols. This is the second wave of non-Aryans which accompanied the Aryans who migrated from Northern India. Due to the earthquake which occurred in that area, the river-bed of the Saraswati river changed, Hastinapur was destroyed and probably the great-grandson of Parikshit, named Nichakshu of Pandava-Kula, had to change his capital from Hastinapur to the East, about 100 miles away at Koshambi on the banks of the River Jamuna (near present Allahabad). Some Puranas say that in the time of Nichakshu, there took place an attack of locusts and a complete drought followed for about twelve years. As a result, all the people around the River Saraswati from part of Punjab and Kanyakubja dispersed elsewhere, and some of those people, step by step, came and settled in Goa, probably in 1,000 B.C. and not later. In these groups, the Kol tribe who migrated from Goud, the place around Kanoj, established themselves first at Kushathali—present Kuthal (Cortalim) village, Salcete taluka whose deity is Mulakeshwar, now present in the precincts of the Shree Mangesh of Priol.

This deity in the Portuguese records of the 16th century is mentioned as 'Gopinato' (corruption of Gopanath, meaning the deity of Shepherds), and some writers analysing the Sanskrit work Mulakeshwar (which is in a 'linga' form) say that these Gavdes are original settlers of Goa, considering that the word 'Mulaka' means original set-tler. But this meaning does not correspond to the truth, as is seen from the following example.

In Madkai village of Ponda taluka there is a vast 'Khazan' land belonging to the village-commune (comunidade in Portuguese). Khazan land means riverine silted land brought generally under paddy-cultivation by constructing protective bunds. In that Khazan land there are two plots named Madhyachem-mulak and Paychem-mulak, which mean respectively first piece of Khazan brought under cultivation by Maddo and the other one by Pay, both the names being surnames of two families of that village in ancient times. The same meaning is obviously of the word 'mulak' in Mulakeshwar. The second wave of the Brahmins named Goud Saraswats who migrated from Gaud, located near Kanoj, to Goa in about 1,000 B.C. along with the Gavdes probably by the same route, firstly established themselves in Kushasthali (Kutthal) in Salcete taluka, and from that part spread along with the Gavdes to other villages. At that time, Kutthal was part of the Shankhawali (Sancoal) village occupied by the Bhargava brahmins who had settled earlier. They gifted one part of that village to the newcomers. In the ancient documents of the village-commune, Kutthal is named as "agrahara" (gifted land) and not "grama". These documents correspond to the very beginning of Portuguese rule and are written in Goem-Kanadi (some call it Hale-Kannad) script [79]. So, the designation of 'Gavdo' for this tribe is obviously derived from the word 'Goud'.

The Satarkar Gavdes

That leaves a type of 'Gavdes', different from those described above, who were traced by me, very recently in the year 1981, when I visited Savai-Verem village for research. In that village there is a very small temple, a niche, which is in decayed condition. A black stone named 'Gavdo' is placed there. A person of the Satarkar caste of that village narrated the following story, confirmed by other Satarkars of the same village:

The Satarkars of Savoi-Verem were originally from Advai village of Sattari taluka. It is not known for what reason, but all the Satarkar families of that village had to abandon it, and with the Santer deity of that village they started their journey in search of new areas for settlement. When they reached Savoi-Verem village, their headman considered the village suitable for settlement. But it was already occupied by families of Gavdes, and these Gavdes were not those which we find at present in Ponda taluka. (The Satarkars do not call themselves Gavdes. By this name they designate only the Kelshi-Kutthalkar Gavdes). The headman of the Satarkar did not want to settle there under the supremacy of those Gavdes, so he forced the headman of those Gavdes to show the complete boundary of the village, and thereafter he killed him. Fear struck the Gavdes and they fled with their families, but it is not known where they settled afterwards. Very soon the Santer was established on Khamin dongor, where it exists at present and her path upwards is marked by carved holes on the rocks. The corpse of the headman was buried and a black stone was planted on that spot. To appease the spirit of the slain headman, animal sacrifice of a cock is made before the niche by the Jalmi (religious headman) of the Satarkars. The deities established by those Gavdes, the Ganaroudhuro and Khaminrouduro, came to be worshipped by the Satarkars, along with all the other rituals performed before.

The names of those deities were in pure Mundari language and I had presumed that these deities were established by the Satarkars or say, by the first Kol tribes and as such I had said so in my articles in Marathi. But when I referred to the "Tale of Bali" (67) *(Balichi-Katha)* as evidence of the advent of the people from Sumer (now part of Iraq), I was confused because the person named Tilasur in that tale is pious. Otherwise, the Asura is always considered malevolent. But the evidence of 'Gavde' of Savoi-Verem ended my confusion, since the 'Gavdo' was of the tribe of Asur or Asur-Munda which is found in Chota Nagpur. And from the Asur-Kahani published by Rev. Haffmann and by Roy (already cited), it is known that in Chota Nagpur they had gained the knowledge of the use of iron ore to fashion tools. The Satarkars defeated the mundas who fled. Some families remained as blacksmiths. Here, in Goa also, the Satarkars and the Kols, who knew the use of iron ore, used it in the same form as the Mundas in making implements. However, I do not know in what caste they are included now, but I presume that they are in the caste of the blacksmith, sometimes named as Kansar, as I said before. In Priol village near Savoi-Verem, the amalgamation might have operated differently as that tribe at the time of the tale of Bali, it appears, was a matriarchal one.

So, the word 'Gavdo' has two main origins: one derived from the Kannad and Telagu word 'Gavunda' meaning villager or gaonkar and the other derived from the word 'Goud', meaning originally from the area of northern India with that name.

The 'Hebars' or 'Shabaras'

I have already referred in the preceding chapter to the four quasi-circular remnants of houses seen by me in the year 1932 in Talauli hamlet of Bhati village and two houses, in 1935, in Surla village of Sanguem taluka. These remnants were named as 'Hebaranchigathanam' (remnants of the houses of the Shabers). The word Hebar is obviously a corruption of the word "Shabara'. In the year 1942, I found at Rivem village of Sattari taluka, a schist slab in natural quasi-oval form. On one face was carved in bas-relief the outer lines of a human figure up to the knees and it might be considered as a woman because the hands were shown with bangles and her name is Shambra-Devi. This Devi was not under worship because the villagers were of the Maratha caste and this deity was considered the deity of the former settlers named by the villagers as Hebars.

Which was this tribe and when did they settle in Goa? The designation of the Shabaras might have been given in Bhati village by the Hawik or Hawig Brahmins who had settlled there in about 1,000 A.D. They had come on the invitation of the Kadamba kings, but we have no evidence on whether those Shabaras were living or not at the time of the Hawigs arrival. Near Bhati there is a village named Viliena and it appears that this name is corruption of Bhillivana (forest occupied by the Bhills). The Ramayana narrates an episode of Shabari offering jujub fruits to Shree Rama. She is identified as Bhillina of the Bhill tribe. The historian Rajwade considers Bhills to be an ancient tribe living on the mountains of northern Konkan. However Dr. Iravati Karve, in her cited book considers the Shabara tribe different from the Bhills living in Orissa.

Passing now to the symbols placed in Hindu temples which represent the tribes or castes established in a village, unless it is otherwise, we find in Pednem taluka the symbols of Pardhi-vounsh in two villages, namely Chopdem and Torshem.

The *Pardhi* is a tribe which in Sanskrit is named Nishada, and their main profession is hunting animals like rabbit, deer, wild boar etc. It is a nomadic tribe which settles in one place only during the rainy season. According to the Bharatiya Sanskriti Kosha, the *Pardhi* is not a proper tribe, but consisted of Bhills and other tribes. Whatever be the present position, it is possible that in ancient times they settled on the hilly tracts bordering Goa temporarily during the rainy season and wandered during the remaining period in search of game, edible roots and wild fruits.

So, it appears that the Shabaras of Bhati and Surla villages of Sanguem taluka were mainly of the Bhill tribe, who established themselves on the border of Goa not before 1,000 B.C. The walls of their residences, as Rajwade says, were made with a type of shrub known locally as *Karavands* which offers protection from white ants due to a special type of fluid contained in the plant. Sometimes the walls were plastered with clay and the thatched roof was made of reeds, bamboo and palmleaves. Often, the walls were protected by a continuous wall built of rough stone boulders, sometimes using clay as mortar. According to my knowledge, fifty years ago this type of huts, but without the boulder wall, existed in the village-sites of Sanguem and Sattari taluka. It is possible that similar conditions might have existed at that time in the undeveloped areas of Pednem, and Kankon talukas.

One point regarding the Pardhi-vounsh symbol existing in Chopdem village may be emphasized. The existence of a similar symbol in Torshem village is justifiable as that village is in a jungle area, and lies on the Goa frontier adjacent to the Deccan plateau from where that tribe migrated. But Chopdem village lies far from Torshem, and moreover, on the bank of the salted waters of the Chapora River, near its mouth,where wild animals could not have existed in numbers comparable to the areas to the East of that village. One justification may be that the Pardhi tribe might have changed their profession of hunting wild animals to fishing, and so may have intermingled with the existing tribe of fishermen—locally named as Kharwi caste, at a later stage, as at present there is no Pardhi tribe in that village.

I had been inclined to admit that the Kols and Mundaris were considered as Shabara there, while the name 'Shambradevi' means 'Noseless deity' as, in the carving, no nose is seen. Likewise, at Ponda town, on the slope of a hillock, a deity named "Shembro-Dev" has been installed and this name is evidently derived from the cut nose shown on his image carved in bold-relief. As such Shambra-Devi does not have any relation with the Shabaras as could be thought of.

In Sanguem taluka, for example, in Sancordem village adjacent to Surla village where I had found two remnants of Shabara residences, there are two types of Marathas named 'Zune Marathas' (Old Marathas) and 'Nave Marathas' (the New Marathas). Both belong to the class of Kunbi-Marathas of adjacent Maharashtra state. However, there are some aristocratic families of Marathas with the surname Desai who are considered to be of a high class amongst the Marathas. They do not marry with other Marathas, who are seen as Gaonkars, even though they have the same surname of 'Desai'. The Zune Marathas do not marry the Nave Marathas, and live in separate hamlets. They differ from one another in colour and characteristics of body: the Zune Marathas have a light brown complexion, they are tall, have a straight and narrow nose, a small mouth with thin lips, fine eyebrows, oval eyes and regular cheek-bones, while the Nave Marathas are of a darker colour, short in stature, with a broad nose and eyebrows, large mouth and thick lips, round eyes and cheek-bones elevated near the orbits. It seems that they are a mixture of different tribes, including probably the Bhills. In Bhati village we do not find any person of the Bhill tribe or of mixed caste. So it seems that the Bhill tribe was extinct there for a long time. At present we do not find any tribe like the Bhills or Pardhi in Goa.

From the above discussion, it can be clearly seen that the names considered to be of tribal groups in the Puranas, as well as by history writers and by common people do mean only social groups and not tribal names.

THE MIGRATION OF KOLS

From about 8,000 B.C. waves of people from Southern India migrated to the strip of land brought up from the sea-bed, including the Konkan area. They were probably completely uncivilised people. The first wave which reached northern India due to sudden environmental change, already mentioned before, tried to find shelter in the areas less influenced by that change. They were later named as Kols. They tried to find shelter in the foothills of Sahyadri mountains on the western slopes. About 8,500 B.C., climatic conditions estabilised. The annual rainy season provided an opportunity for the fugitive people to re-establish themselves in the plains. Such an epoch in time is noticeable in cultural history throughout the world. "In Europe, the upper palaeolithic period came to an end during the ninth millennium B.C. when there was, though largely transitory, rapid improvement in the climate (the alleroid oscillation), and a more permanent change in the flora and fauna of Europe. [48]

"The majority of the inhabitants of Europe passed into a new cultural phase, the mesolithic (middle stone age)... Mesolithic man to make ends meet, spent most of his time in hunting the small and freely accessible nut, his tools show considerable progress, wooden saws with tows of small geometrically chipped flints for teeth for example. In the ninth millennium, the banks of the upper Tigris valley and in the eighth, the Palestinians of the Natufian culture were supplementing their meagre fare with wild wheat. Flint sickles and mortars and pestles demonstrate no more than this and the phase 'incipient agriculture' applied to these cultures is oppressively teleological, but the planting of the crop, the final advance needed to carry man out of the mesolithic, food-gathering state and into the agriculture of the neolithic was in fact close at hand. Note: The boat was probably an invention of this period. The dog, which presumably was suffering from the disappearance of its prey... appears as a mesolithic camp-follower". [48] p. 18.

This passage is cited here only to show how climatic stabilization produced a change in human life and brought about the sequence of different phases from the hunting and fruit-gathering stage to that involving domestication of animals and growing of crops.

The matrilocal system of original settlers

It is said by historians that this mesolithic period is characterised by the construction of small huts with dry pieces of the thickest branches of trees and dry grass as a residence and for the keeping of domesticated animals. Further, the matrilocal system was adopted. In this system, kinship was not observed in a conjugal relationship. This system characterises the primitive stage of all ancient people— not only non-Aryan but also of Aryan stock. You find many references to this state as well as further evolution of social formation in the Rigveda, Atharvaveda and even in the Mahabharata. A good account has been given by the late historian Rajwade [49], and it is necessary to note what he has proved, despite the exaggerated importance he has given to the meaning of some Sanskrit words. At the same time we should ignore the realistic view taken by him instead of the allegorical one—for example, his depiction of Soma with his 27 wives in fact refers to the moon and 27 constellations in that hymn of the Regveda.

However, the tenth sub-chapter (Sukta) of the tenth chapter (Mandala) of the Rigveda, cited by him, is clear proof of the existence of a savage system among the Aryan people in ancient times—probably when the Aryans had settled in Baktha, the eastern part of Iran. The sub-chapter includes a talk between Yami and Yama in which the former asks Yama to give her conjugal pleasure, but the brother refuses to satisfy her. At this she cites ancient examples, but the brother does not change his resolve. This sub-chapter gives a historical background of Aryan Society, then in the formative stage of the family system with marriage links. According to Indologists, the second to ninth chapters of the Rigveda are more ancient than the first and tenth. However, their sub-chapters are of a relatively modern time, like Purushasucta. According to these Indologists, though, those chapters include also some sub-chapters which are more ancient than the ones found in the remaining chapters. One such sub-chapter contains the conversation between Yami and Yama. The Mahabharata which contains more and more episodes, like the Puranas, adopting the system of "sum up and continue", provides an account of the sweetest form of marriage as well as of the matriarchal system of Kerala and other parts of the country. This is not the place to discuss different forms of conjugal life prevailing in different countries at various times, but only to show that the matrilocal system without any bonds of kinship was in vogue in all the tribes—even among the Aryans. Further, certain tribes in different parts of India including those of Goa, were obviously matrilocal in the original form.

THE NORTH KONKAN SETTLEMENTS

Rajwade in another of his articles, while referring to the original settlers of northern Konkan, says [50] pp. 49-50, "The first settlers of the northern Konkan were the cave-dwellers and the Katakari of Bhill tribe—both the tribes living in Konkan since about 6,000 before Shaka (Shalivahana Shaka). It is not possible to define how many thousands of years before Shaka those Katakaris were living in northern Konkan. They never settled on the sea-coast nor were they fishermen. They always lived in the forests of Sahyadri mountains and it is not possible to know who, during that period, were living on the sea-coast... The Katakaris lived on the somewhat flat places of the flanks whilst the other tribe lived in the caverns. The Katakari at least knew to use skins of animal".

I have quoted here the opinion of Rajwade only to give an idea of the settlements in northern Konkan about 6,000 B.C. because the new gazetteers of that area do not furnish this kind of account. The Katakaris who are of the Bhill tribe migrated obviously from northern India, mainly from Gujarat and its adjacent area on the East. Rajwade could not identify the other tribe the—cave-dweller—and so he considered that the tribe was extinct. However, I consider this tribe constituted descendants of the latter wave from southern India,—and in Goa they are represented by the Mhar Caste.

THE MHARS AS CAVE DWELLERS

Now, let me describe this tribe as well as the others in subsequent settlements, possibly on a chronological scale, warning that the chronology is tentative upto the advent of the first wave of Aryans in Goa. In the description of each tribe I shall refer to the important cultural trends of those tribes, sometimes referred to as castes, because generally those tribes, especially in later times, formed castes and sub-castes.

Mhar is now a caste in Goa, the plural being Mharam. The 'Mharam' is a corruption of Mundari word 'Marang', meaning 'of the eldest house', and as such, in Goa, the member of that tribe (now caste) is named in Konkani as '*vodelea-gharache*' (of eldest family). This description 'Mharang' was surely given by the subsequent tribes who spoke the Mundari language.

'Mharangana' is the main characteristic of the settlements of this tribe (now caste). The suffix 'na' means 'occupied place'. Compare Konkana, Kolana, Hodkolna, Firangana, etc. The 'Mharangana' has the same significance as the word 'Khunti' established by the Kolarian tribe in Goa who settled after the Mhar. This denotes the place in a village where the Mhars had marked the establishment of their colony by a stone—a symbol like the Khunti of the Kols.

From Ratnagiri district on the north, to the south in Canacona taluka of Goa, we find in many villages and places this name Marangan. Those places also existed in different villages of the Old Conquests (Tiswadi, Bardez, Salcete and Mormugao talukas) which were destroyed by the Portuguese during the fervour of conversion. We can get an account of these places—taluka and villagewise from the Portuguese records published by   Dr. P. S. Pissurlekar. However, I did not find such names in Astagrahar division of Sanguem taluka as well as in the adjacent villages of Quepem taluka. Further, there are no Mhar families there nor have they any connection with village rituals in those areas. This shows that the Mhar families migrated elsewhere (along with other tribes) due to cholera or other epidemics. Such cases were known even in historic times. However, there is clear evidence that the Mhars were the first set-tlers and for instance in Thanem of Sattari taluka, the Holi festival of this hamlet cannot be started unless the same type of festival has been performed first in 'Mharwado' (a hamlet of Mhars). In all the villages of Goa, according to village customs, the Vatandar (holder of hereditary office) Mhar must be present at the time of planting of the symbol of Holi—a trunk of the mango or arecanut tree—and he has exclusive right to all the coconuts thrown on that Holi. It is pertinent to note that in my native village, Kumbharjuvem, the Vatandar Mhar is Christian, even though he continues with his rights not only for the coconuts of Holi but also to 'Balute'—a portion of paddy—from the rice-fields. The cultivators offer him what is due without any cribbing as this custom continues in all those villages of Goa where a Vatandar Mhar resides in the village or nearby.

It is a general concept among the Hindus of Goa that the Mhar was the first settler in the village. So, morally, he is it's owner. Goan Hindus who migrated to southern India due to persecution by the Portuguese in the 16th and 17th centuries, for example to Mangalore side, have a peculiar custom: when any person dies, a person of Mundala caste is called in to prepare fuel-wood. The incineration is generally done in the property of the deceased person. However, interestingly, the person of the Mundala caste is paid on two counts - firstly, as price of the land where the deceased person is cremated and secondly, his wages. But this custom does not exist among the Hindus whose families settled in the same villages before the Hindu Goans came. It is said that this custom at the time of migration was in vogue in Goa, and that is why the Goan Hindus continued it there. The word Mundala is somewhat meaningful — the suffix 'lo', or 'la' means 'alike to'. Compare 'Bapulo' (alike 'Bapuy' = father, meaning paternal uncle), Bhavlo (alike 'Bhav'—Brethren) and Mavlo (alike Mavam = father-in-law). So, Mundala possibly means 'alike Munda'. The caste of the Mundala is untouchable. There are many other castes of lower status than this caste, but all those reside in hilly areas, so the Mundala who reside in the plains are considered as original settlers of the area.

Customs of Mhars

While females of the Mhar caste are not tattooed, females of other castes including Bhats and Brahmins got themselves tattooed before or after marriage, whenever the opportunity arose—when specialist barbers from the Ghats periodically visited the villages. It was a general belief in those castes that the female who was not tatooed was taken forcibly by the 'Janvro' for conjugal relations and nobody could oppose him. 'Janvro savkata' is the proper Konkani phrase in use. 'Janvro' is nothing but a fusion of two Mundari words, 'Juang' and 'Horo'. Juang is the name of the lowest caste of the Mundari tribe which at present lives in Chota Nagpur and Orissa. 'Horo' means man. 'Javam' is obviously corrupted from the word 'Juang'. How did this word of the sub-tribes of Munda from Chota Nagpur and Orissa happen to get to the Goan people? The other word 'horo' gave birth to the old Marathi 'Eru', meaning 'a person' while in Konkani the word took another form—'her' meaning common (man). Dr. Iravati Karve considers that the Juangs from Orissa migrated to northern Maharashtra. In the same way, it is probable that the same sub-tribe from Chota Nagpur migrated to the Konkan and so to Goa about 5,000 B.C. and mixed with the already settled tribe which constitutes the present Mhar caste. On the other hand, there could be another reason for tattooing. It appears that a woman, after attaining puberty, was considered impure unless tattooed. [37].

The Mhars are linked to the sacrifice of the male buffalo made before the village deity at Torshem (Pednem taluka), Vodocon (Ponda taluka) and Poinguinim (Canacona taluka). The neck is severed by the Vatandar Mhar, and he takes its flesh, leaving the head at the place of sacrifice, which is removed by him the next day. The offer of sacrifice at Torshem and Kakodem (Cacora) is annual while in the other two villages it is triennial. The Mhars used to eat the flesh even of dead cattle, but the new generation has abolished this practice.

In certain temples, in rituals of great festivals, the Mhars enjoy priority to enter first with small oil-lamps of clay (divjam) upto the entrance hall (Subhamandapa). This practice is seen in the temple of Shree Deuki-Krishna at Marcela (Orgaon village, Ponda taluka), originally from Chodan (Choraon) island, in Shree Navdurga temple of Cundaim (Ponda taluka), originally of Ganci-village (Tiswadi taluka) and in the temple of Poinguinim village of Canacona taluka. In the Shree Shantadurga temple of Kavlem (Ponda taluka), Mhars have the right to enter the temple upto the sanctum sanctorum (garbhakuda) on the day following the annual great festival. It is said that this privilege was offered to them as they had dismantled and shifted their huts so that the place could be used for the temple, as the deity was transferred from Kelshi (Quelossim) of Salcete to that place due to the persecution of the Hindus by the Portuguese in the 17th century. Among the families of Pednekar Goud Saraswat Brahmins, on the annual religious feasts (*deukarem*), food is ceremonially offered to a Mhar couple in addition to a Brahmin couple, thereby honouring the Mhar caste.

Goan Hindus believe that the rituals performed by a Mhar can nullify the effect of the evil eye and so a Mhar used to be summoned when a child was offered a prize or was commendated in the school or when the child was sick. The Mhar of my native village is a Christian; even then he was called to perform the rituals. He used to make two human figures of wet rice-flour mixed with turmeric powder, one male and other female, painting *"kajal"* on their eyes and a moustache for the male figure. The torches were then put on fire. Each of these figurines were then taken in hand and the Mhar used to move in a circular motion, three times, before the face of the child, chanting '*dista vachum*' (let the evil eye go). After that he used to take a portion of water in his hand and sprinkle it on the face of the child. Then the child was given a full bath.

Fifty years ago, in Usgaon village (Ponda taluka) I remember a cobra had once entered a Brahmin's house. They had brought blessed rice given by a village Mhar and thrown it out according to his instructions including even into the household shrine, without bothering about any superstition of untouchability.

In Goa, there are many families of Gavda and Kumbhar (potters of Christian religion) castes as well as Gurov and Bhagat, who for generations practice the profession of sorcery and witchcraft, but for the removal of the effect of the evil eye, and protection from cobras, the Mhar is the only person relied upon. This form of rituals produce a psychological effect on the child, fortifying his inner consciousness. I have myself experienced this effect in childhood. I presume that the Mhar tribe had from the beginning, like the Neanderthal man of thousands of years ago, a concept of the spirit in a vague form. They believe that the spirit exists in the human body even when alive. This concept is seen in other tribes in different forms and its primitive form existed amongst the Mhars.

The Mhars have their totem (kula) defined by a tree or plant. It appears that these were adopted by subsequent tribes which settled in the village. The Mhars of Thanem of Sattari taluka have 'Kalama' tree as a totem which is also the totem of Maratha Gaonkars (village members) of that place. However, a people with a common totem do not intermarry.

ARRIVAL OF THE PASTORAL TRIBE

Subsequent to the Mhars it appears that a pastoral tribe came from southern India. The Mhars lived by hunting and gathering fruits and edible roots for thousands and thousands of years. The pastoral tribe came not earlier than 4,000 B.C. This tribe domesticated buffaloes and was of the matrilineal system. They were not agricultur-ists. Probably, they held a religious belief in the worship of ancestors, said to be in

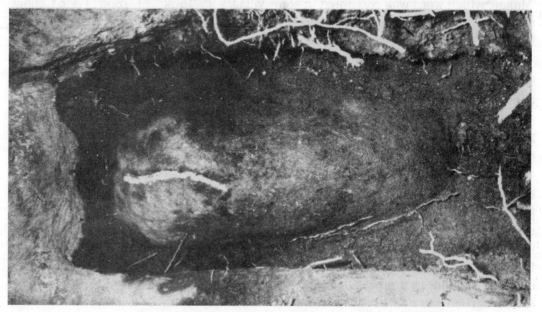

ill. 9 : "Matari". A memorial of the high priestess of God Anu (Ne-an) at Silvado, Savoi-Verem, village Ponda taluka, dated c. 2,000 B.C.

vogue in the primitive stage of human life, but I have no proof of this. However, certainly they worshipped Nature not like the primitive Indo-Aryans, but like the pro-Australoids of the Indus-Valley—they worshipped the vulva and phallus symbolizing the creators of human kind. The form of creation appeared to them as an incomprehensible task of Nature. In the Indus Valley, rings and erect stones are found separately and not joined together, because for them both elements had a separate identity as male and female elements. In Goa, the same idea persisted though not by any contact with those Proto-Australoids of the Indus Valley. Their famous figurine of the dancing girl is typical of the Indus valley tribe. Here also the tribe was of the Australoid race, and the concept of two separate (and not joined together) male and female elements was due to natural intuition.

Today in Goa, we have only one specimen of the representation of the vulva at Savoi-Vere (Ponda taluka), named *Mhatari* meaning an old woman. *(ill 9)*. The symbol is made of a small black stone, rounded on the top with a sagital groove running in the middle of the top surface. A similar specimen was present at ancient Cundaim village which was changed later on to an idol. It seems that this representation of 'Yoni', meaning vulva,was later changed as Bauka-Devi.

The archaic symbol Moko

The male element represented by an erect stone came to be named as 'Moko'or 'Makaji' which word was corrupted in some villages as 'Tonko' or 'Topo'. I don't know if this name was given initially or later on. Now we shall verify what factual history furnishes in respect of these male and female symbols and the respective tribe.

In Portuguese records of demolished temples, it is mentioned that 'Moko' was situated in Gandaulim village. In some other Portuguese records, the name 'Moko' has been mentioned as the deity of the shrine first demolished and which was situated in Dhawaj (Daugim), a hamlet of Ela village adjacent to Gandaulim. So, it appears, the recorder made a mistake. Dr. P. S. Pissurlenkar corrected this error in his publication.

Even the shrine and the symbol of 'Moko' was removed by the Portuguese. The Hindus therefore placed, near the original place, a black-stone symbolizing 'Moko', known generally as '*Rakhneacho-Dev*' (Shepherd's God), by the side of a road, and all the persons passing by that road used to offer him a leaf of a jungle-plant existing there. On the day of *Dhenulo-Padvo*—the festival corresponding to Bali-Pratipada—the Hindus of Kumbharjuvem village, as well as of Gandaulim village took the image of Shree Krishna in a procession starting from that place. Many Hindus, owners of the properties situated in that hamlet as well as those with 'Dhavajkar' as the surname, offer Him a bunch of plantains, supposedly because He is a symbol of 'Mokho', meaning plantain tree.

The origin of the name of the deity and rituals shows that the pastoral tribe who established the symbol had noticed that all the plants were produced from seeds except the plantain tree which was produced from the roots of the mother tree. This was for them a miracle shown by Nature and since it was produced without seed and had the shape of the male genital organ, it symbolised for them the male element. This concept was reflected in the female symbol also. In some areas 'Moko' was transformed to 'Betal' when idolatry was adopted copying the Sumerian system after 2,000 B.C. This will be described in the chapter relating to "Goa's Sumerian Connection". "*Bauka-Devik na ghov, ani Betalak na bail*" is a saying in a Hindu household, meaning 'Bauka-devi has no husband and Betal has no wife'. It is very interesting to examine this, but let us pause here to see how such worship was introduced by a pastoral tribe which had no idea of agricultural processes at that time.

Here I must make a note in respect of the plantain tree. It is said by historians that the plantain tree like the coconut is a foreign one, introduced by the people of South East Asia who brought and evolved their culture in India. For justification they depend on the nomenclature. But I refuse to accept this view. In 1932, I saw *Ran-Keli* (jungle plantain trees) growing on hills in a forest area like Bhati village of Sanguem taluka, producing plantains of a rough variety named '*Ran-Kelim*', not very sweet and with too much of gum and therefore used only for making vegetable dishes. In 1943, I saw also on the hilly area in Rivem, Golauli and Surla village of Sattari taluka plaintain trees of the same type. It is possible that its domesticated variety had been imported.

The hamlet where 'Moko' was established is named Dhavaj, obviously a corrupted form of "Sthawaj" of the Malayalam language, meaning homestead of the Nayars of the matriarcal system of Kerala. There the ancient area of the homestead was afterwards parcelled and each of the parcels was named 'tarawad'. The village name where 'Dhawaj' is situated is Ela. Ela is a word in the Kannad language meaning 'Soil' or 'animal'; hence 'rest place' (of cattle). Adjacent to this village is Gandaulim village. This name is Sanskritized as Bhagal-pallika, pallika meaning a small village and 'Bhagala' is derived from the Sanskrit word 'bhaga', meaning vulva. This Sanskritized form of naming of a village is found in the copper-plate inscription issued by Prithvimallavarman of the Bhoja dynasty ruling from Chandor of Salcete taluka, and dated the later half of the 6th or the first half of the 7th century A.D. So, the name of the village Gandaulim is relatively ancient, it appears that Ela and Gandaulim villages, in ancient times, formed only one village.

Besides the existence of a temple of 'Moko' in Dhaugi hamlet of Ela village, there were, according to the same Portuguese records, in the following villages of Tiswadi taluka: temples of Bauka-Devi and Moko in *Neurem* (Neura-de-Grande=the Great village of Neura) and of Bauka-Devi, alone, in Bhati, Chodan (Choraon) and Vanci villages.

At present, there is a black stone named '*Rakhnneacho-Deu*' at Carambolim village (Tiswadi taluka).

The primitive form of representation of Bauka-devi was changed to an image but the stone representation of 'Moko' continued as such in many localities. But in many castes such kind of representation of the male element was also changed to the idol form with the name of Betal in other talukas, as we will see further. Taking into consideration this view, it is evident from those records that an idol of Betal existed in Bhati village.

We have had an account from Tiswadi taluka. Now we will pass on to Ponda taluka. In this taluka, there are three interlinked villages, Priol, Kundai (Cundaim) and Madkai (Marcaim). In the copper-plate of the Kadamba king Tribhuvanamalla, dated 1099 A.D. Priol village is designated as 'Piriela' and according to a legend dated about 2,000 B.C., which will be referred to at the proper stage, all those three villages then constituted only one village under the name 'Piriela'.

The Tonko shrine

At present, in Priol, as ancient deities, there are temples of Shree Betal and Shree Santer. In Kundaim there is a hamlet Dhawaj and a shrine of Bauka-Devi; in Madkai there is a hamlet named 'Gana' and a shrine of the God 'Tonko' represented by a black-stone. The idol of Navadurga deity was transferred from Ganci village of Tiswadi taluka to Madkai due to the persecution by the Portuguese. The devotees visit the shrine of 'Tonko' on the first day of the great festival of Navadurga, obviously because it was the primitive deity of that village.

The name 'Tonko' is probably derived from the word '*tank*' meaning (a) reed or bamboo worshipped by the Naik caste; (b) it could also be an alteration of the word 'Moko' i.e. plaintain tree produced from the roots (not seed) of the mother plant.

The name 'Piriela' is obviously formed of two words, 'Piri' an altered form of 'Per' meaning 'vast' in Kannad language and 'Ela', as seen before, meaning 'land' or 'resting place of cattle'. I have already said that at the time of primitive settlements, there was only an Austric language, and the Tamil, Kannad, Mallyalam etc., and even Mundari language are its derivations. So some words which are found in the same language do not appear in other languages of the same origin and this is seen in the Marathi and Konkani languages derived from the Prakrit.

In all these three villages, '*Dhenulo Padvo*' is celebrated annually, but village-wise and there is no connection to 'Tonko'. This is understandable since the formality was changed during the intervening period as the population increased. However, the presence of the hamlet named Dhawaj, the existence of the shrine of Bauka-Devi and a hamlet named 'Gana' sufficiently demonstrate that the area—part of Ponda taluka—

was originally occupied by a pastoral tribe, like in Tiswadi taluka. In Gavnem hamlet at Bandodem village of the same taluka there is a shrine of 'Tonko' under the name of 'Purwachari', this word meaning 'first occupier of the land'.

Sacred phallic worship

Now let us move to another site of the same Ponda taluka—to Usgaon and adjacent Khandepar villages. In Usgaon village in an open yard there is an idol of Betal—a male deity in nude form—corresponding to 'Moko' or 'Tonko' as the phallus symbol. And in front of this idol there is an idol of a female figure in a standing pose again, but the body is covered with cloth. Both idols are of black stone. The female idol named Bauka-Devi, is worshipped by Bhavina, servant of the village Gods, and so of the Devadasi caste, and the rites of Betal are performed by a Bhat (Brahmin priest).

Near the boundary of Usgaon and Khandepar villages there is a black-stone kept near the road which is named 'Dhawaj-Rouduro' and his rites are performed by a 'Jalmi' of Naik caste—Jalmi being the designation of the headman of the local settler's caste.

Now, let us consider Salcete taluka. In the Portuguese records of demolished temples and shrines we find the name of 'Makaji' at Margaon, the first shrine demolished in that taluka. The policy of the Portuguese to demolish first the shrines of deities of inferior status in each taluka was to test the reaction of Hindus of the principal village of the taluka. After demolishing them, the next act was of confiscation of the properties of the deities. The rent from these properties was ordinarily used for performing all types of rites and festivals of the deities. These lands were transferred to Christian priest societies like the Jesuits, Franciscans, Dominicans etc. There are Portuguese records of such confiscated lands compiled taluka and village-wise and in the lands situated in Margaon, among others, it has been mentioned that a plot was granted and possessed by a person whose name is recorded as "Roxo Goully". The word "Roxo" is a Portuguese word meaning 'violet', which in Konkani means '*Jamblo*',—so, the name of that person was Jamblo Gouli. Gouli is a name in the milkman's caste, so it is obvious that the person was performing duties of the rituals of Macaji. There is also other proof—on the first day of the great festival of 'Shigmo' at the temple of Shree Damodar at Zambaulim of Rivona village, the inauguration is celebrated by the persons of Dhangar and Gouli castes assembled in an open yard in front of the temple. They dance and throw on each other red-lead mixed with red powder (*gulal*). Shree Damodar was shifted from Madgaon to Zambaulim due to persecution by the Portuguese. This form of ritual shows the link of the persons of those castes with the original village deity.

According to the same Portuguese records it is seen that there were idols of Bauka-Devi and Betal in Chinchonem village. In Bardez taluka too, idols of Bauka-Devi and

Betal (named Vetal in the records) existed in Pilerna village.

In Dicholi (Bicholim) taluka we find in Amonem village an image of Bauka-Devi at the right side of the entrance to the temple of Shree Betal. The daily worship is made by a person of the Bhagat caste, who puts a flower on the devi while elaborate worship is made of Betal. On the grand festival days a woman of the 'Bhavina' caste conducts worship (Puja). In Narvem village there are shrines of Bauka-Devi and Makdeswar (this probably being a sublimation of 'Moko' of Tiswadi taluka).

In Canacona taluka, in the village Canacona, there are images of 'Paik' (alias Paika-dev, God of Paik sub-tribe) named Bhangel-Paik, Ranzan Paik and Tanki-Paik, the last being probably a sublimated form of 'Tank', which in Ponda taluka is named as 'Tonko'. Somewhere in the surrounding area, there is in all probability, atleast a stone of ancient times representing Bauka-Devi, but the local people ignore its existence, so, it is not traceable.

None of the above mentioned deities are known in the New Conquests, viz. Sanguem, Quepem, Sattari and Pednem talukas. It seems that the representatives of that pastoral tribe did not reach there, and some of the families sporadically seen now in some villages of those talukas may be the descendants of the families which may have migrated in a historical period. There are some temples for example in Torshem village of Pednem taluka, where there are some idols but their names are ignored by the people.

It is worth noting that the worshipper of the 'Tonko' of Madkai (Marcaim) mentioned earlier, who is of Naik caste, on a fixed day of the festival, gains a state of ecstasy, falls down, and remains in a rigid posture with the bamboo held in his hand. Afterwards, two persons carry him, one holding the head and the other at the feet. Thus they go to the open yard in front of the small temple of "Tonko". Interestingly, during this time the body of the worshipper maintains its straight rigid posture. The tirth (holy water) of the deity is then sprinkled upon him, and the worshipper regains consciousness and becomes normal.

The Purvachari tradition

On the full-moon day of Kartika month the grand festival of Shree Nagesh of Bandodem village begins. On that day, a member of the family of Vani caste with the surname "Mulavi", starts running from the temple of 'Purvachari', carrying in his right hand a huge bamboo with a symbol of 'Purvachari' fixed on top. During this run, he is in a state of ecstasy and it is believed that the spirit of "Tonko" has pervaded his body. After running some distance, he hands over the bamboo to a person of a different caste, who in his turn, after running some more distance, passes the bamboo to a third person of another caste, who, again after covering some distance, passes the bamboo to the first person with the 'Mulavi' surname. He continues running up to the front of the temple. There he stops but his body is found shaking; Two persons of the Naik caste support and hold him, while he, in a full state of ecstasy, throws the bamboo on the floor of the main hall (sabhamandapa), in such a way that the symbol fixed at the top of the bamboo touches the plinth of Shree Nagesh-linga. Immediately he falls down in front of the temple. The tirth (holy water) of Shree Nagesh is then sprinkled upon him, and he gains his normal state. All the three persons are in a state of ecstasy during the time they have the bamboo in hand.

The designation of 'Purvachari'—meaning the first occupant of land—given to the 'Tonko' is very important for our present case. The Mhars were the first settlers, but the pastoral tribe were the first to occupy the land and utilize the natural sources of water. They grew grass and plants for nourishing buffalo-stock and after centuries succeeded in cultivating cereals using the crude slash and burn method.

There are many temples in Ponda and Dicholi (Bicholim) talukas where we find niches with a symbol-stone named 'Purvachari' which represented 'Tonko'. Even though I did not find Bauka-Devi or Tonko in Pednem taluka, there are, in some villages, stones installed in the temples which go by the name of 'Pur-vouch', 'Purvecho-vounsh' etc. which presume to represent 'Tonko'. It is possible also that this symbol represents members of families of both sexes as the word 'vouch' is representative of those together.

The definition of the word 'Purvachari' given above is correct as can be verified from the meaning of the word 'Kulachari' existing in Goa from historic times. This word means the first who brought under cultivation uncultivated fields (Kul); and so, besides the Gaonkars in the village, there were, in each village-commune those who were not descendants of Gaonkars but were settlers who had brought under cultivation uncultivated lands. In the 'Foral de Afonso Mexia' (charter prepared by Afonso Mexia) compiled in 1526, they are named as 'lavradores" (cultivators).

The cultural synthesis

This pastoral tribe had probably invented agriculture by the slash and burn or say, 'Kumeri' system cultivation. For the purpose of agriculture and for buffalo-keeping they employed the services of the servant-tenant (Dhangar, a Mundari word meaning tenant) from the tribe of newcomers. With the advent of the people from Sumer, their customs were also adopted by the tribes which had settled earlier. One of their customs was the construction of temples and a special form of mode of worship. The Aryan also copied some of their customs, and consequently the other tribes of a lower status. So the pastoral tribe, now agriculturists, were divided into two main groups: one group employed themselves in the service of the temple, and the second continued their original form of agriculture. The first group was divided in two classes according to their services: one class was devoted to singing and dancing in the temples, the female element being named 'Kalavant' and the male one 'Gana'. (But in Pednem taluka it is called 'Gadra'). The remaining service in the temple like sweeping, vessel washing etc. was done by the second class, the female element being named 'Bhavin' and the male one 'Deuli'. The female element of the second group is also named 'Chedum' and its male element is named 'Chedo' or 'Bando'. After Muslim dominion, they were known as 'Fargent'. This was because they served in the armed forces of their masters (Desai & Sar Desai) and were entrusted with security and collection of revenue. Before this, Desais and Sar Desais were designated as Nayak under the Vijayanagar dominion. But before this period, may be even in the pre-historic period, it appears that this second group was linked to the upper status families like the Saraswat Brahmins, Chaddes and Marathas. By virtue of this, this group was always devoted to the master of the family. There are many cases in my own knowledge in respect of this group. Especially in the families of Saraswat Brahmins, at least sixty years ago and before, a usual custom was to send a 'Chedum' to accompany the daughter after marriage to her new home, naming her 'Dhedi'. The 'Dhedi' used to look after the income of the family on behalf of her mistress but never thought of acquiring private property or a house except when her mistress had done that for her.

Dr. Kosambi's observations

Dr. D. D. Kosambi, a Goan by birth, a Buddhist by religion and with leanings towards communism, describes living in his own family household from the time of his grandfather. He says: "The Hindu households are not patriarchal but still contain enough of the older style of living to show by careful analysis what the patriarchal household must have been. Anyone brought up in an enormous abode house where 150 people were fed every day, where servants could not be hired or dismissed, where the women's world was separate from that of the men without the Mohammedan harem seclusion, and where hospitality went to the extreme of feeding even a stray guest at the risk of the host's going hungry needs less stretching of the imagination than one who has to reconstruct the older days from books alone". He continues: "Being the first male child in the direct line after the death of my grandfather, I automatically inherited his soul, his nick name and his name given to me on the twelfth day of my birth. Though my widowed grandmother's favorite grandson, I was addressed by her respectfully the way a modest woman of that class talked with her husband, so real was considered by her the transmigration of the soul of her husband in me. Yet my grandfather was so strict in his observancies that even after talking with any of his numerous Christian friends, he would go home and take the rite bath of 'purification'. When he migrated during his boyhood with his aged parents to the deserted community of Sancoale (which had reverted to Jungle after some unknown epidemic, perhaps the plague, of about 1785), he was seeking his fortune as the pioneer, for one Gama who had taken the deserted property on a nine-year lease hold, and for a distant relative Naik, who had agreed to supply the labour. The family had then migrated for the second time in its tradition after having been driven out of the nearby village of Loutolim in the 16th century to become feudal landlords in what later became the New Conquests. But these feudal acquisitions were lost by the incapacity of my great grandfather. On the second migration, the small family was followed by two servants who worked in the fields and turned their earnings over to 'their' family though there was no organized market as in the USA, slavery was not a recognized institution, and nothing except tradition held the servants to the decayed feudal household". [38] p. 158.

The servant class

This quotation gives us a clear picture on how a family of Saraswat Brahmin lived two centuries ago. The expression "servants could not be hired or dismissed" refers exclusively to the persons of the caste 'Bando', mentioned before, which literally means 'serf' or 'slave'. This type of institution in Goa certainly started earlier than four thousand years ago, when the Mundari tribes settled under the hegemony of the Kols as 'protectee'. Later on in Konkani this came to be called as 'Mundkar' which differed slightly from the "Bando" system. This subject will be discussed at the appropriate stage.

The 'Kalavant', meaning adept in art, has no special duty towards worship and the caste-deity is the same where they perform their duties in the temples through generations of the female line. The 'Bondo' caste have the deity of their masters as their own. But the 'Bhavin' caste, besides performing their duty in the temple where they work, have also a deity named Bauka-Devi which is exclusively worshipped by the village-Bhavin. Bauka-Devi is a word derived from two Sanskrit words, 'Devi' and 'Bhataka' or 'Bhati'. The latter two words mean hire/rent in Marathi and Konkani, and the word is derived from 'bhadem'. So, Bhatika means one who hires herself. The word 'Batik' is derived from that and is current in northern and southern Konkan. The word Bhatoka in a corrupted form became Bauka. Hence, the word Bauka-Devi means goddess of the hired woman, or say prostitute. In Goa, in villages with Hindu temples the existence of a 'Bhavina' is a must. So, in the jungle areas adjacent to two or three villages, there is a 'Bhavin' for the service of temples. In many villages of some talukas we do not find the Bauka-Devi. This may be because the installation of the temples had taken place too late or the existence of the symbol of Bauka-Devi, in the form of black stone marked by the primitive pastoral tribe, was unknown to the new-settlers, as mentioned before.

The worship of ancestors

This tribe, in its initial stage of pastoral life, might have made use of the flesh of buffalo as food. Probably they made sacrificial offerings of the flesh to their deities. The food taken by a people is always offered by them to their deity. So the sacrifice is justifiable. Moreover, eating of the flesh of a buffalo cannot be considered a savage custom. It is mentioned in the Bhagwata Purana that the Yadavas, at the time of Shree Krishna or say about 1,400 B.C., ate the meat of buffalo-calves. The Indo-Aryans ate cow flesh in the Vedic Age, at least when they were in the area surrounding Bakth in Iran, and so the guest is designated by the word 'Goghna', meaning 'slayer of cow'.

It is obvious that this pastoral tribe also domesticated goat, dog, fowl, etc., but for them the sacrifice of a buffalo was important as it was the most valuable among the domesticated animals.

But any scholar may ask me to justify my main view that this pastoral tribe came from Southern India. This is an obvious question.

The worship of dead ancestors was in vogue for millions of years, or say, when mankind had gained the state of 'homo sapiens', if not before. This view has been accepted by all historians. And this feeling after thousands of years naturally changed to the worship of ancestors symbolized as the original parents of the tribe.

Worship of the Mother Goddess

In the excavation made at Satal Huyk of Asia Minor a clay statue of a nude woman sitting on a bench dated 6,000 B.C. was discovered: the so-called 'Mistress of the animals'. In the same area, shrines dated 6,000 B.C. have also been discovered, depicting painted scenes. "These scenes depict women giving birth to bulls' or rams' heads. Model plaster reliefs depict female forms, possibly deities, while male counterparts are represented by symbols: the bull, the ram, and less commonly the stag, leopard and boar. It has been suggested that the scenes represent a concentration of symbolism dealing with aspects of fertility, fecundity, and death. It is not difficult to imagine an early farming community concerned with the primary aspects of fertility, both human and agricultural". [10] pp. 84-87.

I have cited this evidence only to prove how far back the idea of representation of male and female elements, be it as symbols, was being done. The representation by a clay statue shows that it took place at an advanced stage of a community that had taken to agriculture. It is obvious that before this advanced step, the symbols were the only representation of the male and female elements.

What is the evidence in this respect in India, out of Goa? For this we will have to give an account from the South, say from Kerala.

R. C. Dhere in his book 'Lajjagouri' in Marathi provides a good account on this subject. The ancient symbol of female represented by her genital organ is found in Kerala carved in black stone in the form of a conch shell. This representation may be later than the plain symbol of 'Mhatari' (meaning an old woman) existing in Savoi-Verem village which is a type of a small 'linga' with a ditch in a straight line artificially carved at the middle on the top—the ditch is obviously a fine line.

Dhere produces photos of statuettes which represent the later step of the representation of the same nature: a headless and nude female figure with outstretched lower limbs, legs bent at the knees and sitting in the squatting position. Female figures under different names are worshipped, in some villages to bear a child or for easy delivery, and are found, in Andhra Pradesh, Karnataka and in some areas of Maharashtra. Smilar statuettes are also found, often with very little variations, in Vindhya Pradesh, Uttar Pradesh and even in North-East India (here with head). At Bhedaghat in Madhya Pradesh a female genital figure carved on a rock is worshipped under the name of Chousastha-Yoguini. (In the temple of Mhalsa of Priol there is a 'Chounsastha-Yogini-Yantra under worship). It is to be noted that the statuettes of Northern India as compared to those of Southern India are relatively modern as can be verified by their sculptures. [51]

The nearest to the symbol of 'Mhatari' is the one of Kerala; so, the origin of the worship of that symbol in Goa demonstrates that the pastoral tribe which established itself in Goa came from Southern India, and that their arrival goes back very far in historical times.

It is certain that the cult of the phallic symbol like 'Moko' or 'Tonko' in Goa is not recorded in the history of Southern India, but this happened probably because phallic worship was considered a long time ago to be connected to Shiva, perhaps without deep investigation.

Another point: from the Portuguese records it is seen that in *Vernem* (Verna) and *Kolwem* (Colva) villages of Salcete taluka there were temples of 'Lambesvor' and 'Maculespor' respectively [52].

From the inscription on a pillar of a carved cave of Badami (Karnataka) dated 578 A.D. (of the period of Mangalesh of the Chalukya dynasty) it is apparent that a gift of a village named Lanjiswar was made. Nearby that cave there is a temple named Mahakuta where lies a statue of the deity Lanji or Lanjika, which is named in other parts as Mukuteswari [3].

At the time of that inscription, the area of Goa was ruled by Vantuvallabha Senanandaraja of the Sendraka family, under the sovereignty of the Chalukyas [53]. The Portuguese recorders have made many mistakes in the spelling of vernacular words, and I presume that a dash was omitted across the alphabet 'T', which should be 't', so the name Mukuteswari is the real word. The word 'Lambeshwar must be Langeshwari, so both these deities were probably feminine ones. New names might have been given to these deities instead of the ancient ones, or the deities might have been newly installed. For example the God Anant (Seshashahi - Vishnu) of Savoi-Verem was installed in 16th and 17th century A.D. According to traditional history, the village deity of Vernem held her supremacy over the other village deities not only of Salcete Taluka but even those of Tiswadi taluka; so the villagers or, say Gaonkars of each village used to visit her to pay their respects. Now the point is: what was the name of this village deity? Was she Shanta or Mhalsa, because according to tradition Mhalsa was transferred from the adjacent village Nagvem. I presume that the honour was offered to Mhalsa at Nagvem and when transferred to Verna, the honour was offered to her at the new place. The presumption is based on the original statue in stone of Mhalsa; this statue has no head, so the original form of Mhalsa was probably a female nude statue without a head, like Lajjagauri. Her primitive form was changed according to mythology. Interested readers will find some basic information about the idol through the book by Dhere who talks of Khandoba.

THE MIGRATION OF THE ASURA TRIBALS

In the preceding discussion in respect of the 'Gavda' tribe or caste, you have seen that the Satarkar tribe named the Asuras as 'Gavdo' or former settler, that is, those who settled before them. They, under the name Asura-Munda, lived in Madhya Pradesh for thousands of years, and by the trial-and-error method gained knowledge of domestication of animals and of growing cereals and plants like other tribes living there such as the Kols and Mundaris. Besides this knowledge they had specialized in the use of copper and iron ore, fashioning out crude implements and tools for use in preparation of implements for digging the land for agriculture. They also made utensils from stone and clay for domestic use. This tribe was always subjugated by other tribes which consisted of numerous members and their landed properties brought under cultivation with great skill were appropriated. Their destiny was like that of the Jews always suffering despite their resourcefulness and hard work. In Mirzapur district of Madhya Pradesh we find proof of their skill in the construction of bunds for irrigation.

They migrated from that original place owing to one or more reasons mentioned earlier, armed with the knowledge of creating blades of copper which, after being duly sharpened, were used as knives even for shaving or cutting hair, possibly upto the root. This type of shaving was known as Khamin.

Roy is of the opinion that the Asuras were a tribe different from the Kols, Mundas etc. who lived in Chota Nagpur of Madhya Pradesh. Perhaps they had previously come in contact with the Veda tribe of Sri Lanka [41].

They probably came to Goa by one or two routes mentioned by Dr. Iravati Karve (described by me earlier). Some families of that tribe might have established themselves in northern Konkan under the name of 'Agri' as well as 'Mith-Agri' or 'Mith-Gavdi', engaging themselves in agriculture and later in salt pans for making salt. In Goa, at present, we find some of these families under the latter designation i.e. Mith-Gavdi in some villages of Pednem and Bardez talukas. They probably entered Goa about 3,500 B.C. or say after the said pastoral tribe and before the Kols and Mundaris.

Asura customs

The Asura had religious customs and beliefs similar to those of the Kols and Mundas—so only by traditional history and by some designation of names given to them is the tribe distinguished [54]. The characteristics of this tribe are more visible in Savoi-Verem village of Ponda taluka. Installed on top of a hill named Khamindongor one will find two deities named Gana-rouduro and Khaman-rouduro. The first word Gana-rouduro is composed of three mundari words, namely, gana, roudu and horo; gana means to reduce the number of cattle, roudu means to carve a hole, and horo means a person. Consequently ganarouduro means the 'burier' or say destroyer of cattle. The word Kaman-rouduro is also formed of the words Kaman and rouduro; Kaman means to shave himself after burying the corpse of his relative, hence it means burier or destroyer of human kind.

Nearby, at the base of the hill-slope there is sign of a bund, and it seems that this bund was constructed for catching rain water, creating a reservoir for irrigation. This work probably was of the Asuras.

From the legend *Balichi-Katha* (story of Bali) cited before, it is known that about 2,000 B.C. the Asura tribe existed in Priol village, adjacent to Savoi-Verem. Hence, I could trace there the existence of deities of those types. But in Bandodem village there is a temple of Shree Nagesh where the deity is in the form of a linga and was probably placed there by this tribe under the designation of Nege-Era. In Chota Nagpur these deities exist near a pond and is considered as female. In some villages, the deity is also named as 'Bindiera'. The village named Bandode in which the temple of that deity is situated is significant as it contains the element of that word. In Chota Nagpur, rice without husk or turmeric is offered to her. For the oracle, this type of rice is used at Nagesh temple which is significant. In other temples in Goa, rice is not used for this purpose. There serpent-worship is not in vogue but the people of Asur, Kol, ·Munda, etc., settlers of that area believe that the Naga (King Cobra) is protector of the family, and if anybody kills it, he has to offer Naga-Era rice with husk or turmeric, produced by his own hands in the field. On the top of the mountain named "Parvat" at Paroda village there are two temples of Chandranath and Bhutnath symbolized by stones. It appears that the symbolizing had been made by the Asuras, the Khamanronduro and Ganarouduro. These were appropriated by the Kols afterwards, like Savoi Verem village. Later, the second wave of Aryans propitiated them and since then the epithet 'rouduro' was considered as 'Rudra'. Kamanrouduro was designated as Chandranath and Ganarouduro, his attendant, was designated as Bhutanath. These names continue in the present day.

Vestiges of Asura settlements:

According to the traditional history, in Usgaon village of Ponda taluka there lived in ancient times families of Kumbars (potters) who were continuously harassing the Maratha Gaonkars who had settled there later. Therefore, the Gaonkars called their relatives who were living in Sawantwadi, and with their help and settlement, the potters were expelled forever from the village. The fact is that, in 1939 when I was involved in survey work for a topographic plan, I noticed some remnants of a small house with some pieces of burnt clay, probably of different types of pots. I came to know that there once upon a time resided potters. The place was at the top of a mountain, usually not occupied by people as a permanent residence, more so by pot-ters whose residence should be near a place where clay is easily available. Generally, the number of families of potters are few in a village in comparison with other settlers. So, it appears that the Asuras were living in the village, employing themselves in agri-culture and handicrafts like pottery, and after their expulsion, their profession was reduced to only pottery . And they selected the mountain top as there was plenty of forest for fire-wood necessary for their profession.

Adjacent to this village lies *Khandepar* (Candeapar) a village where there is Dhawaj-rouduro, mentioned before. It is probable that the Asuras might have occupied this village, expelling the pastoral tribe. But the Maratha Gaonkars of Usgaon village ex-pelled them also, so the descendants of the original settlers returned and re-settled. This traditional history deserves some correction. The Asuras were not expelled by the Maratha Gaonkars but by the Kols, like in Savoi-Verem (as already stated) and they settled in both the said villages with the Mundas, and after a long period the Maratha Gaonkars came and settled there and many other tribes did so. From the present religious rites in Usgaon village, which are traditional, and are performed by members of certain castes, we get an idea of the sequence of their settlement. Gener-ally, in each village of the talukas of the New Conquests, there are similar peculiari-ties. The detailed description of the rituals is not relevant to the present context.

THE BHARVANKARS

There are many hamlets in the villages of Salcete taluka and in the adjacent villages Assoldá and Xeldem of Quepem taluka where live the families of Asuras who are designated as Bharvankars.

This designation of Bharvankar is probably a corruption of the word "Barbhumkars" the name given by the tribes (Kols and Mundas) to the Asuras who were known to them as originating from the area known as Barbhum of Chota Nagpur.

The Bharvankars have in each hamlet their headman named 'Budvant' who settles their family litigations, and takes a principal part when any common issues concerning the hamlet are to be forwarded to the land-owner. So he is the leader of the hamlet in the present parlance of social terminology. The Bharvankars work in agriculture as well as in the construction of roads and during the past thirty years they have been working in open-cast mining of manganese and iron ore. The mine owners sign a contract with this 'Budvant' who takes as his commission some fixed percentage of the daily wages of the persons under his leadership, but generally the contract is made on the basis of volume of work. The Christian potters caste live generally together with the families of this caste. Some of them are even sorcerers (Ghadis in Konkani) who enter into a state of ecstasy like a Hindu Ghadi and replies to questions, and people have faith in their replies. The protector spirit of place has different names in different villages, with special names as Sankhalayo in Kumbharjuvem and Sankhli (Sanquelim) village (the first in Tiswadi taluka and the second in Dicholi taluka), Fatarsorvo in Bhati of Sanguem taluka, etc. This type of spirit is commonly known as *Vataro* or *Devchar*. The word Vataro is of the Mundari language and is composed of Vat and horo; Vat means place and Horo means person; hence he is the owner of the place. The word Devchar of Konkani origin is composed of the word Dev and Chari, meaning the 'first occupier' as in the Konkani word Kulachari, so Devchar means the God who first settled in the place. His image (not even a stone) is not planted, but his spirit is considered to have his seat near a tree of any species, but very old and he is propitiated by offering '*soro-rot*' (soro means country liquor and rot means home-made flat bread of rice). He is also propitiated with the sacrifice of fowl of any colour except white but preferably black.

Many persons of the Christian religion of different castes of a lower status from the Old Conquest areas consult the oracle in temples of deities which were transferred to villages in the New Conquests, as they were their original village-deities. This type of consultation is sometimes acceptable if taken directly from the deity-image. But the consultation of a Ghadi in critical circumstances is significant of the traditional belief held by their earliest ancestors.

I mention the above event to show how, despite four centuries of contact with the Christian religion, through generations the ancient beliefs are still deeply rooted in Christian society.

Some customs of Bharvankars

Coming back to the Asuras, some of them are in Pednem taluka and in northern Konkan, known as Mitgavde and Mitagri in Christian society, and as Bharvankars and Kumbars (potters), but they are probably found even in Hindu society amongst the lower castes. I presume that some of them are blacksmiths and potters in Sattari and Sanguem talukas, and some have mixed in the caste known as Kunbi-Vanis. This presumption of mine is based on the link which the Kunbi-Vanis have with the rituals of the most ancient deities of certain villages of Goa.

On enquiry, I learnt about an intriguing custom existing in the Bharvankars. After marriage, the girl continues to live in her parent's residence upto the first menstruation. Soon after, the girl, after taking her meal at sunset, is sent to a house where there is an old woman, where the girls sleeps with her. During that time the old woman instructs the girls as to how she will have to conduct herself when she is alone with her husband. She is informed about pregnancy and delivery, and thus given a clear picture of conjugal life. The girl stays every night with the old woman till she is satisfied that the girl has comprehended everything. She then informs the mother of the girl. Then the son-in-law is informed, and on an agreed day, he takes his wife to his residence.

The important fact to be noticed is that the girl was sent to stay in a different house with an old woman whereas the proper mother could have very well given the instructions. Surely this custom is reminiscent of the dormitory system peculiar and exclusive to the aborigines of Chota Nagpur and other areas. There are such dormitories in Nagaland (56). In some tribes, there are separate dormitories for male and females while amongst others they are common. The nomenclature of the dormitories vary according to the tribes, for example in the Oraon tribe, they are known as Dhumakariya or Jonkarpa; in the Munda and Ho tribes as the Gitiora; in Mudiagond tribe as the Gotul; in the Bhuiya tribe as Dhangar-Basa; in the Botia tribe as Ranga-barg and so on. In the Kurumba tribe of South India there are also dormitories named 'Pundalamanie'.

The dormitories were situated as a rule out of the hamlet, in jungle areas. The dormitories of girls were under the supervision of an old woman who taught them craft, home-work, singing and dancing; Near such dormitories there was an open place named Akhada where the girls and often both the boys and girls practiced dancing and singing. In dormitories for boys, a villager looks after them and gives them lessons in archery and in social rules. The 'Akhada' is here named 'Mand' where the annual festival of 'Dhalo' is performed by Hindu women of a lower status in the month of Pauska.

I have already referred to the place named 'Dhumak' existing in Kumbharjuvem village (Tiswadi taluka) and in Orgaon and Volvoi villages of Ponda taluka. Near 'Dhumak' there is a 'mand' in Kumbharjuvem village. In Chota Nagpur and adjacent areas there lived the Kols with a subtribe named Kharwa. I did not find the name of their dormitories in Chota Nagpur. The Oraon is considered to be a tribe, not aboriginal, and they had settled later, adopting the customs of aborigines. So, it is likely that the dormitory of the Kols and its subtribe Kharwa has the designation of Dhumakariya which was adopted by the Oraons.

Now, a point may be raised about the identification made by me of the Bharvankars as Asuras. Why cannot they be considered to be Kurumbas of Southern India who also had their dormitories? The Portuguese writers designate them as Kurumbis in their writings. This point deserves a satisfactory answer.

The Portuguese writers do not make any distinction between Bharvankar, Satarkar and the Kelshi-Kuthalkar gavdes, and give them a common name—Kurumbim. Surely the Portuguese employed the word Kurumbim as a corruption of Kulambi and nothing more. Secondly, if Kurumba was the tribal name of Bharvankars, what was the necessity to name them as Bharvankars. Moreover, what is the ethnological explanation of that word? There is no other explanation except the one I have supplied.

In Naneli village, Sattari taluka, there is a flat place (plateau) named '*Rangachemmol*' meaning playground, and adjacent to it there is a place named Kasarvornem. This place was once occupied by blacksmiths of the Asur tribe as I have mentioned earlier. This tribe sporadically might have settled in some villages of that taluka with the profession of blacksmith or potter. In Karnataka the potters have the designation of Satarkars [57] pp. 77. The author Nadagonde says that those Satarkars came from Sattari, forming a branch of Konkani Kumbhars, but from a separate caste. At this juncture, I wish to make very clear that these Konkani potters belonged to the Asura tribe and the potters designated as Satarkars were of a separate tribe. Here, in Goa we have no knowledge of a Satarkar who might have embraced the profession of potter.

THE KOLS AND THE MUNDARIS

Toponymical influence of the Kols

I have no evidence to say that both these tribes came and settled together in Goa, but it is evident that the Mundari resided here in peaceful alliance with the Kol tribe, as subordinates of the latter. We have many village-names of Konkan and Goa connected with the Kols but I did not find any one connected to the Mundari tribe. So I think that the Mundari tribe came after the Kols, otherwise the original place of both tribes is the same—Chota Nagpur and other adjacent areas, where, it is to be noted, the Mundas and Kols had separate hamlets and the Mundas considered the Kols to be of lower status. Taking this view, it appears that the Kols came from the area of Chota Nagpur to Goa about 3,000 B.C. by the same route as the Asuras. The Mundaris or Mundas came later. In Kolaba district we find the following villages which appears to have Kol as the basic word. Kalamba and Kalamboli in Karjat taluka, Kalamba and Kalamboshi in Sudhagad taluka, Kalambusare in Uran taluka and two villages named Kalamboli in Panvel and Kalapur talukas (please note here that we have a village named Kalapur in Tiswadi taluka).

In Ratnagiri district there are following villages with Kol as the root word: Hadi Kolavana and Kolambe in Sangameshwar taluka, Kolavandre and Kolathare in Dapoli taluka, Koladhe in Lanja taluka, Kolambe, Kolavana and Kolisare in Ratnagiri taluka, Kolavali in Guhar taluka, Kolamb, Kolavanchuna and Kolvankhadi in Rajapur taluka, Kolakvadi in Chiplon taluka and Kolaganv and Kolazar in Sawantwadi taluka.

In Goa, there are the following village names with Kol as a base root = *Hodkoln* (Odcolna) and *Kholli* (Corlim) in Tiswadi taluka, *Kholli* and *Kolval* (Colvale) in Bardes taluka, *Kulem* (Colem) and *Kolomb* (Colomba) in Sanguem taluka, *Kolwem* (Colva) in Salcete taluka, *Kholla* in Quepem taluka and *Khol* in *Kankon* (Canacona) taluka.

From this account of village-names, we have an idea of the expansion of the Kol tribe.

When they came to Goa, their culture was semi-savage. Besides hunting, fishing and even boating by canoes they knew the art of domestication of animals as well as of growing cereals and fruit-yielding trees. Their tools and weapons were of stone, very well polished, like hand-axes. They had probably studied from the Asuras the art of using iron in a rough form. The hand-axe, referred to in earlier pages and which has been found at the bank of the river in Quepem taluka, if not of the time of the Asuras may be from the time of the Kols. Besides the beneficient gods, they recognised the existence of gods like Sing-bonga, possibly symbolising the sun. The Kols also worshipped the Earth-goddess in the form of an anthill.

Rev. Haffmann, author of the Encyclopedia Mundarika says that the aboriginal tribes of Chota Nagpur go to the forest at the end of the great festivals and cover the anthill with leaves. The reason for this is that in ancient times they worshipped an anthill as representative of the Earth-goddess, or say as its spirit; the sudden appearance of an anthill without any seed or human labour being a miracle for them. But later on Sing-bonga was the principle God and so the worship of the Earth-goddess was given second place, but here in Goa the old system continued. This Kol tribe is known as Satarkar, and many persons consider that they were originally from Sattari taluka, and this is correct. This name was given to them because this tribe first introduced the worship of Santer in Goa and so the word Satarkar is a corruption of the word Santerkar. Their language was Mundari. The anthill is named 'Roeen' in Konkani. This word is derived from the Mundari word 'Rono' meaning with holes, which was translated by the latter Aryans in Sanskrit as 'Santara', meaning also with holes. The other designation given to this deity is 'Bhumika' meaning child of the earth. It was named as 'Mavuli' by the newly arrived Marathas.

Mundari customs

I present here a synopsis of some points of the customs of these tribes recorded by Sharad Chandra Roy in his book 'The Mundas and their country' [41].

The Khunti is a planted stone and represents the place where each class first settled, and it is worshipped by the elder clan.

The village is administered by an assembly of the elders of the village presided over by the village headman, 'Pahan' and aided by a person named Munda. In the Munda tribe, later on, the Pahan's position went to the village-priest, and Munda's seat was occupied by a secular headman. The assembly was like the recently named village-panchayat and the members named 'panch'.

A group of twelve villages formed a 'pati' and all types of issues of great importance as well as appeals on the resolution of the village-panchayat were decided by the assembly of Pahans of those twelve villages, aided by the respective Mundas. The assembly was presided over by the Pahan of the village in which the assembly was held, and that headman was named Manki. The assemblies were held in an open place, and the posts which were first filled by selection, later became hereditary.

There are many deities with different names. According to their religious status, they are propitiated by offering sacrifices of fowls, like red and black ones for special deities. The white fowl is sacrificed only in the name of Sing-bonga. Nage-Era Bindi-Era and Chando are the deities among them. Sing-bonga represents the sun (but Rev. Haffmann does not accept this view) [33] and Chando represents the Moon.

Their deities reside near a tree, rock, spring, brook, water-pond, dense forest, top of a hill or low-lying rice field. The Naga-Era resides in a low-lying rice field, dense forest brook or pond. In some villages she is named as Nage-bonga and is considered to be a female and has a friend named Churang-bonga who is also a woman who has died while pregnant. When Naga-Era desires, she appears accompanied by her friend in the Akhads (the dancing place) and enters the body of any woman. Sometimes both the deities may enter two women when the women are dancing.

The tribes think that all those deities are under the rule of Sing-bonga. They believe that in the live bodies of mankind and also animals, there are two spirits named 'ji' and 'Rou'. When they sleep the 'Ji' continues in the body but the 'Rou' moves out and enters again when they are awake. When the person dies the 'Ji' goes to Sing-bonga to give him an account of his deeds and Sing-bonga accordingly rewards or punishes him. The 'Rou' continues on the earth and resides in the storeroom of his family, in the form of a shadow, and protects his family, and he is worshipped with the sacrifice of fowls. Nobody can enter the room except members and close relatives of the family. After the burial of the dead in the burial-ground of the family named 'Sasan', they plant a stone on the pit. When any pregnant woman dies, her legs are broken before burial and on the footpath upto her residential house, thorns are spread and obstacles are made in order to prevent her from coming back to her house during the night. A tiger when killed becomes Vagh-bonga and resides where he was killed, and he too is propitiated and kept satisfied.

The Mundaris have five or six important festivals, one of which coincides with the sowing of paddy and the other with the reaping of the crop. The most important festival is Mage-parab performed during three days of the month of Poush. It starts on a Monday or Friday and the day is fixed according to the convenience of relatives in the adjacent villages. The main programme is of passing along the village-boundary, the gathered villagers dancing and beating the drums and sprinkling cooked rice mixed with the blood of a cock on the boundary line. The boundary is demarcated with huge stones named sim-bongas, (spirits of the boundary) since time immemorial. The villagers of the adjoining village watch if any of these villagers cross the boundary. If any one dares to do so, he is beaten up mercilessly and sometimes this is responsible for bitter strife between the villages.

The tribes, except the Asuras, considered 'Lutkam-hadam' (hadam in Mundari language meaning 'an old man') and 'Lutkam-budia' (budia in Mundari means 'an old woman') as their ancestors. In Asur-Kahani (legend of Asuras) incorporated in the said book of Roy, a couple of the Mundari tribe (Lutkam-hadam and Lutkam-budia) is described. Sing-bonga became angry with the Asuras because the smoke produced by them while making iron reached the sky where he resides. He took the form of a boy and was accepted by the couple as a shepherd and for thousands of years they maintained his memory through a song transmitted through generations.

According to customs, the waste land cleared for agricultural purposes belonged to the group of families which contributed to the clearance, and the land was divided among those families. But the plots were cultivated in rotation, so that the ownership of a family was not fixed in respect of each plot, but the whole area under cultivation belonged to a fixed group of families.

Recently, when the ceiling was fixed by the Government in respect of agricultural land holdings, this raised an intricate problem in defining the holders of each family, as the whole area of cultivated rice-fields was considered from generations as common property, and was held by about a hundred families. I don't know how the problem was resolved.

Etymology of Barazan

Now we will consider the term 'Barazan' found in many villages. In Savoi-Verem village there is a Khunti, a planted stone and a place named Barazan and the religious headman of the Satarkar tribe performs the rituals. Barazan is a flat place covered with wild trees and there are about a dozen small stone links with the plinth placed here and there. There is also a linga of great size and a stone of black colour under the shade of a jungle-tree 'Kel'. This type of tree always has aerial roots like a pimpal (a holy fig tree) and a Vad (an Indian fig tree). This black stone was placed in ancient times because I found carved on that stone two genuine signs of the Sumerian script which means 'Dwadash-gana' in Sanskrit, meaning Barazan in Konkani *(refer ill.14 at chapter 4 page 126)*. The name Barazan means the place where the headman of twelve villages or hamlets assembled in ancient times to take decisions about the village-administration like in Chota Nagpur. The original function of Barazan changed long ago and it soon became a religious place, the praying and other rituals being done by the headman of the Satarkars standing near the black stone. This headman is designated as 'Zalmi'.

I have already referred to the expulsion of the Asura tribe by the Kols (Satarkars); so the Satarkars appropriated the deities established by them. On the top of the mountain named Khamin-dongor, the Asuras had established 'Khamin-rouduro' and 'Gana-rouduro', already referred to and those are worshipped by the Zalmi, where fowl sacrifices are offered. On a plateau named'Bhut-khamb' on the boundary of Savoi-Verem, common to *Keri* (Querim) village at the site of *Ponda-Keri* (Querim) road, there is a niche carved on the face and the hill where horses of clay and cradle are placed in fulfilling vows. This is done in the belief that a spirit (*Bhuta*) exists there, but nobody could give me the name of the spirit. This type of offering of a horse of clay is made in Sanguem taluka to Paika-Dev, and in *Sankhali* (Sanquelim) village of *Dicholi* (Bicholim) taluka to Sankhalio (special name of *Devchar or Vataro*). I presume that the name Bhutkhamb is derived from Lutkam, the name of the progenitor couple of the Kol and Mundari tribes as mentioned before. The Santer goddess which the Satarkar took from Advoi of Sattari as mentioned before is placed on the Khamindongor near the other two deities already referred to, but the worship is made by a person of the Paddye family who is of the Brahmin (priest) caste. Sacrifices are not done here.

Symbol of Mhatari

I have already referred to the symbol of 'Mhatari' existing in the hamlet of Silvado of Savoi-Verem. Now I must refer to it again. In 1959, when I first visited the place, it was noticed that the Mhatari was symbolized by a stone in a linga form but it was of very low height and on the middle of it was carved a straight line, perpendicular to the opening face in direction, representing the female genital organ inserted in a schist-slab. The small room was also made of schist slabs. Nearby another slab was planted erect. On its face five horizontal parallel lines were carved, crossed at the middle by a vertical one. I thought that these lines symbolized a 'dipasthambha' (light-pillar) as exists in front of the many Budia of Asur-Kahani, naming her Mhatari in accordance with the translation of the word Budia. But later on, my view changed after studying other signs more deeply. The carved lines on the slab was not the symbol of 'dipasthambha' but the genuine sign of the Sumerian script pronounced 'sil' and meaning a temple, so Shivado means effectively *'devulvado'* (a temple hamlet). The second reason was that near the 'Mhatari' stone representing Luthkam Hadam, the husband of Lutkam Budia should have existed and the third one was that the symbols of the couple must have existed at the place named Bhutkhamb, not very far in the hamlet named Silwado.

The festival of 'Mage-Parab'

The main festival celebrated in Chota Nagpur was the 'Mage-Parab' as I have mentioned earlier. Such a festival also takes place annually in the month of Pousha at Savoi-Verem. The main rituals of the Mage parab are checking of village-boundary named Gaddalap with the rituals of sprinkling of 'Charu' (cooked rice mixed with the blood of cocks) on the borderline on the day of the new-moon (Amavasha) of the month of Poucha, while the 'Holi' planting, and the festival ends on the night of the full-moon (Pournima) which is the last day of the festival. The male elements start their procession from a place named 'maand' (like Akhada in Chota Nagpur) and visit each house where they dance to the beat of drums and dholls. The women-folk perform, in the month of Pousha, like the Mage Parab of Chota Nagpur, their annual programme of singing songs and simultaneously dancing but without musical instruments during three consecutive nights, gathering together at the 'maand'. On the fourth day, before the day of the full-moon a ceremony is held in the morning—an act simulating hunting of game. A woman is 'the hunted game' and afterwards is taken to the different castes of the population of the village, all in order of the status of the gods and caste. The dancing in this form is named 'Dhalo', the word having originated from the Mundari language meaning 'to sing with the wind'.

In the male-dances at the 'maand', the musical instruments which accompany the dancing and simultaneous singing are only the 'ghumat' and cymbals. The 'ghumat' is made of clay in a special form but like a vessel with two openings in opposite directions, one hole being small and the other big. The small hole is covered with the skin of a monkey but it is difficult to get because Goans did not like the idea of killing monkeys. For this purpose, persons from outside named 'Makadmari' periodically used to come from the Ghats to sell the skin. So, in general, the skin of an iguana was used, fastening it with straps of leather. A rhythmic beat is produced by the fingers only. The skin of a monkey is preferred because it produces a better sound. This 'ghumat' in Chota Nagpur is named 'dumang' and both the openings are covered by the skin of the Hanuman species of monkey, and in its absence that of the cow.

A special type of rhythm named 'Zula tal' is in use in Goa, according to the Goan expert Malabarao Sardesai. This rhythm is also found in Chota Nagpur and Orissa as mentioned by Rev. Hoffman in his book Encyclopedia Mundarika. [33].

Some strange customs

When a pregnant woman dies, she is buried and grains of Nachni (cereals) are spread from the burial pit upto her house. Thereby, it is believed she could find her place back to her house. It is believed that a woman who dies during pregnancy, continues in a spirit form and causes different forms of harassment to not only members of her family but also to any one known to her. This spirit is named 'Alvatin'. There was a strange ritual to call the spirit and find out her desires. The ritual is known as 'Dank kadap'. The word 'Dank' is probably derived from the word 'Dakini' meaning spirit or from 'Dankh' meaning rancour. The ceremony is somewhat expensive, as it requires the presence of two or three Ghadis (sorcerers) who are experts in many types of rituals. When I was about eleven years old, I had the opportunity to witness the ceremony being performed in respect of a woman of the Kharvi (fisherman) caste near my house at Kumbhrjuvem village.

Culture of the Kols

In Volvoi village, bordering Savoi-Verem there is a place named 'Dhumak' which is probably the short form of the word 'Dhumakaria', the dormitory of Oraons at present in Chota Nagpur.

Describing in brief what I found as the remnants of culture of the Kol tribe in Savoi-Verem and Volvoi villages, I now pass on to relate also briefly the signs of culture of the Kol tribe, as found in other villages of Goa.

The Santer goddess is worshipped in different villages of Goa, from Pednem to

Canacona, and from Sattari to the sea-shore, even in the Ratnagiri district on the North, and in Karnataka in the South. Existence of the temples of Santer in the taluka of the Old Conquests has been proved by Portuguese records. In many villages we find in the sanctum sanctorium an image of the goddess Santer, Bhumika, Mavuli or Shantadurga, and sometimes shaped in the form of a Mahishasuramardini—a form of the goddess Durga killing a buffalo. In India, the goddess Durga is always considered as the goddess of peace. This was first established at Quelossim of Salcete taluka, later transferred to *Kavlem* (Queula) village of Ponda taluka. Her idol is shown with four hands, flanked by two male idols. All the three idols are in a standing position, the goddess being a little higher than the other two. According to the myth, long ago, a battle had taken place between Hara (Shiva) and Hari (Vishnu) which lasted for thousands of years but there was no conclusion. The Gods as well as humanity were afraid. So, on their praying, the Adishakti—the Primeval Divine power—took the form of a woman and put an end to this battle. This type of idol is not found anywhere in India, nor is this type of myth mentioned in any Purana, nor the Durga goddess with the sign of Shant (peace giver). The Santer goddess is represented in a (masked) form, fixed on a vessel of copper or brass or an image of metal, and in the last century in some villages is named Shantadurga without bearing any characteristic of the idol of *Kavlem* (Queula) village.

The words 'Khunti' and 'Barazan'

'Khunti' appears not only in Savoi-Verem village but also in many villages of *Dicholi* (Bicholim), Ponda, Kepem (Quepem) and sporadically in Sangem (Sanguem) talukas where 'Khuntis' are worshipped. In other talukas of the New Conquests, Khuntis are not traceable. In the talukas (Tiswadi, Bardez and Salcete) of the Old Conquests, from Portuguese records, 'Kunti' is also found existing in Davorli village of Salcete taluka, but it does not mean that it did not exist elsewhere. It was a very minor deity—a stone placed in an open yard—therefore probably was not recorded.

As mentioned, the 'Khunti' of Savoi-Verem is worshipped by the Jalmi of the Satarkar caste, in the villages of Assolda and *Kothambi* (Cotombi) of Quepem taluka by a person of Naik and Mhar castes, respectively, in Amona of the same taluka there is 'Mhal Khunti' which is worshipped by a person of the Gavde caste. At Parvat of Paroda village of the Salcete taluka, the 'Khunti' is worshipped by a person of the Naik caste. In Sanguem taluka, at Sanguem town (otherwise part of Cotarli village) the 'Khunti' is worshipped by a person of the Velip caste. The worship is always a hereditary obligation and is performed by the eldest male of the family.

'Barazan' is the highest institution which characterizes, like in Chota Nagpur, the socio-economic aspect of the communal system of life of the Kolarian, including Mundari stock. It continued its existence for millennia and finally was reduced to its religious aspect only. We find at present many places throughout Goa district with this name. There are even some hamlets named Barazan for example in Sattari and Sangem (Sanguem), (Astagrahar subdivision) talukas. In some villages we find installed, instead of Barazan, some images under the name Baravansha and Baradev. According to the Portuguese records, in all three talukas of the Old Conquests, many villages and places existed under the name Barazan where some niches or idols were probably installed.

Similar to the rituals performed in Chota Nagpur of visiting annually the village boundaries named as Mage-parab and performed in the month of Pausha, rituals are performed under the name of Shigmo (Shimga in Marathi) in Goa terminating in 'Holi'—ceremony of planting a tree trunk (generally of mango or areca). This festival is celebrated in the month of Falguna—the last month of the Hindu calendar year, but, it is noticeable that in *Kumbharjuwem* (Cumbarjua) village the beating of the big drum—Dhol—is done in the month of Pausha, announcing the starting of the festival in the place 'manda'. The procession, in which only male elements take part, is accompanied by musical instruments of strident tones like the Dhol, Nagara and cymbals but in the singing and dancing in front of each residential house the musical instruments with a low sound like the Ghumat and small cymbals are used. In the ceremonial and religious festivals before the temples, sometimes accompanied by the female dancing women—the Kalavantinas—in the ritual beating of 'Suari', the musical instruments are the same—the Ghumat and the small cymbals.

Like in Chota Nagpur, in the month of Pausha 'Dhalo', the ritual is celebrated, but without the use of musical instruments and exclusively by women-folk, in 'manda'. This type of celebration takes place in each village of the talukas, even in the talukas of the Old Conquests, except in Sattari taluka, from where the Maratha people expelled the Kol tribe and maintained the Mundaris as their subordinate.

Sing-bonga installed by the Satarkars at Savoi-Verem became the protector deity of a Saraswat family with the surname 'Singbal' (named after him) in the historic period and it figures in the list of Mahajans of Shree Mangesh as 'Singhan Dalvi', probably because their ancestors were captains of the army of Singhan Yadav. The deity is named "Shinhva-Purusha". At *Bori* village, a Saraswat family—Varde Borkars— also took that deity as their protector, under the name 'Shimoyo'. It is important to note that in the temple of Shri Mhalsa of Priol there is a small temple of 'Shibi-purusha' who is considered to be the ancestor of the Mahajans of the Kaushika gotra.

Mundari rituals

At Thane hamlet of Dongurli village in Sattari taluka, two statuettes of black stone are installed at a place named 'Mundal gireachem-mol'. The statuettes are named Kolgiro and Mundalgiro and the first is considered to be the 'Raja' (King) and the second 'Pradhan' (the minister). The word 'giro' in Konkan means 'devourer', so, these two statuettes symbolize the victory gained by the Maratha people over the Kols and Mundaris. In Naneli village, adjacent to Thane there is a hero-stone in bold-relief, probably of the sixteenth or the seventeenth century where this epithet is symbolized.

There is in Goa a system of 'Mundakars'. The Mundkar is a person who with his family resides in the land of another person designated as 'Bhatkar'. The Mundkars do not pay any occupancy rent nor have any obligation, as even fishermen families reside as mundkars. However, as they dwell in palm-groves, they take up the guarding of the coconut groves and they get a percentage of the plucked coconuts.

The Mundari tribe, like the Kols came from the Chota Nagpur area, but they probably came after many centuries, when the Kol tribe was spread throughout the area of Goa, and the Mundas settled here as 'protectees' of the Kols and were engaged in agricultural work. I presume that the Kol tribe might have initiated the worship of 'Pimpal' (the holy fig tree) and 'Vad' (ficus religiosa), and the Mundaris—the worship of 'Kel' (a jungle tree with aerial roots like the afore mentioned trees). In Sattari taluka I have seen 'Kel' trees near temples without any kind of plinth, while the two other trees are generally with the plinth constructed even by the persons of Maratha and Brahmin castes. In 'Barazan' of Savoi-Verem there is again a 'Kel' tree near which there is a stone planted for their 'Jalmi' to stand on and pray. This 'Kel' tree was personified and named 'Kelbai' represented by a sculpture of Gaja-Lakshimi, image of which is seen on the coin of the third century B.C. found in the excavation at Koshambi (Northern India). It is considered as goddess of wealth and it was introduced in South-India in the period of the Chalukyas of Badami in the sixth and seventh century A.D. [57] p. 52.

It is worth noting that when in a village-temple there is a group of female-deities, the Santer is always of the first rank and Kelbai of last rank. The deity under the name Gaja-Laxmi is worshipped as a village deity in different parts of Satara, Solapur and Kolhapur areas and sporadically in other areas of Maharashtra. In Kolhapur area she is named as Bhaveshwari, Bhavka, Bhaukai etc., and is worshipped for easy childbirth. It can be seen how the basic concept changes from place to place.

Mundari was always connected with the Kol tribe, hence, except the 'Kel' tree, other deities were worshipped jointly and their customs were the same. As subordinates, the Mundari tribe had no seat in the village administration; but after the appearance of the Maratha people they separated from the Kols, and in some villages the tribe has its separate 'Jalmi'. In some villages like Priol, persons of Satarkar and Naik castes perform rituals in the hamlets distributed among them. After the arrival of the Maratha tribe, they named them 'Naik' and some of these formed a separate caste named 'Bhandari', with the toddy-tapping profession. In Ponda taluka, for example, we cannot distinguish Naik of the Mundari tribe and Naiks of the primitive pastoral tribe, which may be known only through certain religious customs in which the Naik caste has its seal while in Sattari they had none.

Their village spirits

I have already referred to 'Devchar' 'Vataro', etc., the village-protector spirit. The 'Mharu' is also a name of this kind of spirit which lives near a tree. This name is probably derived from the deity of Chota Nagpur named 'Maha-Buru' or 'Mhaburu' which reside as spirit on the tops of hills. In the story of Buddha a spirit named 'Maru' is mentioned, was disturbing Gautam Buddha while in meditation in Bihar, in land adjacent to Chota Nagpur. In Goa, we find many places as the residence of Mharu. For example in the area of the temple of Shree Shantadurga at Kavlem, so also in front of the house of Pratap Rau Sar Desai at Bandodem and at Mharvasodo of Usgaon village. At the special place of the 'Sodo', persons of different villages pay their vows by placing horses of clay. These kind of deities came to be known afterwards in certain villages as 'Kshetrapala'. In Assolda village of Quepem taluka, on top of a hillock a small temple has been constructed and there is only a stone, named Kshetrapala.

In Chota Nagpur the spirit of the tiger is named 'Vagh-bonga', and in Goa this type of spirit is named 'Vagro' or 'Vaghre Deivat'. This is worshipped in areas of some temples like in front of the temple of Vijayadurga at *Keri* (Querim) of Ponda taluka, and near the temple of Navadurga at Surla of Dicholi (Bicholim) taluka. According to the Portuguese records it is seen that a deity named 'Vaghro' was installed in *Utardem* (Utorda) village of Salcete taluka; the Vijayadurga of Keri was transferred from *Sankwal* (Sancovale) village of Salcete taluka, in the sixteenth century A.D. In Surla village, due to the belief of the settlers, the killing of tigers was forbidden.

Tree worship

In Chota Nagpur the deities were established in forest groves and were maintained without cutting of the trees as they were considered sacred. In many areas of villages in the New Conquests of Goa, we find such forest groves which are maintained intact, where some deities in an idol form or in the form of a vessel of clay are established. At the top of Vagheri mountain in Sattari taluka there is a forest grove named 'Devcharachi-Rai' (grove of the protector spirit) where a vessel of clay is maintained as a symbol of 'Mavuli' (mother-goddess). The word 'Rai' is derived from the Marathi language means grove. This was probably given by the Maratha people when they settled in the taluka. In Sanguem taluka—Astagrahar subdivision—the sacred forest grove is named 'Panna', for example in Bhati village, there are Santeri-Panna, Paika-panna and Karea-Panna, and there is a Santeri-Panna in Cotarli village.

The word 'Panna' is very significant. At Chota Nagpur the worshipper of village-deities is named 'Pahan', and surely the word 'Panna' is derived from the Mundari word Pahan. It appears, the designation of the worshipper passed to the place of worship and the worshipper came to be named 'Jalmi'.

It is curious to note that in Kerala state the headman of the village who performs the rites of the village-deities is named 'Jammi' and some lands in the village were gifted to him through the generations. In Kannada language there is no such word— not even one which is similar. This raises a problem as to why this word is prevalent only in Goa and Kerala. Probably this name might have been given in Kerala by the Nambudri Brahmins and in Goa by the Bhargava Brahmins who settled at the time of Shree Parashurama. The word was derived from Sanskrit one 'Janma' meaning birth and to the first born and thus representative of the first settlers.

It is worth noting also that in Sattari taluka the Maratha people exterminated the Kol tribe but maintained their legacy of rituals. Thus, in the village-temple of Thane an idol of stone named 'Jalmi' is placed near the image of Santer in the style of Mahishasuramardini though this designation is not in use there. The main rituals in that hamlet are performed by the Santerikar Gaonkar linked with the deity 'Santer'.

THE MUNDARI ORIGIN OF GOAN PLACE NAMES

It is noticeable that in Tiswadi taluka there existed a village named Goali-Moula which later on in the Portuguese time was included in the village Bhati of 'taraf' (freguesia in Portuguese i.e. a group of villages) of Santana. According to a copper-plate issued by Madhav Mantri, Minister of Vijayanagar, it was gifted to the Brahmins [58] pp. 41-42. This village name is surely in the Mundari language of Chota Nagpur and Rev. Haffmann gives the following meaning: Goali-Mouli, a place where a certain number of ploughmen, with their own teams gathered to help generously in the ploughing of the fields, especially of a poor man. If this is done in the hot season, they get only a pot of rice-beer for their trouble.

From ten village-names in the genuine Mundari language we get more explanations:

The first point is in respect of ploughing. It is generally noticed by the historians of India that the plough in the Austra-Asiatic language is named 'langul' or 'nangal' which gave Indo-Aryan the word Nangar. The corresponding word in Sanskrit for this is 'hala'. It is obvious that in Goa and in the adjacent areas, the non-Aryans were using the plough as an agricultural implement after their settlement. It is difficult to know if the Kols at the time of their arrival in Goa were using a plough share made of metal or not. Nevertheless, from the account of Asur Kahani it appears that probably the Asuras knew the use of copper and iron ore—may be in a crude form.

The second point is that the Kols when they came to Goa knew the art of plough-ing flat fields; so the regular cultivation of flat fields was made, *ad initio*, and also the old method of cultivation by cut-and-burn, or say, the kumeri system, was in use probably in the hill slopes as well as in the flat lands covered with forest, brought under cultivation for the first time.

The third point is that they had already domesticated cows, the use of bullocks for ploughing was known, so when they came from the North they were accompanied by cows and bullocks. In Goa, at the time of the arrival of the Kols, the existing pastoral tribe had their buffalo-fold. Whether they were using the milk or not is of secondary importance. Perhaps, since milk is the food of calves, they might have not utilized it for fear of depriving the calves of their rightful food.

Rev. Haffmann mentions that in Chota Nagpur there was a custom of human sac-rifice. In his book, Encyclopedia Mundarica published in 1924 by the Government Press of Patna, he mentions this custom, and says that it was done clandestinely. In Goa, perhaps, the Kols might have introduced the custom, but later on they might have abandoned it, but here was another custom of hanging a human body to a planted pole by an iron hook. They used to observe fast for the full day. This type of ritual was in vogue in the annual festival of the temple of *Madkai* (Marcaim) village of Ponda taluka. This procedure was prohibited by a Government order dated 6th December, 1844. However, in Painguinim village of Cancon taluka, this type of ceremony is cel-ebrated with a variation, every three years. It is named *'Gadeanchi-Jatra'*, in which the pole is substituted by a great wooden wheel, on the surface of which some per-sons of a particular family lie with the skin of the back punctured by an iron hook. The wheel is rotated on its axis till the time a person of a certain family says 'stop'. The performance is hereditary and for this that family is gifted a piece of a rice-field by the village-commune. (Comunidade).

In Chota Nagpur the Kol and Mundari tribes believed in withcraft for long, and the power of their Bongas—the spirits—so among them there are persons named 'Soka' or 'Deora' who are soothsayers. They are very powerful in witch hunting. In Goa, the families who practice this profession are designated as 'Ghadi' but this profession is handled by the families of Gavda and Maratha castes who take the surname of Ghadi and Majik, respectively, the latter name being the Portuguese word "Magico" used in translating the word Ghadi. The Bhagats are similar to soothsayers in profession, but 'Deora' is the same as 'Bhagat'. Here in Goa, the Bhagats are considered of the Vani caste and always are worshipper priests of deities of the secondary level like Rawalnath, Betal etc., but I have no evidence to prove that the ancestors of the Bhagats came with the Kols. But as their profession is similar, the designation might have been introduced at the time of the advent of the Buddhist or Jain monks, most probably the latter. In fact, in the festival of Deuki-Krishna of *Mashel* (Ponda taluka) the Bhagat runs in the procession with a wooden pillar with the symbol of an open palm on the top named 'Jainacho-Khamb'.

On the hillslope at about 400 m. altitude there is a village named Zarmem in Sattari taluka. There are about eight rough black stone pillars, ranging in height between 0.8 to 1 metre which the villagers designate as pillars of 'Hebars', so those are of the Kols. Are those megaliths? If so, why are they in so great numbers? Why were they not found in other areas? I have no evidence to assay a reply.

The Kharwa caste

In Goa from ancient times there has been a caste of fishermen and boatmen named Kharvi. The Bharatiya Sanskriti Kosh says that the Kharvi or Kharva is a caste which lives in Sourastra, Katchh, Khambayat, Thane, Ratnagiri and Bombay and the name is of Persian origin and means the boat-man. But regarding the Kharvis of Goa, the Persian ethnology is not acceptable, because the coastal area where the population of that caste was living in great numbers was under Muslim power for only a short period, about 40 years. In 1510 the Portuguese held sway over Tiswadi taluka, the adjacent Bardez and Salcete talukas and were in their actual possession. The other view is that the word Kharvi is derived from the word 'Khar' meaning salt, but this ethnology also is not acceptable as in Daman and Diu those whose livelihood depends on salt water belong to two castes namely Nakhwa (boatman) and Kharwa (fisherman). So, it appears that long ago this caste name was derived from Kharwa or say the Kharvi tribe. This tribe is more akin to the Munda tribe in appearance, and I presume that this tribe came a little after the Mundaris in Goa and lived on the sea and river-shores employing themselves mainly in fishing and boating, and as their customs were like the Kols and Mundaris they continued their religious life like the Kols, worshipping Santer and maintaining the dormitory system. However, as all the area of Goa was under the hegemony of the Kols, they had no 'Barazan' system. True, they might have had a local administrative body for the resolution of quarells between the members of the tribe. The dormitory was named 'Dhumak', as has been described earlier.

Mundari words in Konkani

There is no doubt that the basic Konkani language is derived from the Prakrit. So Marathi and Konkani are sister languages. There are many words of the Kannada language like 'barap' meaning to write, 'duddu' meaning money and others. This was due to the dominion of rulers from Karnataka region for centuries. Interestingly, I found in Rev. Haffmann's work more than two hundred words of the Mundari language found in Konkani . Some of these words are also found in old Marathi.

To relate an incident: In the year 1942, I had been deputed for a cadastral survey of Sattari taluka. While demarcating a property in Thane hamlet of Dongurli village, both the parties who were of the Maratha family told me that their common boundary was passing through a 'haral'. I did not know the meaning of the word, and they were surprised by my ignorance. At the site I found that 'haral' was a brook which in the Konkani of Tiswadi side is named 'val'. From the work of Rev. Haffmann I noticed that the word 'haral' is of Mundari origin and means a brook. In Marathi it is 'Ohol'. The area of Dongurli village is near the boundary of Maharashtra, and all the people of Goa in that village talk a Konkani language mixed with Marathi words. Nevertheless, I found a Mundari word in that area, denoting a natural feature. Moreover, the Maratha family was of high caste, which is surprising.

It is more surprising when one deals with the name of an ornament—'Baikhuri', commonly used by women. Sixty years ago and before that, it was made of gold (amongst the Hindus of high status) and of silver or of copper (amongst those of lower status) in Goa. According to Rev. Haffmann, in the Mundari language, Baekar, perhaps derived from the Hindi 'band' and 'or' is a thin string generally red in colour ending with two red or yellow tassels tightly fastened around the muscles of the upper arm (biceps), or sometimes just below the biceps especially by women. It is only an ornament, though it is occasionally made use of to suspend some amulet or medicine, believed to act by simply wearing it.

In Marathi that ornament is named 'wanki' but the word 'baikhuri' (a Mundari word for it) is in use in Goa. The point is: since the ornament is of a metal, the use of copper or of iron, be it in spongy form, was surely known to the Kols when they came to Goa.

Now the other words in Mundari: Bandi means a large rice-bay containing at least twelve mounds of paddy. In Goa, by 'bandi' we mean a subdivision of the rice-field demarcated by small bund named 'mer' in Konkani. Here we can draw two important conclusions: the first is that the Kols started the first cultivation of paddy in Goa and the second is that one system of measurement was based on the number twenty. A booklet published by the Central Institute of Languages, Mysore, shows that in the

Mundari tribe two systems are in use, one based on the number twelve, and the other on the number twenty. This is the reason why the Gavdes in general measured paddy, coconuts etc. for long in terms of groups of twenty and so we have Kandi of 20 maans (weight and volume) as well as of 20 Kudavs (capacity), and 20 Khandis go to form one khumbha of measurement.

Even though I have collected about 200 words of Mundari in use in the Konkani language, I am not listing them here or even in an appendix form, because my work is not complete due to two reasons: firstly, because I collected only plain words, and secondly, because the work of Rev. Haffmann has been published only upto the alphabet 'S'. From the cited book of S. Roy it is seen that a dictionary (of Mundari-English) was published before the year 1912, and it may be available in some University library. I recommend the youth interested in the study of the formation of the Konkani language to conduct this useful work.

The name Goa is of Mundari origin

The land of Goa is known by the native people as Goen. When the Kol tribe settled and began the cultivation of paddy, they observed that the ears of corn being big and broad were inclined to one side. In the Mundari language, this type of inclination is 'goen', and the paddy is 'bab'. (The Konkni word 'bhobo' meaning a sweet prepared from rice is derived from this word 'bab'. We have land named 'Babsoro' in Velim village of Salcete taluka, originally 'Babsore' meaning paddy-field). So the low-land area being very important was considered as the producer of goen-bab, and came to be named 'Goen-bab', which provide two short words, namely Goen and Gouba. Gudea Enki (ruler) of Lagash (alias Sirlapur) of Sumer (now part of Iraq) who visited this area by the sea-route in about 2,200 B.C. (?) for the purpose of acquiring the precious wood, mentions its name as Gubi on the inscriptions recorded on the broken clay-bricks. And the Greek geographer (2nd century A.D.) mentions it as Kouba which is the Greek corruption of the word Gouba. Goa as Gomant is mentioned in the Harivansha and the name Goapuri for a town of Goa is mentioned in the Suta-Sanhita. V. R. V. Valaulikar has discussed the name 'Gomantak' [60].

SUMMARY

At the end of the fourth pluviation period, about 12,000 years ago, due to the seismic movement, the western sea-coastal area of the Peninsular India along with a portion of the sea-bed adjacent to it was elevated approximately from Vaitarana River on the North to the South upto Kanyakumari. This movement resulted in the formation of theWestern Ghats and a strip of land on the West of these Ghats known in the Puranas as Parshuram-Kshetra or 'Sapta-Konkanas' is where Goa is situated.

Some waves of people which characterize the Neolithic Age of India were out of their shelters in caves in Southern as well as in Northern India, but most probably those of Southern India had sporadically occupied the area of Goa.

About one thousand years later there was a sudden change in climate which became arid and hot, with violent western winds producing cyclones. So, the people had to flee in search of shelter and sweet water.

Mhar

At about 8,500 B.C. the climate condition stabilised with regular rains. It is assumed otherwise without clear evidence that some families which resisted the catastrophe and did not suffer from the cyclones, started their primitive life of hunting, and perhaps fishing. These people about 9,000 years ago began to settle in the neighbouring bases of slopes of the Western Ghats, or say, of the Sahyadri range. These people were named by the later tribe, probably by the Kols, as Maraung which in the Mundari language means 'of the elder family' and who subsequently were named as 'Mhar'. They probably were worshippers of their ancestors, believing in the existence of spirits, and their place of worship is named Mharangan.

Pastoral Tribe

After thousands of years, or say, about 6,000 years ago, a pastoral tribe coming from South India settled in Goa, and those were buffalo-keepers,who knew the techniques of domestication of animals, but not about plants and cereals. This tribe had no idea of a marriage-link, but afterwards formed two main groups, namely the Naik caste and the second group in the matriarchal system consisted of Chedvans, Bhavins and Kalavantans and their brothers. They installed the worship of the female and male elements symbolized by stones.

Asura

Later on, probably, about 5,500 years ago, a tribe named 'Asura' appeared from the area around Chota Nagpur of Madhya Pradesh. They probably had a crude notion of the use of copper and iron, this in spongy form and utilized this knowledge for making ornaments and small tools for shaping the stone implements. They started agriculture by cut-and-burn method, locally named 'Kumeri' system, and produced cereals. They believed in the existence of spirits and installed deities like 'Kaman-Rouduro', 'Gana-Rouduro', and 'Dhavaj-Rouduro'. Some deities installed by them later on changed by *ized by stones.*

Asura

Later on, probably, about 5,500 years ago, a tribe named 'Asura' appeared from the area around Chota Nagpur of Madhya Pradesh. They probably had a crude notion of the use of copper and iron, this in spongy form and utilized this knowledge for making ornaments and small tools for shaping the stone implements. They started agriculture by cut-and-burn method, locally named 'Kumeri' system, and produced cereals. They believed in the existence of spirits and installed deities like 'Kaman-Rouduro', 'Gana-Rouduro', and 'Dhavaj-Rouduro'. Some deities installed by them later on changed by sublimation. This tribe was subdued by the subsequent Kol tribe, dispossessing them of the land. So, the members of this Asura tribe passed on to occupy certain professions. Some became blacksmiths, some potters, some labourers and others formed part of the Vani caste.

The Bharvankar caste in the Christian community is of this stock.

Kol, Mundari and Kharwa

Next, about 5,000 years ago, Kols, Mundaris and Kharwas came from the same area as the Asuras.

The Kols occupied the lands, cultivated paddy-fields and organised a village socio-economic administration, establishing 'Barazan' in the group of twelve hamlets or villages. The paddy-fields were subdivided into 'Bandis' and were cultivated by the rotation system. Probably later this might have led to permanent ownership by various famiies. In this tribe we note the first roots of the primitive communes. Their main Goddess was an anthill named afterwards by the Aryans as Santer and Bhumika, and the tribe named as Satarkar are probably Santerkars, designated after their main deity being Santer.

The Mundaris who probably came after them worked under their hegemony. They had no special cultural trend, except the worship of a forest-tree named Kel. I presume the Konkani word 'Mundkar' meaning 'protectee' obviously is derived from their economic status in connection with the Kols.

The Kharwas probably came along with the Mundaries, but as there was no suitable area from their independent village, they took to the profession of fishing and boating which forms the present Kharvi caste.

The religious customs of all the three tribes were the same like the Sigmo festival of the men folk and the Dhalo festival of the women.

115

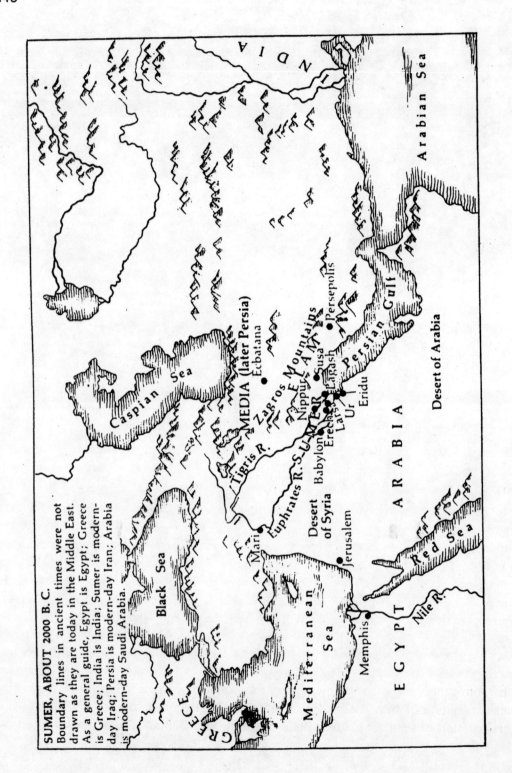

SUMER, ABOUT 2000 B.C.
Boundary lines in ancient times were not
drawn as they are today in the Middle East.
As a general guide, Egypt is Egypt; Greece
is Greece; India is India; Sumer is modern-
day Iraq; Persia is modern-day Iran; Arabia
is modern-day Saudi Arabia.

Chapter - 4
ADVENT OF SUMERIANS IN GOA

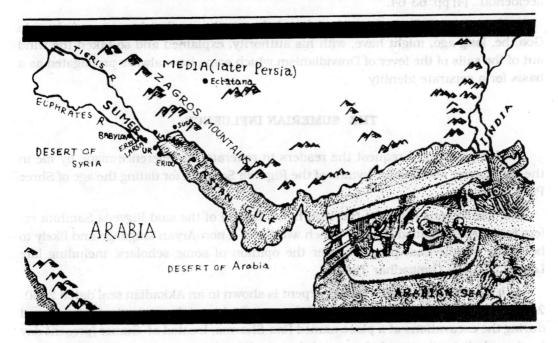

In the first chapter reference has been made to the migration and settlement of the Aryans-Brahmins of the Bhargavas and the Angiras clans to the western coast of India when they accompanied Shree Parashurama in his expedition to the South. This expedition took place about 2,400 B.C.

This event has been recorded by the historians of India, in general, and my findings reported in this regard also corroborates this event. Now I wish to place before you another event that has not been recorded up to now and is unknown to Indologists due to the lack of evidence. It is to be noted that only after the excavations at Harappa which was started in the year 1921, was unearthed the evidence and the link to the word 'Hariupia', mentioned in the Rigveda as being the name of a town described there with details, and now confirmed by the excavations. Thus the history of Northern India was changed by this new evidence. It had been thought that the culture of South India is Dravidian and that it is of autochthonous origin. Some link this culture to that of the Brahmins of Southern Iran. There are, however, a few historians who think differently: one of them says that some Egyptians might have visited the western coast of Peninsular India as merchants. They probably induced the idea of construction of temples in the minds of the people. Nilkant Sastri has pointed out that the structure of the temple, the rituals and their organisation in South India is similar to those of Sumer. He says, "In fact the resemblance is so close that, inspite of the absence of any direct proof of connexion, it is difficult to believe that it is accidental". [4] pp. 63-64.

In fact, if Dr. Nilkant Sastri had found the specimens that I uncovered here in Goa, he, long ago, might have, with his authority, explained and so taken the wind out of the sails of the fever of Dravidianism which some have always propagated as a basis for a separate identity.

THE SUMERIAN INFLUENCE

At this juncture, I request the readers to reiterate the reference made by me in the 1st chapter about some hymns of the Rigveda Samhita for dating the age of Shree Prashurama.

The fourth song (*richa*) of the 18th hymn (*sukta*) of the said Rigveda Samhita refers to a serpent named 'Teimat' which word is of a non-Aryan language and likely to be of the Middle-East people as per the opinion of some scholars, including late Lokamanya Bal Gangadhar Tilak.

As a matter of fact, the 'Timot' serpent is shown in an Akkadian seal dated 2360-2180 B.C. depicting the seven-headed dragon which was drawn in the tablets found during the excavations at a place named Ras-Sharma, located at Sumer (present day Iraq) symbolizing primeval chaos and drought [8] & [9]. Interestingly, the drought is named as Vritra and described also as serpent 'Teimat' in the Rigveda Samhita.

Both the Sumeriologists and Indologists admit that at the time of Sargon I, King of Akkad and Sumer there was commercial contact between his domain and North-West coastal India, a region named as 'Meluha' in Sumerian cuneiform inscriptions. Some scholars place Sargon in c. 2500 B. C. [11] and others in about 2550 B.C. [12].

In Goa we find the Sumerian culture deeply rooted perhaps because the families were of the highest status, or say of the ruler-priest class of sumer area. With these remarks I ask the readers to scrutinize this work carefully. It may be for the first time that a new chapter on the history of India is being opened by me with the finds that I uncovered by chance. I am going to describe at length and show the direct connection of the finds with Sumerian culture from Sumer and not through the Indus Valley culture or any other.

The finds that I made in this respect are from Savoi-Verem and Priol villages of Ponda taluka. I am listing them by the chronological order in which I found them. In the introduction I have already mentioned in which circumstance I obtained them.

Obviously after listing them I shall concentrate on each item separately, considering in proper perspective vis-a-vis what is found mentioned in the history of Sumer.

THE ARCHAEOLOGICAL FINDINGS

The First find: the cave of Savoi-Verem

In the year 1950, the late Padmakar Bhatt Savoikar showed me in Savoi-Verem village a cave carved out of laterite rock with an entrance doorway, on the slope of a hillock. Immediately at the entrance there was a corridor-type room, and if I remember well, a small room carved at the middle of the length. What was most interesting was that the entrance to that room was not through a door but through a rectangular hole carved at the bottom of the carved surface, so that a person might enter the small room only by crawling through. Savoikar showed me also twelve signs carved on the wall and I had copied them in my notebook. Those were surely the signs of the Sumerian script confirmed by me later on.

Second find: place name "Mhatari" and Sumerian idol

In 1959, again in Savoi-Verem village in the area of the 'sil-cum-Inam' property and more adjacent to it, three objects were found, namely: (a) a sacred-place named 'Mhatari' as mentioned before; (b) an intact idol of whitish black stone, of a variegated nature, the legs of which from the knees downwards were like those of an eagle, and separately a broad and long fish made of the same type of rock, but which was in three pieces. The full description of it can be found in the introduction; (c) some clay-bricks dispersed here and there having some lines carved on one face which could not be deciphered.

In the year 1970, I found in the Central Library, Panaji, a French book written by G. Maspero titled 'Histoire Ancienne des Peoples de l'Orient'. I was astonished by the description given therein of the idol of the God Anu. This description was somewhat short, but it gave the most important characteristics of the idol and those tallied exactly with the characteristics of the idol which I had seen. As a result I decided to concentrate on that area and visited once again the spot as well as the surrounding area of Savoi-Verem village and I found the following:

ill. 10 : Frontal view of Oracle-plate of Betal at Barazan Priol Village, Ponda Taluka, dated c. 2000 B.C.

Third find: oracle plate of Betal and two stelae of Priol

In 1971, I visited the place named 'Barazan' of Priol. There I found a black stone with carved lines *(ill.10)* which was an oracle-plate. I also found there two stelae *(ill. 11)* in bass-relief. On one stela there was a symbol of the Bel of Sumer—a tiara with two horns at each side and below that a woman of the Saraswat Brahmin caste standing before a linga of Shiva in the posture of worship. Further down a woman of the Paddye Brahmin caste worshipping the top of a hill, as it is believed that the image of God Betal was first installed on top of the hill situated in that village. This temple is presently situated in the low-lying area. During the great annual festival a procession takes place, and it starts with first, a visit to that place on the top of the hill, where there is nothing except a tree. Next the folk visit the residential house of a family of Paddye caste with Desai as the surname where they take repose for one night and the next day, in the early morning, the procession continues to make visits to other residential houses according to the order already fixed from ancient times.

It is worth noting that the principal family of Paddye Brahmins in Priol village—the said Desai family—worships an idol of 'Tripura-Sundari' (of the Tantrik cult). There is a tale in that family that in ancient times, the worshipper had to offer a drop of human blood every day. This custom might be traced to the custom prevailing in Sumer.

In Sumer, the flesh of goat and sheep was offered daily to all the deities. Obviously the Paddye Bhats continued their custom here, by offering the flesh of the goat, as sheep was not available here. Influenced by Buddhism when it

ill. 11 : View of one of the stelae at Barazan, Priol Village, Ponda Taluka, showing on the top tiara with two horns, symbol of betal.

spread in Goa, the Paddyes might have abandoned the custom of offering flesh.

Sumerian Bel and Goan *Betal*

The idol of the God Bel in Sumer was styled in the form of a King seated on a throne and considered as sovereign of the earth and of the spirit. However, he was also worshipped in different forms, one of these was 'Bel-talal'. The word 'Talal' in the Sumerian language means a warrior, and he was styled in the nude form in the pose of shooting an arrow from a bow. The sculpture of the idols of Sumerians was not realistic. It was idealistic. Hence, the nude form represents virility. In the copper-plate of Tribhuvanamalla Kadamba dated 1099 A.D. [59] the God Betal of this village is designated as '*Bhairava*'. According to the Indian mythology the main Bhairavas are eight in number. Each main Bhairava has seven more Bhairavas in his group. Thus in all there are 64 Bhairavas. However, I did not find any Bhairava from this group described in the nude form. In Maharashtra there are idols in the nude form called 'Nagna-Bhairav' but their sculpture is different: there the Nagna-Bhairava has two hands and holds in the right hand a '*damaru*' (a sort of tambor, shaped like an hour-glass) and in his left hand a '*trishula*' (a trident). A serpent is shown around his waist and a dog is considered to be his '*vahana*' (a vehicle). While Betal holds a sword in his right hand, in the left a half-cut coconut shell, a strip with small bells is found around his waist and there is no vehicle.

Fourth find: the puzzling cave temple of Surla village- Siddheswarachi houri

During field work for drawing up a topographic map of Bicholim (*Diuchal alias*

ill. 12 :   Rock-carved temple of Siddeshwar at Surla Village of Dicholi Taluka, dated c. 1,000 B.C.

Dicholi) taluka, during the period 1938-39, I noticed a cave temple at the base of a hillock in Surla village *(ill. 12)*. I revisited it in 1971 and took measurements, photos etc. and felt that the cave must have been carved long ago. Subsequently, I visited the place a third time (as well as *'Barazan'* of Savoi-Verem and *'Rangache-mol'* at Naneli village and places at Thane of Sattari taluka) accompanied by Mitragotri and other staff of the local Museum of Archaeology.

The influence of Sumerian architecture—Cubit as an unit of measurement

The hillock of Surla village has a shape in which the frontage might be carved in any direction but it is remarkable that it had the magnetic bearing of 227 degrees; the magnetic declination at the time of measuring was about two degrees, hence, the geographic bearing was 225 degrees. This is typical of the Sumerian orientation of temples. According to Hindu procedure the face of the frontage-wall is oriented in the N-S direction so that the entrance is oriented to the East. The remnants (plinth) of a temple at the time of the Kadambas existing in Chandor village of Salcete taluka, shows that the frontal wall was truly oriented in the N-S direction. The second point is that the frontage face was made by cutting the laterite rock of the slope of the hillock, so that a rectangular platform is built before that frontage. One of the sides of this rectangle which is paralleled to the frontage measures thirty metres and the other side three metres. The proper frontage which had somewhat deteriorated due to the existence of iron oxide in the rock, measures 30.02 m. (thirty metres and two centimetres). The dimensions of the remnants of the brick-wall of the temple of Chandor do not tally to the metric system, which shows that while the unit of measurement, probably a cubit, had the length tallying with the present metric system, the unit for measurement in the temple construction was completely different.

It is surprising to note that the unit for marking the excavation of the construction, and the direction, is totally identical with the process of the primitive construction of a temple in Sumer. Anton Moortgert in his book "The art of Ancient Mesopotamia" states:

"The largest buildings of the first phase is the so-called 'Limestone Temple'. The building was constructed on an elongated, rectangular plan 70m x 30m, with its corners facing the cardinal point of the compass" . [61] pp 1-3.

From this quotation it is evident that the direction of the frontage of a temple from the beginning of the construction of this kind was like that of the cave in Surla village and the measurement of the side walls were as if the metric system was used. In Sumer, among others, there was a measure 'cubit', equivalent to 0.495 m; approximately half metre [62]. Around 1899, a committee had been appointed by the Portuguese Government to give a report about the weights and measures in use in Goa and their values in the metric system. That committee found the length of a cubit marked on the wall of an old church in a village (Curtorim?) of Salcete taluka, and computed its value to be 0.4953 m. It is not understood how this value of a cubit being as an unit was not taken into consideration when the temple at Chandor was built. The temple was constructed with a frame of wood, the space between the wooden columns being filled with clay and bricks. It seems that the builder of the construction was a non-Goan, and so, he took a unit different from the Goan one. From this evidence is clear that the Sumerian type cubit continued to be used as an unit up to the advent of the Portuguese.

The cave-temple of Surla has three openings as entrance doors; but I presume that when it was carved the entrance was only one— - the one on the left. The other two openings are carved later in the historical period. I make this presumption based on the memory on the cave that I had seen in Savoi-Verem village in 1950. It is worth noting that both these villages viz Surla and Savoi-Verem are adjacent to each other, though separated by a river.

Through this entrance we enter into an oblong rectangular room. The rock, as I have said before contains iron-oxide; hence, all the faces of this room are intensely corroded. At the middle of the length of the rear face (which is the major side of the rectangular room) there is a door carved in laterite rock which is 1.03 m. wide and 1.73 m. high but it is remarkable that only about 0.60 m. from the bottom, the outer and inner surfaces of the wall, where the door is carved, are badly corroded, while the upper portion of the opening of the door, or say, both sides of the door in the width of the wall are corroded to only a negligible extent. At the right side of the door, there is a carved square hole in the wall admeasuring (60 cm.x 60 cm of side), at a height of about 80 cm. from the bottom of the wall where an oil-lamp of brass was kept. It is curious also that the lateral faces of that hole show negligible corrosion. This shows that the carving of this square hole as well as the conversion of the hole-entrance to a door took place very late, and in the historic period. This conclusion is corroborated by other facts as well.

Siddheswarachi houri

Linked to the rear face of the sanctuary room lies a pedestal of about one metre height and square in form; the upper face is a plain square of 60 cm. on the side, and carved along with the rear face, so that one face of the pedestal is part of a surface which serves as the wall of the room. On top of the pedestal there is a 'linga' of black stone, which is monolithic and formed of a base (Shalunka) which is circular, though somewhat oblong. The proper 'linga' is 10 cm. high, cylindric, the top is curved, and on the top there is a groove 10 cm long, seen as parallel to the main line of the façade. The periphery of the 'linga' proper measures 60 cm and obviously the periphery of the 'shalunka' is larger, and in this part there is no groove on any side. It appears the libation for worship was impossible, because in a cave of such type there is no way of discharging water. The 'Shalunka' is so large that on the top of the pedestal it did not fit safely, and this is the reason why, due to the lateral pressure of

ill. 13 : Linga of Siddeshwar at Garbhakud (Sanctuary) of a rock-carved temple at Surla Village of Dicholi Taluka.

the adjacent surface of wall, the 'shalunka' is broken *(ill. 13)*. It is also to be noted that there is no 'Nandi' there. This cave is named 'Siddheshwarachi-houri', which means cave of Sidheshwar.

Not far from this spot there is a temple constructed of laterite stone where the 'linga' was imported from outside without taking into consideration the suitability of its establishment elsewhere. It is also noticeable that at the middle of the top base of the pedestal there is a shaft-hole. I have found in Candola (*Khandolem*) village (Ponda taluka) a pedestal like this in a small cave, having on the top a shaft-hole. This cave is named as *Vanadevata* (deity of the forest) but there is no idol there.

So, it is clear that a plaque of black stone with an appendage at the bottom was placed on the shaft hole-the appendage being inserted in the hole. A shaft is never used to place a 'linga'. This is another reason to consider that some other deity was placed on that plain surface. What might be the nature of that deity is a moot point.

I presume that the original carving of this cave temple must have taken place about 1,500 B.C. or say, three and a half thousand years ago, if not earlier.

The proof of the builder's skill is that he had knowledge of astronomy and consequently the process of marking on the ground the direction of the true North.

The builder carved in front of the cave a courtyard in the form of an accurate rectangle 30 m x 3 m, as also the pedestal with 60 cm square on the top. The rooms form accurate rectangles if the damage due to corrosion is duly accounted for.

Being a surveyor with experience in different areas of work in land-surveys, I did all the operations needed to verify the accuracy of the work, and concluded that the builder, if he had a cubit as an unit of length, he divided it in five parts and so marked the 60 cm. side of the pedestal. From the marking of 30 m x 3 m. rectangle it is seen that he used the decimal system. The diagonals of the rectangles and square are accurate, which shows that the builder was fully acquainted with all operations of the basic arithmetic with squares and square-roots and had knowledge of geometry.

Worship of Sumerian God Nimirud

It is interesting to note that on the fore-face of the 'linga', a sign is carved resembling a portion of the alphabet 'Shree' of the Devanagari script. I have never seen this type of sign engraved on any 'linga' as heard of the existence of such a sign on any 'linga' in worship in any part of India. There is no reference to such a sign in Hinduism. In Sumer, the symbols of the gods Anu and Bel were their tiaras with two horns on both sides; and that of the goddess Inanna with the symbol of a shepherd's hooked stick, but I could not find symbols of the other deities of Sumer. That sign cannot be considered as a tiara with two horns, because the lines representing the horns must have been carved in a horizontal line or curved upwards. This symbol is quite different, and that is the point. To ascertain this point we have to go back in history.

In Sumer, now part of Iraq, there were many city-states, one of them being Lharsa. All the city-names are obviously deciphered from the cuneiform script carved on the clay-brick found in the excavations. Dr. Waddell, however, does not agree with the deciphering of the name as Lharsa and he says that it is 'Sirlapur' or Sirburla [63] page 20. The main deity of the city was Ningirsu, sometimes named Nimirrud (Nimrod) and the name of his consort was Nimgizidda.

So, a plaque with the couple or a single one of the Nimrod was probably placed on that altar or say, that pedestal in bold relief. According to the Hindu concept of deities, this couple or single one was changed to a 'linga' and it was named by the conjugation of the main names of the primitive deities. The prefix Nim, Nin or In in Sumerian languages means Lord or Lady corresponding to the Shree of the Aryan language. Hence omitting these prefixes, the names were 'gizidda' and 'rud' or 'rod' respectively. The composed word would be Zidda-Rud, and taking for Rud the Rudra of Indian mythology, a linga was selected as a new deity-Siddheswar, the Siddha is an ascetic person-a Jogi, by his specific name. Even on his *samadhi* (tomb) a 'linga' is placed but without '*pindika*'.

According to Dr. Wadell the image of Nimrod as well as of Ningirsu was the same. A man in a standing position holding in the left hand a net with captured fish and in his right hand a fish, the fish being his enemy. As the sign in the Sumerian script is a little different from that of the carved symbol, I am unable to decipher its meaning.

Nimirud and 'Pasupati'

However, at this juncture, I recollect the symbol found during the excavation of the Indus civilization at Mohenjodaro and its similarity to the carved symbol. This figure is that of 'Pasupati' and has some characters of Sumerian origin. The head-dress of Pashupati is shown with two horns; its three faces are seen. It is possible that with the fourth face being at the rear side, it is not visible.

In Sumer we find many paintings showing gods and even goddesses with the head-dress with two horns. Even the king being conducted by his tutelary goddess to the main god at the time of coronation wears a similar head-dress with two horns. These forms of head-dress with two horns even came to be used in Cappadocia. The headmen of Panis were used to this kind of head-dress. The descendants of Panis who came to the East had a custom whereby at the time of marriage the bridegroom used horns.

In the Babylonian period in Sumer and obviously before this period in their proper country i.e. Babylonia, there were a couple of deities named Amarru-each had four faces. Hence, if there is any doubt of the existence of the fourth face in the figure of Pashupati, we have before us the image of Brahmadeva with four faces and his daughter Saraswati is named Chaturwakra (with four mouths); we are otherwise accustomed to see her statuette with one face. The legend of a conjugal link between them is significant.

I cited this fact of history because the clue found even about the origin of the symbol of a headdress is significant to establish the probability of interaction between two civilisations viz, Indus Valley and Sumer on account of their clear contact, not only commercial but cultural as well. The symbol on the linga of the cave-temple of Surla village cannot otherwise be deciphered.

The lost idol of Nimrod

As I have mentioned before, Nimrod came to be represented by a linga representing Rudra-Shiva, his consort Nimgizidda considered as Ninhursag was named Navadurga and her temple was also established in Surla village.

An elderly person of a Gaonkar family of that village, of Ghadi caste, narrated to me a legend in vogue in that village. In the village there were many deities but a spirit-like deity was transforming the vegetarian food offered daily to other deities into flesh and so the deities were starved for centuries. Finally they got an opportunity.

The Goddess Santer was passing through the village and all the deities met her and prayed for solace. She took the form of a woman and got a well excavated deep with plenty of water and laid down in that well a bunch of plantains. She then called the spirit-god to go down and take that bunch, but with the condition that he should go down with his head downwards. The bunch had been thrown attached to a heavy stone, so it was at the bottom of the well under deep water. As soon as the spirit-god reached the bottom of the well, the Goddess Santer poured stones and mud into the well and completely closed it, putting upon it a black stone. She told the spirit-god to stay there and promised that annually he would be offered the flesh of a cock. Goddess Sater then went away and settled in the neighbouring Kothambi (Cotombi) village. From this legend it appears that the idol of Nimrod is buried in that place where the slab is. I could not excavate there, firstly because of the faith of the villagers and secondly it would have needed my continuous presence there, which was not possible.

Fifth find: Sumerian script at Barazan in Savoi-Verem village

In December, 1973, I visited the place named '*Barazan*' situated in Savoi-Verem village. Near a block of black stone of an irregular shape there was a jungle tree, known as *kel*, the aerial roots of which had circled one portion of that rock. After the roots were cut, two carved signs appeared, one on the top, and the other on the face of the stone (*ill. 14*).

The sign on the face is like a parallelogram of crossed or say, in the form of the logitudinal section of a '*damaru*' drum. The parallel sides measure 6.5 cm and 7.5 cm, the crossed lines 5 mm and the depth 3 mm. This sign, according to Dr. Waddell's cited book, is of the Sumerian cuneiformscript pronounced as '*Gana*' and means also '*Gana*' in Sanskrit which corresponds to the Konkani word '*Jana*'. The sign at the top consisted of two parallel lines, with the following dimensions: one 5.7 x 0.9 x 0.6 cm and the other 9.0 x 1.0 x 0.8 cm. On the right side a line perpendicular to those lines disap-

ill. 14 : Black stone at Barazan, Savoi-Verem, Ponda Taluka with Sumerian signs in Sanskrit language meaning "Dwadash-gana", dated c. 1,000 B.C.

peared because on that side the piece of rock was broken by the destructive action of the aerial roots. G. Maspero in his cited book shows that the sign is as of the Sumerian script and gives its pronunciation as 'ud' and the meaning as the Sun or a day. The engraver did not put this sign on the face together with the other sign, because in this case the reading would have been 'udgana' and so incoherent with its true meaning. So, he engraved this sign on the top to indicate that it was related to the Sun. This is the the the definite interpretation.

According to the Indian mythology the Sun, *Aditya*, was not one, but twelve. According to cryptic Indian numerology '*Aditya*' means twelve. In the hymns of Shatapatha Brahmana it is mentioned that Adityas were twelve in number, and according to the view of Sankar Dikshit [65] the hymns of Satapatha Brahmanas were composed around 1,500 B.C. So, this concept was surely in use before those hymns.

Be that as it may, the facts that emerge from the discovery of the two signs are: the signs are surely of the genuine Sumerian cuneiform script; these signs write down the Sanskrit word '*Dvadasha Gana*'. This word in Konkani means '*Barazana*' which is the name of the place where the carved signs were found.

The two parallel lines are 6 and 7 cm. in length respectively, depth and breadth being about 3 mm; the shape of the carving is like the 'U' of the English alphabet, but carved at the bottom. The lines of the parallelogram with crossed sides are somewhat narrow in breadth and the depth is more or less the same. The stone is very hard, of fine texture. The cutting of the line could have not be done without the use of a hardened iron tool.

The Sumerian script and the Sanskrit language was known to two peoples: the Sumerians of high caste and the Aryans of the Bhargava clan [9]. It is known from history that there was an Indian interpreter in Sumer. There is evidence of the presence of Indian merchants in Susa and Sumer in the early chalcolithic period. "A piece of sculpture (of the period of Gudea about 2,200 B.C.) also depicts a humped bull." [65] pp. 35 p. 47.

ill. 15: Frontal view of the oracle-plate of the God Anu discovered in an arecanut garden at Silvado, Savoi-Verem village, Ponda Taluka, dated c. 2,000 B.C.

The Saraswat Brahmins in whom the original Bhargavas are included, settled in Savoi-Verem village in historic times and as such they are of the Kulkarni vangad of the village commune while the Paddye Bhats are Gaonkars of the same commune. It is likely that the engraver of those signs was from the clan of Paddya Bhats.

Sixth find: the Oracle Plates of Anu and Inana

In April 1981, I visited 'Mhatari' of Savoi-Verem, and while climbing the steps two oracle-plates were found used as steps in different staircases. After pouring white powder on the grooves of these plates brought to my residence, I was astonished to note that one oracle plate showed the symbol of the god Anu-a tiara with two horns *(ill. 15)*. The 'tiara' is a bass-relief and the elevated part of the 'tiara' is a natural elevation proper of the stone-perhaps the shape of this natural form might have been regularized on its outer border by rubbing on that side. The horns are relatively small in length and their lines are carved like other lines on the plate. Close to the tiara, at the right side, the figure of a fish is carved and its tail, instead of being carved in the inverted 'V' form is carved in the form of two adjoining rectangles, perhaps the symbolic form of a tail. Both the sets of lines constitute parallel lines as said before, except one at the bottom of the right side set which is somewhat inclined. It is remarkable that on the top-most face there is a carving in the form of the English alphabet 'H'. The dimensions of this slab are: 53 x 32 x 9 cms in maximum. On the portion corresponding to the thickness of the slab of the right side, parallel lines are carved and similarly they must have existed on the left side but this portion was broken and lost which is easily traceable. The second oracle plate was of Goddess Inanna with the symbol of a shepherd's stick. The dimensions of this oracle-plate are 44 x 40 x 6 cms. *(ill. 16)*.

ill. 16 : Frontal view of the oracle-plate of the Goddess Inanna discovered in an arecanut garden at Silvado, Savoi-Verem village, Ponda Taluka, dated c. 2,000 B.C.

It is remarkable that while all the script lines in both the oracle plates are carved on the surface, the natural cut projection of the plate is oriented as the tiara proper. The priest had selected this schist-plate as the figure was a mystic symbol, impressive to create faith. In Shree Chandranath temple of Parvat, Parodem (*Paroda* alias *Paddem*) village, Salcete taluka, the original image of Shree Chandranath is similar to this type of projection of a rock-plate and is considered as a 'Swayambhu' (self-existent) linga.

i) The origin of oracle-plates

From the symbols it is quite clear that the idea is solely of Sumerian origin and represents a direct link with the gods Anu and Inanna of Sumer. I have not taken into consideration here the similar oracle existing at Barazan at Priol village, despite its being of the God Betal, only because there is no visible symbol of the God Bel or Betal.

It is interesting to understand the main sentiments behind the consultation through the oracle. Elizabeth Lansing in her book '"The Sumerians" says: [65]

"Completely enslaved by the immortals, man had no control over his own destiny. Neither was there any way for him to know what the capricious gods had in mind for him. His sense of helpless dependence is shown in the lines of a poem: 'Mari man - his days are numbered ...... whatever he may do, he is but wind'. (Mari is the name of the Sumerian city-state)".

"Even the kings of each city-state were no more than temporary tenants of the God who owned it. Since the God rules, all citizens were equal in his service. Sumerian society was co-operative, with every detail carefully planned. In Sumerian documents the workers of the temple estates, priests, herdsmen, fishermen, gardener, etc., were referred to as 'people of the God'. Inspite of this concept of equality in the eyes of the God, it must often have occurred to some of the toilers in the fields that the high priests and great kings were more 'equal than they.'"

ii) The temple diviners of Sumer

But how was the divine will disclosed? Another writer says:

"The Sumerians do not seem to have been so deeply addicted to omen-reading as their Semetic successors. They do, however, appear to have consulted the Gods in this way over important appointments-such as that of the high priest. It was the Akkadians of the Old Babylonian period who began the systematization of the divine's art, writing down a mass of observations for the future generations.

"Omens could be either sought by men anxious for divine guidance or vouchsafed by the divine goodwill. Of the first type the interpretation of the entrails of sacrificial animals, especially of the liver and lungs of sheep, was probably the earliest. It was never abandoned, but in later times it was surpassed by astrology. Models of sheep's organs were made in pottery and inscribed with interpretations very much like the ceramic heads of all phrenologists. A typical report sent to the king at Mari reads.... 'At the monthly sacrifice, I examined the omens. The left side of the 'finger' was split, the middle 'finger' of the lungs was over the left. It is a sign of fame. Let my lord be happy'. Diviners showed an understandable desire for omens to be good; they might recast them again and again if the signs were depressing. [10] p. 233.

"The Lord of Wisdom text has already shown how normal it was for a private citizen to appeal to the divine (and also to the interpreter of dreams and the exorcist). Sickness, as in this case, was a frequent reason for such consultations, but they might also concern chances of having children, business ventures, or the choice of a wife". (Note: In Goa, the Hindus consult omens, say oracle, in all the above cases, especially in the acceptance of a bride; the Christians, in general also do; dreams are also interpreted in this way).

"The demons provoked sickness and maladies; a demon was creating asak (plague)". (Note: the word *asuk* in Konkani in use 60 years ago meant small-pox).

Magical devices for defeating hostile demons must have preoccupied all the humble people in times of trouble. Sympathetic magic and the use of effigies were among them. (Note: in Goa, for the removal of the 'evil eye', the Mhar prepares two effigies-male and female-of rice-flour for the ritual named '*dist kadap*' in the Konkani language. For instance, dust would be gathered from various melancholic, demon-haunted places, moistered with bull's blood and modelled into a figure of the devil monster (demons were often in animal shape) and enclosed in a pot. 'Shamash' would then be evoked to judge in favour of the sick man and against his foe and the pot was buried in a desert place. Note: sixty years ago, here in Goa, a *Ghadi* or *Bhagat* or even a Muslim magician were engaged in such witchcraft, inserting a ghost-*bhut* in Konkani-in a bottle which was then tightly closed and buried in a barren land).

Even these superstitious fringes of religion were not entirely removed from the higher forms of temples. The evocation of 'Shamash' just mentioned would be addressed to him in moving words as the bringer of light and warmth to the people and a source of justice to wronged men and women.

A priest of the first class bore the title of 'mash mash', but from the earliest times the functions have been divided, and he whose mission was to appease the hearts of the angry gods by psalms, was called 'kalu'. On certain fixed days he visits the temple to offer sacrifices, and to intone the sacred lamentations, accompanying himself on various persecusion instruments [62].

It is known that the Akkadian period in Sumer started with the ruler named Sargon I whose reign is calculated to be between c. 2700 - 2600 B.C. [66]. We may take here the later date. And from this date upto 2000 B.C. (ibid) p. 103, the time when the

Amorites and Elamites attached and captured the city of Ur and forced the people of Sumer to migrate, the system of omen-consultation was perpetuated at their new settlements.

Introduction of Sumerian rituals to Goa

The Sumerian priest-kings were known as "Patesis". These Sumerians were of the highest class-the present Paddyes were overly bound to religious rituals. These rituals for them were like the need for daily food, clothes and shelter. For omen-consultation a sheep was needed and in Goa this was not available, hence a substitute was chosen, and so the oracle plate was prepared. The Sumerians migrated from the Persian Gulf about 2000 B.C. and they might have taken about three years' time for their journey to the Goan coast by the sea-route. So, about 2,000 B.C. they must have made the mud-houses with roofs of palm-leaves for housing their deities along with the oracle plates. Hence, these oracle plates are relics of the most ancient times of the people who came from outside India. If one puts aside the finds discovered in the Indus Valley, there is no room to consider that these people migrated from the Indus area, as no object for omen-finding is discovered so far. Moreover, no sign of temple-construction has been found in the areas of the Indus civilization.

The proof of migration of those people to Goa in the time period mentioned above will be put forward later. However, the two oracle plates as well as the two symbols of the genuine Sumerian script found carved on a rock at Barazan, and the fact that all these proofs have been found in the same village, Savoi-Verem, is more than sufficient to believe that the people did come and settle in that village even though, unfortunately, I am not able to produce the idol of the god Anu shown to me in 1959 by the late Padmakar Bhatt Savoikar and later submerged by him in the river as he told me in 1962. I was of the opinion that an idol of Inana also must have existed in the same place where the idol of Anu was found. In the temple of Shree Anant, as Sheshashahi-Vishnu, a metallic mask named 'Hurnia' was preserved and was worshipped only in the festival of Navaratra in the temple of Shree Santer of the same village. I had, in my previous article in Marathi, opined that the mask was of Inanna of Urek and that the name was corrupted from the word 'Urek-Anna'. Now with the discovery of the oracle-place of that deity, my presumption has been consolidated.

Drawing a parallel with the Sumerian temples, Hindu temples generally have the *dipasthamba*, instead of the huge bamboo, in front of them. Instead of a water-tank at the corner of the temple, we have it generally in front and rarely behind the temple. An exception has been made in the case of some temples of Santer of the fore-comers, or when the deities were established on the top of hills or at any site where no water existed.

Even in small Hindu temples, the entrance door is named '*sinvhadwara*' (with or without the lions' heads), then there comes a hall named *sabhamandap*, and finally *'garbhakud'*-the cella. The priests in service of the deity of wealthy temples have differ-ent deities and accordingly they are named as Gheisas, Abhisheki, Pujari, Devari, Jotkar, Haridas and Puranik. In the precinct of the main temple or nearby, there are temples of minor deities connected to the main deity named *'pariwar devata'* (retinue deities) and it is interesting to note that the powers of the main deity for consultation of the oracle are sometimes delegated to one such minor deity or even a demigod-*gramapurusha*. Examples are Ravalnath on behalf of Deuki-Krishna at Marcela and Grama-purusha on behalf of Mangesh of Priol, both in Ponda taluka. It is worth ob-serving here that Shree Mangesh is considered as an incarnation of the god Rudrashiva, or say, Mahadev, and so he should be worshipped only with white flow-ers. However, during oracle-consultation, buds and petals of flowers of red colour of a shrub known as *'pitkuli'* are employed and this custom shows undoubtedly that the flowers and buds, especially of red, were selected only because this was a substitu-tion for the lungs and liver of a sacrificial sheep. Presumably, the use of oracle-plates found by me as of the god Betal at Barazan at Priol villages were utilized for such consultations with the use of petals of the flowers of the red *'Jaswandi'*.

In Sumer, as well as in Akkad (where the deities and many customs from the Sumerians were copied), historians have found some paintings at Mari (a city-state) and scenes demonstrating an intermediary deity, generally a goddess, between the king and the main god. Here in Goa too there is a similar custom among the Gaud Saraswat Brahmins, who besides the clan-god/goddess (*kula-daivat*) have a tutelary deity (*Palavi-daivat*). It may be noted that inspite of having the same deity as the clan-deity, the tutelary deities may be different according to the families. For example, out of the families which have Shree Mangesh as the clan-deity, some have Mhalsa of Priol, while the others, Mahalaxmi of Bandoda as their tutelary deities. The Paddye Bhats may have different clan-deities but the tutelary deity is Annapurna; the karhadi Bhats have Mahalaxmi as their tutelary deity. At the time of marriage the bride goes to the husband's house with the image of the deity of her parents (in the Bhatt caste only).

In Mesopotamia the same deity had a different name, at different times in the same place, and also was in a different form in different places. For example, in the city-state of Lagash the city-gods were Ningirsu and Nimgizidda. The Sumerian deity Inamma was named as Ishtar and was depicted mounted on a lion and in the dress of a warrior, but was considered as the goddess of love.

Similarly, in Goa, the goddess Santer was originally symbolized by an anthill. When it was transformed into an image it took different forms: at Queula (*Kavlem*) the image is in an attitude of (peace-giver) Shantadurga, while at Thanem of Satari taluka it is represented in a fighting posture Mahishasuramardini (killer of Mahishasura-a demon in the form of a buffalo) *(ill. 17).*

The Portuguese records prepared in 1595 mention Shantadurga of Quelossim (*Kelshi*) as Santer and Mangesh and Mulkeshwar of Cortalim (*Kutthal*) village as Manganath and Gopinath respectively.

In a scene depicted on a cylinder-seal of Sumer, the city-god of Nippur, Enlil or Bel is shown seated on a stool. Behind and to the left is seen the head of a bull, his vehicle and on tope of his head there is his symbolic tiara. Inanna or Ishtar has the lion as her vehicle as mentioned above. Enlil was the supreme god (in Konkani *Mahadev*), so his vehicle had passed his successive incarnations. It is to be noted that in front of Manguesh (otherwise *Mahadev*), there is a *Nandi* (sacred bull) while the vehicles of Shantadurga and Mahalaxmi of Bandodem village are lions.

ill. 17: Idol of Nava-Durga (Mahishasura Mardini) at Surla Vil Dicholi taluka.

SUMERIAN CULTURE — SOME OUTSTANDING FEATURES

I shall highlight the main features of Sumerian culture, which is rooted deeply in the society of Goa. But before moving to this topic, I think it is necessary to prove the dating of migration and to find out which circumstances compelled them to migrate from their native place. For this purpose we have to consult the history of Sumer, the southernmost part of Mesopotamia (present Iraq). The quotations given below are based on the data collected from the work of three writers on the Sumerian Civilisation [62], [65] and [66].

This land of Sumer is situated between two rivers-Tigris and Euphrates, with the Persian Gulf as its southern boundary. The evidence of its civilization is found to be from 5th millennium B. C. onwards. The land was originated from silt deposits only, without any type of rock, almost a plain. There was no rainy season. Its agriculture is dependent only on the flow of water from the rivers and their tributaries, which are fed by the water resulting from the melting snow of mountains on the Northern boundary. The network of canals was the backbone of agriculture and even for providing drinking water to the population. The main sources of livelihood were cattle breeding and growth of cereals. There were orchards scattered here and there. The land was fertile and some historians say that the proportion of produce of cereals to the seeds in certain places was in the ratio of 33:1!

The city states

Most of the Sumerian historic cities had been established during the protolitrate centuries at the southernmost areas of Mesopotamia, namely Eridu, Ur, Uruk, Erech, Babilon, Nippur, Suza, Lagash and Larsa. (Please refer to the map of Sumer).

The northern areas of Mesopotamia were occupied by Semites and who by then were called the Akkadians. The Sumerian language and culture remained entrenched in Uruk, Ur and all the old southern centres of Mesopotamia.

There was an increasing struggle to capture power between the Akkadians and Sumerians.

Sargon of Akkad and his successors

"The world's first civilization had been created in Mesopotamia under Sumerian leadership. But, about 1,000 years later, the world's first empire was created by Semitic (Akkadian) leadership so Sargon of Akkad (C 2,600 B.C.) and his empire appear at once as the model for many successors down to recent times".

Elam was geographicaly linked to Sumer, so Elamites from the East and other ehtnic groups namely Gutians from the North entered Sumer and established themselves there.

"The Gutians were now ruling over a considerable part of Mesopotamia, including the Northern Plain. They adopted the cuneiform script and the Akkadian language for their official inscriptions, but these 'mountain dragons' appear to have remained essentially barbarous.

"Among the city-states, one was Lagash, which the second dynasty had again raised to pre-eminence. Outstanding among this line of Ensis (governors) was Gudea (2134-2124 B.C.) whose calm, strong face is so well known to us from the many fine sculptures unearthed from his capital city (Lagash). Lagash and all the southern cities were profiting from the fact that the Gutians had ruined Sargaon's river port of Akkad. Gudea, indeed, seems to have built up a peaceful commercial empire comprising nearly all the lands which the Sargonids had won and held by force. Even the black diorite in which Gudea's features were recorded for posterity had been shipped on the Gulf from Makan (Lakrom).

"Within a decade of Gudea's death Lagash seems to have been losing ground, and the city of Ur was in power under the leadership of its king Ur-Nammu. He continued the trade. Ur-Nammu celebrated the return of the ships of Magan and Meluhha (India) into the hands of Nanna (the moon god of Ur).

"Like Gudea before him Ur-Nammu was active in temple-building and irrigation works. He must have been an excellent administrator, and, so far as is known at present, was the first king to draw up a code of laws. So long as they prospered, he and his line ruled as absolute monarchs with an imperialist outlook. The king was now the supreme judge, the head of every service; Ensis had become no more than governors with delegated powers. Indeed kingship was recognized as divine. Hymns were addressed to the king, shrines dedicated to him, sacrifices made to him, and from the reign of Ur-Nammu's son Shulgi (2093-2046 B.C.) his name was written with the divine determinative. (Yet even now these Sumerian kings were far less exalted in the hierarchy of gods than the Pharaohs in Egypt)".

Amorites - the desert enemies

"Amorites had been drifting into Mesopotamia since the day of Sargon. These nomad Semites can in fact be seen as successors to the Akkadians but they appear to have been less ready to settle and become good citizens. Very soon after the accession of Ibbin-Sin in about 2027 B.C., they began to harrass the Akkadians and Sumerian by force."

"Ibbin-Sin, however, continued to rule over Ur and the south for a number of years, and when at last, in about 2003 B.C., he and his proud and venerable city fell, it was not at the hands of Isin but of Elam."

"Ur could be restored, Nanna returned to his temple (no one knows what happened to Ibbin-Sin), but Sumer had lost its greatness. Civilization had been kindled there, sparks had leapt to Egypt and to India. Now, so far as Mesopotamia was concerned, its heat and light, its main centres of creative energy and their resulting wordly powers, were to shift northwards, leaving the south as something of a burnt-out land". [66] pp. 95-103.

The Great Exodus

History says that about 2,000 B.C. "the civilization of Sumer had been kindled there, sparks had leapt to Egypt and India". The Book of Genesis informs us that Abraham with his Semitic people began his wandering from Ur to the land of Canaan and step by step to Egypt. But what about the spark in India? It is surprising that while the Indologists speak of the contact between peoples from Sumer and India, in the Rigvedic Age, identifying Meluhha to the Indus Valley area, no single reference is made to this great episode. It is worth noting that some historians mention that at that time of Ibbin-Sin, the city of Ur had a population of 100,000. This is only the account of one city, and we have to add the population of other cities lying on the banks of the Euphrates river. According to some historians the famine was created artificially by the Amorites by diverting the course of that river, and that, when the Amorites arrived at Ur, they restored the original course. The water overflowed and produced inundation, as the canals were silted since the annual desilting was not done.

Now the point is: how was it that the people possessed the knowledge of the route to India? It is known that c. 2100 B.C. Ur-Nammu celebrated the return of the ships of Magun and Meluhha (India), Gudea, as the records prove, carried on trade in gold, cedar and copper with countries as distant as Egypt and India [59] p. 39. And before Gudea, "Sargon I of Akkad may even have made forays into Egypt, Ethiopia and India. (ibid) p. 38. And we hear of an official interpreter of the Meluhha (India) language in his time."

These facts prove undoubtedly that the exodus of the people (non-Semitic) of Sumer to India was by the sea-route. Now the next point: what is the proof that they came to Goa?

Gudea, according to Dr. Waddell, mentions in his inscriptions the names of the places from where he collected the material for construction of the temples: "It is admitted by Assyriologists that Gudia (2143-2134 B.C.) personally visited and ransacked for material to build and adorn his temples... from the mountains of Megan (Sinai) and Gubi and Dilman, via the Persian Gulf and Indian Ocean he brought precious wood and diorite blocks for his statuettes and friezes by ships to the port of Lagash and states that for these purposes he travelled from the lower lands to the upper lands." He states: "My patron saint-my beloved King Ninirrud (Nimirud), the son of Lord Sakh opened the way for me from the upper sea, (Mediterranean) to the Lower Sea (Persian Gulf and Indian Ocean)". [63]

Historians have identified all the places indicated in the inscription of Gudea, except Gubi, saying that this place should be anywhere on the western coast of India.

The Greek geographer Ptolemy mentions the name of Goa as Kouba, as said in an earlier chapter. So, taking into consideration the finds, it is clear that undoubtedly, Gudea's Gubi is Goa. The emigrants from Sumer knew about the location, environment and facility for settlement in Goa through tradition. Moreover the existence of the Bhargavas in that area, who were known to them as well as the knowledge of the sea-route, led those people in this direction.

I have given here a summary of the history of Sumer of about three thousand years, because I wish to point out that the intention of the emigrants was not invasion nor temporary residence but permanent residence. They brought with them their ideas, customs, etc. which took root in Goa and in South India.

The races of Sumerian colonists

The people of Sumer, at the time of migration consisted of five different races. In respect of the most ancient settlements in Sumer there are divergent opinions. My account is based on the works of three writers mentioned before. [62, 65 and 66].

It is said by some historians that these Sumerian people had migrated from the Indus Valley area. The western component of the ethnic spectrum was predominantly Semitic and its first manifestation started probably about 2900 B.C. It is less easy to date the first impact of the eastern component, but Elam was geographically linked so closely to Sumer that reciprocal influences were an almost constant factor from the beginning. Keeping aside the Hurrians, the last factor of component of ethnics spectrum was of Gutians, who from the North were trying to enter Sumer and came and established themselves there soon after the death of Naram-sin, son of Sargon I of Akkad. The Sumerians called themselves 'black-headed', perhaps in opposition to the Gutians who were white headed. But it is possible also that the word 'black headed' might have been employed in respect of their black hair while the Gutians had hair somewhat of a golden colour. The feature of the Gutians was fair. Here I am reminded of a bust of a priest of the Indus Valley who had covered his body also with a shawl, the right hand being bare. The Gutians were surely of Aryan stock, while the Elamites were of Irano-Aryan one.

The mystery of the Elamites

The people of all those races except the Semitic one migrated to India. But what is the proof that Elamites also were part of that exodus? We get an answer from an inscription of Gudea. He describes how he built the temples with precious metals: "He caused the craftsmen in precious metal do well therein...; he brought the smiths, the priests of Nin-tu-Kalam-ma, who, before her, are more than professional craftsmen, they are priests, and their work requires the presence of the goddess, their patroness. This is perhaps an exceptional cause, and certainly in later times smiths do not rank as priests but in none of the crafts was the God very far away. Just as medicine was half magic, so in the instruction for performing what we should call a straight forward technical operation, we find some ritual act interpolated, some verbal charm has to be repeated to ensure the success of an experience ... The crafts were largely hereditary,and the knowledge of them was confined to the initiation... Thus Gudea for his temple brought in skilled smiths; labour from Elam and Susa as Saloman..." [66]

So those Elamite smiths who had obviously come with their families and with an idol of their goddess In-tu-Kalm-ma might have settled there. In-tu-Kalam-ma means in English Lady-Mother-Kalamma and in the Goan language *Shree-Maya-Kalamma*, and as such is established at Cansarpale of Bicholim, (*Divchal*) taluka. Sixty years ago the deity was named as *Kalamba* and now it is known as *Shree Kalika-Devi*. It is the deity of copper and gold-smiths, who call themselves Deivadnya Brahmins.

Besides these families of Elamite smiths, some other families of other classes of Elamites with professions like those of the Semites might have accompanied them.

So far, there is no direct evidence available from Indologists about the voyage of the Sumerians to India except that given in the previous pages stating that at the time of Sargon I, King of Akkad and Sumer there was commercial contact between his domain and the North-West coastal area of India and that Gudea collected some material for construction of temples from Meluhha (India). However, we may conceive a mental picture of their march of migration which was by the sea route taking into consideration the following probabilities:

It is likely that their ships sailing along the coastal line of the area covered by the Indus civilization might have reached at different points of the western coast of India. Some berthed in Gujarat, while others might have advanced more and more towards the South, halting for food in exchange for fabric etc. at different Southern coastal areas. Some ships, probably caught in a hurricane or some other kind of catastrophe, might have sought safe embarking sites, such as the creeks of Chiplon (Maharastra) where they were given shelter by some Bhargava Brahmins, inhabitants of that area. Those rescued were probably the Elamites who are named Chitpavan Brahmins. In the same way other ships moved towards the South and disembarked on the Goan coast. Some families took shelter on the shores of Salcete taluka, others entered the bay of Mormugao. Once these ships were inside the bay, it was safe to disperse to the banks of the Zuari and Mandovi rivers. The Bhargavas and Angirasas had already occupied, may be sporadically, the lands of Tiswadi (in Portuguese Ilhas), Bardez and Salcete talukas, hence the newcomers had to be under the hegemony of those Aryan people. The seashore area did not have sweet water, cereals and vegetables throughout the year. Hence some families, unencumbered by the settlement of the Aryans, travelled with their allies to the shore of Marcaim (*Madkai*), then part of Piriela (now *Priol*) village of Ponda taluka. The tale of Bali is full of this Migration [68].

The tale of Bali

This tale is recited during the marriage ceremony days in the families of the Gauda caste in Ponda taluka. Thus it has continued for over 4000 years like the Vedic hymns.

According to the tale, there was a state named "Mangal" with fertile lands, which gave three crops annually. Once a great battle took place among the inhabitants of the place. Three hundred and fifty men who went there to find out the cause were butchered. Their bodies fell in the waters of the Priol-Ganga (river of Priol) and drifted towards seawater. Their wives tried in vain to empty the seawater with their pots. A sparrow communicated this incident to the brother-in-law of one of them (husband of her sister) named Tilasur who rescued the bodies. But the wives could not identify the bodies of their husbands because they were cut into halves. Moved by their despair, Tilasur invoked help from Chandravati, wife of Indra, who directed the wives to join the halves of their husbands. But half of one body was missing. A crow brought mud with which the body was restored. Chandravati sprinkled 'Sanjivani' (the juice of a plant which brings the dead to life) and thus the bodies were animated. This person restored with mud was named Bali. He dug fields and began their cultivation. Thereafter he got married.

Demystifying the tale of Bali

As Pargiter says, this tale probably carried some truth. What is this truth?

In Konkani 'Gal' means a land originated from silt-deposit and so is very fertile. The word 'mand' means a plain and vast land. So, 'Mandgal' means a vast plain of fertile land which characterizes completely the Sumerian land. Since conflict was raging in that place, three hundred and fifty families came by the sea-route to the shores of Priol village. Bali is the changed form of the god Bel, now worshipped as Betal in Priol as well as in the adjacent village of Marcaim (*Madkai*). The number 350 of the families is significant. These comprised what are now the Paddye Bhats of the Brahmin caste and Fotte and others of the Vani caste who are Gaonkars of different villages of Ponda taluka as well as a family with the surname 'Maddo' considered as the first settler of the village *Madkai* and so it had certain privileges in the village rituals. It had the right to receive one 'pad' (about one litre) of rice from each family settled in *Madkai*, per week.

The 'God of Storms' in toponymy

Enlil or Bel, the god of storms and sovereign of the earth and of the spirits was the city-god of Nippur, the religious centre of Sumer, and so had supreme powers, like Anu, the god of the sky. And so, in the assembly of gods, 'Anu might preside with Enlil at his side'.

Now, it is understood why the idol of Bel was established in Priol- it was a sign of the first settlement of the people from Sumer. The god Bel was being worshipped also under different names like Bel-talal, Bel-Marduk, Bel-Dakan etc. Mardol is a hamlet of Priol village and Dhakan is one of Madkai village. I think those names were given after Bel-Marduk and Bel-Dakan respectively. The next settlement was occupied by one part of the people from Urek who gave that name to the village known as Verem, establishing the idols of the god Anu and the goddess Inanna. It is noticeable that in copperplates this village is named 'Veraka'. The opposite bank of the river was occupied by the people originally from Lagash (otherwise Sirlapur) and that village is named Surla at present. According to the tradition among Gaonkar-Ghadis, there existed a family of paddye Bhats, long since extinct, and it is said that the widow of that family entrusted them to take the administration of the village in their hands.

Sumerian settlement in Goa

Thus, many areas of Ponda taluka were occupied by the people from Sumer. But before these settlements or may be simultaneously, some people from Sumer settled in Bardez taluka-backing this event are the village names like Beti-Verem and Serula and Varka village of Salcete taluka. It is impossible to identify the deities of Sumerian origin as all of them had taken Purana deity forms and moreover the very ancient signs of civilization were destroyed during the terror of Christianity.

Sumerians Settlement in South India

All the people who migrated from Sumer could not have sheltered in Goa, so that people travelled to the south of Goa by the sea-route. It appears that the families of the highest class, Paddyas, settled in Goa and persistently maintained their customs whereas the families of other classes, mainly artisans and craftsmen-and perhaps some families of the highest caste-travelled to the south where they might have amalgamated their customs with those of the original settlers of these areas.

Sumerian influence on Goan society

Impact on religion

The religion of Sumer was closely bound to its culture as a whole. Most of our knowledge of economic activity comes from the archives of temples, which, under royal or priestly patronage, frequently monopolized industrial and commercial life. Hence, while talking of religion, other subjects will be naturally referred to.

In the excavation of Eridu city located at the bank of the Euphrates river a terracotta male figurine (1 ft. 5 1/2 in.) of the early Uruk period c. 3,700 B.C. has been found (Hirmer Fotoarchives) - [10] P. 112. The city-god of Eridu was Enke (the god of water and wisdom), but besides the city-god, temples of other deities also existed. This figurine is surely of the God Bel. He is in the nude, holding in both hands a narrow long plate, probably a sword in use at that time. His tiara does not show horns, and this may be due to their loss with time or it is also possible that the tiara with horns might have been introduced in later times. The comparison of the figurine with the present idol of Betal in Goa, provides evidence about migration of the Sumerian in Goa. In Dicholi taluka there is a village named Virdi, on the bank of the river Volvota, a tributary of the Mandovi river. Among other deities, there is an idol of Betal in that village, which is remarkable in this context.

All these changes at Uruk as well as at other sites are well documented. A Sumerian myth says that 'Oanes', being half-fish and half-human, emerged from the sea to teach men in writing, all the arts and sciences and then disappeared under the waters [8] p. 13. Oanes is probably a corrupted form of 'Ushands', the name of an "Indo-Aryan Sadhu", and this name appears in the ninth chapter (Mandala) of the Rigveda as a composer of some hymns. Enki, city-God of Eridu, the god of wisdom, surely personified that sage who came with his people by the sea-route and settled first at Eridu and, later, one section of these people passed to Uruk. They probably were of a tanned complexion, like the Bharadwaja clan.

Sumerian temple and land administration

It was during the Uruk period that the basic expression of Sumerian society was formulated. This is most evident in three main developments seen at Uruk:

(1) the construction of monumental temples,

(2) the masterful production of cylinder seals and

(3) the evolution of cuneiform writing.

Many temples were built in Uruk itself, and they are reminiscent of those of the Ubaid period at Eridu. The similarity of buttressed façades and a long central room surrounded by small rooms testifies to the persistence of both architectural traditions and belief systems. The city of Uruk, like all Sumerian cities, was dedicated to a specific deity. Uruk was dedicated to the two great Sumerian Gods Anu (the Sky God) and E-Anna (Ishtar in Babylonian texts), the Goddess of love.

"There seems no doubt that throughout Mesopotamia (Sumer, Babylon and Akkad together) the image of the god that was kept in the cell (a womb type sanctuary in Konkani meaning 'garbhakud') of the temple was not only worshipped closely but also from afar. He was served by the priests as a living being. There was a divine wardrobe, with clothes changed at appointed times and for festivals. Twice two-course meals were laid before the image, one in the morning and one at night; there were also lighter meals or divine snacks. This was the regime at Uruk in silent (non-festival) times, and it was probably traditional. Before eating, the god's hands were washed. While the god was taking breakfast or dining, curtains were drawn round him probably to screen the mystery from human gaze". (Rituals comparable to those observed during puja of a Hindu deity).

How near ordinary citizens were allowed to approach the image is not known-and this may have varied with time and place. It can be assumed that the cell was forbidden to them. In some temples aligned doorways may have allowed a distant glimpse of the figure on its pedestal. Generally, however, it seems that the citizens had a clear sight of the images only when they were carried through the streets on the occasion of their festivals. They seem to have been fastened to beams that rested on the shoulders of bearers (the 'lalkhi' type in use for the festival at Shree Mangesh at Priol). (Note: but in paintings at Mari, Inanna is carried in a 'machil' by the bearers in the procession. The 'machil' is replaced in Goa by 'palkhi' type vehicles). This procedure of carrying holy figures is still, of course, a familiar practice in many parts of the world, not the least in Catholic lands where saints and madonnas are taken for such outings, borne shoulder high through great crowds of devotees. (The 'lalkhi' appears to be an imitation of the Catholic practice). In huge temples, besides the image of the god in the cella, his/her prototype also was installed in a shrine on the top of a 'ziggurat', which was visited daily by citizens climbing up and descending down through two passages on the two sides. The third passage, the axial, was reserved for the king, his family and relatives or say to the nobility, as well as to the priests and priestess. The rooms for the dwelling of the high-priestess were always closest to this shrine of God, she being his human wife.

There was another way in which ordinary citizens could approach the divine images-and indeed remain in their presence. This was through their own images. In early dynastic times, worshippers could arrange, by what system of observances and payments we do not know, to have sculptured stone figures of themselves in an attitude of devout prayer placed in the temple. A sculptured stone form of the person who bore the expense for the construction of a temple was always placed in front of the cella, in standing posture with a lamb in both hands symbolizing the sacrifice offered to the deity. (In the temple of Shree Mangesh of Priol, the image of Gram-purash, who symbolizes the builder of the temple, is placed in front of the Garbhakud in a seated posture, holding a coconut in both hands. This image is placed on the straight line between the Linga of Shree Mangesh and his vehicle Nandi. Otherwise, according to Puranic rules this attitude of seating is prohibited. It is said that in the original temple at Kutthal (Cortalim), the position was the same and as such this custom was maintained). The idea of offering sacrifice can be linked to the more dignified form of the Christian worshipper placing a candle before the altar of his deity. (Note: Hindus offer oil for 'Nandadippa' before the image of God).

It seems that, in fact, some part of the god's food was transferred to the King's table and that the eating of this blessed food was symbolically recognizing royal prerogative. Considering the distance separating the palace from the temple cells it is a bit difficult to understand how this was done-but there seems no doubt that it was.

This feeding of the king with the 'divine jelly', as it were, is interesting as it is another link between divinity and the royal executant and servant. The setting of the meal on the god's table was, however, at the centre of a vast system of temple sacrificial offerings of substantial economic significance. A large number of beasts, most of them sheep, were brought daily to the temples to be offered across the sacrificial tables.

Great numbers of loaves made from both wheat and barley flour were supplied, the miller being charged to utter a certain prayer while he ground the flour and the cook to utter another prayer when he kneaded the dough and when he took the loaves from the oven. Sweet concoctions were sometimes made from cream, honey and dates (sometimes specified as Dilmun dates) and there were innumerable libations of milk (reserved for the morning meal), prime beer and wine. These liquids were first presented in vessels -those for wine and beer usually of gold, and those for milk in alabaster. Large quantities of oil were also offered. The frescoes at Mari (where things may have been ordered differently) show the simultaneous presentation of a triple libation and a small burnt offering (like the *panchyamratra puja* for Hindu deities).

There were also a few prohibitions. Certain birds and animals were never to be offered to certain gods and goddesses. In connection with rituals for the repair of a temple, omens announced that the entry of a dog into a temple means misfortune for the people, whereas the entry of a rare beast of the desert into the city would mean its utter destruction.

The principles by which all this food and drink were transferred to the priests, craftsmen and others by the vast temple household are only partially known. With the king receiving at least part of the actual meal set before the chief god, it seems likely that the distribution was carried out on hierarchical lines, with humbler groups supplied from the humbler shrines within the precincts. Sometimes precise allocations were made for services rendered.

As regards the serving of the meals to the images, the offices of the priests by day and by night involved a round of exactly prescribed rites, including sacrifices accompanied by appropriate prayers and recitations. (According to Sir Wooley, the priest in a nude position, in the cella, besides libation, prepared a small fire with aromatic wood (like the *Aryan hom*). There was a regular festival for the new moon and on the last days of the month. Some idea of these priestly duties is conveyed by one of the Seleucid texts from Uruk concerning the rituals prescribed for the sixteenth and seventeenth days of one month.

These details serve to convey some idea of the ceaseless, ordered activity of the priesthoods in all their main grades and the sanga (in Sumerian terms), down to the humblest hierodule. The names of different classes of priests are known in both Sumerian and Akkadian, but their functions remain uncertain. It is thought that the Sumerian ishib priest may have been in charge of libations and lustrations, while the gala may have been a poet and singer. The personnel undoubtedly included many singers and instrumentalists. The service of Inanna demanded an exceptionally large number of eunuchs and hierodules.

The diurnal round of the temples were inturned and self-sufficient; the meals were in no sense mystical or concerned with communion. Prayers and sacrifices were not directly on behalf of the people. Rather these services represented the temple carrying out on behalf of society its obligation to work for the gods, to supply them with their needs so that they themselves were freed from toil. It may have some meaning to say that this obligation brought about a kind of 'social contract' between gods and men; the temples which by one means or another were supported by the entire community, saw to it that the contract was maintained.

There were, however, occasions when the temples opened their gates and looked outward to the people. As well as the monthly festival on the fifteenth and sixteenth days, there were a number of seasonal festivals, such apparently as the 'Eating of Barley' and the 'Eating of Gazelles'. No doubt the populace took part in these festivals. At the height of the summer drought came the popular rites of lamentation for Dumuzi. But really, the great occasion that brought the temples, their divine images, the king and the people all together in feeling and in action, was the celebration of the New Year. This was essentially a celebration of revival, of the promise of fertility in the renewed cycles of the seasons. In some places, including Ur, it was celebrated as the death of late summer. But the principal celebration, and the one known to us from a well-preserved Neo-Babylonian text, took place at the beginning of spring and at the month of Nison, coinciding with the spring equinox (Makara-Sankrant of the Hindu calendar).

To draw a parallel ritual during the Hindu festival in Goa, like the festival of 'Eating the Barley' in Sumer, we prepare sweets made out of new rice on the day of *Panchami* or say on the day before Ganesh Chaturthi and this festival is named '*Navem*' (New). This is a domestic festival. Besides this, the village commune celebrates on a fixed day which varies from village to village, a social festival named 'Festival of Ear (of paddy)'. Like 'Eating of Gazelles' in Sumer, we have a similar form on the last day of '*Dhalo*' designated as '*Savaj-Marap*' (hunting of game). Where there is no festival of '*Dhalo*' like in Satari, a day is fixed for '*Devachi bhoundi*' (hunting in the name of god) It is to be noted that hunting as a ceremony did not exist in the primitive tribes who settled before the people from Sumer.*(ill. 18a)*.

Now, a point may be raised at this stage: if idolatry appeared in Goa and South India from direct contact with the people from Sumer, did it appear in North India too? At the time of Cyrus and Darius of Persia, around the 5th century B.C., Indians were admitted in their army which invaded Babylon and even went westward. These sol-

ill. 18a : Devachi bhoundi (hunting excursion) in the name of God in Sattary. Copied from India Portuguesa by Antonio Lopes Mendes, 1870

diers came with the idea of idolatry in the temples. Before that time, simple idolatry did exist but without public temples. This was the state of affairs even at the beginning of the Indus Valley Civilization as attested to by archaeology. At the time of the Kushanas in North India (c.138 A.D.) we notice the idol of goddess Nana mounted on a lion on the coins of that period. The historians of Alexander the Great (c. 327 B.C.) mention that an idol of Heracles (probably of Shree Krishna) was worshipped in some areas conquered by him.

Devdasi system at the service of God

Our main point is not of idolatry but of its worship in the temple with certain rituals and rites which are prevalent even today. Even the idols are worshipped from ancient times in the temples. The institution of the Devdasi system is a characteristic feature differentiating the South Indian system from the Northern. This system is surely of Sumerian practice and was introduced in Goa and Southern India and later spread to all strata of Hindu society.

This Devdasi-system in Sumer began way back at least 3,500 B.C. A daughter of each family was offered to the deity, and the daughter of the ruler (Patesti) was their head-high-priestess named Nin-An. The word 'Nin' also means noble or of the highest class and the other girls were 'Salme'. Nin-An was the human wife of the god, a high priestess and it was expected by traditional customs that she be celibate. The Salme might indulge in business, commerce etc. and might marry but the husband should not have conjugal contact with her. So she had to offer the husband, her substitute, that is, one of her female-slaves. She could have children but the father's name should never be known. They could have private property which passed to her heirs after her death. Their work in the temple was to maintain the temple clean, wash the vessels in use in the temples and dance and sing. The distribution of services was done by the high-priestess.

In Goa, the dancing-woman (*Kalavant*) is designated 'Nhene'. There are two castes amongst them. Bhavina of the lower caste is in charge of cleaning the temple and its precinct as well as the cleaning of vessels and oil-lamps in daily use in the main temple and others in the precincts. Their brother '*Devli*' is in charge of other lamps. The other group is of higher caste the 'Kalavants'. They are in charge of dancing and singing and their brothers '*Ganans*' called these days as '*Mridangui*'-one who plays the '*Mridang*', a percussion instrument and had the duty of accompanying the '*Kalavants*' in their professional work.

These services, like those of the priests were and are hereditary, and so, the old system of gifts of land in compensation for services called '*Namashi*' (land gifted by joining the hands, meaning never to be reverted) continues to be possessed by such families. They also get the shares, in the prescribed form in kind and cash, of the offerings from the devotees, like in Sumer.

In the cella (*garbhakud*) of the temples of Bhats and Saraswat Brahmins, only worshippers (*pujaris*) and the descendants of the Mahajans-founders of the temples and members of their caste-are admitted just like the Sumerian custom where only the worshipper, the ruler and his family and his relatives could enter the cella.

Temple and land administration in Sumer

"All these temples were built at enormous expenditure of organized, communal labour. They served not only as centres of worship but also as storerooms for surplus agricultural produce and administrative centres for redistribution of temple goods. Hundreds of temple labourers and craftsmen (who formed a distinct class within the tightly stratified society) were supported by agricultural surplus. While this surplus must have come from agricultural communities outside the urban centre, there is little evidence to suggest that during Uruk times political (temple) authority and centralization extended beyond the village immediately adjacent to the cities.

"These specific factors converged in the rise of the temple-palace administrative complex. First was the irrigation system itself. In order to maximize agricultural production, water resources had to be managed. Successfully doing so assured a surplus; it also demanded a great deal of labour. Canals had to be dug far upstream to deliver water to the distant fields, and after that, continuous maintenance was necessary to prevent the silting-up of the canals, which were often over 25 miles long. A second factor was the need for a voice whose authority surpassed all of the special-interest group in the society.

"The temple-palace played a crucial role in mediating the relationship and disputes between farmers, herdsmen, fishermen, craft-specialists, and the State. A third factor in the comparatively rapid growth of the Great Organization might have been the lack of natural resources in the alluvium. Meeting the every increasing demand for resources was the responsibility of temple agents who acted not only as private merchants but as emissaries representing the city-state.

"It seems clear that the hereditary possession of patriarchal families were increasingly purchased by the nobility... Analysis of the deeds of sale indicates that the families were unable to compete with the increasingly larger estates of the nobility. When large tracts of land were sold, the approval of the entire family acting as witnesses (this preventing their later protestation) and the approval of the entire assembly were required. Diakonoff's views are of early bureaucratic dealings of the assembly and extended families over land as being the primary cell for the creating of the State." 172-175. [66]

Assembly of citizens

"The doubts about the distribution of ownership and power within the state are necessarily very much involved with authority of a more political kind-though by now it must have become obvious that the political function cannot be separated from the religious function. This question of authority concerns the existence of an assembly of the people on the one hand and the supreme ruler of the state on the other. It will perhaps be easier to begin with the first-if only because so sadly little is really known about the subject.

"The first direct documentary evidence for the existence of a popular assembly functioning in Mesopotamia dates from Old Babylonian times (from 2,000 B.C. onwards). There was a council of elders led by the town or precinct Mayor. Large cities appear to have been divided into precincts, each administered from its own gate, there was also an assembly, called in Akkadian the Puhrum, which appears to have consisted of a gathering of all free male citizens who cared to attend. It is unlikely, although not totally impossible, that women could take part. At this time the function of both bodies seem to have been entirely judicial, the mayor and elders judging minor cases, while the more important were referred to the Puhrum.

"This assembly was empowered to deal with civic pleas such as the ownership of houses and gardens and paternity cases, and also with criminal matters including seditions, utterances and murder. While the king had supreme judicial power, he sometimes referred cases to the assembly. On one occasion, for example, a man who had been arrested for seditious by a royal official was sent before the Puhrum for the charge to be proved before he was imprisoned". [66] pp. 176-77.

Here I have quoted a summary of the temple and the land administration, to give a broad idea of the evolution of the institution in Sumer upto 2,000 B.C. when the people migrated. We shall compare this with the corresponding system in Goa - at least the last paragraph in respect of laws of sale of land.

Sumerian Social and Political Hierarchy

Land tenure system

In respect of land-ownership in the city-state of Sumer, historians have different opinions, according to their political leanings. The Russian writers put up their theory that in Sumer the private land system was very well developed while the American are of a different opinion. In fact, in the history of Sumer, even before the sovereign of Sargon of Sumer, in the city of Lharsa, for example, there was anarchy and the kings as well as nobility had encroached extensively upon the lands of the temple.

Utukagina, the ruler of Lharsa before Sargon, promulgated drastic legislation confiscating all the privately occupied land, even of his own palace-use and incorporated it in the temple-estate. So the writers chose the period and place according to their political views and wrote their version of history. I prefer the balanced view of the historian and writer of 'The First Great Civilization', who provides an account of the situation around 2000 B.C. [66] The reader will come across some systems and words existing in Goa.

"Otto Edzard judged that the contrast in the documentary evidence between the Sumerian south and the Akkadian north is not likely to be a chance one. He would not say that private land-holding was prohibited (or, presumably, that merchants and artisans did not trade and work on their own account), but to him the evidence suggests that in the traditional Sumerian city-state the temple was the great proprietor of the arable soil. In short, it would appear that one of the chief differences between Sumerians and Semites in the land of the Two Rivers, is the frequency of private property".

"It must have been a fundamental belief of the society that each of the dozen or so city-states into which the Sumer was divided belonged to the presiding deity to whom it had been allotted when the world was made".

"The temple was an enclosed, self-supporting unit in which the maintenance of the temple cult with its daily routine of sacrifices and its seasonal festivals was at the centre of a great economic organization involving agriculture and stock-keeping, fisheries, manufacture and commerce.

"Farming and the storage of its produce was of course the basic activity of temple community, providing rations, wages and special payment for all those employed. It also provided great numbers of sacrificial animals-which were in fact, it seems, largely eaten by the personnel of the sanctuary and perhaps by ensi and his immediate circle".

"The temple land, which was inalienable, was of three kinds. There was the *nigenna-land*, which was used directly for the support of the sanctuary; there was the *rurra-land*, some of which was assigned to farmers working the nigenna-land and some to craftsmen and administrators as payment for their work and services. This land was not heritable and could be taken from the cultivators if the administration so decided. The third category of land was the *urula-land*, which was allotted to various individuals, much of it to temple personnel, as a boost to their income".

"In addition to grain, vegetable were cultivated. Cattle were kept, perhaps mainly for sacrifice (including milk offerings) and traction, and very large herds of sheep that served for food but, more importantly, provided for the temple weavers. There were, of course, bakeries and breweries to supply the whole community".

The payment of rent (payable by the cultivator) was in kind only and rates were according to the 'Law of Nisab and Honey' which existed in written form. The conditions were as follows: in cereal-cultivation if the seed was furnished by land-owners, the share of the owner was half of the gross, otherwise, one-third of it. If any cultivator (tenant) maintained the land uncultivated, the tenant was obliged to pay in proportion to the produce obtained in the adjacent land. In case of fruit-bearing trees, if plantlets were furnished by the land-owners, he had the right to get two-thirds of the gross produce, otherwise one third of it. If the dues were not paid within the prescribed time, the tenant had to work as a slave of the land-owner for the duration prescribed in that law, and if this was repeated the land-owner could withdraw such piece of land and pass it to another cultivator. All the tenants of a plot of land were obliged to collectively repair the dykes and canals without any wages.

The Goan word 'Bhageli' (shareholder of crop) is derived from that type of tenure, and the distribution of shares of crop varied according to the nature of law, location, etc.

Sumerian Units of Weights and Measures

Linear Measures

Finger				=	0.0165 metres
Mason's hand	=	10	fingers	=	0.165 metres
Open hand	=	15	fingers	=	0.2465 metres
Foot	=	20	fingers	=	0.330 metres
Cubit	=	30	fingers	=	0.495 metres
Reed	=	6	cubits	=	2.97 metres
Pole	=	12	cubits	=	5.94 metres
Half-cord	=	60	cubits	=	29.70 metres
Surveyor's cord	=	120	cubits	=	59.4000 metres
League	=	130	cords	=	10692.00 metres

The unit of area in the third millennium B.C. was the sar or 'reed', a square with a side of one 'pole'. Its subdivisions are the 'sixtieth' and the 'barley corn' which is a third of a sixtieth. Its multiples were the 'gan' or "field of 100 'reeds' ", and the bur of 18 gan. On this data the corresponding modern measures are:

Barley corn	=	0.196 acres	(0.196 sq.m)
Sixtieth	=	x 0.588 acres	(0.588 sq.m)
'Sar' or 'Reed'	=	35.2836 acres	(35.2836 sq.m)
'Gan' or 'Acre'	=	3528.36 acres	(3528.36 sq.m)
'Bur'	=	6.351048 hectares	(6,35,10.48 sq.m)

The basic unit in measures of capacity was the ga (about 8.42 decilitres).

The author gives a detailed account of weights and measures but does not mention some measures in the first decimal digit [62] (pp. 224-226.)

Sumerian influence on Goan village administration

Soon after the conquest of Goa, the Portuguese saw that the village and taluka administration was completely different from the one in vogue in Portugal. The government therefore ordered a compilation of the local laws for preserving the system, and as such, the compilation was published in 1526 with Charter amendments concerning the sovereignty of the Portuguese. This is known as the "Foral de Afonso Mexia" (Charter of 1526 about the use and custom of Gaonkar and Peasants in Goa). [68].

Section 18 reads: If any Gaonkar or other person wants to sell any inheritance in any of the said villages, he will not be able to do so without the permission of all the Gaonkars of that village (Note: obviously in an assembly). And thus in the same way nobody will be able to buy without the said permission. If any sale or purchase is made without the said permission, it will belong to nobody and each time when the Gaonkars might want all will be unmade for the good of the rent which is bound to be paid to us (Government) for which purpose they shall have to be satisfied and knowing about these rents, they shall hold their letter with the declaration of the rent they must pay.

Section 19 reads: When any sale deed is to be made of any inheritance it will not be enough if it is signed by the very seller but it should also be signed by all the heirs even though some among the heirs may be minors. A declaration should be made if any person signed on their behalf. And if any one fails to sign for all time, the sale will be nullified and the amount returned to the purchaser. And if any improvements were made, the buyer will forfeit them.

These two sections are similar to those of the Sumerian law. Leaving aside the 19th section which is identical for the undivided properties of the Hindu family, according to the Hindu Law, the 18th section of the Charter is very interesting. There was no such law in the whole of India, except Goa. The history of South India talks of co-operative institutions and village assemblies, their committees and sub-committees which reflect the influence of the Sumerian mind, but there was no such rule (18th section of the said Charter) existing in Goa. That law by itself is sufficient to prove the existence of the Sumerian mind in Goa, and this law could not have existed without the settlement of the people of Sumer. It is quite surprising that the custom mentioned in the 18th section of the Charter continued over a period of 3,500 years without interruption! The village assembly, according to the records of the 16th century A.D. (as per the documents in the Directorate of Archives in Goa and Portugal dated from 1511 A.D.) was formed of elders of the Gaonkars of the village and the approval or decisions had to be unanimous. A single 'naka', meaning 'no', of an elder Gaonkar was sufficient to sabotage the decision of the assembly for sale and for purchase. It is not known whether this custom was existing in Sumer. Otherwise, in Gram panchayats in India a majority of votes is enough to come to a decision. During this period many non-Goan ruling dynasties governed the land of Goa; however, the basic structure of the village and taluka administration continued unchanged.

I have described here the cultural background of Sumer and there is no way of summarizing it. I think it provides a vivid reflection of Goan society in all facets of life. Various ruling dynasties and powers with different concepts like the Muslim and the Portuguese dominated the region but the fundamental concept of the Sumerian type, with very slight inevitable change due to different environments continued for thousands of years upto 1964 A.D. Surprisingly, some words in land-tenure continue to be used to this day.

Now let me focus on some designations. In Ponda taluka as I have mentioned earlier, where families of Paddye Bhatts are concentrated, there is a word '*Kar*', originally meaning the land gifted without obligation of payment of rent by the tenants of areca-nut gardens and rice-fields. This was subject to obligation of services of the owner's land without payment of wages. This system in Sumer was applied to the tenants of the lands of the temple-'nigenna-land'. This system was applied to private lands also. Probably around five centuries ago-the dating cannot be fixed due to lack of documentary evidence-free-holding lands were subjected to a fixed and perennial annual rent in cash. In some areca-nut gardens, the tenants pay a fixed rent, also under the same designation, for possessing banana trees and graft-mango trees. In case of rice-fields, the same type of rent is paid by the tenant as for banana trees, whatever may be the number of such trees. There is a popular saying in Goa that *"Kundaichem Shet karak mharag"* (rent payable for the paddy-field of Kundai village is heavy due to rent payable as *Kar*).

The word *kar* cannot be considered as a corruption of the Marathi word 'kar' (meaning tax), because it does not exist in the Satari taluka which was first occupied by the people from Maratha country. Secondly, because '*kar*' meaning tax is variable according to many reasons given by the government, but *kar* is not variable.

Now, regarding the niginna-land. If I remember well, I had noticed in the Portuguese records of the lands of Hindu temples, which were confiscated by the government of Salcete taluka, a name of a paddy-field recorded as '*Nagonen-Sheta*'. I was surprised. This name might have been changed to *Gimonem*. In Chinchinim (*Chinchonem*) village of Salsete taluka as well as in Pilgaon village of Bicholim taluka there are places named *Gimonem*. This word apparently seems to have been derived from the word '*gim*', derived in its turn from the Sanskrit work 'Grishhma', meaning 'very hot season'. But there is no paddy-field of the vaingon type which produces paddy in that season. So, it appears that the word 'Gimonem' is a corrupted form of niginna.

Now in respect of agricultural lands and measures, in Goa, a field of paddy is named *sarem*; and "*sar*" or '*sair*' in the Sumerian language means a square with a side of one 'Pole' and this measured 12 cubits (*haats* in Konkani). This measurement is recorded in the said Portuguese Charter dated 1526, a measurement of a paddy-field. Another Sumerian measurement is a 'Reed' equivalent to 6 cubits and this measurement is also recorded in the Charter for the areca-nut garden, which is always under artificial irrigation as were gardens in Sumer. Only bamboo of 18 cubits utilized for the coconut garden as a measure and which is recorded in the Charter is not found in the Sumerian list. Perhaps because there was no such tree in Sumer! This type of different measurements of bamboo for the fixing of rent was in use as far back as a century ago in Goa. Further, this measurement existed only in Goa.

Now in respect of the value of a cubit, I have already referred to this unit when I wrote of the dimensions of the fore-courtyard of the Sidheshwar temple of Surla village. The Indian cubit from the time of the Kushanas (1st to 3rd centuries A.D.) measures 18 inches, while the Sumerian and Goan cubit measures to 19 1/2 inches.

God as land-owner

According to the Sumerian concept, the ownership of the whole land of a city-state was vested in the presiding god or goddess and the ruler was his/her steward. This concept was rooted in Goan villages and continued upto the advent of the Portuguese in 1510. Afonso de Albuquerque, the Conqueror of Goa, was surprised by this concept. In Portugal, at that time, the land belonged to the crown or to the nobility, or to the eclesiastic bodies; whereas in Goa, the Gaonkars controlled the administration of the village on behalf of the presiding deity of the village. The village-servants, craftsmen etc. were servants of that deity. In his second letter dated 1511, Afonso de Albuquerque, informed his king (of Portugal) saying: "Here the land does not belong to anyone so, it belongs to the King. His Majesty will be pleased to send some young men of good families to get married to beautiful girls on this place, and, will then be gifted with lands. And by this form the domain of His Majesty will be perpetual". Imagine how far sighted the thinking of Albuquerque was!

The eclesiastic bodies were named in Portugal as 'Communidades eclesiasticas'; so, the village communes came to be designated as 'Communidades'.

Collective farming

Before the advent of the Sumerians, the administration of the village was run by an assembly of elders, but the cultivation and appropriation of produce was individual; this system changed to collective farming, with all the obligations of maintenance and repairs of dykes and the irrigation system being transferred to the cultivators. So, excepting some private lands, the arable area was under collective farming-the commune-after the advent of the Sumerians.

Surnames of Sumerian origin

Now let me pass on to the system of surnames. It is presumed that surnames entered as the designation of a family around the 10th century A.D. onwards, but the surnames linked to the profession might have originated long before that.

I have already referred to the Padye family with the surname 'Desai'. When I visited a residential house of that family at Panchamem hamlet of Priol village, an elder of the family informed me that according to tradition their surname was originally 'Kale' and later on was changed to 'Desai'. The surname 'Desai' is the corrupted form of 'Deshpati-

Deshawayi', a designation existing in the time of the Yadavas of Devgiri (1000-1350 A.D.) and applied to the person entitled to collect the government revenue of a province. But at the time of the kingdom of the Kadambas this type of designation did not exist nor was it evident from the cited copper-plates of Tribhuvanamalla dated 1099 A.D., where the order was issued to a 'Devaraya' as the collector of revenues. 'Devaraya' surely represents the Sanskritization of the word 'Devari' with two meanings: a priest with the duty of ornamentation of the cella as well as of the *Palkhi* (vehicle used in processions). It could also mean a person who falls into a state of ecstasy as a result of a divine spirit entering his body. This is generally noticed in the principal festival of Betal, in Amonem (Bicholim taluka). In the temple of Betal at Priol, this family of 'Desai', being the first in the hierarchy, has a special seat near a pillar of the '*sabhamandap*' of the temple. There is a Paddye family in the adjacent village of Kuncoliem with 'Devari' as the surname. Hence, it appears that this 'Desai' family had the surname of 'Devari' at the time of the Kadamba kingdom, and not that of 'Kale', as is generally believed. However, there were 'Kallus' at least 2,000 years ago, meaning priests (in the Sumerian language).

I wish to put forward my opinion that like the temple-system, medicine also was influenced by the Sumerians in South India. The checking of a patient's pulse under the name of 'Nadi-pariksha' is a part of the Ayurvedic system. From my own experience I was told to consult an oracle-diviner on the suggestion of an Ayurvedic physician. This form of practice of '*Veiz*' (Ayurvedic physician) tallies with the Sumerian system.

Sumeriologists gives the meaning of the following Sumerian words: Kallu = priest; Ayagall = men of medicine; and, Nigall = scribe of a queen. We have dealt with the word Kallu before. Now, in respect of Ayagall, there is a Padye family in Goa, with their ancestor's house in Querim (*Keri*) village of Ponda taluka with 'Vaidya' as their surname. Their profession has been that of a physician through the generations and so ancient that not only private families have made gift of lands but even some village communes (communidades in Portuguese) present a vatan (gift) in cash annually. These gifts were made because a physician is not supposed to take fees according to the Dharma-Shastra.

This family probably resided originally in Sancoale village, Salcete taluka, and at the time when conversions became rampant, they migrated to Queula (*Kavlem*) (Kapileshwari hamlet), and later on to *Keri* village. Afterwards when the Portuguese changed their policy, allowing Hindus to reside with some restrictions in the area of the Old Conquests, one person of that family came to Panvel village near Old Goa. An order of the Viceroy says that the Hindus are prohibited to use '*Palkhi*' or '*Machil*' (vehicles transported by men), except their own physician, and this was certainly from that Vaidya family. In late eminent physician Dada Vaidya's geneological lineage list, his ancestor is mentioned as 'Ayangalu'-his surname. Information obtained from descendants of that family indicates that Dada Vaidya was of the opinion that the surname originated from the Kannad language and that his family had migrated from Karnatak. But this surname is surely derived from the Sumerian word. This means that the family is continuing its medical profession through the generations from four thousand years ago.

Now, the word Nigale. There are families in the Paddye caste with the surname 'Nigale', and the same surname appears also in the Karhade Brahmin caste. According to information provided in 1959 by the late Padmakar Bhatt Savoikar, there were two residential houses of the 'Nigalie' family in Sil-cum-Inam property situated at Savoi-Verem village, already referred to before. Those families became extinct as they had no heirs. Their houses had mud-walls and probably roofs of palm-leaves. Savoikar had cleared the mounds for a plantation of areca-nut and some pieces of clay, which were in fact clay-tablets with carved lines, were scattered around. I presume that those families were 'scribes of the queen' and priests of goddess Inanna.

Origin of the word 'Paddye'

Sumerian history says that in about 2,500 B.C. (though some would now date it much earlier), this title (King of Kings, showing hegemony) was claimed by Masanapadda (alias Mesannepadda), whose name heads the first dynasty of Ur in the royal list. The overlordship of the great southern city probably represents the height of the Sumerian resurgence after the Semetic penetration [66] pp. 94-9. His successor was named A-an-ni-pad-da [66] p. 47.

The city of Ur lay on the shores of the Persian Gulf, from where emigrants began their voyage. Probably the name Orgaon, a village of Ponda taluka is derived in this way. At the time of migration that city was under the rule of the descendant of the family of Mesannepadda, who had been pioneers of Sumerian resurgence against the foreign Semitic power. So, the families of the highest class named themselves as Paddye and similarly, with slight deviation, the families of lower class named themselves Fatto and another family as Maddo. This last family settled in the area now known as Marcaim (*Madkai*) which is probably a version of Maddaki, as the word 'ki' means land in the Sumerian language. There is another village named Betki in the same taluka, and I suspect that the name may be a variation of the word 'Betki', meaning land of Belit, this being the name of the wife of God Bel. One branch of the Paddye family settled in Priol village and a junior branch of the family might have taken the worship of the wife of Bel with them.

Human sacrifice

Rev. Haffman in his 'Encyclopedia Mundarika' writes on the practice of human sacrifice even among the aborigines of Chota-Nagpur. We even have recent proof of the practice around Nipani area in Maharashtra, which was reported in the newspapers about seven years ago. From the tale of Shuna-Shespa of the Vedic Age, it is known that amongst the Indo-Aryans this practice was prevalent. In the Indus Valley Civilization, the scene of the sacrifice of a woman in front of a tree in which is hidden a spirit is depicted on a seal. According to history, in front of Marduk, city-God of Babylon, the holy fire burnt continuously for twenty-four hours a day and the mothers used to throw their first-born child in the fire as an offering. Babylonia was located close to Sumer, and I found in the pages of history that the sacrifice of children of the slaves was sometimes performed but I did not find for which deity.

However, there are two cases of the sacrifice of children of the Paddye families, both in Ponda taluka and both involving artificial reservoirs. The first happened in Khandepar village. There is an artificial water-reservoir, and at the corner of the dyke there is a very small temple with an image of black stone nameed '*Kumari*' (child-girl). It is worshipped annually. The myth says that it was proving impossible to get the dyke standing firmly, and so finally the Paddye families resolved to offer a human sacrifice. The tank was full of water. They threw a bunch of bananas in it and asked a small girl to catch it. She was innocent, and did what she was told. The dyke now stood firm, and in the memory of the drowned girl, her image is worshipped. The second case is also similar. At that time only one family of Paddye Brahmin resided in Betki village. The members of the family at that time were only a widow and her daughter and son. Both were very young. The other gaonkars were of lower status, and they thought that to make the dyke stable, it was necessary to offer a human sacrifice, preferably of a girl exclusively of the priest-class. Hence, the gaonkars resolved to make a sacrifice of that girl of the Paddye family.

An image of the sacrificed girl, as they say, was constructed in her memory, and which is worshipped under the name '*Mandodari*'. The water-reservoir is named after her as '*Mandodariche-talem*' (tank of Mandodari). An article by a priest published in a Goan Marathi newspaper claimed that the word '*Mandodari*' is derived from Sanskrit, the word '*Manda*' meaning water; but in the dictionary 'Sanskrit-Pakrit Kosh' compiled by Madhav Chandroba, 1970, an authoritative dictionary, no such meaning is given. Moreover, Mandodari is the name of the wife of Ravana, king of Lanka, and she is declared in the Puranas to be the daughter of Shesha, king of Patiala, so the name cannot have a Sanskrit origin.

It is remarkable that the brother of Mandodari is named *Narbando*, and in his memory there is a stone on the bank of a brook. On the festival day, Mandodari visits that stone. The word Banda in the Sumerian language is similar in meaning to

Nigall, 'a scribe of queens'.

Houses

"In Sumer workers, farmers and families of such low earning classes lived in flat-roofed one-storied mud-brick houses. These presented a blank wall to the street, except for their low doorways and tiny windows near the flat roof. Behind that wall a family might live in crowded discomfort. But this house was the owner's castle, where each family member had rights and privileges.

"In a prosperous section there were imposing houses that lined the wide streets. Here where wealthy citizens lived, the way of life was vastly different from that in the workers' quarters. The houses were built of mud bricks to be sure, but the bricks were whitewashed and imbedded with brightly coloured stones and tiles set in rich mosaic patterns. The windows in the high outer walls were larger and had bars, made from the same mud bricks. In each house, a wide doorway opened into an entrance hall. Another showed an open courtyard beyond. This was the heart of the house.

"This courtyard was a large, light-flooded area, encircled by a two-storey balcony from which hung woven tapestries. The inner walls were also whitewashed and provided a quiet backdrop to the brilliant colours of the hangings. Behind the columns surrounding the door was a shadowed walking space where statuary was set in niches in the wall. Large glazed pottery jars caught and reflected the light from the sunlit open space.

"The rooms opening out from the inner court were hidden rooms. One of them was set aside as the house-hold shrine, dedicated to the worship of the personal god who has watched over the daily life of the master of the house and his family. Prayers and offerings were made every day to this god. As a result, the god was expected to take special care of the worshippers. The entrance hall was furnished with highbacked setees and chairs, and the floor was covered with bright reed matting. This was the place where a guest such as he might be received by the master of the house and his wife, if he was bidden to dine. The rooms on the lower storey were occupied, as cuisine, storage, dining-room, and the quarters for slaves; and the rooms of the upper storey were occupied by the members of the family" [36]. According to Sir Wooley, in the latter group of houses, a vessel filled with water was kept at the doorstep for partial wash of the persons before entering the house.

In the Indus Valley the system of construction of houses was the same, with the difference that the entrance door was in the lateral wall with a small passage linking the house with the main street. There was a blind wall adjacent to the main street.

Now, let us compare this form of construction to a typical Goan Hindu house. The

ill. 18b : a vessel shaped pit, carved in laterite rock found at Savoi-Verem

houses of well-to-do families always had an inner court named '*rajangan*' surrounded by columns. The walls adjacent to the corridors had openings for doors of lateral rooms. The main entrance door directly connected the house to the main street. Near the entrance, a vessel of water was kept and it was taken inside during the night. It is curious to note that I found a vessel shaped pit, carved in the laterite rock, with a depth of 1.48 mts. near a house of the Paddye Bhat at Savoi-Verem. I was told that it was of the time of the Nigalie family and it was meant for water and named '*ranjan*' (*ill. 18b*).

Schools

"The schoolhouse, in Sumer, the 'edubba' was connected to the temple and stood within the shadow of its walls. The way to it led along a narrow, twisting street. A Sumerian school boy of 2,000 B.C. could scarcely be blamed for playing truant. He started school when he was a small child and stayed there until he was a young man and a graduate scribe. The school day began at sunrise and lasted until the sun set. Discipline was immediate and harsh; the cane was punishment for sloppy work, for inattention of the slightest infringement of the rules. Even the big brothers, the monitors, who assisted the head teacher, were free with the stick.

"On an average day, the Sumerian schoolboy studied the table he had laboured over the day before. His assignment might be to copy an ancient myth or epic, the usual form of exercise in the long process of learning to form the cuneiform signs neatly and correctly. When the tablet had dried, he could only review his mistakes: he could not correct them.

"Thousands of these practice tablets, some of them marked in very shaky script and obviously the work of the very youngest students, have been dug from the ruins of early Sumerian cities" [65].

The Sumerians who settled in Goa obviously continued their art of writing, teaching it to their descendants probably seated near the temple. And this custom of using the precincts of the temple for teaching continued as far as sixty years ago in the areas of the New Conquests, especially in Ponda taluka. Later, this system disappeared in the areas of the Old Conquests as Christian zealotry destroyed the Hindu temples of that area.

Craft, industry and trade

In Sumer, the people had constructed huge buildings, ziggurats, as temples but construction had been made with the use of clay-bricks cemented with asphalt and inner faces of walls were plastered with lime-stone, as this material was available in plenty on the mountains situated at the northern border of Sumer. They knew also the use of iron. The weapons of kings and their commandants were made from mete-orite-iron, and sometimes from iron-ore which was also found in this mountain but its price was higher than gold, and the metal obtained from the ore was somewhat spongy. "It was not until the second half of the second millennium B.C. that the essential process of carbonizing, or steeling, by repeated heating in the presence of charcoal, and hammering was fully mastered" [61].

In Goa as well as in South India, the system of construction prevalent in Sumer could not be applied as asphalt was not available. But black-stone of a different kind was in plenty. Moreover, since ages past, iron-tools were in use. "A pre-Mohenjodaro iron shelter and forging plant in a Satavahana brick enclosure had been discovered during an excavation by the Andhra Pradesh Department of Archaeology. The excavation had helped uncover iron objects such as nails, chisels, rings, sickles and copper objects like rings, bangles and stone objects such as saddle querns, daggers and pestles" [66].

So, the Sumerian artisans who went to the South of Goa could make use of that black-stone and with tools of iron and the generous help of the kings they could develop their art of building. Thus they effected temples like ziggurats, and that sculpture is called Dravidian while it is in fact of Sumerian origin.

In Goa, black-stone was not available in the proximity of the settlement of the Sumerians, and there was no king to help them in the transportation of such stones. So, it was only much later that they constructed the temple of Shree Mahadev at Tambdi-Surla. Probably there was help from an unknown king as near that temple there is a step-stair named 'Ranichi-paz' (step-stair of the queen).

Mode of living

The Sumerians, through commerce with India, were aware of the mode of living in this country especially in the Indus Valley area. But in Goa due to the heavy rains the mode was a little different. Here, nachni and rice were the main food cereals, the roofs of houses could not be flat and clothing was of cotton and not of wool like in Sumer.

The difficulties in adaptation were overcome with the help of the Aryans-Bhargavas and Angirasas and the local aborigines, and so, as a token of gratitude, the Paddye Brahmins offer a meal on a certain day to some couples of the Satarkar caste in Ponda taluka. Some families which lived among these Aryans might have mixed with them through marriage. All the Paddye families improved on their agricultural system introducing ploughs of a special type, iron implements, and taking recourse to an advanced irrigation system, reclamation of river land, construction dykes and utilizing such land for paddy cultivation. The primitive village commune agricultural system was moulded on the Sumerian style. The patidari system was changed into the common type with the principal that the village land belonged to the presiding deity of the village. The Sumerians, as foreigners could not improve on their ideas of village-administration followed in the Sumerian city-states. However, the Aryans adopted their views and ideas and a mixed form of administration came into being. The village was the basic unit. It was some sort of a village-republic from the theocratic democracy of Sumer to the oligarchic democracy in administration.

In respect of industries, the Paddye Brahmins and others who had migrated from Sumer could not maintain such standards, not only because raw material like wool, copper, lead and bronze were different but because agriculture was of primary importance not only for subsistence but also for the barter system. However, some of them might have employed themselves in timber-products and wood carving- shaping dolls, toys as well as making furniture. Women especially might have busied themselves in textile manufacture *(ill. 19)*.

ill. 19 : Idol of a woman in terracotta of Goddess Inanna from Ur (City of Sumer) dated c. 2000 B.C. Photograph from "The Sumerians" by Elizabeth Lansing

Sumerian medicine

Like craft, medicine was also a secret, and continued through the generations. Unlike the down-to-earth physician, most 'scientists' of ancient Sumer were priests who ascribed all their knowledge to the gods and were very careful to keep their knowledge to themselves. Except for the scribes, they were the only educated people in Sumer. In order to maintain their position, the priests made a tremendous mystery of their knowledge and its divine sources. As a result, religion and science were inseparable in the mind of the average Sumerian.

There was the divining and omen-interpreting physician, the Asipu who foretold the patient's fate from signs, and the practical doctor, the Asu or Azu (meaning doctor of water) who worked with a handbook listing symptoms for every part of the body and appropriate doses and treatment for their cure.

The division is not as intellectually simple as might be supposed. It was the Asipu who seems to have observed the patient's symptoms most objectively and individually, concerning himself with his pulse, his temperature and the colour of his blood. It is in fact from the Asipu's text that we have learnt most anatomical and physiological terms. Yet the symptoms were studied as omens on par with such particulars as the time of day and the date. At the same time, while, as we shall see, the Azu used a number of effective drugs among the 'simples', their working may very well have been regarded as in a sense magical, not to be distinguished from the supposed potency of ingredients similar to those used by Macbeth's witches or from the prescriptions and actions based on sympathetic magic.

The Sumerian tablet from Nippur, dated to the last quarter of the third millennium B.C. and therefore the oldest known pharmacopeia in the world, omits the symptoms. It contains fifteen prescriptions, five of them with directions to apply as a poultice, three in which the "simples" are to be infused with beer and made drunk, and four that include washing the affected part with an elaborately prepared solution, sometimes rubbing the part with oil and covering with ashes or other dry stuff.

As for the very numerous later tripartite Asu texts, often referred to as the Summa Am lu books because each item begins with these words meaning when a man (is suffering from...), some are rational in the same sense as the Sumerian specimen. The following compressed examples refer to a lung complaint-possibly pneumonia.

"When a man is being devoured by pain in his breast, his epigastrium and his belly, he is ill in his lungs. If he is hot and coughs, has sputum, spittle... and water stand in his breast... the breath of his mouth pricks, when his spittle has blood he has reached the crisis...

"The man with the lung disease should have mustard, emmer grains and malt, ground and mixed with oil spread on a skin and bound to his chest and abdomen. He will get better". (After naming several more herbs for further treatment the prescription ends, 'He shall drink fine beer and will become healthy')."

"The Asu's materia medica was very largely of vegetable origin; indeed the same word 'sammu', was sometimes used for both plant and medicine. Many of the plants were therapeutic and have remained in use until today. The Asu's bag contained such narcotics as opium, hemp, belladonna, mandragore and the potent water- hemlock. He might also give camomile for stomach upsets, mustard water as an emetic, and mustard seed as a laxative. He also used the versatile but dangerous hellebore for what purpose we do not know. All this is enough to show that the practitioners inherited a pharmacopeia based on generations of empirical observation. On the other hand it was used uncritically; many different ingredients, the majority of which we should consider non-effective or magical-such as the powdered water snake already encountered, powdered tortoise-shell and the like. The minerals employed were mostly of the same sort-such as powdered copper and lapis lazuli-but also included salt and bitumen oil. The liquids that often served as vehicles for the other ingredients may have had more effect on the patient's health and spirits than the 'drugs' themselves: milk and honey were nourishing, while the beer and wines so often recommended made for a sense of well-being and gratitude.

"Childbirth was largely a matter for midwives and no doctor, involved a mixture of experienced skill and magic. Well-to-do women might consult the medical diviners, and the medical omen texts already quoted do in fact end with a section dealing with pregnant women and new-born babies. In a difficult birth the mother was to fast and drink beer infused with herbs-probably solanum and houndstonge—'she will give birth rapidly.'

"These texts do not conform with either the medical omens or the Asu hand-books. It is possible that they originated among women practitioners of midwifery? There is a single record of a woman doctor. She was attached to a court in Old Babylonian times.

"Medical texts hardly refer to surgery. Yet the laws of Hammiurabi (c. 1895 B.C., founder of the New Babylonian dynasty) decree payments for successful surgery and punishment of cutting of a hand, for causing death or the loss of an eye. The laws mention 'major operations' and opening of the eye socket, all to be done with a bronze lancet, also the setting of bones and the healing of sprained tendons. The inclusion of these items in the national law suggest that surgery was not so unusual as the dearth of texts might suggest".

It is interesting to note from the Sumerian records that Ur-Ningirsu, son of Gudea, Ensi of Lagash sent during times of sickness, missions of doctors to foreign courts. It may also be noted that oil of bitumen, one of the ingredients of Sumerian prescription-Shilajit according to Aryan Ayurveda-is in use even today. In both cases it is mixed with different herbs for purifying. The powder of turquoise-shell was substituted in Goa by powder of the conch-(shunk). This was the drug for rickets-basically calcium-and was given during childhood. It is worth emphasizing that according to Sumerian medicine texts 'sammu' was used as both plant and medicine. It is known that Indo-Aryans from the Rigvedic times, if not earlier, used to offer the juice of the 'soma' plant with special rituals to gods before drinking it. So, it is possible that the Aryans who migrated to Sumer introduced its use there.

Linking Ur-Ningirsu's missions, I am tempted to quote here the Puranic legend of 'sea-churning' through which Dhanvantari, a master of medicine, as well as dancing girls like Rambha and Urvashi, appeared from the sea along with other specimens and objects. Urvashi appears to be a Sumerian name, and her talk with Puruava is mentioned in sub-chapter (sukla) no. 95 of chapter (mandala) No. 10 of the Rigveda. Dr. D.

B. Kosambi, in his book 'Myth and Reality' has referred to this legend and given his version. But I would like to put forward the following points: Urvashi possibly might have been Nin-Ah, high-priestess, and if so, she should never be pregnant, and thus she had entered into contract with Purarava. Secondly, she was accompanied by 'Salmes', other priestesses, designated in the Rigveda as her female friends. Thirdly, their complexion was red; while it is known that the Gutians are considered as white headed or of white complexion, and in a state of excitement the complexion will naturally appear reddish. It is possible that she might have returned to Sumer and might have revisited India with her son and gone back. It is possible also that Dhanvantari might have continued to teach medicine in India.

Entertainment

"Probably the art which meant most in the everyday life of men and women of all classes was music. Court patronage from early times is reflected in lavishness of the instruments at Ur during their burial with the royal dead. In Pu-a-bistomb (4,000 B.C. above) a beautiful harp is found which is the most ancient. [60] pp. 141-142 - The First Great Civilization music instrument found in the world so far. We know from several literary references that music and dancing was a regular feature of the public square. Perhaps they were performed partly by local professionals, partly by visiting groups: Both singing and instrumental music were an important part of the temple services. There was a musical reflection of a custom that must have begun in wealthy circles in Sumer and lasted ever since. On a so-called 'standard' of Ur, itself almost certainly the sounding boy of a stringed instrument the king and his entourage are drinking, a man plays the lyre and a woman sings". [67] p. 266.

This custom spread not only in Goa but also to South India, especially around temple rituals. Even at the time of dining in a feast, divine or private, the singing of 'shloks' is substituted for music - otherwise, according to Hindu customs, no persons should talk while dining.

Games

Among the many ancient Goan games we find one named tabul- falem, which is surely of Sumarian origin. In the excavation at Ur a game board was found. It is made of shell, bone and lapis lazuli with seven bits of yellow colour and

ill. 20: Game board made of shell, bone and lapis lazuli found at Ur (City of Sumer). Note that this is the original form of the Goan game "Tabul-falem".

seven of black *(ill. 20)*. It is remarkable that the colours of the bits, named in Goa as Ghulos, are the same as found in Sumer. In Goa, the game employs four small pieces of bamboo or timber curved on one surface of red colour crossed by two blue or black lines at both ends of each piece. Those four pieces are named tablam, a name with no origin in the Indian language. I think that such pieces of bamboo (tablam) had deteriorated and hence not found in excavations at Sumer. The specimen found is kept in the British Museum.

This kind of game exists only in Goa and in the adjacent area of Sawantwadi, perhaps spreading there in the beginning of the 9th or 11th century A.D. when the 'Senavayi' Brahmins went there for the purpose of administration. The 'tabulfalem', besides the game of 'tablam' includes three other games namely 'kangam', 'hande' and 'wagh' (tiger). Those too probably were of Sumerian origin, the two lions being changed to two tigers with bits of red colour. There is also another game called 'gutfalem' which also appears to be of Sumerian origin.

SUMMARY

This chapter throws light on the influence of Sumerian culture on Goa. The archaeological findings of the author establish a direct connection to Goan society of Sumerian culture and not the Indus Valley civilization or any other heritage.

The laterite cave at Savoi-Verem and the Sumerian signs found there by the author lays the foundation for the discussion on comparative architecture and units of measurement employed by the Sumerian migrant families. The unit used in the construction of the Surla cave is identical with the process of the primitive temple construction in Sumer.

The place name 'Mhatari', the discovery of oracle plates, the worship of the Sumerian god 'Bel' in the form of "Betal" further corroborates the author's views.

The Sumerian god 'Nimirud' was worshipped in Goa in the form of a 'linga'. The 'Sumerian-script' found at Barazan in Savoi-Verem and its mythological origin is discussed. The discovery of the two signs establishes the fact that they are surely of the Sumerian cuneiform script and inscribed by an engraver of the Paddhye clan.

The Sumerian settlers in Goa followed the age-old practice of temple-divining. The origin of this practice in Sumer has been discussed. This practice of omen-consultation was brought to Goa by the migratory Sumerian priests as can be verified from the oracle plates of Anu and Inanna at Savoi-Verem.

The origin of city states in ancient Sumer, the mighty rule of emperor Sargon of Akkad and his successor has been reviewed and the fact which led to the great exodus of Sumerians in about 2000 B.C. has been discussed.

The Sumerian had trade-contacts with India dating from 2100 B.C. The great exodus of non-Semitic Sumerians led them to Goa by the sea-route.

The intention of the emigrants was not invasion but permanent settlement. The Sumerians brought with them ideas and customs which took root in Goa and South India. The history of five different ancient races of Sumer has been sketched. The tale of Bali has been interpreted to reveal its deep-rooted socio-religious meaning.

The first settlement of Sumerians was established in Ponda, Bardez and Salcete talukas. The identification of the old Sumerian deities is difficult due to Sanskritization and destruction during the Portuguese colonial rule.

The Sumerians pioneered the art of huge temple buildings in South India. Thus the original Sumerian 'Ziggurat' form was modified in South India, which is wrongly attributed to Dravidian culture.

The institution of the Devadasi system has been shown to have originated from Sumerian practices. Festivals like 'eating of barley' were carried to Goa. The origin of surnames points to the Sumerian influence among the Paddye class.

The Sumerian influence can also be found in the practice of medicine in Goa. The rituals of human sacrifice followed by the ancient Sumerians took the form of 'Sati' in Goa. However, the Paddye Bhatts of high rank did not continue this custom in Goa. It was very rarely practiced by other classes.

The Sumerian land tenure system closely compares with the Goan land tenure system. The Sumerian concept of divine ownership of land was deeply rooted in Goan villages and continued up to the advent of the Portuguese. The architecture of residential buildings in Sumer also influenced Goan Society. The Sumerians continued their art of writing and teaching on the clay-tablet to their descendants near the temple.

Sumerian craftsmen improved on their metallurgic prowess in Goa. There is proof that the smith class also came from Sumer. The Paddye families improved their agricultural system by introducing a special type of plough using iron-share, taking recourse to an advanced irrigation system, the reclamation of river-land, the construction of dykes and utilizing such land for paddy cultivation. The primitive village commune agricultural system was-moulded in the Sumerian style. The theocratic democracy of Sumer was transformed into oligarchic democracy in village-administration in Goa.

The Sumerian influence on Goa can also be traced to entertainment and games like 'Tabulfalem'.

The wealth of archaeological, socio-religious, cultural, anthropological, socio-political, legal evidence as well as the comparative study of ancient Sumerian society and its impact on post-settlement Goan society has opened a new chapter in the his-

tory of India. Most of the traces of Sumerian influence might have disappeared in the mist of colonial carnage but the solid facts unearthed for the first time have unravelled and demystified certain age-old rituals, law practices etc. found in Goan Society.

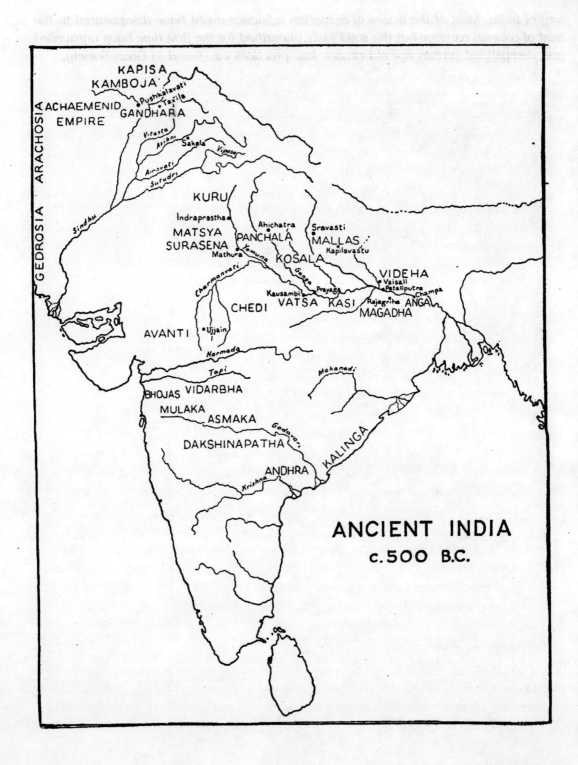

ANCIENT INDIA
c.500 B.C.

Chapter - 5
THE SECOND WAVE OF SETTLERS

The first chapter made clear that the Brahmins of the Bhargava and Angirasa clans accompanied Shree Parashurama on his expedition, around 2,400 B.C., and those clans constituted the first wave of the Aryans to the south. The existence of shrines of the deity named 'Eklo Vir' in Salcete taluka, registered in Portuguese records, testifies to the original settlement of those clans of the first wave in that taluka.

The second wave of settlers consisted of Aryans (*Saraswat Brahmins*) and (Kshatriya-Bhojas and Cheddiyas, named together as *Chaddes*), accompanied by non-Aryans from the Gaud Kingdom and named here as *Gawdes* in about 1000 - 700 B. C. This settlement was followed by people from the Deccan Plateau (named here as *Marathas*) at about the beginning of the Christian Era.

What were the cultural trends of these two Indo-Aryan waves ?

Etymology of river names

First of all, let me present here the evidence regarding the names of the rivers as we know that migrating people adopt the names of their original home-site for the area where they settle afresh. We know that the Indo-Aryans held great reverence towards the river. Their first wave had settled in Tiswadi, Salcete and Bardez talukas, these areas being crossed by two major rivers known at present as Zuari and Mandovi and a narrow river joining both now known as the canal of Marcela which is between Cumbarjua village and Marcela hamlet of Orgaon village of Ponda taluka. These three rivers were named as Asikni, Gomati and Vitasta, respectively, the first two being the names of the tributaries of the Indus river, and the third one a sub-tributary of the Asikni river. The name of this river was distorted by the transposition of the syllables as Akshini (fashioned in the Sahyadri Khanda purana as Aghanashini, similar to Asaghni, meaning destroyer of sins) with the result that the village on the bank of this river came to be known as *Agshi* (in Portuguese Agaçasim). The name Zuari had, presumably, been given by the Arab navigators. Similarly, in the island of Choraon (*Chodan*) there is a village named Golti, a corruption of Gomati. The word 'Vitasta' means in Sanskrit narrow, as the canal of Marcela is in fact narrow; at the junction of this canal with the Gomati, there is a small island named 'Vantso', corresponding to 'Vitasta'. The Gomati came to be named as the Mandavi, because as some historians say, the Muslim kings had installed a custom-post at Old Goa, which in the Farsi language is named 'Man-Dubi'. It is also possible that the Gomati was named as the Mandovi river by the Aryan settlers themselves because to the east of Ayodhya there was a river with such a name.

Rigvedic form of worship

The Rigveda in the tenth mandala (chapter) records a sukta (sub-chapter) under number 110 composed by Rama Jamadagnya (Parashurama), which besides throwing light on the period in which that sage lived, also depicts the cultural trend of the Aryans, at least of the clans who accompanied him. This sukta comprises eleven hymns, and is more or less identical to the other suktas named Aprisuktas. What is remarkable, however, is that hymn no. 8, consists of prayers of the goddess Ila, Bharati and Saraswati, in human form, invoking them to occupy the seats already arranged near the yadnya (holy fire).

In all the mandalas of the Rigveda we find, excluding this hymn, another hymn in which there is reference to the idol of Indra (IV, 24, 10) but there is no clear mention of his worship; so, that hymn is of the utmost importance.

According to different interpreters, the characters of each goddess vary. But they are unanimous about the character of Saraswati, who is a river. According to one interpreter, Ila represents food, and Bharati speech, while according to another, Ila refers to the land, and Bharati to Bharatwarsha (Indian land). It is noticeable that according to the copper plates dated 1106 A.D. of Gandagopal Keni of Kadamba times, who had established a Brahmapuri (a college for teaching religion, astronomy, astrology and medicine at Old Goa), it is mentioned that an image of goddess Bharati was installed in that place which was transferred to Marcaim (*Madkai*) village (Ponda taluka).

It is in the form of the goddess Sharada, the goddess of knowledge. So the interpretation of the first interpreter is a valid one.

The evidences show clearly that the Aryans who migrated around 2,400 B.C. engaged in the rituals of yadnya (holy fire) along with the worship of idols of those three goddesses and this system continued with respect of the idols, at least upto 1106 A.D. Connecting the name 'Bharati' to an idol of Sharada is very significant, and there is no prior evidence that Sharada was ever designated with the true ancient name of Bharati. This is the third case which focusses our attention on the tendency of people to continue the tradition in defense of the good conduct of society and when the different sects of Hinduism and even Buddhism had taken their own ways in the respective area.

What is true about iconic worship, must also be true about knowledge of the script. It may be true that in the ancient period the Aryans did not have a notion on the art of writing. But later they came in direct contact with the Sumerians. This evidence taken together with the fact that the script existed in the Indus Valley, makes it difficult to accept that the Aryans in the later period, or say the time of Parashurama and onwards, did not have knowledge of that art. For this purpose the Aryans might have employed mud-tablets which probably were reduced to powder and so disappeared with the passage of time. A similar thing must have happened in Goa.

The contact of the Rigvedic Aryan people with that of Sumer has been conceded by historians, but I did not find any influence of the Sumerian religion on the Aryan in the history of India relating to that period. For this reason, I think this fact changes the previous view about the Sumerian influence on Rigvedic Aryan culture in the early phase.

RIGVEDIC CULTURE

Now, let us examine the cultural trends in the Rigvedic Age. Parashurama is to be considered of that Age or may be of a later time.

It is seen that during those times the inheritance right passed from the father to his sons, and the daughter had no such right as the father had given her dowry at the time of her marriage. When a person had no son, he adopted the son of his daughter who came to occupy the residential house of his grandfather. The sons had equal shares in their father's property. However, there is no reference to the kind of property. And, as the next hymns refer to cattle, it can be presumed that cattle constituted property. The name of the compositor sage is Kushik Ayshharathi or Visvamitra Gadhinah, the latter being the maternal uncle of Parashurama. Hence the procedure was of that time, and it is obvious that the same procedure was followed in respect of land-tenure. From other suktas it is evident that a widow without child had the right to get a share from her father's property, and this resolution was taken by a council of elders gathered in the town-hall. From this, it appears that the political as well as the defence head was the king, perhaps elected by the elders, but the civil pleas were decided by the council of the elders of a clan.

References to the life of a widow are very few. We get only glimpses of some aspects of the life of a widow. It was not characterised by so many restrictions and austerities as in later days. X. 18.8 and X. 40.2 of the Rigveda convey that a widow was taken charge of by the brother of the deceased who could marry her with the permission of the elders. This custom must have been in vogue for a long time at least in Rigvedic India, as it has been recorded in the course of the funeral rituals.

In the Rigvedic Age the dead were buried and not cremated, and the custom of immolation of the widow, sati, was prevalent. Marriage with the brother of the deceased was voluntary.

Some hymns of the Rigveda are attributed to female rishis like Apala and Ghosha Kashivati who at that time were in their maidenhood.

The position of woman in society can be gauged from some of the hymns of the second Mandala of the Rigveda ascribed to Paruchchapa, the son of the Devadasi. Otherwise, children were generally named after the name of the father. But this exception to the rule indicates the existence of the Devadasi system - women dedicated to the service of gods, a system which can be traced to the Indo-European period. For we find the same custom prevalent in other branches of the Indo-European stock (Note: This system appears also in Sumer, and it is possible that it was introduced about 3,100 B.C. by the people who migrated to Sumer, and were probably of Indo-Aryan stock).

According to the hymns of the second Mandala, it is evident that the Indo-Aryans at that time knew the area of Katheawad upto the Narmada river. They knew the decimal system.

Instances in which women out-stepped the code of morals, such as abortion as we understand it today, are found frequently in the Rigveda. The way in which they are introduced in the hymns show that such actions were not looked askance at by society.

The Goddess of Dawn, for instance, is often described as a woman dressed in variegated colours, like a dancing maid, appearing on the stage to exhibit her beauty. References to the existence of illegitimate love and the abandonment of off-spring are also to be found in the Rigveda. That there were women who were professional dancers is evident from the description of the dawn.

The question naturally arises as to how far this picture of womanhood painted in the Rigveda can be claimed as the heritage of India. The hymns, as we know, were not all composed in India, nor are they of the same period. Some of them were composed at a period about which history is silent. Others reflect the dawn of Indian history when Aryans entered India through its north-western gates for the first time, and settled in the Punjab.

Thus we find in the Rigvedic age things common to earlier stages of civilization such as rituals round the two primary phases of life—marriage and death—being developed into social institutions. The eighteenth and the eighty-fifth hymns of the tenth Mandala record them. We cannot ascribe these to any legislator of that time.

Through the Rigveda, especially in the earliest books, monogamy was the established order of society. It is only in the very late collections that we come across references to polygamy. (Note: It can be noticed that at the time of the Mahabharata (c. 1,400 B.C.), the Nyoga system for procreation was accepted when there was no alternative as in the case of the impotent king Vichitravirya and also king Pandu. Later on in similar circumstances, the polyandry system was accepted in respect of Droupadi, though without any moral justification. [69] pp 21-32.

In brief, it can be said, the picture of woman-hood given in the hymns of the Rigveda is far different from what we find in later literature. The existence of a festival like Samana where men and women joined in, the unconventional life of a young girl, the pursuit of the Sun-god after the goddess Usha was very much like the scene of Apollo and Daphne, the custom of dedicating women to the service of gods, the winning of a maiden by feats of chivalry, the burial of the dead and various other customs are common to European branches of the Aryans family. They are to be found among the Greeks and the forefathers of the Latin-speaking people. Hence, the status of women of this period cannot be said to have grown on Indian soil but an Indo-European one transplanted by the Aryans.

First wave of migration of the Aryans

We have already referred to a gathering of elders, but it is necessary to provide a more extensive description as the first wave of migration of the Aryans started at least at the end of the Rigvedic age. This is evident from the fact that a sukta composed by Shree Parashurama is included in the tenth Mandala of the Rigveda.

Dr. A. S. Altekar in his book entitled "State and Government in Ancient India" mentions that in some primitive societies, the Government may have actually arisen owing to the operation of 'Matsya-nyaya' (behaviour of fishes), the strong eating the weak one. But as far as the Indo-European communities are concerned, the institution of the patriarchal joint family seems to have been the germ out of which the

State was gradually evolved. The evidence of the comparative philology shows that even when the Aryans were in their original home, they were living in joint families consisting of the grandfather, father, uncles, nephews, sons and daughters-in-law. The patriarch had full power over the members of the family. Some Vedic legends show that the father could blind or sell a guilty son by virtue of his patriarchal authority (R. V. I, 116, 16; A. Br. VII, 15). The position of the patriarch in pre-historic times was more or less like that of a king amongst all the Indo-European communities. His jurisdiction increased, though perhaps his powers diminished as the joint family expanded into a big federation of several natural families springing from a common ancestor, real or imaginary, and living in the same village. The senior member of the senior-most family in such a village was regarded with great reverence by the whole community and used to be entrusted with most of the governmental functions to be discharged, no doubt, in consultation with other elder persons of the locality. The Rigvedic evidence shows that the Aryan society in that early period was constituted in a hierachical order into families, janmans, vishas and janas or tribes (R. V. II, 26, 3).

"Janman' seems to correspond to a village consisting of people claiming a common descent, and a number of such villages joined together by a bond of kinship seem to have constituted a 'vish'; its chief was known as a Vishapati. 'Vishas' were closely knit together, and on the battlefields battalions were often arranged as per the 'vish' to which they had been recruited (R.V. X, 84, 4). Several vishas made a jana or tribe, which had its own Janapati or the king. This organization among the Vedic Aryans shows a striking resemblance to the condition prevailing in Rome in the early days."

"The available evidence thus shows that among other Indo-Aryan communities, the state was evolved in India also in pre-historic time out of the institution of the joint family. The patriarch of the family was instinctively revered and obeyed; and social traditions and atmosphere inspired a similar respect for, and evoked a similar obedience to the head of the village and tribe, who generally acquired the status of chiefs and kings. The power of the kings gradually became more and more extensive as states became larger and larger."

"The institution of the joint family thus gradually led to the evolution of kingship. It also presupposed the rise and acceptance of the notion of family property, and also of the inviolation of the sacred family ties and relationships, especially connected with the institution of marriage. Molestation of women had to be stopped and the peaceful enjoyment of property had to be ensured. This could be guaranteed only by the rise of the institution of State. The institution of the family with notion of the family property thus played its own part in the origin of the State.

"Our writers again and again revolve round the same type of state, viz. Monarchy; only a few of them passingly refer to the Sangha (Republican) State. We have shown already how for a long time the state was tribal. Apart from the frequent references to Vishapatis and Janapatis the Rigveda (c. 2500 B.C.) frequently refers to specific tribes like the Yadus, the Purus, the Abhiras, the Turvasas etc. Vishvamitra's (maternal uncle of Shree Parashurama) prayers are said to have protected the Bharata people." [70] pp. 34-36.

The Aryan village administration

Dr. A. S. Altekar does not give any designation of the headman of the village in the Rigvedic period, but Prof. Mahajan, citing the opinions of different scholars, says: "The family was the unit of social organization. It was under a head called Kulapati. Many families combined together to form the Gram or village which was under a Gramani. Above the Gram was the Vish. However, it is difficult to state whether the Vish of the Rigveda was a local division or a blood kinship like a clan. Above the Vish was the Jana. There is a reference to Pancha Janah, Yadava Janah and Bharata Janah. The king is referred to as the protector of the Jana or people (Gopa Janasya). The word Rastra was used for the whole country."

"Ministers - the king had ministers and foremost among them was the Purohita. He was the alter-ego of the king in all religious matters. He also assumed leadership in political matters. He accompanied the king to the battlefield and strengthened him by his prayers for his safety and victory."

"The kings entourage also included the Senani, 'leader of the army', and the Gramani, the leader of the village for both civil and military purposes. There must have been Gramanis in a kingdom, but the texts seem to contemplate only one as being in the royal entourage, possibly as a representative of the rural interests and population". [71] pp. 97-99.

Mode of living of Aryans

"As regards the dress of the people, the Rigvedic people had two or three kinds of garments. Some people put on garments (Nivi), a garment and an over-garment. Some people put on garments of various colours or those embroidered with gold. Ornaments such as necklaces, ear-rings, bracelets and anklets were used by both the sexes. Hair was combed and oil was also used. Women wore their hair plaited. Sometimes men arranged their hair in the form of coils. A maiden arranged her hair in four plaits. There was the practice of growing beards but shaving was also known as there is a mention of razors being sharpened on stones. A barber was called Vapta".

Dr. D. D. Kosambi says that "each class (of Brahmins) retained their distinctive hair-dressing in later times. The Bhrigus had shave-patches, Goutamas and Bharadvajas had five hair-crests, Atreyas three hair-twists, Vasisthas a single twist to the right. The Vasistha type of hair-braid is not discernible on Indus seals; but the Egyptian statue of Khonshu has such hair-dressing. It is seen more clearly in a solitary figure (a priest?) in an Egyptian relief illustrating a group of Hittite prisoners (Gurney, The Hittites, plate 2, bis). This fits the Vasistha description 'dakshinatas-kapardah'." [72] pp. 109.

But, in the Puranas, Shree Parashurama, who was of the Bhrigu clan, is described as an anchorite, in an antagonic form to that mentioned by Dr. Kosambi. Moreover Dr. Kosambi does not give the sources. So I have reservations about accepting his views.

"Milk and its products were the most important part of the food of the Aryans. They also used a mess of grain cooked with milk. Cakes of rice or barely were mixed with ghee and then eaten. Porridge was prepared from Yava grain. Meat of goats and sheep which were sacrificed, was used. The cow was considered to be sacred and could not be killed (Aghanya). Soma and Sura were used but the use of Sura or liquor was condemned. The whole of the ninth Mandala of the Rig-Veda is devoted to the Soma drink.

"The Aryans of Rig-Vedic India were not nomads. They lived a settled life and built cottages of wood and thatch for their dwellings. Their cottages have been described in these words: 'Columns are set up on firm ground, with supporting beams leaning obliquely against them, and connected by rafters on which long bamboo rods are laid, forming the high roof. Between the corner posts, other beams were set up according to the size of the house. The crevices in the walls were filled with straw and reed, tied in bundles and the whole was to some extent covered with some material. The various parts were fastened together with bars, pegs, ropes and thongs".[40] pp. 61-62.

The land tenure system of Aryans

One cultural trend still remains to be mentioned and that is with reference to the land tenure system.

I have already referred to the case of movable property and residential house which could belong even to a woman by inheritance. In respect of rural cultivated property, this type of property is called 'Kshetra' or 'Urwara', in the Rigveda and there are references of measurement of this type of land. It appears that such properties were of private ownership. The following expression of a woman and named Apala is significant. She says that the cultivated land of her father is like the hair of her head. [73] p. 15. This expression shows that the cultivated lands were inheritable and daughters without brothers inherited them.

With these main features of cultural trends, the first wave of Aryans—Bhargavas and Angiras—settled in Goa. Their settlements were of a few families only, occupying the coastal area probably in Salcete taluka which, perhaps sporadically, was occupied by others, who according to the Aryans, were Janmans. Afterwards the headman of these earlier settlers came to be designated as 'Janm', a distorted form of 'Jalmi'.

These Aryan families obviously held hegemony in the villages where they settled, possibly because they were superior to the earlier settlers in defence strategies. However, they did not interfere in their social and religious ways of life. Their 'Barazan' system and festivals continued and it is possible that the presence of Aryans might have contributed to the peace and order in the area occupied by them and their successors for about three centuries.

Whatever be the development in agriculture and other types of economic progress, the settlers could not remain stable without up-to-date weapons and allied pursuits and this has been proved time and again from ancient times up to the present. In this respect the author of Aryatarangini writes: "In Rigvedic hymns, there is a clear mention of steel. Iron (ayas) is described in the Samhitas as both malleable and ductile, tough and strong. Steel is also referred to as "tikshana-dhatu" in subsequent literature, because of its sharp and penetrating quality. From all available data, it is certain that the vedic Aryans knew how to make swords, armour, etc. of steel, about 4,000 B.C. In Vedic India, the cuirass (varman) was lined with steel, over a skin base. The helmet and the hand-guard were also of the same metal, but in the case of nobility they might have been gilted with gold". [73] pp. 171-172.

The Aryan Sumerian cultural synthesis

About three centuries later, the people from Sumer came and settled in Goa, obviously under the direct and indirect protection of the Aryans, but without joint settlements in the villages of Ponda taluka, occasionally in Virdi, and in Amonem, Pilgaon and Bicholim village of Bicholim taluka, and in Beti-Verem Serula, and other adjacent villages of Bardez taluka. Barbara-desh is a place name derived from 'Baveru' meaning Babylon, the land occupied by the Sumerians [74] p. 156. Near the boundary of Virdi village there is an image of a god named 'Babro-Dev' whose name must have been derived from the word Baveru meaning taluka. The main features, besides those mentioned in the preceding Chapter, are the reclamation of lands— marsh lands on river coasts brought under rice cultivation—called khazan lands. The second feature was the creation of common ownership of the village-land which belonged wholly to the main village-deity, like in the Sumerian administrative set-up introduced into Goa.

Besides, there were many common social and political customs at the time of arrival of both the peoples, Aryans and Sumerians. The Devadasi system among the Aryans was named 'Devadanis'. While in the Sumerians, there were 'Neons' (high priestess) and 'Salmes' (priestess), the Aryans had no temples, so they had no such link with Sumer. The Indo-Aryan kings were accompanied in the battlefields by their purohitas (priests) who sent prayers to the gods, while the Sumerian Ensis and Patesis in such cases were accompanied by their priests (diviners) who communicated to them the answer of the city-god through the signs of a sacrificed ram.

The existence of a gathering of the members of a clan-Janah is mentioned in the Atharvaveda and named Sabha and Samiti (some historians consider Sabha as the place of gathering), and that Veda is considered to be later than the Rigveda. However, we find that the Veda includes the names of serpents, as mentioned before, which are similar to the Sumerian names of the time of Sargon the first. So, the names Sabha and Samiti might have existed at the time of the Rigveda. Historians consider the political system of that time as an oligarchic democracy and it continued to be so in the time of Shree Krishna, installed as king after performing the rituals of Rajyabhishheka mentioned in the Atharvaveda.

But in Goa, at the time under reference, all the three main sections lived together (namely the former settlers, the Aryans and the Sumerians) and continued with their ideas of democracy. The hegemony of the Aryans obviously prevailed followed by the Sumerians. Life continued peaceably, and if any litigation arose beween the early settlers, the Sumerians, as foreigners, did not take cognisance of it, as they were not affected and they consisted in any case, of very few families, perhaps three or four in a village.

The milk of the cow and its products was the main diet of the Aryans. So obviously while migrating the Aryans were accompanied by cattle. And so cattle-breeding was first introduced by them wherever they settled—from Goa to the South.

SECOND WAVE OF ARYANS ACCOMPANIED BY NON-ARYANS

Route of migration

It is said that in the reign of Nichikshu, a descendant of Parikshit (fifth king in his lineage) an earthquake struck with the result that the bed of the Saraswati river disappeared, the Ganges overflowed and Hastinapur was almost destroyed. Very soon a large area around both the rivers experienced a drought for about twelve years as a result of swamps up to Koshambi (near present Alahabad), 100 miles to the East of Hastinapur [75] p. 32.

The birth of Parikshit was around the time of Bharat-war or say about 1,400 B.C., hence the drought must have occurred around 1,200 B.C. It is natural that with the catastrophe the affected people migrated elsewhere and probably some from the areas of Kosala, Chedi and Saraswata or Brahmayarta migrated in the direction of Mathura-Ujjein (Satwat-desh) and thence to the South by the Western coast, to Lata, a part of Gujarat and from there to Goa. They did not come straight to Goa. Some came by the land route and some probably by the sea route. They did not settle permanently in the former areas because they were newcomers and perhaps they might not have found suitable commodities to live by. Some families might have migrated from Lata by the land route and settled in Kudal (Maharashtra) Pernem and Bardez area on the northern border of Goa.

The first agraharas of Brahmins

After settling in Lata-desha, some families of Brahmins took up trade by the sea route to the South and then came to settle in Salcete taluka. At that time or say about 700 B.C., if not earlier, the villages of that taluka had a well established administration in the form of the village-commune, managed by a committee of elders, in the mould of an oligarchic democracy. The villages of Sancoale and Loutolim (*Lotli*), adjoining one another, gave some areas of their villages to the newly arrived Brahmin families of the Vatsa and Kaushika gotras-sub clans of the Brigu clan. The families of the Vatsa gotra and Kaundinyc Gotra had the area named *Kutthal* (Portuguese: Cortalim) separated from Sancoale and Nagvem villages and those of the Koushika gotra possessed an area named Quelossim (*Kelshi*) of *Lotli* village [76] pp. 83-84 & [77]. As those areas where gifted, they were named as Agraharas, and not simply Gramas, and so even in the Portuguese period, in the records of villages written in the Goen-Kanadi script (according to the publisher Shri Gajanan Ghantkar it is the Hallekannad script), *Kuttal* village is recorded as Agrahara Kushasthali Grama dated 1614 A.D. [78] p. 55. Kushasthali was the capital of Southern Kosala ruled by Kusha, son of Shree Rama who established his new capital and gave that name. His brother Lava who was ruling Northern Kosala continued to govern from Shravasti, which was the capital of the whole of Kosala before its partition. Kushasthali of Kosala later came to be named as Kanouj. Some historians say that Kushasthali established by Kusha was situated on the Vindhya mountains, but this view is untenable as at that time the capitals were established on the banks of rivers. [76] pp. 122-126.

Migration of Chaddes

Northern Kosala was named Goud [79] pp. 211-212. In this second wave there were families of the Kshatriya caste named Bhojas reinstated in their original home around Ujjain (Satwat), Chaddes, originally from the Chedi kingdom and some families of Vaishya caste—all of Aryan stock and some families of artisans and of non-Aryan stock from Goud named here as Gaudes. Soon after the drought some families from Chedi migrated also to East Punjab and those are considered as of the Khatri caste named Chaddas. While some families continued with their surname, others took the name Uri, Puri, etc. Some families abandoning their martial professions, chose to become merchants and so came to be considered as of the Vaishya caste.

In Goa the Chaddes tried and held their hegemony in some villages of Salcete taluka. Some became members of village communes. The Vaishyas also had been members of village communes of Tiswadi and Bardez taluka. I have not taken into consideration here those who came from Sumer and are considered to be of Vaishya caste in the Ponda and Bicholim talukas.

The immigration from the North was not suspended. According to the 'Sahyadri Khand', Shree Parashurama settled 66 families of Saraswat Brahmins of 10 clans (gotras) in which were included families of the Koudinya gotra [80] pp. 132-134. But this book, the 'Sahyadri Khand' makes reference to the Kadambas, Havig Brahmins and even to the Madhvacharya's sect of the thirteenth century A.D. So, the book was composed around this time or was being composed earlier but some chapters were introduced afterwards, based on summarized legends which were in vogue at the time of writing.

Kudaldeshkar, Pednekar, and Bardeskar Brahmins

I have already referred to a wave of Saraswat Brahmins who migrated by the land route. That wave occupied Kudal and then travelled to Pednem and Bardez talukas. They are known respectively as Kudaldeshkar, Pednekar, and Bardeskar Brahmins. They had no idea of the Sumerian system adopted in other talukas, and continued with their way of life in the cultural trends brought by them which I have already shed light on. However, some original settlers had their own system of primitive agriculture and the village communes existed with a rudimentary form of administration. Those Brahmins maintained village boundaries and private ownership of the land. The kingship system may also have been introduced but there is no proof of this. With the expansion of family members, they came to occupy other villages, and after centuries they came into close contact with the people of these talukas. Some sporadic changes were also made in the village administration system and forests and pastoral lands were considered to be of common use to the respective villagers.

The Mhal administration

At the time of the settlement of the second wave of Aryans the administrative set-up, not only of the village, but also of the taluka was already established. There was no kingship in Goa. The village administration was conducted by a committee of elders of the families named Gaonkars on behalf of the main deity of the village. This concept was adopted from the Sumerians and so idolatry form of worship and the Devadasi system of the Sumerian kind was introduced. The talukas were probably named 'desha' or 'mhal' which were considered as original places of settlement of the Aryans. Committees of the representatives known as 'Mhalgades' of the principal villages were formed.

Mhal is not a corruption of 'Mahal' as some people tend to believe, but has the same connotation as when the word is employed to mean the first cluster of ripened coconuts. Thus, the Salcete taluka committee was formed of 20 delegates of the 10 principal villages, two delegates representing each village (one being of the eldest family and the other of the family in charge of village-records, later named Kulkarni), the eldest of the first vangad and one of the second vangad families, respectively. Their meeting place was named *Mhalgaon* (*Madgaon*, in Portuguese Margaon), being the village of the first order or hegemony. Similarly, the Tiswadi taluka committee was constituted of 16 members from 8 main villages and the meeting place was in Neura village. The Bardez taluka committee was of 18 members from 9 main villages, and its meeting place was Serula (original name being Sirlapur) village. Meetings were held under the leadership of the *Mhalgado* of the place where the gathering took place, and the second delegate of the same village served as the record-keeper of that committee. This committee dealt not only with appeals against the resolutions of the village-committees or of village assemblies, but also considered all cases of political, social and economic nature. In fact, the system was (as now named) a welfare state, as conceived by the mind of the highest class of that time. The system may also be considered akin to that of Sumer in some of its city-states like Lagash. Differences always exist— for instance, slavery did not exist in Goa like in Sumer, and the resolution of an assembly or of a committee had to be unanimous (as said in the Rigveda) and not based on the majority like in the Sumerian system. This system continued for thousand of years with slight changes from time to time.

The families of the second wave adopted the system in force at that time. The adoption of the system can be seen even today in the organization of the Mangesh temple of Priol, originally from *Kutthal* village of Salcete taluka. It is worth noting that designations like Gramani (headman of the village) and Vishapati (headman of the group of villages) which, according to some historians, existed from the time of the Rigveda, never existed in Goa even at the time of the first wave of Aryans. As such the village assembly maintained its designation as 'Gaonpan', which in about the ninth century A.D., if not earlier, came to be named as '*Mahajanki*' at least in the villages of the Aryans.

Before the advent of the Portuguese the village commune administered all the temples existing there, but due to Christian fervour the temples in the talukas of

Tiswadi (then Ilhas), Bardez and Salcete were demolished, so the deities were spirited away elsewhere. The members of village communes were designated Gaonkars, but now the village commune was separated from the Hindu temples. So the members of Hindu families associated with the temples had to use the designation as Mahajanas which was in use in the adjacent area where new temples were established for the transferred deities.

Scrutinizing the dating of migrations

The families of the second wave of Aryans and non-Aryans migrated about 1,000 B.C. but the date of settlement cannot be definitely determined due to lack of clear evidence, but the dating cannot be later than 700 B.C. Scholars like Dr. R. Bhandarkar and others also offer this dating of the settlement, though evidence of the arrival of the Sumerians in Goa was unknown to them.

Now, we have to scrutinize one point. The Bhojas appear in later history as the most ancient rulers of Goa. The point to be considered is whether those people came at the time of the second wave or later. Following the death of Kaunsa at the hands of his nephew Krishna, Jarasandha, his brother-in-law, assaulted Mathura and the surrounding areas called Shurasena Mandala (where a region named Satwant was included) several times. The Kshatriyas residing in this region were named Satwant, a branch of a big clan named Yadu. After the last invasion of Jarasandha, the Kshatriyas resolved to leave that area, and so, some from Rajasthan came to Sourashtra where Dwaraka was established, and others from the West coast migrated to Maharashtra, Karnataka and even to Tamil Nadu where they established their colonies. Many kings of southern India considered themselves Satwants and linked their genealogy to Shree Krishna. The invasion of Jarasandha took place about half a century before the Great War, or say about 1,450 B.C. Aitareya Brahmana Samhita refers to Satwats as the people residing in Southern India (VIII, 3, 14), and according to scholars, the compilation of that book is dated about 1,500 B.C. This Satwat sub-clan from the beginning had adopted a special sect named Satwant Sampradaya — who worshipped God under the designation of Vasudeva, Vishnu and Narayana, in the form of Bhakti (deep devotion), a form of worship without the rituals of Yadnya. [83]. But copper plates of the kings of the Bhoja dynasty (4th to 6th century A.D.) does not provide any information in respect of Satwat Sampradaya, nor is there any image of Narayan or Vishnu found in the area of Chandraura (not Chandrapura and the present Chandor village of Salcete taluka), capital of that dynasty. So, it appears that this Bhoja dynasty was probably one of the clans of Chaddis in the second wave of Aryans.

The families of the second wave of Aryans came and settled in Salcete taluka. The Chedis or say Chaddes had even become members, or say gaonkars, of some villages, but all these families, Brahmins and Chaddes, though they governed their villages, had no right to send their representatives to the Mhal-administration, as those Mhalgades were only of 10 main villages and only of the Saraswat caste.

The Chaddes, that is the Kshatriyas of Chedi and Satwant area [83], always enjoyed hegemony in their original area, so some families of Chaddes tried to select a new area not so far occupied by the Aryans of the first wave. The areas of Salcete, Tiswadi and Bardez were already occupied by those Aryans. Ponda taluka (then known as Antruz) was more or less occupied with the hegemony of the Paddye-bhatts. The adjacent and suitable area for occupation was later named Chandravadi, an area further south. However, the Chaddes needed the help of the Saraswat Brahmins of the second wave due to five reasons: firstly, because they had direct contact with the Brahmins of this second wave; secondly, because the Brahmins of the first wave had recognized them as of their own clan and so treated them accordingly, so they would not interfere in the area which they might have occupied. Thirdly, as merchants by profession for generations, they possessed vast knowledge of the social, political and economic situation of the coastal area and the behaviour of the respective people. Fourthly, because they were versatile in script, accountancy and general administration. Fifthly, they knew that the Brahmins never dreamt of kingship, so their hegemony would go unchallenged.

But the Brahmins would not accompany them in their capacity as simple Purohits; they wanted a financial guarantee as they were abandoning their usual profession as merchants. It may be presumed that the Chaddes promised to give them one-third of the cultivable the land of the village, maintaining two-thirds for themselves, except the forests which would be the common property of both, or say, the village commune. Even though there is a copper plate inscription of Devaraja Bhoja recording that he had lived in the 4th century A.D., I presume that long before, perhaps in the 6th century B.C., the three groups might have established themselves first in Chandravati and then spread out gradually.

Around that time, or say, about 6th century B.C. Chandravadi was under the hegemony of the Satarkar (alias Santerkar) Kols with their headquarters in Amone village. The Chaddes repulsed them and they fled to Astagrahar and the neighbouring area. At present, some families exist in Rivona village and occupy the area around that region. The people of other castes like the Naiks and Mhars continued to live in the original settlement because for them this change did not cause any obstacle to their normal way of living and their rituals. The Saraswat family which accompanied the Chaddes was of Quelossim (*Kelshi*) village, of the Koushika gotra, who came to be named 'Nadkarni' with the surname 'Rege' meaning writer (recorder), and with the expansion of the family, the occupation spread to neighbouring villages. A similar form of occupation occurred also in the families of Chaddes.

The origin of temple worship

It has already been established that even the mother-goddess was under worship among the peoples of the Indus Valley in about 2,000 B.C. The worship was only of a domestic form. There was no temple for public worship. The Rigvedic Aryans also worshipped the three goddesses at the time of a Yadna, as mentioned earlier. There was, however, no temple for public worship. At the end of the Vedic Age and at the beginning of Brahmanas like Shatapatha Brahmana, Rudra and Vishnu came into prominence and Rudra took the place of Prajapati. Vishnu was identified with sacrifices. [75] p. 108. But nowhere in all this literature is there a mention of a deity being worshipped in a temple. In Rigvedic time Rudra was considered as the maleficient head of the Marutas and Vishnu as Upendra or adjunct of Indra, but in the time of Yajurveda, Rudra came to be considered as a beneficient healer of diseases and Vishnu maintained pre-eminence; but their worship is not mentioned. It appears that the construction of temples began possibly when North Indians were recruited as soldiers in the army of the Persian emperor Cyrus and his son Cambuses (528-521 B.C.) and later on in the army of their successor Darius (521-485 B.C.) In Western Asia, those Indian soldiers noticed the existence of the worship of gods in temples and so, when they came back they might have adopted the same mode of worship. Greek sources say that King Pouras appeared with an idol of Heracles in the battlefield against Alexander the Great (321 B.C.). The most ancient remains of a temple of the third century are found in Veirat village near Jaipur. Jaipur is situated in the ancient area named 'Satwant' and is obviously of a very later period — after the families of the second wave had left the place en route to Lata-desh (Southern Gujarat). This means that the idea of construction of temples in the villages of Goa was not brought from Northern India.

Etymology of Mangesh

It appears that the first settler or perhaps leader of the Saraswat Brahmins, who settled in Kutthal village, was a family of Vatsagotra, so the eldest member of that family was considered as 'Grama-purusha'. The Aryans of the second wave probably adopted the idolatry and worship form of the Sumerian, as mentioned earlier, and a temple was constructed with a Shiva-linga named Mangish, Mangesh or Mangirish. The 'Sahyadri-Khanda', in its second and third chapters named 'Gomanchalakshestra Mahatmyan' from the first to the third hymn, mentions the original place of establishment of a linga as 'Mangish'. [7] p. 128. The linga was established by Brahmadeva on a hill named Mangirish in a place called 'Thihotraka'. In the Portuguese, records of the destruction of Hindu temples, the name 'Mangish' has been mentioned as Manganatu (Manganath) and the name 'Shantadurga' of Kelshi as 'Santer', and in the poem 'Krishnacharitrakatha' composed by Krishnadas Shama the said deities are mentioned as Mangesh and Shantadurga respectively. This poem was composed in the year 1526 and those Portuguese records were compiled in the year 1567. It therefore appears that both names were used at different levels of social status. [7] pp. 44 and 47.

Bhargava in his book [81] p. 70 says that at the time of Manusmriti (200 B.C.), the area between the Sarasvati and Drishadvati rivers was named Brahmavarta, while before, in the Rigvedic period the area between the two rivers and the third named Apasa was designated as 'Manisha'. A village with an identical name existing in this area was near the present village of Keishala. The portion of this area but adjacent to the Saraswati river was known as 'Sapta-Sarasvata', and later on the same area came to be named as 'Mangana'.

So, the leader of the Saraswat families who obviously knew the name of the original place of his ancestors, named the Shiva-linga as Mangananatha, corrupted as Manganatha as well as Manganesha, and later abbreviated to Mangesha or Mangirish. In respect of Gopinatu or Mulkeshwar, I have already given the explanation earlier while discussing the names of the 'gauda' caste.

From the above evidence, it is proved that the time of the beginning of migration of the second wave cannot be later than 1,200 B.C. Now let us consider when this wave settled in Goa.

Shree Mangesh Temple and its rituals

I have taken here the design of the Shree Mangesh temple of Priol as an example. The height of the entrance door of the sacred room (*Garbhakud*) is less than the other doors of the temple. This symbolizes the Sumerian type of womb. In the main hall, in front of Shiva-linga, his vehicle-bull (*Nandi*) of black stone is placed. According to the rituals, nobody should sit on the straight line between these two idols. However, an image of Gramapurusha has been established on the straight line. This is in the form of a man in a sitting position with curled head gear and with a peeled coconut (*shriful*) in the hollow of both palms. At the back there is a beautifully carved plate known in Hindu rituals as *Prabhaval*. On the body of the idol there are conventional points where, when the consultation of the oracle is required, buds and petals of red flowers of a plant named '*pitkuli*' are stuck with sweet water. Formerly, 49 points—six for buds and forty-three for petals—were established, but now, out of them, six for buds and seven for petals are used.

It is said that the system of placing the image of *Gramapurusha* and that of consultation of the oracle is the same as in the original place—*Kutthal* village. Those systems are copied purely from the Sumerian temple system, with slight modifications and were required at the time of the first settlement at *Kutthal*. It is presumed that the leader of the families of the Vatsa gotra constructed the temple and so, according to the Sumerian system and style, his image was established in front of the sacred room. The image is shown with a coconut in both hands in a praying posture. This is akin to the custom in Sumer where the statuette of the builder was erected offering in both hands a lamb for sacrifice. According to the rules of worship only white flowers should be offered to Shiva, while for the oracle red buds and petals are used. The justification for this custom lies in the change made by the Saraswats to the Sumerian system. The Sumerians consulted the oracle using the lungs and liver of the sacrificed lamb, and so that a portion was obviously covered with blood. So, flowers of the colour of blood were used as a substitute. Before the advent of the families of the second wave of Aryans, the Paddya-bhatts had already brought about a change in the oracle-plates, mentioned before, using red coloured petals of the flower-tree named 'Jaswandi'. It is noticeable that the Shiva-linga of Mangesh is not phallic, but like a simple natural rock—this type is rare and is designated 'Rudrakshalinga'. This type of linga exists in Goa—including Mallicarjuna of Canacona (*Kankon*).

According to the Sumerian system, rituals with different functions were established in the precincts of the temple and the same system was adopted in the Mangesh temple. A tall bamboo was erected in front of the Sumerian temple. Here, the bamboo was substituted by a light-tower (*dipastambha*). At the corner of a Sumerian temple one could always find a tank. Similarly, a tank is placed in front of the temple of Shree Mangesh. It may be noted that a Mahajan of the temple after his marriage. when he visits the temple with his wife, has to take a ceremonial bath named 'ganthawal' and then only can he enter the temple. This is because his wife who was of a different clan, now enters in the clan of her husband after marriage. In Sumer, only the performer of daily worship, the ruler of the city-state, his family and his close relatives could enter the sacred room of the temple. This system continues even today and in the sacred room only the Mahajans, their families and other. Saraswat Brahmins considered as their relatives are allowed entry.

We have seen from the inscriptions of Gudea, ensi of Lagash and the paintings of Mari that each family had its tutelary deity besides the main city-deity. So, when they prayed to the main god, they always took the help of the tutelary deity. Here the tutelary deity is named '*Palavi deuta*'. The families of Mahajanas of Shree Manguesh have their separate *Palvi deutas*. Some families have Shree Mahalakshmi of Bandodem, others Shree Mhalsa of Mardol, and the remaining two families have Shree Aryadurga of Ankola (Karwar). Originally those deities were respectively from the villages of Colvem, Verna and Sancoale of Salcete taluka. Mahajans offer worship in those temples and are also considered as their Mahajanas.

The Satyavant Lad

Shree Mangesh of Cortalim (Kutthal) village was transferred in about 1568 A.D. The members of the village commune of (*Kutthal*) were of two (gotras) clans—Vatsa and Koudinya. The eldest family of the Vatsa gotra has been designated from old times as Satyavant Lad, while that of the Koudinya gotra as Satyavant Bhandari. What is the origin of these two surnames? Let us first consider the surname 'Satyavanta Lad'. Bharatiya Sanskriti Kosh (in Marathi) gives an account of the Lada Brahmins under the heading 'Latya Brahmana', but the information given there is somewhat incomplete. These Brahmins are also named Lada Bhrahmanas, and there are some Lada Goud Saraswat Brahmanas who, from Lata-desha, migrated to Usmanabad in Maharashtra state and from there due to the persecution by a Hindu king and later by the Muslims, had to migrate to Varhad (Barar), Nagpur and Khandesh and are considered at present as Dravida Brahmins! They continued their original profession as merchants which they practised in their original Lata-desha. At present there are no such Brahmins in that area. However, Marco Polo who visited India around 1280 A.D. refers in his work written in about 1300 A.D. to the Lada Brahmins residing in Lata-desh as truthful merchants, engaged in the commerce of diamonds, pearls etc. and travelling upto Kanyakumari by the sea-route for this purpose.

The expression 'Lada Goud Saraswat' conveys the original place of those Lada Brahmins, and it is clear that from those Brahmins some families came to settle in the areas of *Kuthal* and *Kelshi* villages. Now about the word 'Satyavanta'.

There is no evidence in history to suggest that 'Satyavanta' was an honorific title, gifted by a king, so the origin has to be searched for in a different way. We have already marked the route of migration of the Goud Saraswat Brahmins who had settled in the area of Mathura-Ujjein (an area which then was known as Satwant Pradesh) before migrating to Lata-desha.

It is said that Shatrugnha, brother of Shree Ramchandra had expelled the people called Satwat who had settled in Mathura. [12] p. 195.

From this evidence it is clear that the surname 'Satyavanta Lada' is a corrupted form of 'Satvant Lada'. When surnames did not exist, the Sanskrit form of designation was arrived at the following way: first the name of the kula, then the name of the original place, then the name of the father and lastly the proper name along with his epithet, Sharma, Varma, etc. based on the 'Varna' which denoted the caste. It is noticeable that in the Dravida Brahmins of South India the same form is used, for example, the name R. M. Krishnappa means Rudrapattanasya Mutannasunu Krishnappa (Krishnappa, son of Mutanna, from Rudrapattana village).

The eldest family of the Vatsa gotra which presided over the village-committee, maintained such designation as a surname, while the eldest family of the Koudinya gotra whose eldest member was the accountant-cum-treasurer and record-keeper (Kulkarni) changed over to Satwant Bhandari as the surname — Bhandari meaning treasurer. Both the posts came to be hereditary for thousands of years, but the designation changed during the period of kingship. This will be discussed in the next chapter.

Etimology of Daivadnya and Thavai

The families settled in *Kutthal* and *Kelsi* villages continued their main profession as merchants—a profession which continued for generations. At the time of migration (about 1,000 B.C.), besides Brahmins, Chaddes and Vaishyas, artisan families also migrated. According to historians, in that period the caste system was already established.

In the Vedas we find the names of Twasta, Ribhu, etc as prominent artisans. In Taitareya Samhita and Shatapatha Brahmana the name of Kashap is recorded as an eminent artisan. His book 'Kashapsamhita' is available, along with two others named 'Brigusamhita' and 'Mayasamhita'. Besides, there are 12 more Samhitas which are relatively modern and I have referred to them to trace the significance of some words in use in Goa.The 'Kashapsamhita' recognises four classes of technicians/artisans in which 'Daivadnya', meaning assistant to an engineer, is put in the second class. Their work was like that of a draughtsman or evaluator. Astrology began from this class, and astrologers are considered as 'Deivadnyas' [82] pp. 5, 43, and 45. There is no doubt that the word 'Daivadnya' means astrologer, but it is not known how the gold-smith caste of Goa call themselves 'Daivadnya Brahmins'. There is no reference that links the goldsmith profession to 'Daivadnya'.

Now let us examine the word 'Thavai' which in Konkani means carpenter. This word is derived from the word 'sthapati', which appears in the Mayasamhita and denotes a technician of the first class, meaning an engineer and all-round technician. Identical qualities are described in 'Sutradhara' ,which provides the word 'sutar', meaning also carpenter, in the Marathi language. The construction of sumptuous buildings like temples, palaces, etc. in Goa involved the use of carved laterite. However, we have exceptions in the form of the temple of Shree Mahadeva at Tamdi Surla of Sanguem Taluka and some columns of black stone in the old temple of Mhalsa at Verna village, Salcete taluka, and columns which were found lying at Old Goa—probably remnants of the palace of the Muslim rulers of Adilshahi. So, in Goa, 'thavai' was the most important class of technicians involved in building. After the advent of the Portuguese, this was substituted by the word 'mest', a corrupted form of the Portuguese word 'mestre', meaning a man with full knowledge (of a certain art or science). And so, we find in villages of the Old Conquests, that lands were granted to them by village communes. These gifts were known as 'Mestanchi nomos' (nomos, derived from the Sanskrit work namashya—gift not to be reverted, given to hold through generations), and in Portuguese referred to as 'Nomoxim dos carpinteiros'. Their *Purushas*—image of the original ancestor existing in some temples—were designed as *Mestancho Purush*. In those temples they are listed in respective statutes as Mahajanas, among others of different castes. However, in respect of goldsmiths we do not find their '*Purush*' in the temples, except in the temple of Mhalsa where Sonal Bheirava is one of the retinue deities and in the temple of Kolamba (recently named Kalika, which was under litigation between the Sonar also known as *Shet* (goldsmiths) and *Kansar* (coppersmiths), situated at Kansarpale and now considered exclusively of the goldsmiths).

We notice from the Portuguese records that generally in a village or in a small group of villages, blacksmiths, barbers, washermen and mhar families existed and village communes granted to these families some rice-fields for their subsistence. But all these families were linked to the temple of the main village-deity and were considered servants of that deity and not of the villagers, despite the fact that they were under the vigilance of the village-commune committee. Besides those lands named namashes, the elder of the family was entitled to a certain portion of paddy, conventionally fixed. These people are named in Marathi as "balutidars" and the paddy taken by them is called Balutem. In Konkani, despite the existence of that custom there is no distinct designation, though there is a measure—Maddea-podd—measuring about one litre used for distribution of the grain.

Besides, those village-artisans and servants, there were also some families considered as original settlers, and generally the elder of the eldest family is named *Zalmi*. He is entrusted with some annual rituals on the occasions of sowing and ripening of the paddy-fields and these rituals known generally as 'fudlik' consists of offering a cock to the kshetradeva (spirit god of the place). In these cases, though the rituals are conducted by a *Zalmi*, the flesh is used by the Satarkar or Naik family (in Ponda taluka for example). In Astagrahar area of Sanguem taluka, for example, the *Zalmi* of Gaonkars makes the rituals, but does not eat the flesh of cock, so it passes on to the Naik of that village.

This custom may have existed before the arrival of the second wave of Aryans, but it seems that with the introduction of worship of idols in temples, this custom might have been initiated.

CULTURAL IMPACT OF THE SECOND WAVE

Science, religion and the political system

Both these groups of Aryans had no check on the governing bodies of adjacent areas, so they were in Chandravadi with the right to put their ideas (expurgated from those in vogue in Northern India at the time when they left that area) into practice. The thoughts and actions obviously were according to the era of the Epic Age—or say, of the time of the Ramayana and Mahabharata. For details the readers may refer to the Epic Age described in the book 'History of India' by V. D. Mahajan.[40] Here I shall quote some portions of this book which are pertinent to show the reasons which impelled some changes in the system formerly established in Goa:

"Great sanctity was attached to cows and vegetarian food. At the beginning of the Epic period, the clothes of people were simple ones. There was very little of tailoring. The dress of a man consisted of two oblong pieces of cloth, one which was tied round the loins and the other round the body. When men appeared in public, they tied their turbans. Young people used coloured turbans and the old ones white turbans. The dress of women consisted of two oblong pieces of cloth, the lower piece of cloth was like a Sari and the Uttariya cloth was used for covering the head. Widows covered the heads with white cloth and married women used colourful cloth. Women put coloured powder on their heads. Ordinary cotton clothes were used by the people but occasionally, silken clothes were also used. The Kshatriyas kept long hair but the Brahmanas shaved their heads and their chins.

"Astronomy had made great progress in the country. The people had knowledge of the twelve Rashis. They had knowledge of the movements of the moon among the 27 Nakshatras. All astrological considerations were based upon the conjunction of the moon with Nakshatras."

"Religious conditions - Important changes took place in the religious field in the time of Epics. The Vedic gods were superseded by Brahma, Vishnu and Shiva (Mahesh). Indra, Surya and Varuna were relegated to the background. Gods and goddesses like Ganesh and Parvati became popular. The Avtara or the doctrine of various incarnations of Vishnu became popular. Rama and Krishna came to be worshipped as the incarnations of Vishnu."

"Political condition - During the period of the epics, there were a large number of states in India. The ordinary form of government was kingship but there were also republics. The king was not an autocrat. He was required to rule according to the principles of justice and morality. The people had the right to depose a wicked king. If a king in any way injured his subjects, the latter were allowed to kill him "like a mad dog". The king was required to consult the people on certain occasions. It was the duty of the king to respect the laws of the Pugas (village communities), Shrenis (guilds), Jatis (castes), kulas (clans), Janapadas (regions)".

Ancient Republics

"As regards the Republics, there were two kinds of them. There were individual republics and confederations of republics. The name for individual was Gana and the name for a confederation of republic was Samghatana. The great difficulty in the way of the successful working of a Gana was the lack of unity and every precaution had to be taken to avoid internal dissension. The same difficulty was found in the case of confederations of republics. We are told that republics of Yadavas, Kukuras, Bhojas, Andhakas and Vrishnis formed themselves into a confederation or Samgha and Lord Krishna was chosen as its President or samgha-Mukha. The heads of the various units of the confederation were called Ishvara. It is stated that there was rivalry going on among the party-leaders and Lord Krishna complained about the same. However, Narada asked Krishna to keep the confederation strong by removing the internal dissensions.

"Reference is made to various kings and nobles in the state and those were the Mantris or the members of the Cabinet, Amatyas, Sachivas, Parishadas, Sahayas, Dharmikas, Arthakarins etc. The various heads of the departments of the state were known as Mantri. Purohita, Chamupati, Dvarapala, Karagrahadhikari, Dravyasamchyakrit, Yuvaraja, Pradeshta, Nagaradhyaksha, Karyanirmanakrit, Durgapala, Atvipalaka, Rastrantpalaka, Sabhadyaksha and Dandapala."

"The Grama or village was the unit of administration, it was under a Grammani or head-man. Above the Gramani was Dashagrami, Vinshapati and Shatagrami of Granma-shatadhyaksha. These officers were in-charge of 10, 20 and 100 villages. Adhipati was in-charge of 1,000 villages. The money was collected by the different agencies but ultimately it was sent to the king."

"The state recognised the private ownership of land in the country and contented itself by claiming only one-sixth of the produce as land revenue. The mines were considered to be the property of the state and were worked departmentally. The people had the right to use jungles freely. The king was entitled to demand forced labour from the people once in a fortnight or 10 days. The Brahmanas learning the Vedas were exempted from taxes but those Brahmanas who were not learned the Vedas had to pay taxes. The taxes, on the whole, were not oppressive. The king was to be very careful about the finances of the state and attend to same daily. He was always to see that the income was more than the expenditure and there was always a large sum in the reserve fund."

"Justice was administrated by the king with the help of a minister and a council of the caste. Witnesses were examined by the parties. There was also the system of ordeals. Fines were imposed on the rich and the poor even thrown into prisons. The jurors were employed from the locality but there were no pleaders. The system of arbitration seems to have been popular. It was considered to be the sacred duty of the king to punish the wicked. It was sinful to accept bribes. The offence of theft was punished with great severity."

"The army was regularly paid and every soldier got both in cash and in kind. The commander-in-chief was in-charge of the whole army. The foot-soldiers were armed with a sword or a spear. Strong-bodied persons used the "gadha" or mace. The use of armour was common. Archery reached the zenith of its glory. Warriors fought to the music of drums, Nadyas and Mridangas. It was the age of chivalry. Fighting was the duty of the Kshatriyas and it was most shameful to run away from the battlefield. He who died in the battlefield went straight to heaven. A warrior was not to fight a woman or a person resembling a woman. A person who was wounded or who fell in the battle-field, was not to be attacked. However, the destruction of the country of the enemy by fire was considered to be legitimate".

This is the summary of the cultural trend, mainly of the people of the Kshatriya caste of the second wave of Aryans. It was constituted mainly of Bhojas and Chediyas. The Bhojas had their tradition of Oligarchic republic while the people from Chedi had witnessed only a constitutional monarchy. (The reader may note that Shishupala, enemy of Krishna, was a king of Chedi), but in respect of land, both the groups had a common idea—that of exclusive existence of private-ownership of land. The idea basically was against that of the people of adjacent areas like Salcete and Ponda (then Antruz) talukas. But the Saraswat Brahmin family which had accompanied them might have convinced the Kshatriyas to bring the land under cultivation, as well as to continue to cultivate the lands already brought under cultivation in a cooperative manner—all the families working for it and the net produce being dis-tributed to all. The members of all castes were direct cultivators. The Saraswat fam-ily was of only one gotra, and its members must have been numerous, so their branches were established in the principal villages along with the members of the Kshatriya families. Later on, cooperative farming was abandoned as lands were dis-tributed, creating private ownership by such families. This is what I have gathered from the traditional history of Chandravadi (now Quepem) taluka. Obviously very soon after the settlements, the administrative set-up was fixed village-wise, and kingship was established with headquarters at Amonem (*Amone*), which had also been the headquarters of the Satarkars.

SETTLERS FROM DECCAN PLATEAU

Stela of Rangachem-mol

We do not know the cause of the migration of people from the Deccan Plateau to Goa. They entered Pednem and Sattari talukas, but the exact time cannot be deter-mined due to lack of evidence. Presumably, these people settled in Goa about the beginning of the Christian Era. In respect of the invasion of these people there is not only a legend but a stela commemorating that invasion. *(see ill. 8, Pg. 65 of Chapter 3)*. This stela was probably carved during the time of Vantuvallabha Senanandaraja of the Sendraka (Sinda) clan, ruler of Goa and maternal uncle of Pulakeshin II (610-

642 A.D.). The carving, in bas-relief was found at Rangachem-mol of Naneli village in Sattari taluka. The stela shows four portions, and starting from the bottom to the top, the pictures are as follow:

The first shows a person standing with a type of mace held erect in his right hand, with another person behind him. Both wear simple turbans, and at the feet of the first person a man is seen lying on the ground. Nearby there is a fire, and at the right of that fire some persons are shown beating drums. This scene represents the slaying of the headman of the original settlers (Satarkars). The second picture (on the second step) shows two persons (the same as above) in an erect posture and two women are seen seated. The first woman is offering "Shela" to one of the two persons. This scene indicates that the wife of the principal person is honouring him for his victory over the original ruler. The third step depicts a scene showing the back of a couple standing together, with an arm around each others shoulders. At the right, there are some persons standing, looking at the couple with either sorrowful or astonished faces. The scene means that the principal person has died and his wife has immolated herself on the pyre. Lastly, on the top, there is a Shiva-linga which means that the couple, after death, went to heaven—Shivaloka. The Shiva-linga represents an amalgamation of male and female elements i.e. the couple in heaven.

At about a kilometre east of this site, is found a memorial in the form of a round oblong slab, vertically placed, and about two mts. in height on the bank of a rivulet, which is named 'Sati'. Obviously this was the place of immolation of that woman. Similar kinds of memorials are found in different areas of the Deccan Plateau, which surely represents the ancient form of a memorial to sati.

This stela, along with other plates of deities, was found when a bulldozer of a drug-manufacturing company was levelling the soil. The fact came to my notice in the year 1979. But long before, in 1943-44, while working for a cadastral survey of this area, I had heard a legend, recounted below, from villagers about this incident which now stands confirmed subsequent to the discovery of the stela.

The legend of the subjugation of Hebars

Long long ago, Maratha families came down from the Ghats to settle on the plains, but the original settlers would not allow them. At that time the area of Satari taluka was occupied by the Hebars, and their chief lived at Rivem village in a castle built of mud and stones, the walls being about four-and-a-half metres in height. There was only one entrance and it was formed of two folds of very thick timber. There were three thick cross bars of timber placed at three different points along the length of the door. The weight of the folds was so great that to close and open them, two persons were needed and the sound could be heard a long distance away in many surrounding villages as the closing of the door was done soon after sunset. In the castle there was a big residential house of the family of the headman. There were also some houses of his dependents, besides cow-sheds. The constructions were of mud and stone and the roofs were covered with straw, grass and jungle-palm leaves.

The Deccani people were waiting for a proper occasion to attack the Hebars, and soon found it. There was a wedding ceremony of a member of the headman, and the Deccani people, seizing this opportunity, collected dry grass and kept the bundles dispersed in the forest area around that castle. This was done with utmost secrecy. The wedding ceremony was in the house of the chief of the Hebaras. Obviously, all the headmen of the village of Sattari taluka with their families were present in the castle. All the male members were drunk. When the ceremony ended, the guests retired to their dormitories. The doors of the castle were closed. When the sound was heard by the Deccani people, they collected in groups and brought the bundles of dry grass and piled them outside the walls. Some ladders of bamboo were also ready. With the use of a '*chakmak*' (a flint and steel piece to strike fire), bundles of grass were set on fire and the attackers on ladders threw these in the castle. The roofs caught fire. The residents and wedding guests woke up but many were drunk. Some tried to open the door, only for about ten Deccani males to strike them dead with maces and other weapons. Not a single Hebar, male, female or child, got out alive. Thus, the Hebars were subjugated in their headquarters. Now the Deccani people slowly occupied the villages, and the Heberas from other areas ran away. Their dependents stayed on in the villages and were afterwards named 'Naik'. Now these members of Deccani families took the designation of Gaonkars. The members of one family took kingship while other families occupied the adjacent seven villages. So, they are considered a brotherhood and that is the reason why they cannot marry inter se.

Soon, another family appeared from the Deccan Plateau and occupied the villages of Zorme, Poriem and Surla. They also had links with other nine villages which now are in Belgaum district. Hebars is a corruption of the word Shabara, but they were of the Kol tribe as can be seen by the name given to the semi-gods established in Mundalgireache-mol at Thanem hamlet of Dongurli village. Later, the Deccani people erected idols and though the exact nature of these symbols is not known, they were named Kolgiro and Mundal-giro. Kolgiro means the devourer of Kols, and Muldal-giro, devourer of the Mundari, the first is considered to be the king and the second his chief minister (Pradhan). At that time horse ridding was in vogue. So the images were shown on horseback in the form of crude carvings. Later carvings show a metallic helmet, "Mukuta", perhaps a head-dress worn at the time of Vantuvallabha Senanandaraja. The existence of two male persons as promoters—one principal and other as adjunct—represented in the stela found at Rangachem-mol, tallies with these two idols and provides clear evidence of my exposition.

The adoption of local customs

The Maratha people had absolutely no idea of the administrative system in the talukas of the Old Conquests, Ponda (Antruz) and Chandravadi taluka. They continued their administrative system which was in use at that time in the areas of the Deccan Plateau. However, the Deccani people adopted some customs and religious rites of the earlier Satarkars. This included the village deity Santer, under the same name or similar names like Bhumika and Mavuli, as well as the village administration system. Each village had its boundaries fixed and the council of elders with the help of other members of gaonkars resolved and even today resolve litigations and appeals. The decision is final but formal confirmation is required from the elder member of the eldest branch of Mokasdar of the villages under his jurisdiction.

A village council meeting

There is an interesting case of the village Zormem, which does not fall in the jurisdiction of any Mokasdar. This village lies on the slope of the mountain Vagheri of Sattari taluka as the plain area is too small, with only one well at a corner of the hamlet. Due to scacity of water some use water from a spring. There is no way for expanding the houses already constructed, and to construct a new house was a great problem, not only because the construction involved excavation of the slope but the water source would be at a great distance. The married young persons had to sleep along with the old folk, and by the mutual consent of brothers and cousins, some were taking recourse to their residential houses for a few hours at night. I had noticed this fact in the year 1937 when I visited the village in connection with aerophotogrametric topographic maps.

One day, in the morning, I heard a Naik shouting '*Meleak yeare*' ('Come for the gathering', *melo* meaning gathering). The Gaonkars started assembling in the open place in front of my residence. There was a bench where three persons were seated— the elders of the three main families. The Gaonkars sat on the ground and the *Bhavina* (unmarried maid-servant of the temple) sat in one corner away from the seated group of Gaonkars. The Fousdar of the village, a reporter nominated by the Military Commander of Sattari taluka, with more powers than a simple administrator (now mamlatdar) was present. Though a Gaonkar, the founder has no right to speak. His job was to maintain order and peace in the meeting, under the direction of the President. The president consulted both elders and ordered the claimant who stood up and narrated the claim. Then the President ordered the defendant to speak. Then he asked for evidence. First he heard the testimonials of the claimant, and afterwards of the defendant. The President made up his mind but looked at the *Bhavina*, who seemed distressed. The President realized that *the Bhavina* knew about the case.

He consulted the two elders and ordered *the Bhavina* to disclose whatever she knew. At first she expressed her hesitation but after much persuasion by the President she asked permission of the gaonkars assembled, declaring that she would refuse to give information if even one 'no' was heard from the gathering. She began her narrative with:

"My grandmother told my mother and my mother told me, and based on that information I give my statement solemnly as if it is being given before Santermaya (Santer is the main deity of that village)". For the President this narrative was new but some aged Gaonkars were convinced of her story. Her eyes were focussed on the ground. She completed her long narrative. There were points of mortgage, its payment, change of residence of a family, and several other details. When she finished her narrative, the President asked her: 'Then who is the owner of the house, according to you'? She replied: 'It is for the Gaonkars to decide. I should not interfere in the resolution of the Gaonkars. I am a servant of the village'. Then some Gaonkars sought some explanation from her, which she gave, gazing fixedly at the soil. Now, it was the time to pass a resolution. The President consulted both the elders and they agreed to his decision. He then declared that 'the house belonged neither to the claimant nor to the defendant; it belonged to a person who lived in one room of that house with his children. It is up to him to accept one of the litigants in his house for residential purpose. However, it is my advise to both of you to start constructing new houses right now, because the children of that gaonkar will grow up and they will require the whole house. The assembly is closed'. And saying so he stood up, the other elders also rose and the *Bhavina* went to the temple of Shree Santer. The true owner had tears in his eyes. I have described this account at such length to demonstrate how a village assembly used to resolve issues in the past. This account also shows that the *Bhavina* had narrated the history of about sixty years beginning with the construction of that house. In that sense, she was the true bard and record-keeper of the village.

The monolithic monuments of Kols and Mundaris

At this stage I am reminded of the procedures at Thanem. The place where Kolgiro and Mundalgiro are placed is named Mundalgireachem-mol. The people make vows and pay to the Mundalgiro (Mundalgiro is Pradhan, the Minister, and Kolgiro the King). They say that Mundalgiro makes promises after taking due consent from Kolgiro. The fact remains that all sacrifices and offerings are made to the Mundalgiro.

In 1937, I saw near the temple of Santer some columns of black stone of about a metre in height. The villagers consider them to be gods of Hebars, classifying them as Rakshas—devourers of human flesh. I presume, as mentioned before, that they must have been Khaminrouduro and Ganarouduro like in Savoi-Verem. But there are also about six more of them. At that time I could not make up my mind, but I think those other columns may be deities of a lower stage. All those deities are probably of Asuras or Asur Mundas. Later on the Satarkars captured that area, expelled the Asuras and established their deity Sater, and when the Deccani people expelled the Santarkars they appropriated that deity, and much later in about the 7th century A.D., imitated the Matrika worship. This in good iconic form can be seen from the carvings of different deities like Brahmani (ill. no. 27 p. 244), Gaja-Laxmi (ill no. 28 p.246), etc. found unearthed at Naneli village. But in Zarme those deities are represented only by natural black round stone placed on plinths made of mud. They are under different names of Matrikas, and the villagers even arranged hunting programme named 'Devachi Bhoundi', and the game was brought near those temples. Lard was offered to all the Matrikas, except to Brahmani because she is considered to be strictly vegetarian as her name was Brahmani. So, even though the change of rituals took place, the worship of deities in the form of simple blackstones, like those of the Asura mundas, continued. I am not in a position to check the real position of those eight column-stones considered to be of Hebaras, but I suspect that, excluding two which are near the temple of Shree Santer and considered to be the deities of Satarkars (Kols), the remaining six columns may be representatives of the ancestors of the Kols and Mundaris or may be monolithic memories of the tribes, like the Hero stones found in Karnatak and the Deccan Plateau.

THE SETTLEMENTS IN HEMADBARCEM (SANGUEM)

The Deccani people, after occupying the area of Sattari taluka, went on to occupy the Hemadbarcem division of Sanguem as well as a part of Bicholim taluka, expelling the Satarkar families, but sparing the Mundari tribe and naming them as Naik. They accepted the deities like the Santer of the Satarkars and gave her names like Bhumika and Mauli in some villages. They also introduced deities of their original place like Jogayi, Layirayia, etc. After some centuries, certain families of the Chaddes also migrated to Sattari areas. This is how we find *Chaddo Purush* in Pariem village and Gaonkars of Pissurlem village of Chaddo caste, both villages being in Sattari taluka.

The leader of the Maratha expedition was a Sendraka family of high status and could not obviously administer all the area occupied by the Deccani people. So, he probably bought some families from their original place and established one at Surla of Hemadbarcem which is now known as Surlakar Desai and others at Kudnem village, Dicholi taluka. But at present their descendants are unknown. At this place the images of Uma-Mahesha and of Kudneshwara of the time of the Chalukyas (7th century A.D.) were found. Both these families ruled independently, admitting the supremacy of the Sendraka ruler, as no conflict has been recorded in the annals of traditional history. There is in Calem village a family of Kalekar Desai, which I presume to be a branch of the Surlakar Desai family, or perhaps of a different family, but installed there probably in the same period when the Surlakar Desai clan was put up there or a little later.

The Sendraka family had two separate branches which ruled, upto the 10th century A.D., the area of the northern border of Goa. They are known as Parmikar Desai and Usapkar Desai. Recently a copper-plate was found in Pednem taluka which appears to be issued by a member of one of these families. According to traditional history, the Sendrak family of Sattari now known as 'Bivamrao Desai' cannot have matrimonial links with those two families who are considered to be of the same brotherhood.

Evolution of the script

I have already referred to two words carved on a rock in a genuine Sumerian cuneiform script meaning 'Dwadasha-gana' (*Barazan* in Konkani) found at Savoi-Verem village of Ponda taluka. This is of very great importance not only in the history of Goa but also that of India.

Even though the sign found consists of only two words, it is sufficient to prove with the help of other finds that about 2,000 B.C. the Sumerian cuneiform script was introduced in Goa. The two signs of the Sumerian cuneiform script are in syllabic form but we do not have evidence as to the time when this syllabic script was transformed into an alphabetic one. This script is known as 'Goen-Kandi' or 'Kandevi script' and Kandeva appears to be the name of a Havig Brahmin who delineated the line of the water-channel named 'Ramanathacho-pat' which starts from the bank of the river on which every year an embankment is constructed at a place named 'Kandevacho-pantho' at Kurpem village, Astragrahar division, Sanguem taluka. From the historical records of the Chalukya (Badami) dynasty it is seen that king Vijayaditya II (693-733 A.D.) had granted in the year 708 A. D. the village Colomba of Astragrahar to eight Brahmins of Bharadwaja, Koushika, Kondinya, Moudagalha, Atreya, Kashypa and Vatsa gotras. It is important to note that the name of the person of the Vatsa gotra was Dasavarma (and not Sharma or Sharman). [85] pp. 179-180. So, they were Brahmins and Kandeva probably was a son of one of these families, thus this intelligent person in about 730 A.D. might have brought about the change in the script to make it suitable for rapid writing—the alphabetic Goen-Kandi script. Before him the cuneiform Sumerian syllabic script must have taken the alphabetic form after a few centuries of the arrival of the Saraswat Brahmins, who, as merchants by profession, were using another script which was in use in their original place.

As the Goen-Kandi script differs from the current Kannad script, some writers call it Halle-Kannad (Old Kannad), but there is no reason to accept this view. What might have possibly happened is that the script so styled by Kandeva might have been introduced by the Having Brahmins who had also established themselves in the area named Nagara-Khand in Karnataka. At present, they are found in the Sirsi area of Karnataka. About their settlement in Goa, we will make appropriate reference to it in the next chapter as they appear after the rise of kingship in Goa. The style of that script continued even upto 80 years ago in Tiswadi taluka. There are many records of accounts written in that script in the temple of Shree Mangesh of Priol and old records of many village-communes in the beginning of the Portuguese domain in Salcete taluka are found written in that script, the language being a curious mix of Konkani-Marathi and even Portuguese words.

The art of writing

Shobhana Gokhle has written a well researched book in Marathi on the Epigraphy and Palaeography of India [85]. It begins with a review of the Vedic Age. The book refers to different forms of material used for recording. Here I refer to a particular form of recording when paper was either not available, or the people wanted to economize. The records of the village commune whenever they referred to permanent resolutions, were prepared on cloth and maintained in safety, as the Bhurjaepatra or Tadapatra in use was outside Goa and not available here. For recording the accounts of village communes and letters use was being made largely of tender leaves of banana-trees. Pieces of those leaves were cut and kept on flat soil in the shade for slow drying. The corners of the pieces were kept under the pressure of stones. When dry, those pieces became flat and were given a rectangular shape and proper size for inserting them in a carved wooden plank, the carved having room generally for six leaves. The ink in use was made of a decoction of the juice of banana-flowers and black betel leaves mixed with triphala-churna (powder of areca-nut, gall-nut and yellow myrobalan). The mixture was then bottled. Black of oil-lamp (*kajal*) was kept separately in another bottle. At the time of writing, a mixture was prepared of the two in such proportion that the colour would be dark black. Writing was done with a wooden pen, generally of hard bamboo. These leaves were kept for some hours in the shade. Thereafter the leaves were inserted in the hollow plank and covered with another plank of the same size and tied with a rope of cloth. Then this wooden box was inserted in a bag of cloth with a shoulder strap like a postman's bag. A messenger would carry this to the indicated house.

SUMMARY

The first wave of Aryans came and settled in Goa in about 2,400 B.C. They came with the ideas of the Rigvedic Age. In about 2,000 B.C. people from Sumer appeared and introduced their way of life with the result that the ownership of village land remained vested in the main village-deity; co-operative farming turned into a common holding of villagers who were considered to be founders of the village-commune and its administration took a form of olegarchic democracy. The Aryans of the first wave accepted this type of administration and improved and applied basically the same method for administration at the taluka level, in the area occupied by them or say in Salcete, Tiswadi and Bardez talukas. There is no such evidence in Ponda (Antruz) taluka which was at that time exclusively under the hegemony of the Sumerian people, mainly the Paddye Brahmins.

After the arrival of the second wave of Aryans in about 700 B.C., if not earlier, no noticeable change took place in the areas of the talukas, where they settled along with the Aryans of the first wave. This second wave consisted of Bhojas, Chediyas—both Kshatriyas and Sarawat Brahmins, the last having migrated from Lata (South Gujarat) by the sea route.

Some families of Kshatriyas wanted a degree of independence like some Paddye families who migrated to Antruz area and selected the areas adjacent to Salcete taluka, which was named later as Chandravadi (now Quepem taluka). They moved there with a large family of the second wave, of the Koushika gotra already settled in Quelossim (Kelshi) village. The Kshatriya-Bhojas and Chediyas, named together as Chaddes, expelled the Satarkars who fled to the south up to the village of Rivona in Sanguem taluka and occupied the villages and established their headquarters at Amonem village. They, however, kept the Mundari tribe as well as other families of the original pastoral tribe in their service. They established the system of kingship under the hegemony of the Bhojas, which is the first kingship to appear in the area of Goa in about 600 B.C. However, the village-administration system of adjacent Salcete taluka was adopted with slight modifications. In the beginning of the occupation the three main clans held common ownership of the land and cooperative farming was practiced, the net income being equally distributed among those three subgroups, but later on, the lands were distributed among those three member-clans, while the forest and pasture lands, villagewise, were kept under common ownership.

The areas of Kudal and later on of Pednem and Bardez talukas were occupied by the families of the second wave of Aryans consisting of Saraswats who had arrived there by the land route. They continued with the system of private ownership of the lands. Later, around the beginning of the Christian Era, the people from Deccan Plateau appeared and settled there and entered the local administration. However, there is no clear evidence as to whether these people gained hegemony or equal status as compared to the Brahmins who had settled earlier.

In Sattari taluka, the people from the Deccan Plateau came from the Western Ghats, about the beginning of the Christian Era. They entered through Rivem village, attacked the Satarkars who had occupied that area and expelled them. The leader of these people was a member of a family known as Sendraka who had already settled in the area of the Western Ghats known at that time as Kuntala. This leader came to be ruler and later on his descendants became kings. The expansion of these people continued in Hemadbarcem division of Sanguem taluka and in a part of Bicholim (Dicholi) taluka. As occupation progressed, the ruler brought families of his matrimonial relations from their original home and established headquarters at Surla of Sanguem and Kudnem of Bicholim (Dicholi) talukas. It is possible also that another family might have settled at Colem village of Hemadbarcem. It appears that those families ruled their respective zones independently, admitting nominal sovereignty of the Sendraka family. After some centuries, may be around the 9th century A.D., two branches of the Sendraka family migrated to the northern border of Goa and are presently known respectively as Parmekar Desai and Usapkar Desai. The main family of Sendraka is known at present as Bivamrao Desai and they live at Thanem and Dongurli villages. The tradition among these three families continues to be of brotherhood and they cannot have matrimonial links inter se.

Now in respect of the Goen-Kandi or Kandevi script, with the advent of the people from Sumer (especially the ruling families known as Paddye Bhatts), the cuneiform script was introduced in Goa. The script was syllabic, but afterwards came to be alphabetic. The period of this transformation is now known. Later on in 8th century A.D. the writing style was changed to Goen-Kandi (Modi) and this was in use up to 80 years ago, the Devanagari (Balboth and Modi) existing side by side.

201

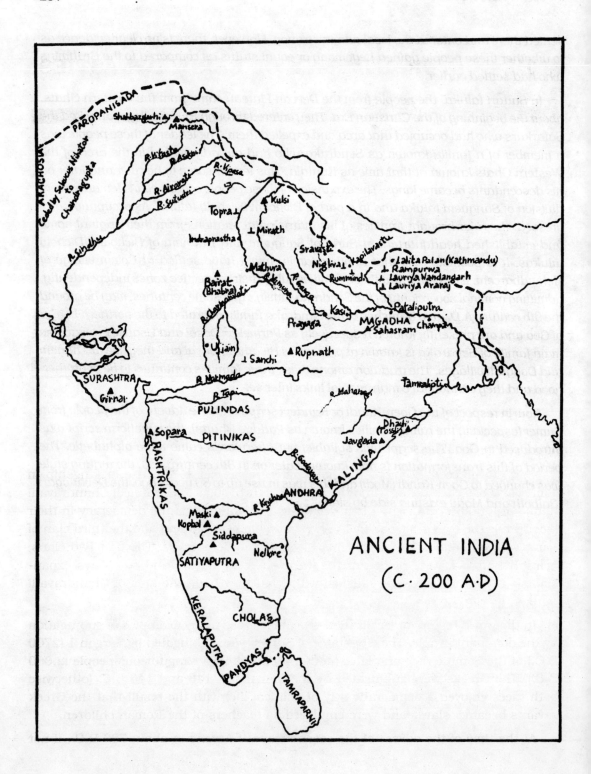

ANCIENT INDIA
(C. 200 A.D)

Chapter - 6
THE CULTURAL IMPACT OF EARLY DYNASTIES

INTRODUCTION

The early inscriptions

In the preceeding chapter, I have made references to the rise of kingship in some parts of Goa, starting with the kingship of the Bhojas in the area of Chandravadi taluka around 600 B.C. The Bhojas had the seeds of aristocratic democracy in their blood while the Chediyas an absolutely monarchic bent of mind and the third clan of Saraswat Brahmins were proponents of oligarchic democracy. The first two clans, being Kshatriyas, were belligerent or warrior-like by nature and so always expansionist. They could never be satisfied with what they had—the area of Chandravadi taluka.

In the world history of civilization we come across many examples of subjugation by the dominant people. The city-states of Sumer were subjugated by Sargon 1 (2700 B.C.) of the Semitic race and later on by the Amorites, a sanguineous people (2,000 B.C.). The Greeks were subjugated by the Romans in 148 and 146 B.C. (otherwise both races enjoyed a democratic way of political life) with the result that the Greek savants became slaves and were employed as teachers of the Roman children.

At the time of the advent of the second wave of Aryans in about 700 B.C., if not earlier, the village-committee used to appoint some watchmen, *talls* in Konkani, to guard not only the crops but also to police for thefts, adultery and various conflicts. But they never thought about raising a permanent army as there was no reason to suspect invasion. The most important factor was the demarcation of village-boundaries, but these were already fixed since time immemorial or say by the original settlers. Besides, annual checking involved in the religious rituals in the month of Pousha in some villages of Antruz taluka and in the month of Falgun in other areas saw to it that no conflicts arose. In certain doubtful cases the signs of *Surya-Chandra* (Sun and Moon) were carved together (round representing the Sun and the quarter crescent the Moon)—indicating that the boundary would last till the Sun and Moon continued to shine—Yawash Chandra Divakarou—in Sanskrit) on the rocks, which can still be seen in certain village boundaries of Surla of Ponda taluka and Virdi of Bicholim taluka. But the Chaddes in Chandravadi taluka maintained an army (to which they were accustomed) obviously with weapons in use at that time. They probably hired existing village artisans and perhaps might have brought skilfull ones from adjacent villages. And step by step they increased their sway, first on the adjacent Salcete taluka, later on the Antruz taluka, and so on. This has been proved by the six copper plates of the Bhoja dynasty which are considered to be from the 4th to 6th century A.D. Now we shall scrutinize each of those copper plates to ascertain the kind of administration practised by that dynasty, as also other aspects dealing with the socio-economic conditions of the time.

Goa under Mauryan empire—an assumption

Let me first clarify certain points raised by some writers. Historians like Dr. Gune mistakenly think [18] p. 65, that the Bhojas referred to it in the edicts of the great Mauryan Emperor Ashok are those who had settled down in the semi-independent kingdom on the southern border of the empire comprising the Deccan and the Konkan coast. The Bhojas referred to it in the edicts of Vidarbha [18] p. 102. One of the edicts of Ashok refers to the land named 'Aparanta' as located on the border of his empire, but this area is the same which lies between the Tapti and Vashisthi— rivers very far to the north of Goa (ibid) p. 102. So, we can surely conclude that the Ashokan empire did not include Goa nor was it ever under its sovereignty.

Satavahana rule in Goa—an assumption

Let us now consider the Satavahanas rule. Dr. Gune considers, (vide the same articles) citing the Maharashtra State gazetteer (history), that Krishna, the brother of Simuka (C. 200 B.C.), had subdued the Bhojas of Goa, but this affirmation is baseless, and there is no evidence in this respect. Moreover, the Satavahana empire was bounded (and not included) by Konkan territory. It was only at the time of Gautamiputra

Satakarni, following the defeat of Nahapana Satrapa (C. 125 A.D.) that the Aparanta (northern Konkan) passed to the domain of Satavahan but it did not include Goa. [86] p. 27. However, we find some words in use in Goa similar to those found in the book 'Gatha Saptashati' (Sattashayi) [85] in the Prakrit language compiled by Hala Satavahana. These words are Tattill (*Tall* in Konkani) meaning watchmen; Wodahi (*Wodavi* in Konkani) meaning a girl who has not attained puberty (Kumari in Marathi); Dhuwa, derived from the Sanskrit word Duhita (*Dhuv* in Konkani), meaning daughter, and Gahawayi derived from Grihapati (*Gharkar* in Konkani) meaning head of household, husband [86a]. According to Joglekar, Hala Satavahana reigned about 43 A.D. and Gautamiputra Satakarni, about 76 A.D. Admitting the new dating of the last king as about 125 A.D. fixed by Dr Mirashi and the difference of 33 years between those two kings, the new dating of Hala may be C. 92 A.D. But the existence of similar words in the Konkani language does not constitute any evidence of supremacy of the Satavahanas on Goa. It may only prove that Konkani and Prakrit are sister languages.

The correct dating of copper-plates of 'Devaraja Bhoja'

Dr. Gune also refers to the Kshatrapas, Abhiras, Trikutas and Kalachuris, but in fact these families have absolute no link with the history of Goa. But he has omitted the Chuttu family of southern Kanara which is mentioned in passing by late G. A. Pereira [87] p. 16 and 20, while describing the content of the copper-plate of Devaraja of the Bhoja dynasty, he refers to the expression meaning "the twelfth year of the victorious and prosperous reign" and says, "king Devarajah hadn't to face any serious encounter with other chiefs in the neighbourhood. It is in this context that his reign is referred to as 'victorious' even if he had some rivals he must have routed them".

From this expression on the inscription it is clear that Devaraja was in conflict with some people or king and he had defeated them. Historians have closed their eyes to the presence of that expression, but it is possible to clarify this point based on the information obtained from the above mentioned book of Dr. Mirashi. [86]

Dr. Mirashi says [86] pp. 36 & 42, that after Shak Satkarni of the Satavahan dynasty, the Konkan area was under the domain of Vinhukad of the Chuttu family who governed from Vanavasi (Badami) of North Kanara. Its evidence is found in the form of inscriptions at Vanavasi and at Kanheri (near Bombay). At the same time the Khatri who was of a family named 'Kur' occupied Western Maharashtra. A king named Beliokuras has been mentioned by the Greek geographer Ptolemy (C. 140 A.D.) (ibid) p. 40. Dr. Mirashi says that after a few years, Vanavasi city was occupied by the Kadambas, putting an end to the Chuttu dynasty. So, from this evidence it can be inferred that the Chuttu king had invaded Goa territory and Devaraja had expelled him. Dr. Mirashi mentions only two names of kings of the Chuttu dynasty (otherwise considered to be a branch of the Satavahanas) in Vanavasi. So, if we consider that they held sway on Goa may be for 50 years, it must have ended about 190 B.C. The time of the defeat by Devaraja must be during this period 140-190 A.D. So the copper plates of Devaraja must be of the 2nd or of the beginning of the third century A.D. and not of the 4th century A.D. as some writers tend to believe.

Titles in vogue during the Bhoja dynasty

It is possible that during the time of the Chuttus some families of North Kanara might have come and settled in the areas of Salcete like Cuncolim (*Kunkalli*), *Balli* and in Canacona (*Kankon*) talukas. They might have accepted the kingship of the Bhojas, establishing the village-wise administration under their hegemony. On the other hand, it appears that many centuries before Devaraja, the Bhojas of Goa expanded their dominion out of Chandravadi to Salcete, Tiswadi, Bardez and Ponda (Antruz) talukas, without interfering in the ancient village and taluka administration. They only imposed an annual tribute on each taluka, which was distributed among the villagers, under the name 'Bhojika', for the purpose of administrative expenses, covering the collection of revenue and for the maintenance of a permanent army for defence purposes. The taluka administrative body (of communes) accepted this without hesitation, since there was the need for defence against any invasion. Later on during the Kadamba dynasty (980 A.D.—1355 A.D.), the second innovation was that they fixed customs duty. The third innovation was that in the village-commune, areas of undeveloped village administration like in Antruz taluka, the ownership of the uncultivated lands, forest and pasture lands was vested in the State—so practically in the hands of the king. The fourth innovation was that the headman of the village, whatever be his caste was named 'Bhojak' (a petty chieftain) so he was made an aristocrat, and was given direct connection to the Bhoja king to execute orders without the necessity of going through the previously established channel of the taluka-committee. After the Bhojas it appears that the old system was re-established with the surname as 'Prabhu'; he was the former '*Mhalgado*' or representative of the main village in the taluka committee. Those persons or say the '*Bhojakas*' and 'Prabhus' might also occupy official posts in the central administration, without prejudice to their original posts which were hereditary. It is not known what was the percentage of the 'Bhojika' as well as of customs duty, and we cannot make any affirmation in this respect due to lack of evidence.

It is noticeable that the designations of posts of the Bhoja time do not appear in the administration of the Satavahanas; so this is yet more proof that Satavahana rule, direct or indirect, did not exist on the area of Goa or say on the Bhoja kingdom. Shaka era (Shalivhana Shaka) was unknown both to the Satavahanas and Bhojas which was introduced by the Western Kshatrapas in the Southern India. Dr. Mirashi (86) p. 128, regarding the social position of the time of the Satavahanas, considers that Apastamba-Dharmasutras (3rd to 5th century B.C.) might have been in use in the Deccan and Andhra territories. One of the most curious rules followed by those theological rulers was that the adoption of a boy as son was not acceptable because it represents a kind of purchase, meaning that one could instead get a child with contact of a man other than the rightful husband! This kind of concept never existed in Goa, so it is clear that the people of Goa continued with their own customs which existed at the time of migration.

COPPER PLATES OF THE BHOJA DYNASTY

After the bird's eye-view description of the administrative form, I pass now to scrutinize each of the copper-plates of the Bhoja kings.

I - Devaraja—Shiroda copper-plate

This copper-plate formed of three pieces was found by the historian the late Dr. P. S. Pissurlenkar in the possession of Gopal Sinai Gude of Shiroda (Ponda taluka). He collected it from him with the promise that it would be returned after use. At the request of Dr. Pissurlekar, C. R. Krishnamacharlu an eminent historian came in 1933, to his residence at Fontainhas (*Mala*) hamlet, Panaji. Dr. Pissurlekar lived there with his parents. I also lived there as Dr. Pissurlekar was my maternal uncle. As soon as he arrived, he began the work of clearing the copper-plate by himself for a couple of days. Satisfied that he could decipher them, he went with Dr. Pissurlekar to a local photographer and took several pictures. Besides, he made many prints using ink with his own hands. The next day he left with those prints and photographs. Dr. Pissurlekar went personally to Shiroda and returned the copper-plate to Gude. I have to emphasize here that Krishnamacharlu, despite being an officer of high rank, personally did the work of cleaning the copper-plates. He was in fact an eminent scholar [88].

Interpreting the copper-plate

The copper-plate was issued from Chandraura (not Chandrapura), present Chandor village of Salcete taluka on the verbal order of Devaraja of the Bhoja family. It makes it known to the Bhojaka, Ayuktak, Gramiya etc. that Devaraja had sanctioned the gifts made by Prabhu Naga Bhojikamatya to two Brahmins of the Bharadwaja gotra named Govindaswami and Indraswami in the area of Thaniyark of Kottika of Jiyaya (Vishya?). The gifts are in the form of a piece of land for the household and another piece for grazing cattle (including the right not only to grass but also to wood). Some historians say that the gift also included the right to the tolls (custom duty) due to the State, but I could not find any evidence of this. The place Thaniyark or in Konkani 'Thanear' was situated in *Kutti* village, Ponda taluka which during about 1792 A.D. was a custom-post. Upto this year the collection of custom-duty was being auctioned [89]; and this system continued in the Portuguese time upto the 19th century A.D. when the auction system was abolished and a special Government office was established with necessary staff to collect customs duties directly.

For nearly a century the contract was operated by the Dhume family whose main house was in *Kumbharjuwem* village (Tiswadi taluka) and one member of this family resided at *Thanear*. This family was the contractor for such collections not only in the area under Portuguese domain, but also parts of the domain of the ruler of Soundhem as well as in the areas of Bicholim and Pednem taluka of the kingdom of Savantwadkar Bhounsule.

Later, the contract passed into the hands of Punda-Kamat of *Panwel* (presently Ribandar), and the house abandoned by the Dhume family went to the Kaisare family who were their assistants, through generations. It is remarkable that the annual procession of Shree Vithal of *Kutti* (in Portuguese, Curti) starts with the *palkhi* being taken to that house. It is possible that the temple of Shree Vithal was established by the merchant class and they might have established such a privilege. Some historians consider the gifted lands were from the village Cortalim (*Kutthal*) (Salcete taluka) which is wrong as Cortalim (*Kutthal*) village was a village-commune of Brahmins and named 'Senawayi', a corrupted form of Shrenipati, or say merchants by profession and there could be no person with the 'Prabhu' epithet to make the grant.

Scrutiny of the inscription

This is the most ancient copper-plate found in respect of the area of Goa and the characters of the inscription belong to an archaic variety, and though mainly in Sanskrit there are, here and there, expressions in Prakrit.

The inscription is dated in the twelfth year of the victorious and prosperous reign of King Devarajah, on the twelfth (*dwadashi*) day of the dark fortnight (*Krishna paksh*) of the month of Magha.

It was issued from Chandraura. From the word Chandraura, it is clear that during that time the village was not named as Chandrapura, and was only known as 'Ur'. The Bhojas after holding supremacy over Salcete taluka, transferred their headquarters from Amonem village to this village which was more suitable for communications by land as well as by river to the sea. The Bhojas were of the Lunar clan, and as such they named the area previously occupied as Chndravadi and the principal deity of that area as Chandra-Chuda or Chandreshvar. This is installed on the top of a hill known as 'Parvat'. Later on when they established their headquarters to 'Ur', they named it Chandraura.

The order on the copper-plate is addressed to the Bhojaka, Ayaktak, Gramiya and others. The post of Bhojaka does not appear in the Satavahana administration, but it does in Northern India during the period from 6th to the 4th century B.C. V.D. Mahajan says [71] p. 201-202: "...The share of the king varied from 1/6 to 1/12 of the produce. This was collected through the village headman who was known as the Grama Bhojaka. The latter was either elected by the village council or was a hereditary officer. The village council consisted of all the elders of the village and was known as Grama-wriddhas. The village council helped the headman to maintain law and order and also to carry out public utility work such as the laying of roads, the construction of irrigation channels, the digging of tanks and the construction of halls and rest houses.

ill. 21 : Idol of Gautam Buddha of Colvale Village, Bardez Taluka, presently kept in Father Heras Museum, Mumbai.

Large holdings were rare. In addition, to the Kshetras which were individual or family properties, there were common pasture lands known as Vana. The number of persons living in a village varied from 30 to 1,000 families. A family was a comprehensive unit including not only father, mother, children and grandparents, but also the wives and children of the sons. The herdsman was known as Gopalak.

"The arable land of the village lay outside the mountains. Fences and field watchmen guarded the fields from beasts and birds. All the fields were cultivated at the same time. The irrigation channels were laid by the community and the supply of water was regulated under the supervision of the headman. No individual was required to fence his part of the field. There were common fences. Each family took the product of its share. A shareholder of the land in the village could not sell or mortgage his share of the village field to an outsider. Around the villages, there were woodlands or uncleared jungles, and the villagers collected fire-wood from there".

So, it is clear that the designation of 'Bhojak' to the headman of village was imported from Northern India, the original place of the Aryans of the second wave and was perhaps made known by the Buddhist monks who had been in Goa; The idol of

Buddha found at Mushir of Colvale village, Bardez taluka, is dated by Father Heras to the 1st or 2nd century A.D. (This idol was worshipped by the Hindus under the name 'Goutama', according to the Portuguese records of the temples demolished by them). *(ill. 21)*.

Bhojaka and ayuktaka—the village officials

It is surprising that the designation of 'Gramabhojak' as village headman of the Brahmin community and moreover 'Deshabhojak' as chief executive official of a large division existed in Tamil country, as can be seen in the Chola inscriptions of the 10th and 11th centuries A.D. The Gramabhojaka, village headman, was leader and mediator with the royal government. How he was appointed and whether the office was hereditary, cannot be determined. The village elders are also mentioned in particular besides the headman and the assembly.

The history of cultural expansion is interesting. The constitution of the village-commune with its assembly and headman with the designation of Grama-Bhojaka, existed in Northern India about 6th century B.C. The same type of village constitution with the identical designation 'Bhojak' with the same deities appears about the beginning of the third century A.D. in Goa, and then, in the 10th and 11th centuries of the Chola kingdom. This phenomenon could never have existed without the migration of the Saraswat Brahmins who had settled in that area long before the dates of the inscriptions of the Chola kings. A traditional history inserted in Konkan-Mahatmya [90] p. 392, mentions that a Saraswat Brahmin with his family had gone on a religious tour to South India and when he returned, he settled in *Kutthal* village. He was of the Koudinya gotra. This history shows that long ago many families of Saraswat Brahmins of different gotras had passed to South India where some of them settled. Some came back, and it appears that from that time there was mutual contact during various periods of history. It is worth noting that according to the history of South-East Asia [91] p. 21-22 & 118 it is seen that in the first and sixth centuries A.D. the Brahmins of Koudinya gotra went to Kambodia and Funan respectively. It is worth stressing here on what Dr. V. T. Gune says [18] p. 70: "The ancient traditions of the Bhojas about navigation and shipping are recorded in the Sanskrit manuscript 'Yuktikalapataru'. In A.D. 673, the Chinese traveller J. Tsing noticed Indian colonies of Bhojas in Sumatra, Kalingas in Java and Bhojasparasa in Bali. It seems in some cases the emigrants named their colonies after the place-names from where they migrated from the west coast as Bali, Banda, Sunda, Gowa, etc. As late as the 17th century there was in the island Madagascar, a kingdom by name Gowa, ruled by a sultan with whom the Portuguese in Goa has trade relations".

Now in respect of the post Ayuktaka—I did not find this word in the Sanskrit dictionary but found the word 'Ayukta' meaning appointed, substitute, and minister

(Mantri). Dr Altekar [92] p. 215, mentions that, "the district officers—the Vishayapatis or Vishayadhyakshas in the Mauryan administration—like the modern collectors were responsible for maintaining law and order in their districts; they had also to supervise the collection of government taxes and revenues. They were naturally assisted by a large subordinate staff: the Yuktas, Ayuktas, Niyuktas and Vyapritas who are exhorted in numerous records, and as Dhruvas in Gujarat in the post-Gupta period".

Even though we do not find the word 'Ayuktak' in that book, it is entirely plausible that this word means 'Ayukta of lower rank' like the word 'pallika' meaning small village with the basic word 'palli' meaning village.

We find that in village commune constituted exclusively of the Saraswat Brahmins, like *Kuthal*, there was a clan designated 'Bhandari' whose eldest member was the treasurer of the village-commune and so account-cum-record keeper.

But in underdeveloped areas where the headman as well as the members of the village commune were illiterate (generally of the gauda caste), for example in the Ponda (Antruz) taluka,— for maintenance of records, accounts and treasury and for the purpose collecting different types of dues and taxes it was necessary to post literate officers. And so, the post named 'Ayuktak' was created. The incumbent was appointed obviously by the government in such areas, while in other areas he must have been nominated by the assembly of the village-commune. Later this post came to be hereditary up to the time of the advent of the Portuguese. The village-commune used to give the 'Ayuktak' cultivated or uncultivated land which he might bring to cultivation. This can be seen from section 14 of the Chapter on the Uses and Customs published in 1526 in the Historical Archives of Goa (93) p. 4. Besides this land, in some villages he was given a fixed annual amount named 'Kulkarni/Vatan' (Ayuktak was later named Kulkarni). This designation of 'Kulkarni' appears in an inscription dated 1212 A.D. in Mardi village of Solapur district which mentions that Dholapeya Nayak was 'Kulkarni' [94] p. 79.

The village names

Now, let us deal with the expression "Sthaniyadya vaktayah". Here 'sthaniya' means the successors of the original settlers or say Gaonkars and so, members of the village commune. The word 'adya' means others, that is to say the cultivators, artisans, etc. who were permanent residents in the village. The word "bhavishad" means in future, that is to say for ever.

Now in respect of the expression, "Jiyayasu Thanniyarka— Kotikayya-parivrittena". It means at Thanniyarka of Kottika situated in Jiyaya. Here the word 'Antar' has been omitted while mentioning the district or Vishaya; so the effective word was Antruz or Antraz. The word 'Vishaya' also was omitted. In this copper-plate the words 'Grama', or say 'Pallika', as well as 'Vishaya' are not carved, which appear in the copper-plates of later kings of the Bhoja dynasty. I presume that the person who drafted the writing did not take necessary care, believing that the localities were generally known by everybody.

The village name is Kottika which is the present Kutti (Curti in Portuguese); Thaniyarka is a Sanskritised form of the Konkani word 'Thanyar' meaning at Thanem. This means a post of Police or Customs, and now the locality is named 'Metar'. The basic word 'Meta' is a Portuguese one with the same meaning.

About Prabhu-Naga-Bhojikamatya and Bhojaka relations

Now, with reference to the expression "Prabhu Naga Bhojikamatya". The name of the donor has been mentioned with his epithets. His proper name is Naga, and the epithet Prabhu has been prefixed to his name. Had this been a surname or only an honorific, it would have been suffixed to the word 'Naga'. Hence the epithet 'Prabhu' is indicative of 'Mhalgado' or say, the representative of one of the principal villages that constituted the committee of 'Vishaya' (district, at present taluka). So, we can say that in all the other Vishayas those members in the 2nd century A.D., were designated as 'Prabhu'. Obviously, the members of Quelossim (Kelshi) and Cortalim (Kuthal) village of Salcete taluka had no seat then in the 'Vishaya' committee, perhaps because it was named Mhalgaonpan or Mhal Mahajanaki, as the village assembly was then (and before) named 'gaonpan' or Mahajanki. Naga, besides being 'Prabhu', was also Bhojikamatya, and the historians have translated this word as "the Secretary of Revenue". This brings us to the question —whether this post was of Central status or a provincial (referred only to 'Vishaya') one.

The word "Bhojika" obviously means dues from Bhojak, in other words, the 'Rajabhaga', that is the amount in cash or kind due to the State, this being the responsibility of the Bhojak—headman of the village. As the copper-plate is addressed directly to the interested parties of the village and not to the representative of the district (Vishaya), nor has indirect mention been made to the direct body, it appears that Prabhu-Naga was the Secretary of Revenue of the district (later taluka) of Antruz. It appears that besides the collection of Government dues, direct administration of the Government lands was also entrusted to him. Further, he had powers to make gifts of lands within his jurisdiction, like the Amatyas (otherwise Vishya-patis) of the time of the latest kings of the Shilaharas. However, confirmation from the king was a must. So, it seems that the word 'Bhojakamatya' is to be translated as direct collector of revenue.

Now in respect of the expression "Prabhu-Naga"—is it only 'Prabhu' or

'Deshprabhu'?

The epithet 'Prabhu' existed long before the kingship of the Bhojas and continues up to the present date. The copper-plates do not mention the designation of 'Desha-Prabhu'. So there are two possibilities: one is that the headman of the principal village of the district was designated for long as 'Prabhu', and all the interested parties of village-communes were named Gaonkars. In Sanskrit they were named 'Mahajans'. The village accountant was named Bhandari. Secondly, it is interesting that the Sanskrit word 'Prabhu' passed to Karnataka after some centuries. In the time of the Chalukyas of Kalayani (973-1200 A.D.) the designation of Prabhu, Urodeya or Nayak meant the headman of villages. This can be seen from the copper-plate of 1074 A.D. [95] pp. 25 and 62. Nadaprabhu or Nadarasa meant head of Nada (group of villages), [12] p. 96. The designation of Prabhu as the headman of the village might have been adopted, since the word 'Prabhu' is a Sanskrit one, and secondly because this designation existed only in Goa. At that time (and before) in Northern India and Maharashtra the headman of the village was designated as Gramani or Gramakuta (in the Satavahana kingdom) and Pattalika in other areas. In Southern India he was named Gavund.

In conclusion Prabhu Naga Bhojikamatya was the Bhojak of the village which constituted the headquarters of Antruz district (Vishaya) and was also the district collector of revenue and taxes.

That brings us to another point. What was the name of the village which constituted the headquarters of Antruz district?

Bori (Borim)—the ancient headquarters of Antruz

We do not find any reference in this respect either in the copper-plate or in traditional history. We get relevant information from traditional history and the copper-plates of the latter periods of Salcete, Tiswadi and Bardez talukas, but nothing about the other talukas of Goa. As mentioned earlier, the copper-plate was found with Gopal Sinai Gude of Shiroda of Antruz taluka. In adjacent Borim *(Bori)* village there is an ancient residential house of a family with the surname (Prabhu Saukar). They are Paddye caste Brahmins. Long ago there was a controversy in respect of matrimonial relations between this family and the Paddye-Karade Batts. The late Narcinva Chintamana Kelkar was requested to mediate; and this controversy was called the "Bhatta-Prabhu Eykya Prakaran" (case of the integration of Prabhu and Bhattas). I think Gude had obtained the copper-plate from the archives of that family which was the second copy of the copper-plate maintained by the donor in his capacity as Bhojikamatya. And so Prabhu Naga Bhojikamatya was the ancestor of the family of Paddya Brahmin and Borim *(Bori)* was the headquarters of Antruz district.

The epithet Swami

Now in respect of the epithet Swami of the donees: the names of the donees recorded in the copper-plate are Govindaswamin and Indraswamin of the Bhardwaja gotra Brahmins. In other copper-plates, concerning Goa territory we do not find names with such epithets as 'Swamin'. So, it is necessary to find its origin. The general idea of the word 'swami' in Goa is that, he is the head of a Hindu monastery (*Math*) or a person who lives a solitary life, wears clothes of a tan colour and is a celibate throughout his life or is a sanyasi (an ascetic). Many times the word 'swami' is used in addressing a letter to a king, lord or a person of higher post of any caste. The husband is also referred to as 'swami' by his wife. But here the case is different. The donees do not appear to be ascetic. We find the explanation in another copper-plate.

In the copper-plate found at Malhara of Vidharba [86] 2nd part pp. 146-155, it is shown that Adityaraja of the Brahmin caste, gifted ten villages to Brahmins of the Bharadwaja gotra in about 270 A.D. The Brahmins are Matulaswami, Bhattaswami, Dityaswami, Dronaswami, Nannaswami, Surayswami and Kalisharma. The copper-plate was issued from Venakheta, probably capital of his kingdom and makes known the gifting of villages to the following officers of the Tahshil (Bhoga):Upareka, Kumaramatya, Dandapashikas, Chata, Bhata, Kashthika, Dootapreshhanika, Vinyaktaka and others.

The copper-plate is very important for a comparative study of similarity and dissimilarity of the administration in both these areas. However, here we are concerned only with the epithet 'swami'.

In both the copper-plates, the Brahmins are of the same Bharadwaja gotra. In the copper-plate of Adityaraja, though the Brahmins are of the same gotra, all of them except one have the epithet of 'swami', while one of them, the last, is mentioned with the epithet of 'sharman'. Why this difference of epithets among Brahmins of the same gotra? This view cannot be accepted, because in that case a different copper-plate might have been issued for the Kalisharma Brahmin. Hence all those Brahmins must have been of the same caste of Brahmins. It is most probable therefore, that the elderly Brahmins or say those more versatile in the Vedas, were honoured with the epithet of 'swami', and the young ones of the same caste, and less versatile in the studies of the Vedas, as may have been designated with the epithet Sharma. King Adityaraja was a Brahmin, so he might have had full knowledge of the geneology of the donees.

Even the epithet 'Sharma' which appears in the copper-plate dated 270 A.D. was not introduced at that time. On the contrary, it must have existed for a long time-perhaps since the time of the invasion of Jarasandha or say about 1350 B.C. I have already mentioned earlier the migration of the Yadavas to Vidarbha and other parts, from the area around Mathura, known as 'Satwant Pradesh'. Some Brahmins also migrated with them and settled in Vidarbha.

At the south of Goa, the Kadamba dynasty was established in the 3rd century A.D. in Karnataka by a Brahmin named Mayurasharma who afterwards assumed the Kshatriya surname of Varma. [3] p. 44. From this evidence it is clear that the Brahmins in Goa in the 3rd century A.D. (and probably before that date) originally hailed from Satwant Pradesh. And so, those Brahmins— the donees—were of the Saraswat caste.

About the term 'Sarvatantraddhikrita Amareshvaras'

The grant was executed by a person named Amareshwara. Now, it is known from accounts of ancient history that all members of the Bhoja assembly were designated as 'Ishvara' and perhaps for this reason the later sovereigns assumed the title of 'Parameshvara'. That means, this person surely was of the Bhoja clan and probably a close relation to King Devaraja. From the copper-plates of Adityaraja mentioned earlier, it is evident that in the administration of 'Bhoja' (Tahsil), Kumaramathy was one of the officials. Probably he was the son of the king. In many copper-plates we notice the presence of Yuvaraja—the presumed successor of the king—as one of the members of the ministry. In all likelihood, that person, the Yuvaraja, had viceregal powers, so the post Sarvatantradrikrita cannot be translated simply as 'superintendent of all Departments' but it would be more correct to compare it to the post of Viceroy or at least Chief Secretary.

From the inscription it is clear that the charter was written by Rayasyadhikrita (private secretary) Prabhakara. The language of the charter is Sanskrit but expressions in Prakrit are scattered here and there. The characters of the inscription belong to the archaic variety. So, Prabhakara was surely of the Brahmin caste, but he does not mention his epithet like Prabhu or Sharman. I presume that he was Sharman but the engraver omitted it as he has done in many instances as in Vartaman, Antara and Vishaye or Ahare. There is reason to consider Prabhakara as a Saraswat of Quelossim (*Kelsi*) and so he was entitled to the epithet Sharman as this Brahmin family had accompanied them in the migration, as mentioned earlier.

The ring of the copper-plate has a symbol of a bird which according to one historian, is a peacock while another thinks it is a swan. Probably, the latter is correct. The dating as the twelfth year of Devaraja's reign marks events in a systematic manner. This type of dating existed up to the times of the Kshatrapas who introduced the Shaka (commonly known as Shalivahan Shaka) era, otherwise introduced by Kanishka or the Kushana dynasty of Northern India.

Devaraja assumed the epithet 'Raja' like 'Aditya Raja'. The latter was of the Brahmin caste, so evidently he preferred that epithet, but Devaraja was a Kshatriya. It appears that the epithet 'Varman' which appears in the later Bhojas, was unknown and perhaps became known when Mayurasharma of the Kadamba family changed his name to Mayurvarma.

Comparing the administrative staff of Adityaraja, who belonged more or less to the same period as Devaraja, one finds that the administrative staff was very limited. The reason was that in Goa, at that time, the administration pattern was generally of self-government in villages and Aharas or Vishayas, thus not requiring a large staff. It may be noted that during the Bhoja era Goa experienced peace and order.

II - Asamkita-Hire Gutte copper plate
The place names

Chronologically, this is the next copper-plate. King Asamkita (the fearless one) of Bhoja lineage, at the request of the Chief Kottipegili (born in the lineage of the Kaikeyas of Nandipalli) gifted away the village Sundarika, situated in the Dipaka - Vishaya to the Arya Sangha (assembly of Buddhist monks) of the Buddhist vihara belonging to them. [87].

The inscription has also recorded the boundaries of the gifted village Sundarika: in the North its boundary extended upto the boulder with the mango-tree, in the South it was bounded by the roaring stream of Maruti-Katter, in the East by Kuruva, and in the West by the waterfall on the mountain.

In Lamgaon village of Bicholim (*Dicholi*) taluka of Goa there is a beautiful artificially carved cave with a plinth and columns named simply as "*Houri*", which is probably the Buddhist vihara belonging to the Arya Sangh mentioned in the copper-plate.

The land gifted is situated in the Dipaka-vishaya, which is a Sanskritization of the district name '*Divchal*', present Bicholim (*Dicholi*) taluka. The land was situated in Sundarika village where presently a place named '*Sundarpeth*' of Bicholim town is situated. The boundaries mentioned in the copper-plate are at present different. However, the natural topographical details can be identified. The southern boundary is a roaring stream, and likewise, at present there is a place named '*Dhabdabeyar*' (waterfall), where at present lies Lamgaon village. After many centuries this Sundarika village was divided, one part passing to the Bicholim town and another part to Lamgaon village, constituting the '*mocasso*' village gifted by the king to a family with 'Visvasrao Sar Desai' as their surname.

About the Kaikeya and Sind families

The grant had been done at the request of the chief Kottipegili (born in the lineage of the Keikeyas of Nandipalli). As chief, surely he was Dipaka-Vishayapati, and I have mentioned before that the ancestor of the Sendraka family had brought at least two families of his close relations, one being established in Bicholim taluka. His lineage has been mentioned in the copper-plate at Kaikeya of Nandipalli. Nandipalli probably is present Nandidurga of Karnataka, the original place of that family. We know from the history of the latter period in the time of Vikramaditya VI (1076-1126 A.D.) that the said king granted Annakonda-Vishaya, modern Warangal, to his General, the Kakatiya Chola in recognition of his military service [27] p. 92. The word "Kaikeya" in the copper-plate must be identified as the word 'Kakatiya' of the later period. It is known from history that the branches of the main family had settled in different parts of India, but did not ignore their original home. It is seen from history that in the period of the family of Chalukyas of Badami, a feudatory of the Sind family whose realm was situated at the north of Aihole was ordered to defeat the Kadambas of Goa. This, despite the existence of the branch of the same Sind (Sendraka) family existing in Goa. At that time, this branch was too weak to chase away the Kadambas, and this is why the Sind feudatory was especially selected to help the Sendrakas of Goa. We will refer again to this case at a later stage.

The copper-plate has a scale bearing in relief the figure of an elephant in motion. The charter is written in the Southern alphabet of the early age, while the language is in Sanskrit. The record is composed in prose, but the invocation and imprecation is in verse.

The inscription starts by praising Lord Buddha, and the epigraph bears no date; but according to P. B. Desai who brought to light this copper-plate, it should be placed by the end of the 5th or the beginning of the 6th century A.D. This copper-plate was found in the possession of Uddanda Bommayya Gaonkar at Hire Gutti, Kumtha, in North Kanara district. From his surname Gaonkar, it appears that his family must have migrated long ago, probably at the time of forced conversions of Hindus to Christianity by the Portuguese.

At this stage, let me take cognizance about any doubts over the identification made by me. The Kaikeya lineage is a corruption of the Kakatiya lineage, and the argument may be made that Kaikeyas may be the people from a land of ancient times known as Kekaya, situated between the rivers Asikni and Vitasta. We know from the epic Ramayana that Kaikeyi, daughter of the king of that land, was the third wife of King Dasharatha, mother of Bharata and Shatrughna. Besides, the Chalukyas in the later period mention that their ancestor had migrated to the Dakshinapatha from his original place, Ayodhya. Similarly, the ancestor of the Kaikeyas might have migrated from that land of Keikaya to the Dakshinapatha, and settled in Nadipalli or say Nandidurga.

Apparently, the argument appears to be correct, but historicaly baseless like the case of the Chalukyas. It is perceived from the scrutiny of historians that the Chalukyas had no Northern Indian origin but were Kannadigas like the Kadambas. [3] p. 66. So, the argument that Kaikeya might be of Northern Indian origin is unteneable.

III - Asankitavarman Kapoli copper-plate

The village names

Through this copper-plate, a grant is made of the village named Vamsavataka situated in the Sollundurka—twenty in Palasika -Vishaya—to one Nagasharman of the Haritagotra who was endowed with all the qualities of a Brahmin. The grantor is Chief Elekilla from the Kaikeya lineage, and the grant had the approval of the king. In fact, the gift was given by both the king and the chief, with libation of water and free from tax (panga). It is executed by the king himself. The king is designated as Maharaja.

The record is dated in the fifth reignal year of the king and the gift is registered on the full moon day of Jyestha. The charter is written by Madhava, the son of Govindabhojika (alias Bhojaka) and the writer of Royal Charters [96] pp. 234-35.

This copper-plate (consisting of three plates) was found by an agriculturist, buried in an iron box at Khopoli Khanapur taluka in Belgaum district.

According to A. M. Annegeri, the village Vamsavataka of the grant may be identified with Khopoli while Palasika-Vishya should be Palasige—twelve-thousand.

The characters of the grant are in a Southern alphabet of about the 5th or 7th century A.D. The language is Sanskrit and the composition is in prose, except for two lines which are in verse.

Gerald Pereira's arguments

Gerald Pereira, who has provided an account of both the copper-plates, considers that the Asankita and Asankitavarman were two different kings. The former had praised Buddha and gifted the land to the Buddha-Vihara, so he was a Buddhist, while the latter is referred to in the inscription as a great devotee of Shiva. Besides, the inscription of the former, going by the form of the characteristics of writing, is placed by the end of the 5th or the beginning of the 6th century while the inscription of the late king is placed by the 6th or 7th century A.D.[87]

I don't agree with this view. The reasons laid down by Gerald Pereira are quite inadequate to prove that they were different kings. We have proof that the Satavahan kings and queens of the Deccan made gifts, invariably to Buddhist monks and nuns as well as to Hindu Brahmins. However they were performing rituals of the Vedic and post-Vedic Hindu religion, and those are approximately of the time of Devaraja Bhoja [3] p. 36. At the time of Asankitavarma, we note that the kings gifted lands to Hindu temples while their wives gifted lands to the Jaina-maths and also maintained Buddhist-viharas. "But by and large, the members of the Royal family (of Chalukyas of Badami) were the followers of Shaiva or Vaishnava ways of life, as the titles of Paramamaheshvara and Paramabhagvata assumed by the Chalukya kings show. The principle of religious tolerance adopted by the rulers of the dynasty was largely responsible for the prevalent religious harmony among many existing creeds. This in turn gave tremendous impetus to the construction of Brahmanical and Jaina temples". [3] p. 77. So similarly, the Bhojas were devotees of Shiva or say Chandreshvara of Parvat, with their capital at Chandrapur. Another important proof is that both the rings of copper-plates bear the symbol of an elephant.

Evidence of the rule of the Kaikeya branch

The land gifted was situated in Khanapur taluka, and from this grant it is clear that Asankavarman had expanded his kingdom to that area, when Satavahan rule had weakened there. The chief of that area is of the Kaikeya lineage like that of Dicholi taluka at that time. From this evidence it appears that both the chiefs were of the same family—moreover, their names terminate in the 'li' syllable. From this evidence it appears that, like the Sendrakas of Goa, one branch of the Kaikeya lineage continued to exist in Belgaum district, while the other was posted by the Sendrakas to Dicholi taluka, as I mentioned earlier. The branch in Goa, giving up their alliance with the Sendrakas ruler, admitted the sovereignty of the Bhojas and the branch of Belgaum also followed suit, perhaps owing to matrimonial relations to the Bhoja king.

The Bhoja kings had not interfered in the existing form of village and district (Ahara or Vishaye) administration as also in the creeds of peoples like, the Satarkars, Paddyes and Saraswats, maintaining *status quo ante*, in those areas. But some changes were brought about in areas like Chandravadi, where the people of high status did not exist. Similarly, the Asantika king also maintained the *status quo ante*, in Belgaum district, where the village-commune system like in Goa did not exist. The area was very far from Chandrapura, capital of the kingdom, so the chief of the Palasika-Vishaya, had the status of king (*Raja*). It also appears that the epithet of Varma, then in use by the kings of the adjoining area, might have been adopted by him and continued afterwards in his generation.

The grant had been made to a Brahmin named Nagasharma of the Haritigotra. He was surely a Kannadiga like Mayurasharma, founder of the Kadamba dynasty who was also of the Haritigotra, known in greater detail as Haritiputra Manavyagotra. The Brahmins like Mayursharma had abandoned their duties of the Brahmin caste and embraced those of the Kshatriyas, changing in the process their own name Mayursharma to Mayuravarma, (Varma being the epithet of the Kshatriyas). The inscriptions do not limit themselves to the name and gotra of the donee but mention that he was performing the duties proper for a person of the Brahmin caste.

About the word 'Panga'

Finally let me draw the attention of readers to the word 'panga', meaning taxes. This word exists even today in the Konkani and Marathi languages and means debts subject to payment. It is known from the copper-plates that 'Bhojek' means the amount due to the state as Rajabhaga by each village, and 'panga' was the amount due, or say tax, which each cultivator had to pay in the respective village. This was the amount consisting of the proportional part of 'Bhojek' (the rent payable from the gross or net produce to the village commune) plus an amount corresponding to the proportional part of expenses due for repairing of the tanks, roads, etc. for public utility and also maintenance of the public temples and expenses for worship and public festivals which were known as "Grama-Kharch". The maintenance of bunds of rice-fields and reservoirs for watering the vaingan crop of paddy (summer crop) was the duty of the respective beneficiaries, who were the Gaonkars, and that work was practically done by the group of direct cultivators named '*Bhousa*'. This was the system in use in the areas of Goa where the village-commune existed. In Belgaum, since it was under the influence of the Satavahana king's rule, the administrative system of that area was different from the one in Goa.

The practice of village communes

"The administration of satavahanas was but a continuation of the administrative traditions established by their erstwhile masters, the Mauryas, with some striking innovations. The king was the hub of the administration. They had in addition to the ancient title of Rajah, the title of Swamin. Gautamiputra Satakarni is called Rajrano, i.e. 'king of kings'. He was the supreme commander of the armed forces and the fountain-head of justice. He led the army in person to the battlefield.

"The Satavahana rulers were well educated in the 'Kautilya system of administration for the princes'. Gautamiputra Satakarni is said to have 'properly devised time and place for the pursuit of the Tivage' (i.e. Trivarga) and sympathised fully with the will and woe of the citizens. Like the Mauryan monarchs, the Satavahana kings looked after both the material and spiritual welfare of the people. The king was assisted by a council of ministers whose number is not known. The scanty information in the inscriptions when pieced together indicates the existence of the central service. It consisted of such royal officers as the Amatyas who acted as the governors of the Aharas, the Rajamatyas who attended on the king and were members of the advisory body; a Mahamatya who was entrusted with the execution of a special task; the Bhandarika or the superintendent of the stores; the Heranyka or the treasurer, the Mahasenapati or the commander of the army; the Lekhaka or the Secretary of State who drafted the king's documents and the Nibandhakaras who were charged with the task of registering the documents. The appointment of the Mahasenapati dates from the time of Gautamiputra Satakarni and his son. Sometimes, the Mahasenapati also acted as governor. The existence of these officials and the detailed procedure that was followed in respect of the registration of official documents go to show that the Satavahanas had established a sound system of administration. They must have maintained all essential departments such as those of police, finance, justice, army, commissariat, agriculture, industries, etc., although contemporary inscriptions do not actually refer to any of these."

"The empire was divided into various divisions such as Aharas corresponding to the Rastras of the Pallava records. They were in charge of officers called Amachas (Amatyas) or governors. The Aharas were further divided into Nigmas (towns) and Gamas or Gramas (villages). We do not get adequate information regarding their administration in the inscriptions. The villages were in the charge of the traditional headmen who are referred to as Gramanis [alias Gramani [86] p. 389 in Gathasathasai (Gathasaptshahy) of Satavahana kinga Hala (20-24 A.D.) They looked after the administration of five villages and sometimes ten villages. The official incharge of the administration of the towns and villages enjoyed complete autonomy. The Nigama had an assembly called Nigamasabha which acted as the mouth-piece of the citizens". [3] pp. 32-33.

Joglekar's view cited in the book above, gives an excellent commentary, saying that at the time of Satavahana Hala the headman of the village was named as 'Gamani' as well as 'Pallivayi' (Pallipati), and the designation as 'Patala' (Patel, derived from the Sanskrit word Pattakila) was being introduced. He correctly says that according to the designation of "Pallipati" in the Gathasaptashaye, his right on the village was like a ruler [3] pp. 342-343.

Even in the Shatapatha Brahmana and other books of post-Vedic times, there is reference to the existence of the village-assembly of the elders. I think that this system was in use in Northern India and in Goa, but it was not then in use in the Deccan.

Expansion of the Bhojas domain

As the domain of Bhoja Asankit started expanding the give-and-take method in administration slowly began to change. Thus, Asamkita upgraded the chief of Palasika-Vishaya to the status of king, and probably advised him to introduce the system of village-assembly, which was a success. It began as an advisory board to the village headman, and the system spread to adjacent areas even though not in the Bhoja kingdom. Thus, about the 9th century A.D. we find in inscriptions of the Deccan mention of the village assembly of the elders of a village named Mahajana under the presidentship of Gamunda as mentioned by Nilakanta Sastri [39] p. 106. Autonomy in the times of the Satavahanas mentioned in the cited 'History of Karnataka' was restricted only to the powers of the headman of village but now the will of the headman was disciplined by the advice of the village-assembly, thereby leading towards the creation of a Welfare Stage. [39]

On the other hand some principles of the Koutiliya administration in use in the Deccan were adopted by the Bhoja king; Asamkita, one of them being that the property of a person without any descendant (niputrika) passed to the king.

As the chief of Palasika-Vishaya was upgraded to the status of king, the approval of the grant was made by Asamkita himself, and not through any administrative official.

I have devoted much space to the Satavahan administration system only to show that the expansion of the Bhojas opened a new chapter in cultural trends. In Goa, previosly the properties of the persons without a descendant reverted to the village-commune which had assigned the land.

The charter is written by Madhava, the son of Govindabhojika (alias Bhojaka). This person was surely of the Brahmin caste, and being of Bhojaka lineage, and without the epithet 'Prabhu', he was surely a Saraswat Brahmin originally of *Kutthal* or *Kelshi* village. Probably he was of the Koushik gotra, originally of Kelshi and might have been Bhojaka in a village of Chandravadi. The writer might have been from the lineage of Ayuktaka but was a Bhojak which is significant because he held a higher post of writer of Royal Charters and consequently he was head of department of the registration of records—a post like the one of Private Secretary (Rajasyadhikrita) in Devaraja's time [98].

Between Devaraja and Asamkita there is a gap of about two centuries, according to the epigraphists who have determined the dating based on the system of characteristics of the respective inscriptions. So, we do not have any idea about any innovations made in the administration system during these two centuries. But based on the conservate minds of people of high status, we have no reason to believe that there was any significant change in the general administration, even though the families of *Kelshi, Kutthal* and their allies, the Vaishyas of Colva and Betalbati villages had contact because of their external commerce, with areas on the sea-coast of India and perhaps abroad.

IV - Kapardivarma - Arga copper-plate

This copper-plate records that King Kapardivarman of Bhoja lineage, from his residence at Pansa-Khetiaka, donated as a gift a piece of land called Pukkolli-Khajjana in the village of Sivapuraka, belonging to Aditya Sresthi to Svamikaraja, at his request. The latter re-gifted the Khajjana to a Brahmin named Bhavaryya of the Kaudinya gotra, with libation of water, so that merit might accrue to him.

The language of this copper-plate is Sanskrit, though the characters are in archaic Kannada. The composition is in prose. The charter is not dated but it has been ascribed to about the 6th century by a paleontologist. The charter was written by Krishna Bhojaka and executed by Nandaka Talavara who probably was a high government officer. The plate salutes King Kapardivaraman as Dharmamaharaja (meaning a pious and righteous Maharaja). The copper-plate was found in a temple at Arga about four miles south of Karwar where it was under worship. A. M. Annegeri who discovered this plate in 1946-47 is of the opinion that the Shivapur mentioned in the copper-plate is in Supapetha or in Halyal taluka or Karwar. Dr. P. Pissurlenkar held the view that Shivapur should be in Chandrapur. The fact is that the gifted land was situated in Kudne, adjacent to Harvalem village of Bicholim taluka. The copper-plates might have migrated to Karwar along with a member of the family.

Evidence of ancient Shivapur

In the 'Sayhadrikhandam', in its first part 'Adirahasyam', chapter nine titled 'Shivapuravarname', describes the place. In that chapter reference is made to the lingas existing there.

On the other hand, we find from the evidence of the Archaeological Survey that "there is an inscription in angular Brahmi character on the rectangular part of the shaft (*linga*) which reads: Sambaluravasi Ravi. This linga is situated in one of the chambers of the artificial cave carved on a flank of a hillock in laterite rock, known by the people as "*Pandavanchi Houri*". This is situated in Harvalem village of Bicholim taluka and at a little distance from this place there is a waterfall, where Hindus have a ceremonial bath in the month of Shravana. About fifty years ago, a person of the Bhandari caste constructed there a temple with a Shiva-linga and named it 'Rudreswar'.

The archaelogical evidence

The portion of the 9th chapter of the Sahyadrikhand from Sholas 119 to 138, provides a proper description of Shivapur. The existence of a cave, an idol of Shiva or say Rudra with his wife Rudrani and footprints carved on rock and called Vishnu-pada are all there in the area comprising at present Harvalem and the adjacent Kudnem village. The name Harvalem or Harvalli or say Harapalli corresponds to Shivapura, as Hara is another name of Shiva and Valli or Palli corresponds to 'Pura'. The expression in the Brahmi script on a linga, namely Sambalura, is surely a corruption of 'Sambapura' as Samba is also another name for Shiva. Sambapur and Shivapura are the names of the same village. Dr. P. Pissurlenkar could not designate the village as Shivapura, because an epigraphist had read that inscription as 'Sachipur-che-Sirassi' (58) p. 1.

Identification of place names and the donors.

The land granted belonged to an Aditya-Sethi. A king who was titled as Dharmamaharaja would never confiscate land, and obviously the king had purchased it from the Sethi. The word 'Sresthi' makes it clear that the owner was of the Vaishya caste. It appears that the person was pious and so he established that linga which bears the said Brahmi inscription 'Sambaluravasi Ravih',—Ravih and Aditya are both names of the Sun God. A question may be asked: why did the donor Swaminraj not purchase the land directly from the owner Sresthi ? There may be two reasons for this: firstly, because Sresthi was a rich man, in no need of money. Besides, a person is always reluctant to sell land when it is inherited and the word 'vasi' in the inscription makes this position clear. Secondly, the village-commune system might have taken root there, so the land could not be sold without the permission of all the elders of the Gaonkars of the village. Moreover, the donee Svamikaraja appears to be a high officer (possibly Vishayapati) of the Kaikaya lineage of the Vishaya in which the village was situated—probably Dipaka-Vishaya (*Divchal-Dicholi* taluka) and so the land could not be granted to a person who was not a Gaonkar of that village. But going by the theory that all the uncultivated land of a village belonged to the king, as we have seen in the case of Devaraja Bhoja, and now Asankitavarman, the principle of Kautilya administration having been adopted, the ownership of land was rested in the king. So the king could purchase any type of land and gift it to any person, even though he was not a Gaonkar of village.

'Khajjana' a Sanskritized form of the word '*Khajan*', means riverine marshland brought under cultivation of paddy by construction of a protective bund (embankment) against the flooding of waters at high tide. The king made the gift from a temporary camp at Panasa-Khetaka meaning a very small village-hamlet, named Panasa. A place bearing this name, in the form of a hamlet, may exist today in a village adjacent to Sivapura. The grant was executed by Mandaka-Talavara, but his official post is not mentioned. However, from the epithet 'Talavara' he appears to be a person of the Kshatriya clan. In fact today we have a Kshatriya family with Talvar as the surname. The inscription was written by Krishna-Bhojaka (alias Bhojak), and this person must have been a Saraswat or Paddye-Brahmin, belonging to the family of the headman of the village (as he was a Bhojak and not an Ayuktaka).

The antiquity of Kudnem and Shivapur (present Harvalem)

Bhavarya of the Kaudinya gotra was surely a Saraswat Brahmin as suggested by the epithet Arya. Moreover, the families of the Kaudinya gotra are originally of Cortalim (*Kutthal*) village. Bhavarya and his successors probably obtained more lands adjacent to that (*Khajan*) land in the form of assignments from the village commune of Shivapura, to such an extent that after some centuries that area constituted a separate village, perhaps with the name of Kaundinyapura or Kaundinyapalli which later came to be designated as Kudnem, as is presently known. In this village we find the idol of Shiva with Uma in couple form which Dr Gune considers to be of the early Chalukya period (7th century A.D.) (99). The other part of Shivapur had the name Harapalli or Haravally, the present Harvalem village.

Scrutiny of place names

Now some more details in respect of places. The bund of the granted Khajan is named "Sastar"— evidently this name is derived from a surname or say caste name 'Sresthi' mentioned in the copper-plate. The Khajan is not cultivated in the rainy seasons as it is subjected to inundation of salt water of the river existing on its border, adjacent to the bund. And so, it is cultivated with the vaingon crop of paddy (summer crop), irrigated by sweet water accumulated in the river with a temporary bund across the bed of the river made every year. The river is named "Amonechi nhein" (river of Amonem) as on the other bank lies the village of Amonem. This word Amonem was Sanskritized in the Sahyadrikhanda as 'Amrit' from the basic word 'Amo' for 'Ambo' (mango), in Sanskrit 'Amra'. I have already referred to the existence of footprints which are called 'Vishnu-Padam' in the Sahyadri-khanda. At present, the place is named 'Pavlar', and it lies in Kudnem village near its common boundary with Navelim village.

As the chapter 'Shivapuravarnana' of the Sahyadrikhanda refers to the idol of Rudra with Rudrani, of the 7th century A.D., it proves that upto that time the village name of Shivapura was in use.

Dr. Gune, in his article in the Goa Gazetteer, page 67, has wrongly placed Shivapura in Palasika or Halsi of Khanapur taluka perhaps, solely because the copperplate was found at Arge temple in Karwar. The findings of a plate in a place does not mean that the grant should necessarily be in that area. We have another example of this: long ago a copper-plate was found in Chiplon, which was named the Chiplon copper-plate but the granted lands were situated in Sattari taluka of Goa and were granted by Pulkesin II of the Chalukyas of Badami, at the request of his maternal uncle Vantuvallabha Senanadaraja who was ruler of the whole area of Goa. The historian who found it declared plainly that the site was not identifiable and thus he avoided making any untenable argument.

V - Prithvimallavarman - Bandodem copper-plate A

Identification of place names

This is one of two copper-plates found with a person from Bandodem village, Ponda taluka, in the year 1949-1950. This copper-plate shows that the grant was issued from Vrishabhini-Kheta by King Prithvimallavarman of the Bhoja lineage in the first year of his reign, on the 13th day of the bright half of the month of Jyestha. The granted land was named 'Vrishabhini-Kheta', situated in the village of Bhagala-Pallika and included in the Kupalakath-desha. The grant was made for the merit of the king's mother Chetasadevi, daughter of Nellika, at the request of his brother Shatrudamana. The land was surely purchased from a private owner or from the village-commune and the formal donation was made by the king himself. The donee was a Madhavarya of the Agniveshya gotra. The charter was written by Devasharma-Acharya of the Bharadwaj-gotra. Due to the Sanskritized nomenclature, identification was a bit difficult.

Kupalakathara-desa means Ahora-desha or say a district with its headquarters in Kupalakata. Kata or Kataka in Sanskrit means village, 'kupa' in Sanskrit means well (*bain* in Konkani), and the word 'la' is a Sanskrit one, meaning taking (*ghene* in Konkani); so, Kupala means 'Bainghene' or say '*Bainguinim*' village. This village is in Tiswadi taluka of Goa and lies between Ela and Panvel village. During the Muslim and in the early Portuguese domain, it was made part of Old Goa. Bhagalapallika is also a Sanskritized word, 'Pallika' meaning village. Bhaga is a Sanskrit word coinciding with '*ganda*' in Konkani, so Bhagala means 'Gandala' or the present village Gandaulim. The word Vrishibhim-Kheta is the Prakrit form of Kshetra meaning *sheta* (paddy-field) in Konkani. Vrishabh is the Sanskritization of *Vaijina* (in Konkani meaning midwife). In the cadastral survey records of Gandaulim village prepared in the year 1905, we find under survey no. 47 a property with coconut and cashew plantations named *Vaijini-chem-bhata* (garden of midwife). Under No. 48 there is a similar plantation named '*Vaijinicho-cudco*' and its holdership is recorded in the name of two Christians. Adjacent to those lands there is a paddy-field of the village-commune, and at the corner of that field there is a plot adjacent to those lands and is named as '*Sasan*' under survey No. 52 and recorded in the name of a widow of *a Bhat* (Hindu priest) residing at Cumbarjua *(Khumbharjuve)* village. All that area is named 'Vajemvado', meaning the hamlet 'vajem'.

'*Sasana*' means land held through generations, and the properties with such names were not purchased or appropriated by private individuals through encroachment, due to religious feelings. It was considered that land with such names were gifts made for religious rituals. Hence, even after Christianization of the village, the family of that donee designated in the copper-plate continued to receive the rent on that paddy-field. At first they were living in Marcela of Orgaon village, Ponda taluka which is nearest to the Gandaulim village, and was part of the Muslim domain. Later on in the very beginning of 17th century A.D. the Portuguese, due to the economic downfall of their regime, permitted the Hindus with certain restrictions, to reside in their domain. So, the family of the Hindu priest came to reside in *Kumbharjuvem* village. Around 1904, the widow died without leaving heirs, and nobody wanted to purchase the '*Sasana*' land, Hence after her death the land was incorporated into the adjacent paddy-field of the village-commune. The other lands under survey nos. 47 and 48 were not part of the gift, but were obtained by assignment from the village-commune, so, the Christians purchased it.

About the name "Chetasadevi"

In respect of Chetasadevi, she is said to be the daughter of Nellika (Nellika-balika) or, properly said, girl of the Nellika clan. Prithivimallavarman mentions that she was his mother, but I believe she was his step-mother, and the real mother of Shatrudamana. Nalke is a caste name of a tribe living in southern Kanara [100]. If Chetasadevi had been the real mother of the king, he might have purchased the land directly, but it was purchased by Rudradaman on behalf of his mother. And a Brahmin would not take land from the hand of a person of the Shudra caste. If that woman had not been of the Shudra caste, she would have directly made the grant of land. It is merely my presumption that she might have been a daughter of a ruling family of Karnataka named Nala because in the inscription of Aihole, Nalas are mentioned among other rulers subdued by Chalukya Kirtivarman of Badami (560-598 A.D.). However, it is possible that the Nalas may be a family of that tribal caste.

The writing of the inscription was prepared by Devasharma-Acharya of the *Bahradwaja* gotra, who was surely a high priest and a Saraswat Brahmin.

VI - Prithvimallavarman-Bandodem copper-plate B

About the village names and boundaries

This is the second copper-plate found in the same year in Bandode village, Ponda taluka.

The grant is issued from the victorious Prithviparvatas by Prithivimallayarman of the Bhoja lineage. The object of the charter is to record the grant of a field called Kappotikhajjana, situated in the village of Malar included in Kupalakat-desha and made by the king for his own merit. The donee was one Damarya on the Agniveishya sub-division Pravara of the Bhardwaja gotra. The gifted land is named Pukkolli-khajjana which means Khajan land with that name. The village mentioned, Malar, is the present Malar village situated in *Divadi* (Divar in Portuguese) island, included in Tiswadi taluka. This village, according to the inscription, was situated in Kupalakata Desha, and this 'desha' is the same as mentioned in copper-plate 'A'. It means the district which corresponds to the present Tiswadi taluka. So, from the time of the Bhoja kingdom, Divadi island was part and parcel of Tiswadi taluka. The boundaries of the granted land are given in all four directions. The northern boundary is formed by the river. In the midst of the field is a yupaka, otherwise kupuka, meaning a small well (that is a *fondaro* or *hondko* in Konkani which means a well without any masonry walls, with sweet water) which generally exists in many paddy-fields to water the summer crop of vegetables.

The name of the donee in the inscription is mentioned as Damarya of the Bharadwaja gotra. From the epithet 'Arya' and his gotra, it is certain that the donee was a Brahmin of the Saraswat or Paddye caste.

Nidhivara and Kamboja gotra

The charter was executed by Nidhivara and the writing was executed by Budhadasa of the Kamboja gotra.

The word Nidhivara appears to be the designation of the post of treasurer like Bhojikamatya in the time of Devaraja Bhoja, but his proper name is not mentioned. The writer's proper name has also not been given and is just mentioned as Buddhasuta. Perhaps he might have aimed at such a designation. Kamboja gotra, I presume, does not appear among the Saraswat and Paddye Brahmins. Since only Brahmins of these castes existed in Goa at that time, Kamboja gotra may signify the Kamboja clan. It seems that the writer was a Buddhist, versatile in the Sanskrit language, and perhaps he was an adviser to Prithvivarman, otherwise the king would have not given the status of a queen to his stepmother—Chetasadevi of the tribal caste. This charter was issued from Prithviparvata which was surely from *Parvata*

(Chandranatha Parvat). That means his capital continued at Chandrapur.

INTERPRETING COPPER-PLATES OF THE BHOJA DYNASTY IN GOA

Taking into consideration both these Bandoem copper-plates (A & B), I think it is pertinent to make the following remarks:

1. **The royal epithets - in his copper-plates**

   In these Bandodem copper-plates we do not find epithets like Raja, Maharaja, Dharmaraja etc. which are found in the copper-plates of the other Bhojas. It is possible that at this time the Bhoja domain had diminished, and so the king was satisfied with the epithet 'Varman' that is, 'ruler'. Perhaps he was living an ascetic life.

2. **The administrators and others**

   Both the charters are addressed to the present and future Bhojakas, Ayuktakas, Sthayicas and others (cultivators, artisans, etc.) like Devaraja Bhoja, while the intermediary Bhoja kings omitted this procedure.

3. **The sale deed of land**

   In the second copper-plate (Plate B) it is not mentioned that the gifted land was purchased. However, it must have been purchased from a private owner or from the village-commune. In the first copper-plate (Plate A) the purchase of land has been mentioned.

4. **The royal emblem**

   Both the copper-plates do not have rings. So it is not known what emblem was used for 'Rajamudra' (royal signet). Devaraja had the seal of a Swan, Asamkita-varman adopted the elephant for his seal-probably he had gained the powers of "Maharaja". But we have no idea about the emblem (seal) of Prithrivarman. It may be added that the Swan indicates peace and the elephant, besides signifying strength, is also a representative symbol of Buddhism.

5. **The language of the Charters**

   The Charter of Devaraja Bhoja is in Sanskrit, with some expressions in Prakrit. The Charter of Asamkita is also in Sanskrit, in prose, but the invocation and imprecation are in verse. The Charter of Asankitavarman is in Sanskrit and in prose, except two lines which are in verse. The Charter of Kapalivarman is in Sanskrit prose without any line in verse; and both the charters of Prithivivarman are in Sanskrit without any line in verse. So, it is clear that in the times of the Bhoja kings, principal records were written in Sanskrit. However, Konkani was surely the popular language in Goa since we notice the Konkani word 'Khajjan' , meaning *Khajana.*

6. Dating of Charters

Based on the characteristics of writing, epigraphists assign the following datings to the Charters of the Bhojas: Charter of Devaraja, somewhere in the 4th century A.D; Ibid of Asankita, by the end of the 5th or the beginning of the 6th century A.D; Ibid of Asankitavarman, about the 6th or 7th century A.D; Ibid of Kapalivarman, about 6th century A.D., and both Charters of Prithivimallavarman, the latter half of the 6th or the first half of the 7th centry A.D.

Regarding the dating of these charters as mentioned in the volumes of Epigraphica India, I have some reservations due to the following reasons:

a) The charter from Kapoli copper-plate issued by Asankitavarman refers to a granted land situated in Palasika-Vishya, Palasika being present Halsi, which was its headquarters. Palaeographists have dated it about 6th or 7th century A.D. which Dr. Gune in his cited article, p. 67, says, "The Kadamba king Ravivarma seems to have established in the Palasikavishaya of the Bhojas during the early part of the 6th century A.D." If this is correct we have to put Asankita or Asankitavarman in the 5th century and not in the 6th or 7th century.

b) From the history of the Chalukyas of Badami, the dating is clear because the copper-plates refer generally to the Shalivahana Shaka. In the Aihole (located at a little distance to the North of Badami) inscription, Kirtivarman I Chalukya of Badami (566 - 598 A.D.) is described as the knight of the destruction of Nalas, Mauryas (of Konkan) and Kadambas. From the Bandodem copper-plate it is seen that the Maurya king Anirjitvarman was ruling in South Konkan in the 6th century A.D. He made a grant of land and a house-site to a Brahmin, and his territories in the Konkan were assigned to the feudatory, Swamiraja of the Chalukya family. Hence, the second copper-plate (plate B) by which the land in Lala village was gifted should be dated in the early years of the first half of the 6th century and not at all in the 7th century as computed in the Epigraphica Indica.

Buddhists in Goa

In the charter of Prithivimallavarman - Bandodem copper-plate B, the compositor, Buddhasuta mentions sanv (samvasta) 205 (in number), but the historians neglected the zero and saw it as 25 from the reign of the king. Similarly, in the Bandodem copper-plate of Anirjitvarman Maurya the samvata is mentioned 209 in number, but the historians overlooked the zero and counted it as 29 years from the start of the reign of that king. The fact is that Devaraja Bhoja must have started the counting of years from the date of the 'victory' year. It is probable that the Buddhist monks enjoyed the protection of this king, so they might have established their first Vihara at Colvale village of Bardez taluka, and so they were grateful to that king. The Buddhist monks were methodical in their practical life, writing their accounts, and perhaps recording the principal events. We have not found any writing so far, but a similar procedure was followed in different Bouddha-viharas outside Goa, especially in Northern India and Ceylon. The Buddhists always mentioned and recorded in their books from the starting year of Samvata adopted by Devaraja. Later on, Buddhavihara was established at Lamgaon village of Bicholim taluka, as we have seen in a grant mentioned before. The writer of the charter of the Maurya king also knew that the system was in use in Bardez taluka, so he recorded Samvata 209. From this dating we come to know what within four years from the issue of the charter, the Mauryas of Konkan had occupied Bardez taluka where the granted land was situated, in Kumardwipa, present day Juve island. Considering that Kirtivarman I might have occupied Southern Konkan from the Mauryas in the last days of his reign, say in the year 590 A.D., it appears that the 4th century A.D. dating marked by the epigraphists to the charter of Deveraja tallies with this computation. So the dating of 7th century A.D. is to be rejected but the 6th century A.D. is acceptable. The datings of the charters issued by Asankita or Asankitavarman and Kapalivarman as mentioned by Dr. Gune in his article published in the Goa Gazetteer should be corrected accordingly.

The idol of Buddha, named afterwards as Gautama, discovered by Fr. Heras at Mushir of Colvale village is dated by him as belonging to the 1st or 2nd century A.D. [87] p. 20. While some put the statue in the 3rd century A.D., it appears that the Buddhist monks had established themselves in Goa in the time of the forefathers of Devaraja Bhoja and continued to propagate under Bhoja's sway at least, since we find the idols of Gautama up to the advent of the Portuguese in Goa. This subject will be discussed in the next chapter.

No evidence of Ashoka Empire or Satavahana Empire in Goa :

In earlier pages we have clarified that contrary to the belief of some historians, the empire of Ashok Mourya did not include Goa nor was it under their sovereignty. The same way, the Satavahana empire was not included but only bounded by Konkan territory within which Goa is located. But yes, Goa was ruled for a short time by the Konkan Mouryas.

THE RULE OF KONKAN MAURYAS IN GOA

A maritime power

These Mauryas of Konkan (northern Konkan) with their headquarters at Gharapur near Bombay always had eye on Goa. Its coastline was famous for external commerce by the sea-route. The Greek geographer Ptolemy (C. 150 A.D.), in his book describes Goa as Kouba or according to other writers as Kowa.

Goan sailors were versatile in high sea navigation with experience through generations going back to a thousand years. There were pirates, as Ptolemy says, on that route. So seafarers had to maintain in their ships fighters with appropriate weapons. The fleets were organized by Goans for the main purpose of commerce. There was also commerce by the land-routes.

The Mauryas of Konkan also had their fleets, as noted in the description of their defeat by Pulakesin II (610-611 to 642 A.D.), who annexed their territory to his kingdom. It appears that the Mauryas also maintained their external commerce by the sea-route and Goan commerce was their rival. They tried to invade the Bhoja kingdom with a surprise attack, perhaps on Chadrapura which is on the river bank. But it appears they were completely defeated and since a permanent watch on the sea-coast was maintained with fleets, over the centuries, the Mauryas could not fulfiill their ambition. At the time of Prithivimallavarman, it appears that there was a conflict within with the step-brother Rudradamana, and the Mauryas took advantage of this internal conflict and the Bhoja kingdom was swept out from history. It is probable that the Bhojas might have continued their reign in a portion of territory around Chandrapura, as feudatories of the Chalukyas of Badami from the 6th century onwards, but this possibility is not supported by any evidence.

THE COPPER-PLATES OF THE KONKAN MAURYAS

I have already made reference to them in the preceeding section while talking of the Bhojas. Here we have to scrutinize two copper-plates of the kings of this ruling family.

VII - Anirjitavarman-Bandodem copper-plate

This copper-plate was found at Bandodem village, Ponda taluka. The characters of this record formed of two plates are similar to those of the Bhoja king Prithivimallavarman but the former are box-headed. The language of the charter is Sanskrit and in prose. It is assigned to the period of 6th or 7th century A.D. by palaeographists but according to my views stated earlier it is of the early half of the 6th century A.D.

Identification of place names

In this charter, the Konkana Maurya king, Maharaja Anirjitavarman addressed the inhabitants of Dwadasha-gramadesh (desha or say the district constituted of twelve villages) as well as the present and future Bhojakas, Ayuktas and sthayins, from the victorious Kumaradvipa, that he had made a grant of one hala of Khajjana land, and another piece of land including a house-site, a garden and tank belonging to one Rashtrakuta, and also some land to be reclaimed from the forest (aranya-Karshana) by employing four batches of workers (preshya-kula), to one Hastarya of the Harita gotra.

The gift which was to be exempted from all taxes (Panga) was made by the king for securing the final merit for himself as well as for Nagapadda, Malladatta and Achala. The king himself executed the grant which is dated the tenth day of the seventh fortnight of Hema i.e. Hemanta Savamta 209.

The charter is addressed, like those issued by Prithivimallavarman, to the Bhojakas. Ayuktakas, Sthaniyakas and residents; so, it is clear that the village administrative system existing at the time of the Bhojas was maintained by the Mauryas in the area of Dwadeshagrama-desha. We find for the first time the designation of Rastrakuta in this chapter.

Dr. Gune's arguments

Dr. V. T. Gune erroneously identifies 'Kumara-dvipa' with Kumbharjuve situated in Tiswadi taluka, while this is to be found in Bardez taluka (Dvadasha-grama-desha). In this taluka there are three islands, namely, Khorjuve, Panole and Juve—the last known also as 'Raneache-juve' to differentiate it from another island also named 'Juve' situated in Tiswadi taluka by the side of Kumbharjuve. The Kumara-dvipa should be rightly identified with this "Raneache-juve" not only because it is situated in Bardez taluka but also because of the mention of a house-site which belonged earlier to a Rastrakuta, as this designation corresponds to a person of a Rano family. During the propagation of Christianity, many families of Rane and Desai of the Kshatriya caste fled, and later some families came back and reinstalled themselves in that taluka, and such members of the Rane family settled in one of their original places, the said island of 'Juve'. The island 'Juve' appears with the epithet 'Kumara'. The compositor of the inscription introduced the word 'Kumara' to symbolize the overlordship of the Maurya king. The Mauryas from Konkan and Rajputana apparently claimed descent from the Kumara Viceroys sent to Ujjayini and Suvarnagiri by the Maurya Emperors of Magadha [87] p. 25. The designation 'Rano' is very ancient. We find this designation in a rock-inscription of 273 B.C. before Ashoka in Madhya-Pradesha [100] p. 28.

On the etymology of Bardez

The area of Bardez taluka was divided into twelve divisions named gramas, each gram consisting of a nuclei of people. As the population was very limited in terms of the number of families, when it increased the hamlets of that time came to be named as 'gaon' (village). Thus at present we find a large number of villages. Each 'grama' at that time had its village-committee consisting of a headman (Bhojak) and record-keeper-cum-accountant (Ayuktaka). For each taluka, there was a person of the category of Vishayapati' whom the charter of Maurya designated as 'Rashtrakrita'. It is obvious that the original 'Vishayapati' constituted a large family, like the Bhojakas and Ayuktakas. When they separated and established separate houses, each member came to be named Rastrakuta. This is the reason why we find mentioned in the charter the grant of the house-site of a Rastrakuta. According to the socio-religious customs of the Aryas the property of any person who died without off-spring passed to the king; and so, that house-site (with tank and khajan land) was gifted to a Brahmin. This island 'Juve' is surrounded by the waters of the river Kolvale, and the village of Revadem and Nadodem are situated on the other bank.

Some historian are of the opinion that the name Bardez was derived from the fact that within that taluka were twelve Deskats (given to Desais)—lands owned by the Desais. In fact, the Bhojaka families of that taluka came to be named as Desais later on. In Quepem taluka (Chandravadi) there is no Mokaso and hence they were only called Bhojakas and are currently named Desai.

Origin of the Rastrakuta designation

Now in respect of the designation 'Rashtrakuta'. This designation appears for the first time in the copper-plate of Anirajitavarman Maurya, and was employed obviously because it was in use at that time or before in Northern India. It has no link to the Rashtrakuta in the Rajputana families who belonged to the Moon race (Chandravanchi and of the Atrigotra). This designation referred to the officials charged with the collection of government dues in respect of a district (Rashtra), similar to the medieval designation Deshmukh Deshpande p. 238. They could not change the village-commune system where it existed, in respect of the landings, so the word 'panga' referring to the tax payable to the village-commune, which appears in the copper-plate of Asankitavarman Bhoja, has also been mentioned in this copper-plate.

There is no reference to the name of the compositor of the charter, but I think that the text was prepared by Nagapadda who was surely of a Brahmin of Paddye caste. The other two names, Malladatta and Achala were most probably of two members of the Rastrakuta family who might have had rights to the forest land gifted to the Brahmin. The gotra of the donee is Harita, so probably he was a Brahmin of the Paddye caste.

VIII - Chandravarman-Shivapur copper-plate

The copper-plate was found by V. R. Varde Valaulikar (known as Shenoy Goembab) in Goa [103]. King Chandravarman is described as 'nana-samanta-man-marichibiracharila-padapadma', i.e. whose lotus-like feet shone in the rays of the sun in the form of many feudatory chieftains. The charter records the donation of some land to the Mahavihara i.e. monastery situated in Shivapur, the boundaries of which have been specified in the charter. It is not known from where the grant was issued as the first part of the plate is damaged.

The spread of Shaivism in Goa

Some historians identified Shivapur with Shirodem (*Siroda*) of Ponda which is not correct. Shivapur is the same place mentioned in the Bhoja copper-plate, part of which is present Harvalem village of Bicholim (*Dicholi*) taluka. The Maha-Vihara referred to is the famous artificial cave known as '*Pandavanchi-houri*'. Taking into consideration the religious seats existing at the time, it is clear that one part of that cave was utilized by ascetics of the Pashupata sect of Shaivism.

The Pashupata sect

This Pashupata sect was of very ancient times and was propagated with certain modifications in Gujarat and spread from Indore. The family of Kalchuri ruling northern Maharashtra and northern Konkan, 416 A.D. onwards had adopted that sect, and there is evidence that a queen of that family made a grant to that sect. The Mauryas of the Konkan who were posted by a king of that family to administer Aparanta-Konkana also helped the Pashupata sect.

At the time of the Bhojas a merchant (Vaishya) named Ravi or Aditya probably carved the caves for establishing lingas and as a dwelling for ascetics of the Pashupata sect, and the Maurya king by the charter granted the land for their maintenance. The sect believed in the principle that Shiva was the principal God, and Vishnu was his 'ansha' i.e. his past, and this is the reason why the Sivapura-varnam of the Sahyadri-Khanda mentions the 'Vishnupadam', the sign of foot-prints. I have mentioned its existence at a place named '*Paular*' now situated in *Kudnem* village which was formerly part of Shivapur.

The Mauryas were expelled by Kirtivarman Chalukya from Goa, so the dating of copper-plates determined by historians as of the 6th or 7th century A.D. is to be rectified because those copper-plates could have been issued only in the period of the 6th century not later than 590 A.D.

The Pashupati sect adopted Yoga-Sadhana with certain changes and spread up to Mysore and Tamil Nadu. Their religious concept was against Buddhism and Jainism;

so, due to the propaganda of this sect Buddhism and Jainism declined, and the decline was marked at the time of Shilahara in the Konkan. After the Shilahars, Jainism was introduced by some kings of the Kadamba dynasty in Goa, but that also succumbed shortly as soon as the support of Kadamba kings disappeared when the dynasty was extinguished by the invasion of the Muslims. For a detailed study of the Palshupata sect I recommend Marathi readers to read 'Pashupta Sanpradays' in the Bhartiya Sanskritic Kosha.

The Konkan Maurya administration in Goa

The Mauryas ruled for about 40 years over Goa. They did not have sufficient time to introduce their system of administration. Dr. Altekar gives a good account of that period. He says: "The large extent of self-government was enjoyed in the 7th century B.C. by the village communities of the Shakyas, Mallas, Lichchavis and Vjjanis but those were mountain clans, accustomed to a life of independence, and what was true of them, was not true of the rest of India. There were similar republican tribes in the day's of Samudragupta in the south and south-western parts of the Punjab, but it is equally clear that the rest of India was a stranger to such institutions in the fourth century A.D. Similar was the case in the 6th century B.C. at the time of Amoghavarsha this system was unknown in Magadha."

"The Jataka give a clear account of the picture in the 6th and 7th centuries B.C. For our purpose it is of extreme importance for it will enable us to realize the state of the village community as it actually was at the time when the Aryan colonization of the Deccan began to take place. For the Jataka stories were compiled in the Maurya's period and they undoubtedly refer to and describe the life three centuries earlier.

"According to Jatakas, each village was no longer an independent village republic as was in the case of the Vedic times. It was a subordinate unit of the principality or State, and its head was the village headman who was probably a hereditary officer. He was responsible for the collection of revenue and chief of community. There was an informal council of village elders, which the headman would occasionally consult. There were no regular and periodical meetings of the body as was the case among the Shakyas and Vajjanis.

"Headman (gramapati) as hereditary officer was the custom in the North. The headman in Western India was selected by the people not appointed by the Government, but again was a hereditary officer. Under the Andhras then, the village headman was a hereditary officer and same was the case under the Chalukyas. The Goa plates of king Satyatraya Dhruvaraja dated A.D. 610 describe all the village officers including the headman as shayi or permanent residents of the place."

"In a few communities, however headman does not exist but his absence can be easily explained. This is chiefly in the Ratnagiri and Kolaba districts, and its cause is the 'Khoti' system, which is prevalent there. Khoti system was introduced by the Maratha and Peshwa. Soon the ancient Patels, as headman of villages disappeared. Thus it is that there was no hereditary Patels as headman of villages. However, several Maratha and Kunbi families are styled as Patels in ancient deeds, and therefore we may conclude that in pre-Khoti days, headmen were common even in Konkan (Ratnagiri Gazette pp. 136-142)."

"The name 'Lekhaka' found in Sanskrit (northern writer) must have been current in Western India" [103] pp. XII-12.

SOVEREIGNTY OF THE CHALUKYAS OF BADAMI

Shedding new light on the Sendraka family in Goa

The founder of the Chalukya ruling family was a chieftain in Southern India, but Pulakeshi I fought the Rattas and Pallavas and made himself master of the town of Vatapi (Badami) and established a kingdom of modest dimensions. He enjoyed high sounding imperial titles like Satyashraya, Ranavikrama, Prithivivallabha and Srivallabha as revealed in the Chiplun copper-plate [53].

Feudatories of the Chalukyas

His son Kirtivarman followed his father on the Chalukyan throne in about 566 A.D. and ruled up to 598 A.D. He assumed the usual titles of family. He married the sister of Raja Shrivallabha Senanandaraya of the Sendraka family. He subdued some kings and expelled the Mauryas from Goa, and installed his brother-in-law, the said Shrivallabha as King (Raja). His proper name was Vantu which is explained by other evidence which will be referred to later. The Chiplun copper-plate mentions his name by his epithets 'Shrivallabha-Senandaraja', omitting his proper name. This mistake also occurs in an inscription of Pulakesin II, where only his epithet 'Satyashraya' is mentioned.

THE COPPER-PLATES OF THE CHALUKYAS

IX - The Chiplun copper-plate

The Chiplun copper-plate was obtained by a cultivator at Chiplum, the chief town of Chiplum taluka of Ratnagiri district. It consisted of two plates. The ring, on which the plates were strung, was accidentally destroyed the cultivators. The characters belong to the southern class of alphabets and are of a size regular to the period to which the record belongs. The language is Sanskrit, and in addition to an opening verse in praise of Vishnu, there are seven of the customary benedictory and im-pressible verses at the end.

Translation of the inscription

The inscription is a record of the Western Chalukya king Satyashraya-Pulakeshin II. Here is the translation of the principal part of the copper-plate published in the Epigraphica Indica:

"He, the King (Pulakeshin II) issued a command to the inhabitants of the Avaretika vishaya to this effect: 'My maternal uncle, the ornament of the Sendrakas, the most devout worshipper of (the god) Mahewshwara Srivallabha-Senanandaraja, who has acquired (a knowledge of all) the proper and improper practices of noble people, (and) who has covered all the places between the quarters of the compass with the canopy of (his) fame that purchased by the price of his valour, - he, the king, in order to increase the religious merit of (his) parents and of himself, has given to Mahewshwara, the son of Krishnaswamin, of the Atreya gotra, who has performed sacrifices, these two things, free from the right of entry by the irregular and regular troops, by messengers, and by the king's servants, - (viz) the village of Amravatavaka, and Vishti at (the village of) Avanchapalli on the Charubenna.

"He who grants land, (whether simply) ploughed, (or) planted with seed (or) full of crops, he is treated with honour in heaven, for as long as the worlds, created by the sun, endure. Let prosperity attend the writer, the reader and the hearers".

Mr. Fleet's mistakes and their correction

Fleet who translated the copper-plate tried to identify the places. He even trav-elled to Nashik area but it was in vain. Paramananda Gupta in his cited book has summarised Mr Fleet's views. The reason for such a form of investigation was that the copper-plates were found in Chiplun. They ignored the possibility that a Bhat of Sattari taluka might have migrated to Chiplun at the time of one of the many starvations suffered in the 19th century A.D. in Sattari taluka, due to attacks of locusts etc. V. R. Varde Valaulikar (Shenoy Goembab) was the first to locate the places in Sattari taluka. However, he made an error in identifying Avaratika as *Advoi* village since he located the places only by consulting maps and was unable to visit the area proper.

Avaretika-Vishya means (like in the case of the Bhojas' inscriptions) the district with headquarters at Avaretika. Avaretika is a Sanskritization of 'Ivrem' village. At the time of the inscription there was only one village which later was divided into three namely Ivrem Budruk (Ivrem the big), Ivrem Khurd (Ivrem the small), Budruk and Khurd being Pharsi words. But these villages are named respectively '*Khaile-Ivrem*' and '*Voile Ivrem*', such designations being closer to the Ghats than the others. The third village is named 'Riem' or 'Rivem'. That there was only one village before the division is proven by the fact that the villages or say Maratha Gaonkars of all these three villages, together perform a religious rite every year named '*Bhogaval*' near a tree on the trijunction of the boundaries of Ivrem Budruk, Chorundem and Dongurli (Thanem hamlet).

Now in respect of identification of the village of Avanchapalli. Avanchappalli is a Sanskritization of Askinpalli or Askinpali which like 'Avaretika' or primitive Ivrem village, comprised, at the time of the inscription, Pali and Dongurli villages. The latter village is formed of three hamlets namely Thanem, Bocal (alias *Bakhal*) and Dongurli. The ancient formation of the village is corroborated by the custom existing among the Gaonkars of those villages - that is, if the Gaonkars of the three hamlets of Dongurli are unable to perform certain village-rites, due to any reason, the Gaonkars of Pali village have the right to perform the duties on their behalf, as they are the successors of the eldest brother of the main family. It is to be noticed that the linga existing in a shrine named '*Math*' is a symbol of a Siddha named '*Askin-Siddha*'. At the south of this place lies a ricefield with some coconut trees long before known as *Ishhti*. I knew this in 1942 when I was working as the head of a batch for a cadastral survey of that area. That part of the property belonged to Hirba Babu Bivam Rau Desai, the representative of the eldest branch of the family which owned the two villages namely Dongurli and Rivem. In that year I had seen two blackstone inscriptions about forty cms. high—one showed a bas-relief picture of a male person in a seated position with a head-dress like a *Mukuta* and on the other plate were carved two big signs. Both the inscriptions were found at the base of the coconut plantation, on the right level of the land, while about one metre away, the low-lying area was under paddy cultivation. In the year 1969, when I re-visited the area in search of those inscriptions, I was told that due to flooding in the rainy season these plates had been washed away. I searched for more than an hour with two labourers, but could not locate the inscriptions. The existence of those inscriptions are known even today by persons of my age in that village, but they cannot accurately describe the figures marked on the stones. Adjacent to this property to the south, lies the slope of a hillock named 'Haskin', a name which tallies with the description of the village. Charubenna, mentioned in the inscription, is *Chorounem* village (in Portuguese Choraundem) and not a river or rivulet, as historians seem to think from the last portion, 'benna', of the name. Otherwise, from that inscription it does not appear to be a river but a place-name—a village.

From this description, it is clear beyond any doubt that one of the lands granted is the one described above. Now we shall try to identify Amravatavaka-grama, the village designated as Amravatavaka. The name is composed of three Sanskrit words namely, Amra, Vata and Vaka. Amra in the local language means *Ambo*. Vata, *Vad* and Vaka mean in Sanskrit a vase oblong in form, used for melting metals. So this name identifies with the village Ambede-Budruk. This village has a more or less oblong form in the NE-SW direction. The word Budruk means big which probably was utilized to signify its length, because in Sattari taluka there is no other village with the designation of Ambedem-Khurd.

According to the land-survey report, in the year of 1866 the area of the village is about 111 hectares and was given on permanent lease by Zoitoji Rane Sar Desai on behalf of Sawantwadkar Bhousule, by a charter (*poto*) dated 14th February, 1780, to two brothers of the Chitpavan Brahmin caste with the surname Bhave. The name of the donee in the inscription is Mahesvara, son of Krishnaswamin, of Atreyagotra, and as the charter does not mention the name of the composer, I presume that the same person might have composed it. This presumption is supported by the fact that at the end of the charter reference has been made simply to the writer for merits gained.

The worship of Maheswara and the place name *Mahadevachem Mol"*

One more point is noticeable from the inscription—while Pulakesin II has been described as worshipper of Vishnu his uncle Srivallabha is described as a devout worshipper of Maheshwara. In 1943, I had seen a Shiva-linga at the corner of a place named '*Mhadevache-mol*' situated in Thane hamlet, in a forest grove and without any kind of shelter. It was not under worship on the grounds that this type of stone-carved Shiva-linga had to be worshipped exclusively by a Brahmin of the priest caste, and no such family lived nearby. It is probable that the Shiva-linga was installed by the donee 'Maheshwara' and the worship was suspended when that family abandoned the village. In the last five years a temple has been constructed installing that Shivalinga and the worship rituals are conducted by the Brahmins of the priesthood (*Bhat*). The Shiva-linga is a Southern type, that is, without a 'Shalunka', which is remarkable. Remarkable also is the fact that in the whole of Sattari taluka there is no Shiva-linga under worship, except in Pissurlem and Honda villages adjacent to Bicholim (*Dicholi*) taluka, which is understandable. In Pissurlem village there is a family with the surname "Harapati", known as Pissurlenkar of the Kulkarni vangad of the village-commune. Only one village-commune found in the whole area of Sattari taluka might have installed that Shiva-linga, long ago. This family is of the Saraswat Brahmin caste, Mahajana of the temple of Shri Shantadurga of Queula (*Kavale*), Ponda taluka (the eminent historian Dr. P. Pissurlenkar belonged to that family).

In Honda village there is a Shiva-linga with a shaft about one metre long. It is named '*Hond-deva*' or '*Vyaghreswar*', and is exclusively the family deity of the Bhats of Ambedem village. It is possible that the Bhat family with the Bhave surname might have settled there after arriving from Chiplun side and gaining permanent lease of Ambedi-Budruk village in 1780 when it was already abandoned by the successors of the original donee, Maheshwara of the Atreya gotra.

The Golden Age of temple architecture and sculptures

The epoch of Vantu-vallabha

The epoch of Vantu-vallabha is characterized by the great impetus provided by him for the construction of temples and installation of Hindu gods, on a scale never known before him. [104]

He, it appears, did not impose his own ideas, but helped the Gaonkars in the installations. From various evidence, we can say that his period may be characterized as the Golden Age of Goa.

He was well aware of the legends of the origins of his family as well as of the Chalukyas and he made use of these legends to inculcate in the people he ruled a religious devotion and sympathy in respect of both the families.

According to one of the legends on the origin of the Chalukya family, their ancestor sprang from the Chulka (both hands allowed to hold water) of the creator Brahmadeva when he desired to create a hero at the request of Indra, to protect the earth from evil-doers. Therefore, the Chalukyas claim to descend from the sage Harit of the Manavya gotra. They claim that their ancestor was nursed by the Seven Mothers (Sapta Matrikas) and protected by Kartikeya (who also was born from the Sapta Matrikas). All the Chalukya princes adopted on their banner *Varaha lanchana* or the Boar crest, which they obtained from god Vishnu. The gold coin used by them as currency had the figure of a Boar and was named *Varaha* while their banner was the Boar crest [104] p. 56.

ill. 22 : Idol of Brahmadeva at Parce Village, Pednem Taluka, dated c. 6th Century A.D.

At Aihole, north of Badami, the starting point of the kingdom of this family, an idol of Brahmadeva with four heads was installed. Like-

ill. 23 : Idol of Brahmadev at
Brahma-Carmali Village, Sattari
Taluka, dated c. 6th Century
A.D.

wise, Vantuvallabha installed approximately on the boundaries of his domain six idols of Brahmadeva, viz, the first in Parcem *(ill. 22)*, the second in Vinordem village both in Pednem taluka; the third Brahm-Karmali *(ill. 23)* of Sattari taluka; the fourth in Colomba village *(ill. 24)* of Astagrahar division of Sanguem taluka; the fifth at Reddi island, Sindhudurg taluka; and the sixth existed in *Kurka* village (Curca in Portuguese) of Tiswadi taluka. The last was destroyed in about 1542 by the Portuguese, as can be seen from the Portuguese records published by Dr. P. S. Pissurlenkar.

After gaining sway over the whole area of Goa, Vantuvallabha changed his headquarters from Rivem in Sattari to the hillock known later as Mardangad of Ponda town. According to the legend that his ancestor was of *Nagavansha* or say *Shesha-vamsha*, he made an idol of a man with *Mukuta*, the lower part of the body, being in the form of a serpent in rolled form. This idol was at Talauli village near Ponda town and now is in the Archaeological Museum of Goa at St. Inez, Panaji, under the name 'Naga-devata *(ill. 25)*

Sendraka is a Sanskritized form of

ill. 24 : Idol of Brahmadeva at
Colamba Village, Sanguem Taluka,
dated c. 6th Century A.D.

ill. 25 : Idol of the mythological 'Sinda Nagaraja', ancestor of the Sendraka family,found at Talaudi Village of Ponda Taluka and recorded as 'Naga-devata' in Panaji Museum, dated c. 6th Century A.D.

Sind. The Bombay Gazetteer Vol. XV, part I, gives a full account of that family from the evidence obtained through inscriptions.

There are two legends mentioned in the Gazetteer which more or less are similar. One of those legends says that the Sindhu river had a son from God Shiva who was found by a Nagaraja,who passed the child on to be reared by a tigress. The boy was named Sind and when young, he came to the South and established his kingdom at Karahata (present Karhad). We find the history of this family spread in different areas in Belgaum district and Karnataka, with different banners, from the 3rd century A.D. The second legend says that the ancestor of the family was the son of a Nagaraja named Dharendra born in the area of Ahichhatra on the bank of the river Sindhu, and so named Sind, who was nourished by a tigress, and the further history is the same. So, based on the last legend Vantuvallabha styled an idol in the form mentioned above. The fact is that the designation 'Naga' does not mean a serpent, nor does it stand for the Naga race of the Assam hills. 'Naga' is a Sanskrit word meaning simply the people who lived in a mountainous area, and nothing more.

Five idols of Brahmadeva are worshipped even today, out of the six installed by him. In the Skandapurana (1, 1, 6; 3, 14 and 7, 1, 165) there is a narration that Brahmadeva had started a sacrificial Yadyna at Pushhakar Tirtha, but at the time his wife Savitri was absent. Hence Brahmadeva adopted a daughter of a herdsman named Gayatri as his wife and performed the Yadyna. Savitri became angry and cursed her husband that he would never again be worshipped. The Skandapurana was not composed before the 8th century A.D., so the worship in the 6th century A.D. is admissible. Moreover in that *Tirtha* and at Kumbhakonam in South India the worship continues and every twelve years there is a great festival named Kumbhamela in those places.

All the idols that we find in Goa in the Chalukyan style, except the one in the temple of Tambdi Surla in Sanguem taluka, are of the period of Vantuvallabha who directly imported the carved idols of blackish schist stones from Southern India. It is probable that he even imported big beams of teak wood, the carving of which might have been done here by specialist carpenters brought from the South. Here let me mention only two of the most magnificient works in that style: the first is the temple with the idol of Ananta at Savoi-Vere of Ponda taluka and the second example is of two idols of the Sun god and the other of Uma-Mahesha at Kudnem of Bicholim (*Dicholi*) taluka.

The temple of Ananta is surrounded on all sides by sweet water. Though its structure is tiny it invites the attention of visitors due to its location (surrounded by water) in conformity with the description that Ananta or say sheshshayi-Vishnu resides in Kshirasagar—an ocean of milk. The erection of the main structure is supported by a wooden framework, with exquisite wood-carvings especially on the columns. The idol of Sheshshayi-Vishnu is like those found in Karnataka and at Trivandrum (here named

'Padmanabha', and is of wood). But the later temple is not surrounded by water like in Savoi-Verem. The other idols mentioned were situated in Kudnem village and were noteworthy on religious and historic grounds.

We have already noticed that a linga existing in Harvalem cave represents symbolically the Sun-god and as such, with the same significance the idol of the Sun-god was established in the adjacent place. It is known also that during the time of Chandravarman Maurya of the Konkan, the sages of the Pashupata sect resided in the caves. They worshipped god Shiva with his Shakti (power) as primeval elements of the creation of the Universe (*Yoga-Sadhana*) and preached to the people to adopt this path in worship. This sect later deteriorated into different sub-sects, namely Kapalika, Shakta and Kalamukha, and later on Gorakha-pantha appeared. But at the time of Vantuvallabha only the earlier Pashupata-sect existed. So, to symbolize the principle of that sect an idol of Uma-Mahesha was installed near the Harvalem caves. A similar type of idol of the couple was already established at Aihole, North of Badami, in the time of the Chalukyas.

Dr. Gune in the Goa Gazetteer (p. 73) wrongly identified 'Kundiwataka' village of a Nerur copper-plate (near Kudal in Sawantwadi) with Kudnem village, based on the existence of the idol of Uma-Mahesha in the Chalukyan style. Other historians have since long identified that village with sufficient assurance with village 'Kundi' existing in the same area of Kudal. Dr. Gune does not ignore it, but he made his affirmation without making a proper study of the facts.

Besides the idols of Sheshashayi-Vishnu, Aditya (Sun) of Brahmadeva and Uma-Mahesha, Vantu-vallabha started to change the deities under worship in his original place in Avretika-Vishaya of Sattari taluka, where his family—at least around the first century A.D., if not earlier—had established themselves having come from the Karhad side of Belgaum district. So, we find idols of about the 6th century at '*Rangache-mol*' of Naneli village.

Mother Goddess worship in transition

I have already referred to the system of worship of the primitive Kols. They worshipped the Santer (anthill) (*varula* in Marathi, and *Roin* in Konkani), and their dependant Mundari worshipped a jungle tree named '*Kel*'. The Maratha people who subjugated the area appropriated these deities, and introduced their own Jogayi which was being worshipped in the form of a round granite stone (designated as '*tandala*' in Marathi). In Marathi areas at that time many female deities under the name of Jogayi, Ambayi, Mangalayi, Mariayi, etc. were under worship by different people. Such type of worship, that is, a form of worship of the Mother-goddess is noticed not only in India but also abroad. So, wherever the Maratha people settled in Goa we find such type of worship symbolized by granite or basalt stone, for example Layirayi of

ill. 26 : Idol of Jogeshwari found at Rangachem mol, Naneli Village, Sattary Taluka, dated 6th Century A.D.

Shirgaon village of Bicholim (*Dicholi*) taluka, Morjay of Morgi village of Morjayi Pednem taluka etc. In all there were seven sister-goddesses with their only brother named Khetoba installed in Vainginim village, near Haturli in Bicholim taluka. I will not provide an account of the development of this type of idolatry in Goa, as this is not the proper place. However, it is remarkable that out of these goddesses only Jogayi, under the name of Jogeshwari or Yogeshwari, is found under worship (*ill. 26*).

In Sattari, those three deities were under worship. Vantuvallabha tried to make the idol on the basic principle which governed the establishment of such goddesses. It is remarkable that all those three goddesses are considered as virgins. The Santer (ant-hill) was styled as Maheswari with a trident in the right hand, or in a fighting form 'Mahishasuramardinim', as the main deity which protected the village by killing a buffalo (Mahisha). The third deity is kelbai and *kel* is a jungle tree. This word *kel* is of the Austric language which appears in Kannada, meaning opulence; so it was styled in the form of Gaja-Lakshimi. Jogayi was named as Jogeshwari which did not have the position of Yogeshwari at that time, but was considered as 'Mahalakshimi', so she was styled in that form. Besides these three, Vantuvallabha introduced the fourth named 'Brahmani', but popularly named 'Bahamami'. In the excavation at Naneli only three idols and one Virgal were found. Among these three idols 'Kelbai' as Gaja-Laxmi and Brahmani can surely be identified. Now the idol named by me as 'Maheswari' may be of Jogeshwari, and the idol corresponding to Santer was not made maintaining its form as an 'anthill', as exists in different villages. The idol of this goddess Brahmani is generally styled sitting on a low seat, the legs crossed horizontally, or sited on

ill. 27 : Idol of Brahmani found at Rangache mol Naneli Village Sattary Taluka, dated c. 6th Century A.D.

a lotus flower, and she is the 'Shakti', power, of the god Brahmadeva. But the idol of Brahmani discovered at Naneli village is quite different *(ill. 27)*. This idol of Brahmani is also styled in a sitting posture but only the left leg is folded horizontally while the right leg must have been folded vertically. The idol is found mutilated, but this position can be visualised. The left leg in sitting form lies on a coil of two joined Naga-serpents with their hoods at each side (hood of the right side was found mutilated). It is remarkable that the mukutas Crown of Jogeshwari and Bhahamani are of the same type as that of Chalukya Pulakesi II and that of Gajalakshimi). In short, this deity represents Kelbai which is of a lower stage. So, the sculpture of this idol is surely of the period of Pulakesi II, whose picture is available and published in histories. The representation of the goddess Brahmani in this form is unique in style, so, it requires some explanation.

The unique images of Brahmadeva and Shakti

There are two different interpretations before me. One of them is that Vantuvallabha had installed six images of Brahmadeva. As shown before, he thought of symbolizing His Shakti. At Aihole, the Brahmani was installed among Sapta-Matrikas. Moreover, she was Shakti of Brahmadeva who created, according to the legends, the ancestor of the Chalukyas. This family had adopted as its protector the god Kartikeya, who in Southern India is named Subrahmanyam and is symbolized by a couple of naga-serpents joined in the form mentioned above. In the temple of Mahadeva (in Shiva-linga form) a plate exists at the entrance of the sanctuary showing in bas—relief this type of Subrahmaniam as that temple was constructed in the period of the later Chalukyas. At Panaji Museum there is an idol at 'Dharbandoda (Sanguem taluka) which is of Yogeshwari (Jogeshwari). It is in sitting (*sidhasana*) form, while that found at Naneli is in standing form which I named first as Maheswari mainly because a trident is found in a hand. Later on, I considered it to be Jogeshwari because at Thane hamlet adjacent to Naneli, in the main temple among other idols there is a Jogeshwari instead of Maheswari. Otherwise both the deities are forms of the same 'Shakti', the power of Mahesvara or Shiva.

The second interpretation could be that Vantu-vallabha was honoured with the exclusive epithet of 'Senanandaraja' by his nephew Pulakesin II, and this epithet is of the god Kartikeya, as commander-in-chief elected by the gods. According to the Puranas his vehicle is a peacock and the banner is a cock.

Vantu-vallabha was honoured by two titles: Shrivallabha and Senanandaraja. The title 'Vallabha' was offered among the Chalukyas and Pallava kings to their feudatories who were members of the private council of the king and were consulted in intricate cases of conflict of any kind. The prefix 'Shri' was the highest among Vallabhas. Besides this title, the other exclusive title 'Senanandaraja' was also offered. So, to express his gratitude he might have symbolized the 'Subrahmanyam'—his own symbol but at a low level so as to provide support for the power of the Chalukyas derived from the creator of their ancestor.

In popular language Mahishasuramardini is named Santer, and Gaja-Lakshimi as Kelbay in all villages in Goa wherever we find prototypes of the idols which appeared not only in the villages of the New Conquests but even in the area of the Old Conquests. Gritli Mittelwalner, a German professor of Indology, found in a well near a chapel, an idol of Mahishasuramardini, in *Hadfade* (Arpora) village, Bardez taluka. We find her name recorded as Santeri in the Portuguese records of the destroyed Hindu temples published by Dr. P. S. Pissurlenkar [7] p. 50. The idol of Kelbay (Gaja-Lakshimi) is found in worship in Volvoi village, Ponda taluka, and it is interesting to note that a similar idol is found on top of the mountain Bandol of Usgaon, now in Ponda taluka. *(ill. 28)*.

ill. 28 : Idol of Gajalaxmi (Kelbai) found at Rangachem mol
Naneli Village Sattary Taluka, dated c. 6th century A.D.

It is to be noticed that all the idols and their prototypes are always in bas-relief, or say, in the form of two dimensions carved on basalt rock plates.

It is noticed from history that even the chieftains of the Sind family in different areas had their different banners from the 3rd century A.D. and I presume that as such, Vantu-vallabha had adopted a cock as his banner.

Prosperity in trade and commerce

Since long ago, *Vodlem Goen* (Goa Velha), interlinked to *Agashi* (Agaçaim of Tiswadi taluka, was known to seafarers as an important port of Goa. Ptolemi (C. 150 A.D.), a Greek geographer mentions it as Kouba or Kowa. This natural port found its utility degraded after centuries of continuous silt deposits on the banks of the river Zuari, especially during the rainy season. So, it appears that very soon after the conquest of Goa by the Chalukya Kirtivarman I, Vantu-vallabha, as king of Goa, ordered the silt to be removed and constructed the port with all facilities for big ships sailing to the Malabar coast with horses. It was named 'Sindapura', after the name of his family. This port continued to be frequented by ships and was prosperous in the area. Earlier, Chandrapura (present Chandor) was also a port on the river Kushavati (known as Paroda river) but was becoming non-usable because of silt deposits, and slowly declined to an inferior status, to be used only for internal navigation. Therefore, the Kadamba rulers in about 1038 A.D. transferred their capital to Gopaka-pattana, present *Vodlem-Goen* (Goa Velha i.e. Goa the Old). An inscription on copper-plates issued in the year 1053 A.D. by Jaykeshi I, of the Kadamba family [59] pp. 6-18, makes a gift of customs duties to be paid in that port to a mosque constructed by his Minister Saddan, a Muslim Arab. From this long inscription we come to know of the territories and countries the ships came from. The rate of customs-duties varied. This inscription does not mention the name Sindapura, and there is a reason behind it. There was rivalry through the generations between the Kadambas and Chalukyas and the Sind family was always faithful to the Chalukyas. So, the Kadambas changed the name to Gopaka-pattana. However, its derivation has nothing to do with the word Gopa, as some historians try to explain. The name Sindapura was completely banished, and the writer of the inscription styled the name Goa as Gopaka, and nothing more. However, foreign travellers, according to foreign navigators, continued with the old name Sindapura, at least up to the year 1342-49. Al Idresi and Ibn Batula, the Arab Muslim travellers mention it as Kowa-Sindapur or simply Sindabur. [87] p. 17

Ibn Batuta states: "...on setting sail from this town (i.e. Quga or Gogo in Kathiawar), we arrived after three days at the island of Sindabur (Goa) on which there are thirty-six villages. It is surrounded by a gulf, the waters of which are sweet and agreeable at low tide. In the centre of the island are two cities, an ancient one built by the infidels, and one built by the Muslims when they first captured the island". The city of Ela on the island of Goa must have been built by the Mohammedans after their first capture of Goa in 1313. According to Fonseca, Ibn Batuta visited Goa between 1342 and 1349 (Historical and Archaeological Sketch of the City of Goa, p. 125).

External trade at least from this port must have existed from about 2,300 B.C. onwards though sporadically. I have already referred to the expedition of Gudia from Sumer, who named that port as Gubi. And about 2,000 years later we find from records that the ports of the western coast of India from Bhadoch to the south up to Ceylon and even farther were handling external trade directly from the Roman empire and later on with Arabia, especially. I have already referred to Ptolemy, but more ancient is the record of the author of Periplus (C. 75 A.D.) which describes the trade existing at this time. In this description we do not find the name Goa but it is clear that trade existed also from Goa port as mentioned later by Ptolemy.

The land-tax payment system

In respect of land-tax payable by cultivation, it appears in the inscription from the Bhoja time onwards under the designation of 'Panga'. From historical records of the Gupta age we know that customs-duty existed in their kingdom and there are records of Southern India like the kingdom of the Pandyas and Cholas proving the existence of customs-duty on import from the seaboard. I have touched on this point earlier. There was complete subjugation of the dynasty of the Mauryas of the Konkan successively by Chalukya Kirtivarman I, his brother Mangalesh and his son Pulakeshin II from Puri (Rajapuri at north of Vengurla) on the sea-coast or Gharapuri near Bombay and Revatidwipa (present Reddi village) of Northern Konkan. They extended their sway up to South Gujarat, establishing their viceroys of the Chalukya and Sind families. This had been made mainly to check the piracy caused by the fleet of the Mauryas, obviously to monopolize and command the western coast, as, besides creating prosperity the kingdom was gaining customs-duty. So, it is presumable that custom duty existed from the Bhoja period onwards but the rates are unknown, except at the time of the Kadambas and these also in respect of Sindapura port from the respective inscriptions. However, it is worth noting that such duty did not exist on the import of horses from Arabia and Persia.

Once it is established in principle by a kingdom that customs-duty should be imposed on external trade, by the sea-route, it is obvious the same type of duty must have existed also on imported goods by the land route. In the time of the Bhojas and later, there were a few paved roads and cart-roads, and all the goods were transported by pack-animals only rarely using boats to cross rivers. One such road from the Ghat was from Dhumogod, passing through the Sancordem village of Hemadbarcem of Sanguem taluka. The name Sancordem is derived from "Sank", "Ur" and "dem" all Kannada words meaning respectively, customs-duty, village; and 'dem' is a suffix characterising 'small'. So, it is clear that the village was a customs-port to collect duties and perhaps was established in the last period of the Bhoja dynasty, taking an example from the practice existing in Karnataka, when that dynasty expanded their sway to that side, as we know from the copper-plates already mentioned. We find the same place-names in Goa containing the word 'Samk' meaning surely 'customs-duty', for example, 'Sankwal' village in Mormugaon taluka, on the banks of the Zuari river and 'Sankwadi' hamlet in *Hadfade* (Arpora) in Bardez taluka, adjacent to *Kalangut* (Calangute) village.

We also find in Goa some families with the surname 'Keni' of the Saraswat Brahmin caste as well as those with the surname 'Dangi' of the Sarawat Brahmin, Vaishya and Naik castes. The designations 'Keni' and 'Dangi' are of Kannada origin meaning customs officers. There is a copper-plate of the time of Tribhuvanamalla Kadamba, dated Shaka 1028 (1106 A.D.) from which it is known that a person named Ganda Gopala of the Keni family from Panjarkhani (hamlet of Cuncolim village) of Salcete taluka established a 'Brahmapuri' (Institute of Instruction) at Gopak (present Goa Velha) making grants of lands purchased by him.

Etymology of the term Ghodemanni

Ghodemanni (misspelt as Ghodemodni) is a distorted form of the vernacular word Ghode-Mandani, meaning literally arrangement of horses, and consequently means treatment (maintenance with proper feeding, cure of all diseases etc.) and their training which might be examined naturally by the king through periodical exhibitions to evaluate their fitness . Also inspected were the warriors on horse-back, as at that time, the main weapons used were lances and bows with arrows, the spade being of a secondary level.

The horses were brought from Arabia, Persia and Afghanistan by Arab and Persian merchants by the sea-route to the Malabar coast long before Pulakeshin I (547-567 A.D.). But the merchants never instructed the purchaser about the proper feed and cure of diseases suffered by horses, nor did they bring a single mare, in order to avoid breeding of horses on this soil. Their proper feeding was gram and grass; gram was not produced on the Malabar coast and the local buyers had no idea of a substitute for gram. They were fed with meat, milk, ghee and grass, with the result that the horses died within a few years, providing the sellers the opportunity to sell more horses.

Vantudeva or Vantu-vallabha was aware of the advantage of horses on the battlefield. Sindapura port was frequented by foreign traders. It seems Vanthu-vallabha sent some spies who secretly collected some of the feed after clandestinley entering the vessels. After some tests, it was found that gram might be effectively substituted by the lentil named weaver's bean (*Tor* in Konkani and *Turi* in Marathi). In addition, the flour of *raghi* mixed with sweet water with a small portion of common salt, as well as grass, was used to feed the horses. The results were excellent. As horses are herbivorous like buffaloes and cows, the medicines prepared from different herbs for their diseases were equally efficient, but not for some peculiar ailments. To take care of the horses, some Arab slaves were brought whose descendants at present are at Valpoi and Bicholim. The area of Avaretika-Vishaya at that time had an abundance of such food products. Besides the area comprising Naneli, Pali, Choraundem, Hivrem Budruk, Hivrem Khurd, Golauli, Rivem and Dongurli village with its hamlets Thanem and Bokhal constituted an excellent place as horse shelters. Moreover, the area was the original settlement of Vantudeva's family, so the villagers were faithful to him.

About the title Hayapati and Dr. Pissurlekar's work

Vantudeva had changed his headquarters from Rivem of Sattari to a hill, named later Mardangad, at Ponda town, as soon as he was made king of Goa, including some adjacent areas. The purchased horses were sent to the area mentioned above but surely there was the need of a supervisor living in that area to check on the feeding and training of the horses, including that of the horseback warriors (cavalry). This person was not properly a commander (senapati) in the battlefield, but had the qualities of an instructor, a Hayapati. I did not find any copper-plate with such a designation in Southern India, but the existence of such a surname and other evidence confirms my idea to be a fact.

In Pissurlem village of Sattari taluka, there is a Saraswat Brahmin family known generally as Pissurlekar. This family is of the Kulkarni vangad (record-keeper-cum-accountant) of the village-commune of that village, and the name exists in the records of the Mahajanas of Shri Shantadurga of Queula in Ponda village transferred from Quelossim (*Kelshi*) of Salcete (now Mormugao) taluka, in the 17th century A.D., due to persecurtion by Christian missionaries. The name of this 'Pissurlekar' clan is listed as "*Harapati*" in the second vangad i.e. in the second rank of the pre-eminence (vangad) list among the Mahajans. While in the clan of the first vangad 'Mahale', there are many families with different surnames, in this second vangad '*Harapati*' these is only one family with Pissurlenkar as the surname. The eminent historian, the late Dr. P. S. Pissurlekar belongs to this second vangad.

Dr. P. S. Pissurlenkar was always anxious to know the origin of the surname 'Harpati'. At Panaji, about the year 1927, Prof. Jadunath Sarkar and Prof. Govinda Sar Desai, both eminent historians, were his guests for a week. They had visited him to collect information about documentary evidence in respect of the Portuguese government and the Marathas and Moghuls. At that time, this issue about the name '*Harapati*' was placed before them. Prof. Sarkar informed him that there is no evidence of the existence of a post named Harapati or Hayapati in the history of Bengal, and Prof. Sar Desai also had not found any evidence of any Hindu or Muslim ruler having an officer with such a designation, nor was it any historic title. Dr. Pissurlenkar added: the word Harapati is of Sanskrit origin in which 'hara' means donkey, and in Goan history we do not find the use of donkeys for any purpose. On the other hand, this designation was depicted in ancient records which might have been in the 'Modi' script, (running writing form of Devanagari script in use in Goa from the 13th century A.D. onwards, if not earlier) and in writing, the alphabet 'ra' is quasi-similar to the alphabet 'ya'. So, '*Hayapati*' was recorded as '*Harapati*' in the records of the list of the Mahajans prepared after the transfer of Shri Shantadurga at Kavlem. Even though Dr Pissurlenkar was fully convinced of these errors, he did not ask it to be corrected due to lack of documentary evidence. His slogan was '*Pas document, pas histoire*' (a French phase meaning 'no history can be written without documentary evidence').

The duties of Hayapati

The duty of the Hayapati was limited not only to the feeding and training of horses. He had to look after the supply of allied pursuits, like copper-head-guards, armours and weapons for warriors as well as leather goods, horse-shoes, etc. We find a place named 'Cansarvornem' adjacent to '*Rangachem-mol*' where are found ancient idols of Brahmani, etc. and a stela. I have already referred to this place as existing at the time of the original settlers, the Kols and Mundaris in that region. In Kansarvornem the smiths had been supplied with copper and other material imported from else-where, and the leather work was entrusted to the Mhars. The number of horses must have been at least one hundred, and we can calculate what was the volume of daily-work. It was necessary to maintain the records of expenditure itemwise, and for this reason probably Vantudeva might have selected a Saraswat Brahmin.

The proof of use of the head-guard can be obtained from the dilapidated stone idol of Kolgiro and Mundalgiro found in the area of '*Mundalgireache Mol*' at Thanem hamlet. The head is seen with a head-guard. The remaining portion of the idol was found in the open yard in front of the hamlet temple (*see ill. no. 7a and 7b at p 64 & 65*). This idol surely was made by Vantudeva when he established the deities and stela at Rangachi mol at Naneli village. The idol of the Kolgiro or Mundalgiro existing before was carved without any skill and this is found near a tree. The present idols of Kolgiro and Mundalgiro were established the third time, with the head-dress shown as Mukut about the year 1866, when the present temple existing in the hamlet Thane was constructed and new idols of Brahmani etc. were installed. All the expenses were made by the Mocasdar of village Dongurli in which that hamlet is situated.

The most important duty of Hayapati was vigilance on the daily long-running exercise of the horses. So he had to locate his residence in such a way that he could, from that place, keep an eye all over the area—not only flat land but also the hills intended to be climbed and descended. Such a suitable place was established by him, which continued to be occupied through the generations up to 710 A.D., when the ruling power declined due to the occupation by the Shilahars who are known as Goa Shilahars. The residential area of the family of Hayapati was situated in the hamlet named *Bakhal* (Bocal in Portuguese) at a place named 'Bamanwadi' near the boundary of Golauli village. In the Portuguese records of 1869, we find the name of the ridge of hill behind this hamlet designated as '*Bamnacho tembo*'. In that year on the base of the hill three or four mud houses existed but at present there are no houses there and the total area at present is covered by cashew groves. On that 'Tembo' there is a plateau and from that plateau you can see all the equestrian area.

The daily work of the Hayapati was obviously to supervise the running of warriors on horseback in the early morning. In the afternoon he and his servants, all on horseback, visited each village to check on the maintenance of the horses and the production and supply situation at the smith's and Mhars' hamlet. It is obvious that all the staff were paid. However, we have no documentary evidence of it, but probably the system might have been like with the Chalukyas. It is also noticeable that, besides horseback warriors, there was also the infantry for which warriors were being trained. That also was another duty of the Hayapati, and the trained young staff formed the irregular army, which meant their service was requisitioned whenever the government was in absolute need like in the case of the modern 'recruit'.

It appears that Vantudeva, in alternative years, at the time of the festival of *Sigmo* in the month of Falgun, visited the area in the place of '*Rangachem mol*' and checked the efficiency of the horseback warriors and their skill in fighting. The king at the same time checked on the progress made by the smiths who resided in the adjacent area, 'Cansarvornem', and the Mhars were present with proof of their skills.

Vantudeva, convinced of the efficay of a trained cavalry, probably expanded this form of training in suitable areas of Sattari, Bicholim (Dicholi) taluka. up to Usgaon in Ponda taluka.

The iconic worship of King Vantudeva

I have already mentioned that Vantudeva had a brother named Kandadeva who accompanied his brother-in-law, Kirtivarman I in his campaign against the Mauryas of the Konkan. It appears that Vantudeva could not manage the entire area of Goa, so he handed over to his brother or to the son of his brother the areas of Bardez, Bicholim and Pednem taluka, like his nephew Pulakeshi II had done, passing one part of his domain to his brother.

This branch also continued the work of Vantuvallabha and his descendants, establishing at Morgi village of Pednem taluka a training centre for horseback warriors utilizing the smiths of Cansarvorne of the same taluka to manufacture related and auxilliary items.

Vantudeva had become very popular due to his pious actions subsidising expenses for the installation of temples and idols and at the same time increasing revenues in external commerce. So, people of all strata of society were extremely content. After his death, the Bhats of Savoi-Verem and the people in general in gratitude spontaneously built two idols in different styles. Justifiably, the heir-descendant of Vantudeva residing at Mardangad had the late king's complete support. Now the point may be raised on why two types of idols were carved.The reason is simple, and in elucidation I cite here another example.

At a site between Tamdi and Surla of Hemadbarcem in Sanguem taluka there is a mud temple. In that temple there are two idols, side by side, of the god Betal carved of black stone, in the same style. One statue measures about 2.10 m. while the other about 2.0 m. These idols were established, it appears, at the time of the construction of the famous temple of Shree Mahadeva of Tamdi in about the12th (or 13th?) century A.D. Near that mud temple a festival is celebrated every year named '*Barabhumicho Kalo*', meaning the festival of twelve places - obviously the twelve hamlets of Surla village. The existence of two identical idols of Betal perhaps means that two rival sculptors had competed against each other but it so happened that the villagers couldn't decide on who was better, so both the creations were accepted and were worshipped side by side. ·

More or less the same problem was encountered in selecting the idols of Vantudeva in two different styles, and both were acceptable at different levels. The first, worshipped at Murdangad and created by a person of the Naik caste with Dangi as the surname, is named Shembro-Dev (noseless god). This name has been ascribed to him because there is a hollow at the root of the nose. It should be noted that at the time of carving, the sculptor intentionally made such a hollow because Vantudeva had suffered this injury in the battlefield (and perhaps due to this wound Kandadeva, the brother of Vantudeva, accompanied his brother-in-law Kirtivarman I Chalukya in the expedition against the Mauryas). This sign of a battle wound, especially on the face,

reflected the bravery of a warrior and was honoured by the people. The people considered him as a hero. The icon was fashioned in an allegoric form based on the supposed genealogy of Naga-Vansha and is carved in the sitting posture with each of the two hands holding a serpent and the hood draped over the crowned head-dress *(see ill. 25 p.241)*. The other icon was also in the same area but without allegoric form. This idol was damaged by a Muslim (Moghul) warrior who cut portions of both hands. So, it is not known what objects were in the hands, but from the position it appears that there were some weapons. This idol, a century ago, was transferred to a place known as New Bazar in Ponda town and was covered with a silver cap. In the right hand a sword was shown and in the left a shield. The crown of the icon of stone is styled like that of Pulakeshin II of the Chalukyas, as shown in this idol *(ill. 29)*. The idol is named as 'Atalo', a corrupted form of

ill. 29 : Image of Vantuvallabha under worship in a temple existing at Ponda town, dated c. 7th Century A.D.

Vantuvallabh—Vantuvallo-Atalo. While the first idol is without any shelter, the second idol was installed in a temple with mud walls, but later on the late advocate Sushil Kavlekar had the temple built of laterite stone with lime mortar. The daily worship is performed by a person of the Vaishya caste with the surname Gurava, and his subsistence is derived from the gifts made by the person who appears before him to consult the oracle. I have proof in my own family that even about the middle of the 18th century A.D., when his idol was not under worship, the people made vows and offerings.

I have mentioned this fact here because in the entire history of India we do not find this kind of worship of a King. He probably lived in the period (540-620 A.D.), ruling Goa territory from about 570 A.D. He was never considered an incarnation of any god, unlike Parashurama, Rama and Krishna, nor was he a founder of any religious sect like Mahavira, Buddha or Tirthakara. There is a big statue of Kanishka of the Kushana dynasty installed near Mathura around the 3rd century A.D., but it was never worshipped. This point is important to show that in India there was no other example of a ruler who had constructed huge temples-ziggurats there, and it is ridiculous to say that the Paddye Bhats might have had that memory. Next, we find an idol of Shivachitta Kadamba (Permadi or Hemad-dev), in a standing posture, installed at Uguem village of Hemadbarcem division of Sanguem taluka, who ruled during 1147-48, 1176-77 A.D. in Goa territory. He and his wife Kamaladevi are known in the history of Goa to have performed some pious acts. He is worshipped in this temple, where annually a festival is celebrated. All the villagers of that division believe that it is their obligation to assist in the festival. But the installation may be surely understood on the grounds of the example of Vantudeva at Ponda town.

Historians always had found it difficult to find new evidence in the sequence of ruling dynasties in Goa because they did not try to make the identification of place-names and other elements from the Chiplun copper-plates.

Dr. Mirashi, in his recent work on the Shilahars, says: "Mangalesh, king of the dynasty of Chalukyas of Badami, according to the Nerur copper-plate (Indian Antiquary, vol. VII, p. 161), killed the King (Maurya) Swamiraja (whose capital was Revatidwipa, present village Reddi of Ratnagiri district, 8 miles South from Vengurla), and posted, as ruler of Southern Konkan, his relative Satyashraya Dhruvaraja Indravarma. According to the Goa copper plate (J.B.R.A.S. vol IV, old series, p. 307) in Shaka 610 (A.D. 688-89) he was ruling, from Revatidwipa, on four districts, but we do not find who was ruling afterwards in that area, during a long period. It is most probable that it was under the feudatory of the Chalukyas of Badam—the Sendrakas—because nearby at its south was the ancient Sendraka Vishhaya"[105] 1st part, p. 40. However, Dr. Mirashi further refers to the two successive successors of the Chalukya rulers at the same region, so it is clear that he, from the above mentioned passage, means that there was no cognizance of rulers of the Sendraka Vishhaya for a long period.

SUMMARY

In this chapter, the cultural history of Goa is revealed based on the interpretation of nine copper plates related to a span extending through the periods of four dynasties namely: Boja (c. 600 BC - 520 A. D.), Konkan Maurya (c 525 - 580 A. D.) and Chalukya of Badami (580-760 A. D.). The later transferred hegemony to the Sendraka dynasty in Goa.

There is an assumption that before the Bhoja Dynasty, Chandragupta Maurya held hegemony over Goa for the reasons that the Deccan and Konkan coast that includes the land named "Aparant" was under their sway. The fact is that "Aparant" lies between the Tapti and Vashisti rivers that constituted the border of his empire. So "Aparant" was very far to the north of Goa and as such, it is clear that Goa was never under the direct sovereignty of the Maurian Empire.

Similarly, there is an assumption that Satavahana ruled Goa after the Maurian kingdom. It is true that Gautamputra Satakarni of the Satavahana dynasty held domain over "Aparanta" (North Konkan) in about 125 A. D. but as mentioned above, Goa (as described topographically) was not included in the said area and in the absence of any other evidence, this presumption is not tenable.

Bhoja Dynasty

We began the study of the history of this kingdom from the time when we unearth the earliest evidence from the inscriptions, which means from the c. 3rd century A.D., with the inscriptions of Devaraja Bhoja. But this does not mean that before this period there was anarchy in Goa. On the contrary, from ages past, from about 2,500 B.C., the administration of each village was done through the elders of different families in a democratic way, as the society was mainly agriculturist. This primitive form of administration known in history in general as 'Primitive Communism' was in use by the first non-Aryan settlers. This made way for the Sumerian system which consisted in considering the whole land within the boundaries of a village as common land and so indivisible or unpartitionable. Members of all families had to work together and divide the produce according to their share in the family. The existence of a kingdom did not change this mode of life. However private properties began to appear, providing opportunities to people who had the capacity to employ their skills and bring under cultivation uncultivated lands.

The royalty which rose first at Chandravadi with the hegemony of the Bhojas was invited by the village-commune of Salcete and other talukas on the coastal zone for defence purposes. This was due to the power of a king who could command and unify all human efforts for defence. This necessity first had been noticed when the Konkan Mauryas invaded the coastal areas.

Konkan Mauryan Dynasty

The area under the domain of the Bhojas was in the past subdued by the Konkan Maurayas for about 50 years in Goa. (525 - 580 A. D.) So they hardly had the time to introduce their pattern of administration. The Badami Chalukya Kirtivarman I and subsequently Pulakeshi II subjugated them.

The Sendraka dynasty under the tutelage of the Chalukyas of Badami

Pulakesi II subdued the Konkan Maurya and appointed his maternal uncle Vantuwallbha Senanandaraja who established the Sendraka Dynasty. This later was subdivided into two branches namely, the senior and the junior. Both branches tried to bring prosperity to the people. At that time the importance of the cavalry in the army was understood and so both dynasties tried to bring in Arabian horses. They engaged Arab Muslim slaves as attendants to the horses. The Muslim slaves married local girls of low status in their places of settlement—Sattari and Pednem talukas. As the Arabs did not sell the mares, these were brought from Kathiawad and breeding was thus accomplished. Vantuwallabha, who was the founder of the Sendraka dynasty, moved from Sattari (Rivem village) to Ponda town and established his capital there. He brought about allround prosperity in Goa. He constructed a fine port at Agshi(Agasaim) and named it 'Sindapura'. Thus Arab ships began commerce with the result that the people were prosperous. The Bhojas did not patronise Buddhism, so it declined in Goa. Vantu-vallabha patronized the Vedic and Puranic religion. The reign of Vantu-vallabha may be characterized as the Golden Age, and he was so popular that his idols carved at that time are worshipped in Ponda town even today.

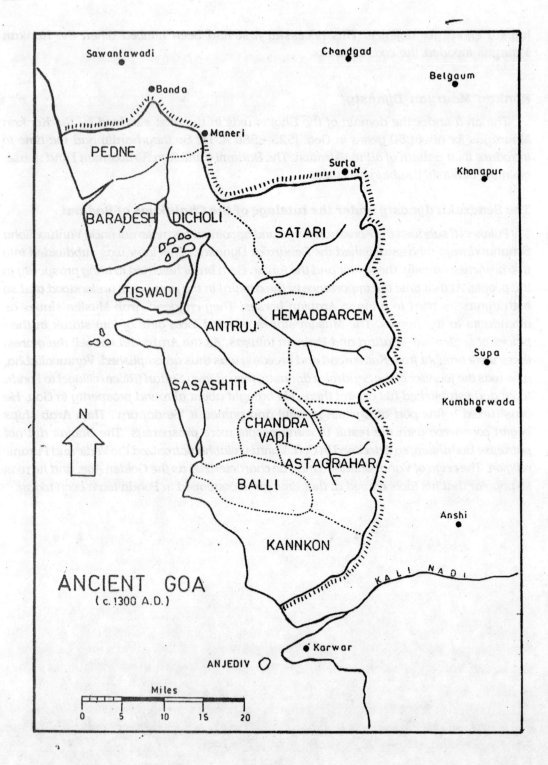

ANCIENT GOA
(c. 1300 A.D.)

Miles

0   5   10   15   20

Chapter - 7
THE CULTURAL IMPACT OF LATER DYNASTIES

THE WIDE GAP

Dr. V. T. Gune in his article in the Goa Gazetteer Vol. I at p.p. 72-82, presents an account of the Konkan Chalukya dynasty ruling on Goa territory, citing the seven copper-plates of Nerur. In the previous chapter I have already shown that Dr. Gune erroneously identified Kundiwatak village mentioned in one of those copper-plates as Kudne of Dicholi taluka. All the other six copper-plates of Nerur refer to the area of South Konkan situated at Ratnagiri district and ancient Sawantwadi state—all out of the area of Goa. Yes, he also mentions the Chiplun copper-plate but does not localize the area mentioned in it.

THE COPPER-PLATES AND INSCRIPTIONS OF THE
CHALUKYAS, SHILAHARAS AND KADAMBAS

So, the history of Goa already compiled does not help to define the ruling dynasty or dynasties from the death of Vantuvallabha of the Sendraka family (c. 620 A.D.) to the rise of the founder of the Goa Kadamba dynasty, Guhaladeva (C. 980-1005 A.D.). But suddenly in an inscription of 1380 A.D., eight centuries later we find a king ruling on a part of Goa named Virakavana using the title, partly, of Vantudeva Vallabharaja Maharaja!

Setting aside the viewpoints of the historians of Goa covering this period, and going only by the data found in the inscriptions which relate to Goa territory only, we find the following:

Period A.D.

(1) **Pulakesin II Chalukya of Badami** Grants the lands situated in Avaretika Vishhaya on the behest of his maternal uncle (Vantu Vallabha Senanandaraja). **Chiplun copper-plate**   611-642

(2) **Shanafulla,** founder of the dynasty of the Shilahar of South Konkan, obtained the lordship of Sinhala (Shimalesha) by the favour of his suzerain Krishna I of the Rastrakuta dynasty— two copper plates of grants issued by Rattaraja of the Shilahars of South Konkan. **Two Kharepatna copper-plates,**   765-795

(3) **Aiyapa**, Shilahar of South Konkan, invaded Chandrapura and is said to have bathed there with coconut water celebrating his victory over the kingdom. **Kharepatan copper-plate.**   820-845

(4) **Avasara II,** Shilahar of South Konkan, son of Adityavarman, succeeded him. The said record says that he also helped the rulers of Chandrapura and Chemulya like his father. **Avasara II copper-plates**.   895-920

(5) **Bhima,** also of the same dynasty, who is said to have annexed Chandramandala just as Rahu eclipsed the moon at the lunar eclipse. **Bhima copper-plate**   945-970

(Note: **Chicodi copper-plate** of Avasara III of the same family gives the dating which corresponds to Thursday, 18th October 988 A.D.)

Period A.D.

(6) **Rattaraja**, probably the grandson of Bhima, admitted the suzerainty of Tailapa, the Chalukya king of Kalyani who had ruled over the Rastrakutas.
Rattaraja copper-plate 980 A.D.

955-1020

(7) **Kantakacharya alias Shastadeva I,** founder of the Goa Kadamba dynasty coming from North Kanara and settling in Goa, occupying the area of Astagrahar of Sanguem taluka and Canacona (Kankon) taluka, along with a part of North Kanara —
Stone record of Curdi (Sanguem taluka),

960

(8) **Guhaladeva I**, grandson of Shasthadeva I , firmly settled in Chandrapur (present Chandor), extending in this way the domain of the time of his grandfather to the area of Chandravad (present Quepem taluka) and part of Salcete taluka, but at that time the area of Tiswadi taluka (an island) where lay Sindapura port of Gova town (now Goa Velha)was under the other king., Guhaladeva I

980-1005

(9) **Shasthadeva II**, son of Guhaladeva I, made an expedition by the sea-route, occupied Sindapura and the surrounding area of Tiswadi taluka, He then annexed the area of the kingdom of the South Konkan Shilahars and subdued the Shilahars of North Konkan and of Kolhapur.
Narendra inscription of Jayakeshi II (1125) and the **Demgave record** of Shivachitta Kadamba (Permadi) dated A.D. 1174.

1005-1042

Period A.D.

(10) **Viravarmadeva,** second son of Shasthadeva II,
had his capital at Gopaka (previously
Sindapura)—
Curtorim copper-plate .   1042-1054

(11) We find a copper-plate issued from Gopakapuri
in the year 1351A. D. by king Solar race (but
the name of his family is unknown as the other
plates are lost), granting land situated at Pedina
(Pednem village of Pednem taluka) to a Brahmin of the Vatsagotra named Ravala Thakur.
This plate was found in Corgaon village, Pednem
taluka, in 1977. The entire copper-plate must
have been formed of three plates; only the second was uncovered and has no ring. The plate
is engraved with10 lines on each side. The language is Sanskrit, partly in prose. The script is
the Nagari of 14th century A.D.
Corgaon copper-plate   1351

(12) An inscription of 1380 A.D. shows that a king
named Vira Kavana, with the title of
Vallabharaja Maharaja, ruled over a part of Goa
at that time—
Vira Kavana inscription   1380

SCRUTINY OF THE COPPER—PLATES

With reference to item No.1 *(Chiplun copper-plate)*, the explanation has been provided in previous chapters.

Interpreting the Shilahara Inscriptions

With reference to item No. 2 *(Kharepatna copper-plates)*. Unlike the other two houses of the Shilaharas, the South Konkan Shilaharas claim connection with the kings of Simhala, using epithets like 'Simhalesha' or 'Simhaleswara', while the other two houses adopted the epithet 'Tagarapuradhishvara'—Tagarapura being identified with Ter village of Usmanabad taluka of Marathwada, which, in ancient times according to the Greek geographer Ptolemy (C. 150 A.D.) and Periplus, was a commercial spot. All the dynasties of South India, even of the Chalukyas, desired to demonstrate their antiquity by linking it to the famous areas of ancient times. So, in respect of the identification of the spot and its antiquity, the epithet of those two houses of Shilahara is comprehensible. Historians try to explain the epithet 'Simhaleshvara' by taking Simhala as the name of Rewatidvipa (Reddi) or Goa (Govem in Tiswadi taluka). All the three houses of the Shilaharas are unanimous in their adoption of the mythological derivation of their family named 'Shilar', connecting their genealogy to Jimutavahana. Hence Simhala must be placed near Ter village. Moreover, it might be accepted that they may have adopted the epithet 'Lankeshvara', referring to any one of the islands mentioned above. But it is incomprehensible and so unacceptable that instead of a Puranic and famous name as Lanka, they might have adopted the synonymous Simhala, which was very rarely known even to the learned person who composed the inscriptions.

The metaphor of Lanka

On the other hand, it is noticed that there was constant conflict between the Shilahars of North and South Konkan, and when any Shilahar of North Konkan subjugated the Shilahara of the South Konkan, he took the epithet 'Nishanka-Lankeshvara', meaning 'sole Lord of Lanka', and here Lanka was a metaphoric designation given to Revatidwipa (Reddi)—the capital of the subjugated Shilaharas which previously was the capital of the Mauryas of Konkan. It is worth noting that between the area occupied by the Shilaharas of South Konkan and Sendraka Vishaya where Tiswadi island was situated, the area was occupied by some Chalukya families upto the 13th century A.D. They were the descendants of the Chalukya dynasty, whose domain the Rastrakuta king had conquered and passed on to Shanafulla, founder of the Southern Konkan Shilahara.

There is more to this: in a copper-plate of the Southern Konkan Shilaharas it is said that they were the highest among all the 'Simhaleshas'. So, the compositor of the inscription knew that all the three branches of Shilahars, Southern and Northern Konkan, and those of Kolhapur, were originally of the same area which the compositor named Simhala, the village Ter being situated in that area. Now the point remains of identifying this area. I presume that the area was known as 'Seuna-desha', the original place also of the Yadavas of Devagiri, and Simhala was a Sanskritization of Seuna as follows:

Seuna - Sihuna - Sihula - Simhala, in the same manner as the name of Simghana Yadava was Sankritized as "Imhaladevara" in an inscription in Virgal [106].

The possibility, even by hypothesis, of the occupation of Govem or Gopakattan by the Shilaharas is totally inadmissible. Historians ventured into such acrobatics because the history of the ruling family of Sendrakas was unknown to them.

The conquest of Chandrapura by Aiyapa

Now in respect of item Nos.3 & 4: (*Kharepatana* and *Avasara II copper-plates*)

History mentions that Aiyapa, Shilahara of South Konkan (821-845 A.D.) conquered Chandrapura and took a bath with coconut water. Who was subdued by Ayapa is not known, nor is there any record to indicate that he transferred his capital from Reddi to Chandrapur or that he appointed there his representative to govern the respective area. From the available records it can be deduced as follows: Vantudeva of the Sendraka family had established Sindapura port and soon that port was extensively visited by Arab and other foreign merchants, thereby giving the king income from tax. There was the necessity to put up a permanent watch for any invasion from the sea-route. So, besides the fleet, the cavalry also was of equal importance and the capital had to be selected keeping these points in view. Sindapura was situated in an island surrounded by the wide rivers of the Zuari and Mandovi, hindering the easy mobility of the cavalry. The next port in importance was Chandrapura which was suitable for the movement of both wings of the armied forces. So, the son of Vantudeva might have shifted his capital from Ponda town to Chandrapura. However, perhaps through the intervention of Pulakesin II, Vantudeva made a partition of his dominion, passing to the son of his brother Kandeva the area comprising Bardez, Pednem and Bicholim (*Dicholi*) talukas, thus constituting a branch, which I designate as the Junior branch. The Senior house or say the direct descendants of Vantudeva continued with the occupation of Tiswadi taluka, and the Junior house of the Sendrakas had designs on it, as they did not have any good sea-port. However, they had developed their cavalry with its headquarters at Morji (Pedne taluka). The ruler of the Junior branch entered into an alliance with the Aiyapa Shilahar, who with his fleet invaded Chandrapura, while the ruler of the Junior branch of the Sendraka a family attacked with his cavalry by the land route with the result that the king of Chandrapur had to submit to the proposal made by Aiyapa, ceding Tiswadi talukla in favour of the ruler of the Junior house. The Shilahara king returned to his capital at Reddi. However, the effect of the treaty was not permanent and both the houses were in constant conflict.

In about 753 A.D., Kirtivarman II, the last king of the Chalukyas of Badami was defeated by Dantidurga Rastrakuta. So any branch of the Sendraka family could get the help of the Chalukyas as mediator, to settle conflicts between them. Hence Shilahar Aiyapa took this opportunity. Moreover, at that time his overlord Amoghvarsha I Rastrakuta (814-878 A.D.) was at the peak of his sovereignty.

This is the appropriate place to talk about the boundary between Sendraka Vishaya and the country of the Southern Konkan Shilahars at the time of Aiyapa. Pulakeshi II Chalukya, to avoid any conflict in future between his two sons, appointed as Viceroy his elder son Chandraditya, and sent him to rule the Konkana area. His dynasty continued to rule there upto the time of Kirtivarman (744-45 to 757 A.D.). At that time of the father of this king, the overlord of Badami, Chalukya Vikramaditya II appointed two young Rastrakutas, Govindaraja in 741 as Samanta (governor) with headquarters at Chiplun, and Dantidurga, in 742, also as governor with headquarters at Chandanapuri, both in Konkan Vishya. This was done to mitigate their lust for more power and land, and in this way the sway of the Konkan Chalukyas was limited to the area which perhaps at present forms Kudal taluka. But it was all in vain. Dantidurga defeated Govindaraja sometime before 753 A.D. and declared himself the sovereign power in the Deccan. Dantidurga died without a child and his paternal uncle Krishna I, who was his successor, conquered Southern Konkan from the Konkan Chalukyas and put Shanafulla, founder of the South Konkan Shilaharas, as the feudatory of that area, as he had helped him in conquering that area.

The boundaries of Sendraka Vishaya

From the time of Chandraditya, son Pulakeshi II, the boundary connecting Sendraka Vishaya was already fixed and was more or less the same as the present boundary of Goa territory and part of Sawantwadi on its north. There was no dispute because both the families were linked by marriage. Dr. Gune (18) p. 79, erroneously identifies the village 'Parishvasu', mentioned in the copper-plates issued by Vijayabhattarika or Vijayadevi, queen consort of Chandraditya Chalukya, dated 659 A.D. with Parcem village (Pednem taluka). In Southern Konkan, now Ratnagiri district, there are two villages with the name Parachuri, one in Sangameshwara and the other in Guhagara. The second reason not to identify Parishvasu with Parcem village is that one of the six temples of Brahmadeva constructed by Vantudeva, installing there his idol, is situated in the said Parcem village which continues to be under worship even today (See ill. 22 at p. 241). Here, there is no room to consider that the Konkan Chalukyas might have installed that idol, because we do not find any temple dedicated to Brahmadeva to the north of Pednem taluka in the whole area of the Konkan.

We do not know whether the village name 'Parachuri' was the same at the time of the inscription. But presuming that it was the same, it appears that the composer of the inscription went into the usual convolutions in his Sanskritization. It seems that he considered the name as constituted of two words, namely Para and Churi. The word 'Para' was transformed into 'Parish', and 'Churi' changed to 'Charu', substituted it with 'Vasu', (person) instead of 'offering to him' (object), and hence the word Parishvasu. We have already seen similar convolutions in a copper-plate of Prithivimalla Bhoja where *Vaijini-sheta* situated in Gaudaulim village is named as '*Vrishabhini-Kheta*'. Excluding the copper-plate of Devaraja Bhoja, all the other copper-plates have this kind of Sansritization which makes it difficult to decipher. What might be the reason for this form? I think that according to religious principles, the gift had always to be a secret (*gupta-dana*), and this is the reason for these acrobatics. On the other hand, gifted land could never be usurped. I have supplied proof of this in respect of the land of Gandauli.

In a copper-plate mentioned before, it is said that Avasara II Shilahara (895-920 A.D.), son of Adityavarman, South Konkan Shilahara, helped the ruler of Chandrapura, like his father (870-895 A.D.)

Surely, he as well as his father helped the rulers of the Senior house of the Sendraka family against the attacks of the rulers of the Junior house of the same family, maintaining the treaty made before with the intervention of Aiyapa.

The feuding branches of the Shilaharas

Now with reference to item Nos. 5 and 6 (*The Bhima and Rattaraja copper-plates*).

Bhima, South Konkan Shilahara (940-970 A.D.), annexed Chandramandala (Chandravadi including Chandrapura) to his dominion. From this record it is seen that the Senior branch had to lose permanently the area and probably maintained Sattari taluka in their sway. The existence of a king in 1380 A.D. with the 'Vallabharaja Maharaja' [44] denotes the sequence of this dynasty. Bhima must have assigned his governor to look after the conquered area.

There was always rivalry between the Shilahars of the North and South Konkan, from the beginning of the occupation of the Konkan by both the houses. But these houses maintained friendship with both houses of the Sendrakas, perhaps due to the close relationship. The South Konkan Shilahars were closest to the kingdom of the Sendrakas, so due to this reason, or because of the close relationship with one or another house of the Sendrakas in each generation, this house of the South Konkan Shilahars was a mediator, trying their best to maintain peace in the kingdom of the

Sendrakas. When they suspected the invasion of the Kadambas, the Southern Konkan Shilahars, noting the weakness in the Senior house of the Sendrakas, occupied Chandrapura and the surrounding areas to stop the expansion of the dominion of the Kadambas. The Junior house of the Sendrakas was in possession of Sindapura (afterwards Gopakapuri) and surrounding areas without touching the area which lay between their own domain of Southern Konkan and the area now conquered, of Chandramandale, and its surroundings.

Meanwhile, the North Konkan Shilahars, aware of the fragility of the Southern Konkan Shilahars and of the Junior house of the Sendrakas, Aparjit, conquered Sindapura and the surrounding areas about the year 983 A.D. It is known by the Janjira copper-plate that their sway extended from South Gujarat at the north to the South upto Chandrapur (in the copper-plate designated as Chandrapuravam-puram), at the West the sea and to the East the kingdom of Bhillam Yadava (upto Khandesh) (105) 1st part, pp. 22-23. From this copper-plate it seems that, like the Senior house, the Junior house of the Sendrakas' dominion was reduced to Pednem and Dicholi talukas and possibly Bardez taluka, perhaps as chieftains under the suzerainty of the North Konkan Shilahars.

The end of the Shilahara dynasty

Now with reference to item Nos. 7 & 8 (*stone record of Curdi and Guhaladev I record*).

The domain of the Shilaharas did not last for too long. Noting the weakness of Rattaraja, the South Konkana Shilahara (995-1020 A.D.) whose kingdom was annexed by Tailapa, Chalukya of Kalyani, the Kadamba Guhaladeva I (980-1005 A.D.) took advantage of the situation and firmly occupied Chandrapura with its dependent area, previously of the Senior branch of the Sendrakas. So, for about 50 years, the Shilahars of South Konkan ruled a part of Goa and the Kadamba Shasthadeva II (1005/7-1050/ 52 A.D.), son of Guhaldeva II conquered the other part of Goa from the Shilahara of North Konkan. Hence the Shilahars in this area ruled for only about 17 years.

FOUNDATION OF THE GOA KADAMBA DYNASTY

Now with reference to item Nos. 9 and 10 (*Narendra, Demgave and Curtorim records*)

The place named "Sindapura" or "Sindhaboor"

The Kadamba Shashthadeva II transferred his capital from Chandrapura (Chandor) to Sindapur and this is adequately proved by the recently discovered Curtorim copper-plate issued by his son Viravarman (1042-1054 A.D.). According to the writing, the copper-plate was issued from Gopaka, and this designation Gopaka is without any doubt a Sanskritised form of the name Gove-town in which Sindapura was situated as a port. The charter was passed during the life of king Shashthadeva, by his son, which denotes that at that time the father was absent from the capital and the son was looking after the administration according to the advice of the council of ministers headed by the elder member of the king's family. So it is evident that Virawarman was not entitled to take any resolution he wanted. The copper-plate issued by his brother Jayakeshi I, in 1053 A.D. granted an additional customs tax to be paid at Gopakapura to a mosque which was constructed by his Muslim minister, the tax being used for its maintenance. Both the charters were issued from Gopaka, while the copper-plate dated 1038 of their father Shashthadeva I was issued from Chandrapura [58] pp. 2-18. Hence, these three copper-plates sufficiently prove that Gopakapura was conquered by Shashthadeva II between 1030 and 1051.

The place-name Sindapura was intentionally or otherwise, omitted by the Kadamba, employing instead the place-name of the whole town 'Govem', used by the common people. This was Sankritized by the compositors of the copper-plate, employing the word 'Gopak' Gopakapuri or Gopaka-pattana. However, foreign travellers like the Arab Al-Masudi (c. 943 A.D.) and Ibn Batuta (c. 1343-49 A.D.) continued to use the ancient names Sindapura, in its corrupted form of pronouncing it as 'Kowe-Sindaboor' (Kowe-Gove) or simply as 'Sindaboor', over about four centuries, even though a new dynasty different from the Kadambas, and probably a descendant of the Junior house of Sendrakas, called it Sindapura. A member of the dynasty adopted the designation Gopakapuri when he issued a charter from that town in 1351, as mentioned below.

Now with reference to item No. 11 (*Bhimabhupala Corgaon copper-plate*)

Recently a single plate of a copper inscription was discovered at Corgaon (Pednem taluka) [107] pp. 49-54. The first and the last plates of the set and the respective rings are lost. From the available plate, it is seen that Bhimabhupala was a famous king belonging to the Solar race of the Kshatriyas which ruled over the Konkan with his throne at Gopakapuri. He granted land situated in Pedne village to a certain Ravala Thakur of the Vatsagotra, on the first day of the bright half of the month of Pausha of the Shaka era 1273. The Shaka era is named as Karn Sanvatsara (which corresponds to 1351 A.D.) [84].

The plate also provides the geneology of twelve persons and their relationship, mentioning that the originator of that family was a certain Dinakara whose son was known as Hindola. He was a boon to the Solar race (Suryavanshi) and the kingdom was conferred to him by the grace of the god Shiva.

Like the Chiplun copper-plate, this Corgaon copper-plate changes what the historians of Goa have said earlier about ruling dynasties. That there was another dynasty in 1351 A.D. ruling from Gopakpuri, the area covering at least Tiswadi, Bardez and Pednem talukas and perhaps Bicholim (*Dicholi*) taluka. But the exact period of the provenance of that dynasty is not known and so it is erroneously considered that the Kadambas ruled at that time and before.

The assault of King Achugi on Goa

A stone-inscription in Kannada dated Shaka 1051 (1129 A.D.) says that a king named Achugi conquered Goa town. [45] In another stone-inscription in Kannada dated Shaka 1084 (1162 A.D.) it is said that king Achugi burnt Goa town. [149] In a copper-plate dated Shaka 1013 (1191 A.D.) in the Sanskrit language, it is said Vikramatyadeva, the Shilahara king of Panhalgad, re-installed a king on the throne of Goa, but his name is not mentioned [85]. During this period the following kings belonging to the Kadamba dynasty ruled in Goa, according to historians : Jaykeshi II (1126-1147 A.D.); Permadi-deva (Shivachitta) (1147/48-1176/77 A.D.) and Vijayaditya II (Vishnuchitta) (1147/48-1187/88 A.D.),—these two brothers ruling together—and Jaykeshi III (1187/88-1211 A.D.)

Neither G. Pereira nor Dr. V. T. Gune refer to the above documents. So, taking only the above mentioned indications into consideration, I presume that the two assaults made by king Achugi, probably by the sea-route, were to extract revenge on the conflict which he might have had with the Kadamba kings in the area of North Karnataka, where they also had some parts under their dominion at that time near the sea-coast. But the third event shows clearly different reasons: a king was re-installed in Goa, and this occurrence surely refers to a king of a dynasty mentioned in the Corgaon-plate. It appears that the dynasty was of the Sendraka Junior house who, having lost the domain of Tiswadi taluka, as mentioned before, had conquered the same areas after the burning of Gopakapur city in 1162 A.D. But before the burning and a little before 1145 A.D. Sovideva Kadamba had dethroned a forefather of Bhimabhupala from Gopakapuri, and after about fifty years that forefather or his successor was re-installed in 1191 by the Shilahar of Panalgad.

The change of lordship from Kadambas to Bhimabhupalas

Now we will refer to two events which are not mentioned by both historians. Dr. Gune, in the Goa Gazette, p. 111, says that two gold coins were found in the name of Sovideva Kadamba. "One of them is dated in the cyclic year Bahudanya Sanvatsara which corresponds to Shaka 1140 & 1218/19 A.D. and probably coincides with the reign of Sovideva named also as Tribhuvanamalla. There is another gold coin of Sovideva of Vishavavasu Samvatsara/Shaka 1167 (1245 A.D.). It reads as Shri Saptakoteshacharana Labdhavaravira Sovideva i.e. Sovideva who had attained prosperity by the favour of God Saptakotesha. On the reverse of the coin this cyclic year is engraved in the raised sole of the foot of the lion passant to the left which was the royal symbol of the Goa Kadambas".

Before entering into the matter proper, it is necessary to remove the discrepancy which is noted in the reigning period and the date of the second coin. The historian indicates the reigning period of Sovideva as ending in the year 1238 A.D., and the date of the second coin as 1245. So, the ending year of his reigning period must be 1245 and not 1238. Shree Saptakotesh is the name of the Shiva-linga established in the time of the Kadamba king Jaykeshi I (1050/52-1080 A.D.) in Naroa village of Divar (*Divadi*) island of Tiswadi taluka. He took that epithet which is mentioned in the second gold coin of Sovideva.But in the first coin that epithet does not appear which means that Tiswadi taluka which was lost was reconquered by Sovideva a little before 1145 A.D. from the hands of the Junior house of the Sendraka dynasty. It appears that the Kadamba rulers continued with the possession of Tiswadi taluka at least upto 1250 A.D.

Dr. Gune, in the cited book at p. 113 says, "We learn from the Goa plate of Shasthadeva that he had to make efforts to regain his lost position and that his brother-in-law Kamadeva helped him in coming to the throne by about 1247 A.D. Kamadeva is referred to in the same records as king Kama or Kanava, the son of Lakshmideva, whose wife Lakshmi was a sister of king Shasthadeva. He is described as the establisher of Sashthadeva. The king Kamadeva is said to have attained fortune by worshipping the god Mallinatha and Shahthadeva is said to have attained the favour of the god Saptakoteshvar. On his accession to the throne, he made a donation of a rice field named 'Kinjalauge' near the temple of Murtinarayana to his family-preceptor Vishnu Sharma Dikshit of Gargya gotra. The rice field was situated in the village *Sulibhatti* to the north of Gowapuri where the presiding God is Goveshwar. The charter was issued in the name of Goveshwara. This Goa plate is dated Sadharna Sanvatsara i.e. Shaka 1173 (A.D. 1250/5) and it is cited as the fifth year of his reign and fixed Kaliyuga 4348 (current/Shaka 1169 A.D. 146/47) as the first year of his reign".

Evidence on Kadamba defeat

But from the Corgaon copper-plate we learn that in 1351 A.D. the king Bhimabhupala of a different dynasty was ruling over Tiswadi, Bardez and Pednem talukas, at least, with his throne at Gopakapur. So, there is no doubt that the Kadambas had lost their sway on those talukas at some time between 1250 and 1351 A.D. and before that period, between 1191 and 1246/47 A.D. So, in this way, the lordship of the Kadambas was changed twice, at least over Tiswadi taluka, the power evidently passing to the rulers of the dynasty which Bhimabhupala belonged to.

Ibn Batuta's account

Now in respect of the second event which is not mentioned by Dr.V.T. Gune,but is largely recounted by G. Pereira in his cited book and by Dr.Morais in his book titled 'Kadamba Kula'[108] pp.125-126. This account is from Ibn Batuta's Travels(Gibbs): "...On setting sail from this town (i.e Quga in Katheawad) we arrived after three days at the island of Sindabur (Sindapur) in which there are thirty-six villages. It is surrounded by a gulf...In the center of the island are two cities, an ancient one built by infidels, and one built by the Muslims when they first captured the Island..."

An internal family feud arose and one of the sons of theKadamba king invited the Mohammedan Nabad Djemal-ud-din to invade Goa, promising that he would embrace islam and marry Nabad's sister (another writer says 'daughter'). Djamal-ud-din accordingly equipped a fleet of fifty-two vessels. On Ibn Batuta expressing his wish to join the expedition, he was made the commander of the fleet, under the personal supervision of Djmal-ud-din. Ibn Batuta gives us a graphic description of the storming of the citadel. On Monday late in the evening, he writes, they arrived at Sindabur and entered the gulf. They found the citizens prepared for the encounter and had already set up their mangonels. Having spent the night off the city, the Mohammadans advanced early at dawn against the citadel. The infidels hurled stones amidst the vessels from the mangonels, one of which struck a man close to the Sultan. At this the Mohammadan soldiers plunged into the water with shields and swords.To facilitate the riding of horses, two tartans had been opened in the rear, where the horses were kept in readiness so that each horseman could mount the horse, don his armour, and march without having to waste a single minute. Before long, it was victory for the Mohammedans. The infidels took shelter in the palace of the king, but with the building being set afire by the Mohammadans, the infidels had to rush out, and were easily overpowered and made prisoners.The Sultan looted their quarters and restored to them their wives and children. The infidel population which numbered about 10,000 souls were assigned one of the suburbs of the city for their dwelling. While the Sultan took possession of the palace and allotted the neighbouring houses to his nobles.

After about three months' stay at Sindapura, Ibn Batuta then sailed to Honavar and from there to Calicut. He returned to Goa five months later. The Kadamba king had already made preparations to march against Gopakapura to recapture it. The infidels fled and joined their king while the Mohammadan troops which were quartered in the neighbouring villages deserted the Sultan. The city was besieged by the Kadamba troops and conditions for the Sultan became very serious. During the seige, Ibn Batuta left Goa and went to Calicut and from there proceeded to Dhabat-al-Mahal (Maldive islands).

Ibn Batuta does not tell us anything about the son of the Kadamba king who had invited the Sultan of Honawar. Nor could Batuta give us the final outcome of the battle for Sindapura, as he himself left the town leaving the Mohammadan king to his fate. It is probable that the Sultan was defeated and the Kadamba king won his last victory.

The folk-narrative of Chandor

Dr Morais recounts a folk-story from Chandor and its surroundings: "The people of the city were happy and prosperous, when suddenly one night the city was invaded by the enemy who murdered the king and many of the inhabitants. The princesses and the ladies of the court destroyed their jewels and committed suicide by throwing themselves into the river, which, it is popularly believed, still leaves gold powder on the shores. The tradition associated with the fort is that the Queen, who was absent in some other part of the kingdom, visited the city one day, but found it in desolation and was given the sad news of her husband's demise. As a sign of her grief she removed her jewels, crushed them and threw them all over the palace and cursed the women of Chandor, them all to be like herself (widow). She came out of the fortress, and stamping her feet four times, said that she would not take anything, not even the dust of her feet from the city".[108]

As I learnt from another story, the absent Queen was in Kolhapur in her father's residence. She returned mounted on an elephant as soon as she received the bad news from a messenger sent on horseback from Chandor. At her arrival, she found that her husbands body had already been incinerated. Grief-struck, she immolated herself and her body, according to her desire, was taken to the other bank of river Kushawati, at Assolda village (Quepem taluka), where soon a sati-slab was placed, showing a woman's hand with a bracelet and a combined sign of two triangles on the palm and a carving at the side. This slab is seen at the base of a small hillock known as 'kshetrapalachi-maddi' *(ill. 30)*.

ill. 30 : Sati - Memorial of Immolation of the queen of Kadambakula at Assolde (Assolda) village, Quepem Taluka, dated c. 14th Century A.D.

Ibn Batuta does not make any reference to the assault made on Chandrapura. So historians believed that Chandrapura was a place different from Sindapura i.e. Goa Velha and considered that the Sindabur mentioned by Ibn Batuta was likely to be Chandrapura, because the Arabs pronounced and incorrectly wrote the Indian names.

Some riddles on Chandrapura

Now here one may raise some points not resolved by historians. From the accounts narrated above, it is seen that the cities of Chandrapura and Sindapura were attacked by the Muslims in the period about 1342 to 1344. Now the point is whether the attacks were simultaneously done, first assaulting Chandrapura and next Sindapura or were those attacks made on separate occasions with a gap of one year between them. Ibn Batuta refers to the attack on Sindapura, but not on Chandrapura. Another view that can be accepted is that Ibn Batuta did not make the reference to Chandrapura because it was of negligible importance. The Nabab of Honawar first attacked Chandrapura, killed the king, and sequestered Chandrapura city. He might have taken, in a very short period, say of three or four hours, to the direction of Sindapura as the city might offer him little resistance with the king being absent. The city was also the richest of the Kadamba kingdom. Now the intention of Nabab might have changed. He desired now to expand his sway over the nearest area, Bardez taluka which was under the lordship of Bhimabhupala. This king, suspecting an attack, might have taken necessary precautions by spreading out his troops. And later Bhimabhupala changed from the defensive to the offensive, with his troops entereing Tiswadi taluka, where the Hindu population favoured and joined the fighters of the Kadamba king, who had been in Tiswadi before but had later fled to his dominion. The Nabab was in a difficult position; he could get supplies only by the sea-route from Honawar which was very far. So there was no other solution for him, except to leave Sindapur and he did so. The compositor of the inscription of the Corgaon-plate does not mention this event while he gives the list of the twelve kings of the dyanasty with their relationship to each other. The omission was perhaps intentional, made to hide the defeat and the dethroning of the forefathers of the donor Bhimabhupala dynasty, which the compositor characterized as glorious. This dynasty, like that of 'Vira Kavana Vallabha Maharaja' of the Senior branch of the Sendraka dynasty (1380 A.D.) mentioned before, ruled as independents or as the feudatory of the Kadambas.

Rule of the Adilshahi dynasty

In 1352 A.D., Allaudin, Sultan of the Bahamani empire, captured Goa from the Viceroy of Vijayanagar. In 1489, Yusuf Adil Khan, a baron of the Bahamani emperor, founded the Adil Shahi dynasty of Bijapur which held sway over Goa territory.

In 1510, the Portuguese conquered the island of Tiswadi. By the treaty of 1543 Ibrahim Adil Shah ceded Bardez and Salcete talukas to the Portuguese, and the area of those three talukas came to be named by the Portuguese as the Old Conquests; and by the treaty of 1571 these became their permanent territories. The remaining part of Goa territory continued under the realm of the Sultanate of Bijapur. This dynasty from the beginning were tolerant of the Hindu religion and maintained friendship with the Hindus and as such conferred upon some the title of Pratap Rau Sar Desai, Jasvant Rau Desai, Visvas Rau Desai and Suria Rau Desai, all these being Saraswat Brahmins, and Bhiva Rau Desai or simply Desai, of the Maratha caste. These persons were in charge of collection of revenue and administration with the obligation of the maintenance of an army for this purpose. They all were allowed villages as Mocassos, and sometimes Inams of lands in different villages.

The Adilshahi system of records

One important system which was introduced by the Sultana of Bijapur was that in each territorial division they had to maintain records in the script and language in use among the local population of high status, who were in charge of the recording. As such in Goa these records were in the coloquial Marathi language in the Modi script, a running variety of Devanagari.

The present descendants of Sendraka

In 1942, when I was in charge of preparing records for a cadastral survey of a part of Sattari taluka, I had seen a copy of a Sanad issued to Desai of the Maratha caste by the said Sultanate which was in Modi script and in colloquial Marathi with some Pharsi words, in which, besides grants of villages and other rights in Sattari taluka, the right of use of a banner with the sign of a cock was also mentioned. This showed the special position of the concerned person because the other Sardesais and Desais mentioned above did not have this right. This family of Bhivam (a Muslim corruption of the word 'Bhima'), Rau Desai with a house in Thanem hamlet of Dongurli village, had a finger-ring of silver in which are carved some signs which cannot be deciphered. In 1942, I had seen with the late Hirba Baburau Bivam Rau Desai old contracts of a lease where the sign on the finger-ring had been impressed as a seal. In the inner room used as a sanctuary, two metallic (panchala) idols are worshipped—one in the standing position named "Vantudeva" and the other on horseback named 'Akari'. Akari means the originator of a family. I think both those idols are of Vantudeva, in two different positions. He was the ancestor of that family, hence that family is from the Senior house of the Sendrakas.

The family every year celebrates Ramanavami with great pomp, offering mid-day meal to hundreds of people of different castes. The event takes the form of a village festival (jatra) during those two days. There is no idol proper of Rama under worship, however, on a bench in the inner open yard there is a niche in which a black irregular stone is installed. On its frontal face is carved the word 'Shree Rama' in Devanagari script, but it is not known when the daily worship of that stone and festival started. From this custom, it seems that this house is of the Sendraka family. Some generations after Vantudeva, they considered themselves to be of the Solar race (Surya-vamshi), and started celebrating Ramanavami, as Rama was of the Solar race.

This Bivam Rau Desai family has two collateral relatives whose families are known as Parmekar Desai and Usapkar Desai. Both these families worship in their houses idols of Vantudeva as their ancestor and as such the members of these three families cannot intermarry.

The Parmeker and Usapkar Desais were, in the early period, barons of Savant Bounsule of Sawantwadi. Parma and Usap are villages of early Sawantwadi native-state now incorporated into Maharashtra. Parmem village lies on the border of Pednem taluka, and Usap on the border of *Dicholi* taluka. Usapkar Desai is a branch of Parmekar.

I presume that these two families are descendants of the Junior house of the Sendraka dynasty which is mentioned as a Solar race and worshippers of god Shiva, while Vantudeva in the Chiplum copper-plate is described as a worshipper of god Maheshwar (Shiva). So my presumption appears to be correct.

I have given a somewhat long account of the Sendraka dynasty showing its present descendants, firstly because I was the first to bring to light the existence of a ruling dynasty unknown before in the history of Goa, and secondly, because this is the only family of ancient rulers whose decendants still exist in Goa, maintaining their aristocratic ways recognized even by the last rulers, the Portuguese, and even today that family has certain privileges bequethed by society through tradition. The family has existed at least for sixteen centuries with an aristocratic hegemony. The other ruling family which resides in Goa is of the ruler Soudhem who came from Karnataka and established itself at Bandodem of Ponda taluka, only two centuries ago.

Now with reference to item No.12: (Vir Kavana inscription)

The kingship did not end in 945A.D. The family like the Junior branch of Sendraka continued to govern some part of Goa as mentioned before, even after Bahamani rule and during the very beginning of Vijayanagar rule as independents or as a feudatory of the ruling overlordship. We find in 1380A.D. a king named Vira Kavana Vallabharaja Maharaja, continuing with the honorary title 'Vallabha' given to Vantudeva in the 6th century A.D. by the Chalukyas of Badami

Sendraka administration in retrospect

The system of administration of the Sendraka rulers in general was not different from that of their sovereign Chalukyas whose system is better known through historians.

"The form of the Chalukyan government was monarchy and all the administrative powers were concentrated on the king himself. Though it can be accused of not being in accordance with principles of popular government as in modern times, it was based on the sound principles of imperial system of the federal type well established in the land. The monarch was not absolute and his actions were regulated by religious injunctions. That the king was benevolent and his beneficent actions were felt over at great distance is noticeable by Yuan Chang. The king devoted his personal attention to details of administration and spent most of his working time in the audience chamber or one of the battlefields as the head of his forces. He toured his kingdom constantly and fixed the camp in different places so as to keep in touch with all parts of the realm. The conquered territories were, in many cases , left in the chieftainship of the respective rulers conquered whose submission was accepted by the Imperial Suzerain, otherwise assigned to the ruling sovereign's brother, sons or very close relative". (Note:Here we have proof of this assignment made by Kirtivaran I to his brother-in- law Vantudeva or Vantuvallabha of the Sendraka family. Some provinces were ruled by feudatories and other by independent allies).

"Grama was the lowest unit of the administration. It had its own popular assembly consisting of heads of all families in the village. They constituted the Mahajana of the town or city. The head of the village assembly was Gauda. The Mahajanas assisted him in the administration of the village. The king sought the assistance of those popular assemblies in administration of the militia in times of necessity and in organising public festivals and fairs."

The empire of the Chalukyas like that of the Rastrakutas was divided as follows: Rastra, Vishayas, Karram and Grama. (Note: The area under sway of the Sendraka family was named Sendraka Vishaya as we have noted before).

In Nothern as well as in Southern India there was always a subdivision between Vishaya and Grama, designated as Bhukti or Bhoga in the North and Bhoga or Karram in the South but this is very rarely mentioned in the copper-plates. However, in the times of the Bhojas and Konkana Mauryas this subdivision did not exist as the empire system did not exist in their times.

About the name Karram (meaning group of villages)

The Curtorim copper-plate of Viravarmadeva Kadamba dated 1049 A.D., edited by V. T. Gune, seems to refer to this subdivision 'Kurram' which probably existed in Goa, introduced by the Sendraka rulers according to their sovereign's system, that of the

Chalukyas of Badami [108] pp. 55-66.

According to the transliteration made by Dr. Gune, the last phrase of no. 42 line reads: *"Litekha shaka - Kammirah (?) shasanae tamra - pattake - Ki - dada— —"*

After the word "Kammirah", Dr Gune rightly puts a sign of interrogation. However, let me postulate my view here: This phrase, I presume, refers to the registration of this charter in the registration office of the 'Karram' (group of villages) and it also was composed by the same person who prepared the inscription, and we note once again the allegoric and acrobatic styles in that composition. The compositor like others might have Sankritized the Kannada word 'Karram' into 'Kammiva', the previous word 'shaka' may be 'shikka' (stamp) or may mean registration in short. I have reasons to think so because the description of the land is recorded as "Kudatarikagraharantarvatti - Tundukapuramnama" (Lines 24-25). The land grants is a 'pura' or say village and not a small piece of land or even a hamlet. Secondly it is said that the land or 'pura' is part of the 'Agrahar' named 'Cudatari' Agrahara in principle is land already granted. Then how can a king make a new grant of land of a part already granted?

Now, there is before us the example of Sindapura which was previously a hamlet of Vodlem-Goen (Goa Velha) but after the construction of the sea-port was named by Vantudeva as Sindapura. This original hamlet attained the form of a town, which was not the case of the village Cudatari which lies in Salcete taluka without any navigable river for canoes. In Portuguese times that village had 37 hamlets and none of these have any names even remotely similar to the names of the granted land [109] p. 332.

About the epithet 'Agrahara'

The epithet 'Agrahara' given to *Cudatari* villages deserves an explanation. In Hindu mythology, already referred to in the first chapter, Shree Parashurama had brought some Saraswat families, granting them some villages of Salcete and other talukas. These villages were considered as 'Agraharas' made by Shree Parashurama, and one of the villages was *Cudatari*. Adjacent to the village lies *Dramapur*, a Portuguese trans-formation of its original designation 'Dharmapur', a gifted village, and so, the village granted by that inscription is this village, without any doubt. The king could grant the village because there was no male descendant of the Gaonkar of that village. At that time such cases were common and it is to be noted that the land was granted to a Brahmin of the Kaushika gotra, without the epithet of Bhatta, the Purohita of the king. So the grantee was a Saraswat Brahmin. The grant was done with the obligation of payment of five big Gadyanas annually. The king might have ordered this in consulta-tion with his council. But the grantee was not the owner of the land but had the right to collect the land-tax and other dues from the village commune. This amount, as I mentioned before, in the Bhoja and Maurya period was named 'panga', and later, from the time of the Sendraka, 'sidaya', a Kannada word meaning tax. The inscription conveys it in Sankritized form—'siddahaya' (line no. 26). The same Sankritized form appears as land-tax in the Konkana Shilahar's inscriptions during the time the Sendraka family ruled in Goa.

Etymology of Siddhaya and Torofo

Dr Mirashi who published in Marathi the history of the Shilaharas makes an important note. He says that all the founders of ancient dynasties in the Konkan area had their original tongue as Kannada, since at that time Belgaum district up to Osmanabad of present Marathwada was included in the Konkan and so, some Kannada words like 'siddaya', the epithet 'payya' denoting high respect to a person, generally of the Brahmin caste, appear in Sankritized form in the inscriptions, otherwise composed in the Sanskrit language.

This Kannada word 'siddaya' I had heard as 'sidav' for the first time in the year 1941, from a Maratha Gaonkar of Keri village, Sattari taluka. This village is a 'Mokaso' (Inam) of Rane Sar Desai, and in a particular case, the Gaonkar said: "*Khashe* (Inamdar) is the owner of '*sidav*', but I am the owner of the planted trees". There was a traditional custom of annual payment of one-and-a-half annas for each productive mango or jackfruit tree, the same rate which was applied when the trees were situated on government land. Thus, it is seen that from the time of the Sendrakas, the old nomenclature 'panga' was changed to 'sidav'.

The system of grouping of villages continued even in the Portuguese period and it goes on even now under different names. The Kannada work 'karram' in the Muslim period came to be named as 'tarf' and was maintained in certain areas as 'torofo' (for example '*Torofo de Cotigaon*' (Taraf of Khotigaon) in Canacona taluka. Now, when the Goa Government adopted the Maharashtra State system of Revenue Survey, copied from their legislation, the word '*saza*' was introduced as a substitution for '*freguesia*', meaning village in Portuguese; the word saza was never known in Goa before.

Sendrakas promoted new village communes

In their Vishaya, the Sendrakas not only maintained the existing village-commune system but also promoted the creation of new ones.

The Portuguese Government Order No. 10, dated 18th April, 1848, prescribed that the quit-rent ('foro' in Portuguese) payable annually by private bodies and Hindu temples to the village-communes of Chandravadi province (now Quepem taluka) under the names of *Pardaus* or *Oras*, should be converted into 6 *asharfis* (xerafim in Portuguese) each, when payable by private bodies, and at the rate of 5:1:15 each when payable by the temples. *Pardau* is a corrupted Portuguese designation for a gold coin introduced by the Kadambas under the Chalukyas of Badami, with the figure of a wild boar carved on it as this was the sign of their banner [110] p. 191.

This order proves clearly that not only in the Old Conquests but even in areas of the New Conquests like Quepem taluka, village communes were already established at the time of the Sendrakas domain and continued in their regular form up to the Portuguese period. They had suffered in their administration for a certain time but were re-established by the Order dated 1771 of the Marques de Pombal, prime-minister of D. Jose, king of Portugal.

Adv. Rui Gomes Pereira's comments

Adv. Rui Gomes Pereira says: "Satari - This taluka had the largest number of villages—eighty-eight—and probably all of them had their communities (village-communes). Prior to or in 1882 there remained only two, those of Ganjem and Pissurlem which are included (for purposes of fiscalization) in the Bicholim (alias Dicholi) taluka.

"The most important communities of the Sanquelim or Sattari talukas were those of Caranzol, Compordem, Golaulim, Mahus, Melaulim, Morlem, Onda and Poriem. All of them were members of the Camara Geral (general body) of that taluka.

"The Sar Desai Ranes seized that Province and established such a regime that forced the dissolution of the Camara Geral and of the communities, to the great detriment of the inhabitants. In order to remedy this situation and prompted by hatred and with a spirit of vengeance against those Ranes, the Portuguese Government revived those communities or rather, ordered their re-establishment.

"As the Ranes indulged in disturbing the Province and had to be punished, the Government in 1853 ordered that the communities be reconstituted with the inscription of Gaonkars and Desais of the respective villages, independently of any prior ascertainment about they being descendants from the original Gaonkars or not. At the same time it was decreed that the lands owned by Ranes and Dubhashis under the title of Mocasso, inams and other such titles be reverted to the national exchequer.

"A few years later, the Ranes surrendered themselves to the Portuguese and swore vassalage and to this, the Portuguese Government promised them protection and rights of citizenship. A decision to restore their old rights was also taken, although the agreement made no reference to it. In 1856, the Portuguese Government revoked its Order in regard to the reversion of all concessions under the title of mocasso and others as a token of friendship.

"The above Legislative enactment did not revoke or suspend the Order for the reconstitution of the communities. However, these communities were never again re-established". [111] pp. 22-23.

These two facts sufficiently prove that under the dominion of the Sendrakas the existing village-communal system was developed and established even in jungle areas, a system which was slightly different from that existing in Northern or Southern areas where this system was only restricted to self-government and the right to village land belonged to the Crown. Here, in Goa the right belonged to the descendant Gaonkars, considered as descendants of the original settlers and developers of the village land.

Collection of taxes

The taxes to be paid in this period were the same as in the earlier period. The land-tax named 'panga' came to be designated as 'sidav'; the other taxes like custom-taxes continued as before, but the rate on land is not known. It is worth noting that the Gaonkars of Golauli village exclusively had the surname '*Khot*' which in Marathi means a man (now a family) in charge of collection of Government taxes, like revenue, customs etc. The derivation of this word is not definitive; some thinks it to be a corruption of the word 'Koits' found in the Aine-Akbari of the Akbar's time. The Gaonkars of the surrounding villages had no such surname. On the other hand, it is said that the village Golauli was the head of the 'Kurram' or 'Bhoga' and so, the headman of the village had a seat in the taluka-committee. It appears that the headman was entrusted with the collection of Government dues under the jurisdiction of the respective 'Kurram' from the time of the Sendrakas.

SOME TRADITIONAL CUSTOMS
Personal

Before the wedding ceremony, a Maratha bridegroom is shaved by the village-barber under the pleas of the assembled musicians. The principal operation was '*Regh marap*' (cutting the hair in a straight line, over the forehead). Later, the shaving may be done according to the wishes of the bridegroom. Forty years ago the Maratha man maintained a 'shendi' (clean shaved head with a shendi at the centre). This ceremony practically was symbolic, and barbers profited with this ceremony.

This ceremony obviously was derived from ancient customs when only sages and Kshatriyas maintained their hair like women, with the difference that the Kshatriyas made a cut of a terminal part of their hair. At a place named '*Mandolgireache-mol*' were two idols of black stone named 'Kolgiro'and 'Mundalgiro'. This was surely installed at the time of Vantudeva with the idols wearing a warrior's helmet and a knot of head-hair (see ill nos. 7a & 7b at page 64 & 65). At that time and later all male members of Hindu families had their heads shaved, maintaining a small portion in the occipital region, except the Kshatriyas. But at Morgi(Pednem taluka), as I have mentioned before, the Junior house of the Sendrakas had a centre for the training of cavalry under a 'Hayapati' who was from a Saraswat family and who through generations followed the Kshatriyas in maintaining a full head of hair (*bhis* in konkani); so the family came to be designated as 'Bhise'. These families emigrated from Morji to Bhati of Astagrahar (Sanguem taluka)and lived there as the Kulkarni Vangad and so were known as Bhatikars.

Ghodemanni festival at Thanem (Sattari)

I have already referred to this ceremony and its origin. Here I will describe briefly the festival at Thanem at Sattari which is important because though this festival is considered religious, it contains the germs of the procedures of village-communes and of their general body.

The festival is celebrated in alternate years in the last days of the general Hindu festival of Shigmo. On a particular day at night the villagers Pale, Dongurli, Rivem, Choraundi, Ivrem-Budruk, Ivre-Khurd and Golauli assemble together.The eldest member of each family puts on his ankle a wooden head of a horse with a leather band and all those members, according to the serial number already arranged in the past, stand erect in a straight line in a fixed site in the Mundalgireache-Mol. Then they send a Mhar (messenger) inviting the Mocasdar of the family of 'Bivan Rau Desai' to the main house, where other members of the same family have assembled. The male members of this family start their march to the accompaniment of the Mhar musicians, the "shinga" being the principal instrument. Approaching the site, the members form a line headed by the members of the eldest branch of the family. This rank, like in the military, reviews the gathering and then stops near Gaonkar no 1. of the Pali. The member of the eldest branch asks "How are the affairs of your village going on ?" Each of the Gaonkars in turn, replies, "Very well by the blessing of God and of Khashe" (Khashe means Mocasdar). Sometimes a member makes a claim, and the head replies: We will discuss at *sadar*"(assembly-hall). Wishing "*Ram-ram*" (a salute made by each member of these Gaonkars), all the members of the Desai family return, also to the beat of music.Then the dancers celebrate the ceremony dancing through the night, and finally the Mhars release the leather bands of the wooden equine heads.The Gaonkar members go to the river to have a bath.

The Mhars were servants in charge of the maintenance of horses as well as the making of leather goods and the readying of horses for daily raids in the ancient times. That work is symbolized by releasing the leather band. Periodically the king used to visit the area and assisted in the cavalry raids, the operation being symbolized by Ghodemanni. The review was made by the Mocasdar family, as a substitute of the king in ancient times.

Old administrative customs at Sattari

When any litigation between the Gaonkars of the village arose, the assembly of elders of the families tried to settle it. If the assembly could not settle the dispute, the claimant appears before 'Sadar' and gives his account to the eldest Mocasdar, whose ancient house still stands in Thanem hamlet of Dongurli village. He sends his Naik and calls the eldest member of the Santerkar Gaonkar of that hamlet who is the first in rank among the other families, namely Yougeshwarkar, Bramanikar and Kelbaikar (this branch is now extinct). He notifies all the Gaonkars of the villages, fixing the time and day according to the convenience of all of them. On the appointed day they assemble in the temple of Santer at Thanem.This procedure is however different from the customs in the temple in Ponda taluka, where no meeting may be held in the area covered by the temple building proper, as no discussion or even conversations are permitted there.

If the assembly arrives at an unanimous resolution, excluding the opinions of the claimant and defendant, then this resolution is communicated by the same Santerkar Goankar, who accompanies the claimant to the Mokasdar who confirms and seals the resolution as final. But if there was no such resolution or if the Goankars did not gather, then the Mocasdar fixes the time and day for such a meeting at the 'Sadar' (assembly-hall). At the 'Sadar', the Mocasdar takes his seat on a large bench of masonry existing at one side of the hall. The Goankars appears one after another, and enter the hall with bare feet, saluting and intoning 'Ram-ram'. The Mocasdar answers 'Ram-ram', without any movement of his hands or change in his posture.

After all the Gaonkars have gathered, the Mocasdar explains the claim and the Gaonkars discuss it. If points of disagreement surface, the Mocasdar with the experience of different resolutions taken before, based sometimes on traditional customs, makes up his mind. But he does not express his opinion immediately and attempts to bring about an accord. The Goankars, noting the inclination of the Mocasdar's mind, may agree to the accord. The Mocasdar says, "All of you have arrived at the resolution unanimously, so I agree with all of you". Then he stands up. All the Goankars do the same, expressing 'Ram-ram'. The Mocasdar leaves the 'Sadar' and enters the house and the meeting is over. I know about this procedure because in 1942 I was present at such a meeting.

THE CULTURAL HERITAGE OF GOAN SOCIETY

Sculpture and architecture

That Buddhism was in Goa in the times of the Bhojas is evident from the idol of Gautama discovered by Father Heras at Colvale (Bardez taluka). It is considered to be of the 2nd or 3rd century A.D. At Rivana village of Astagrahar division of Sanguem taluka, in the property of S.S. Desai a life-size, headless statue of Buddha was found *(ill. 31)* sitting on a heavy pedestal. It is now kept in the local Government Museum at Panaji. It is one of the biggest statues of Buddha found in the western region of India. In the same place there are two caves named 'Wivaram', on top of a rocky hill named 'Pandavamsodo'. One cave is large and probably artificial while the other is smaller with some artificial features. V.R.V. Valaulikar says that when he visited the area he was informed that this cave was found in 1904. When the finder dug into the cave, he found almost circular seals of clay, with some indecipherable signs carved on one face. Valaulikar thinks that those signs were of a script similar to those of Brahmi found by Pandit Bhagawanlal Indraji in 1882 on a rock of a hill named Padna in Salsete island near Bombay. That script according to Bhagwanlal, is of the 5th or 6th century A.D. In the caves at Kanheri in the same island, seals of clay made by Buddhist monks were also found—some with an image of Buddha and others with scripts of mantras of Buddhism. This script, according to E.W. West, was probably of the 10th century A.D. [60] pp.14-15.

Idols of Buddha

In Goa, we find only two idols of Buddha in places far from one another. In the Portuguese records of the destruction of temples, we find at least two names recorded as 'Gautameshvar' but, these probably were Shivalingas, firstly because the epithet 'Ishvar' always referred to 'Shiva' generally represented in the form of a 'linga' and secondly, perhaps because of the surveyor's style of recording the names of the deities. For example Surya- Narayan and Laxshimi-Narayana were recorded as 'Narayana', omitting the prefixed word.

In the Chiplun copper-plate Vantuvallabha has been described as worshipper of Maheswara. The grant had been made to a Brahmin who had performed 'Yajna-Yaga', rituals of the Vaidic religion. This proves that he did not patronise Buddhism. Hence it is clear that if Buddhist monks were living in Goa at this time, it is certain that in the middle half of the 8th century A.D., Buddhism was not prevalent in Goa. So, the idol of Buddha at Colvale in Bardez taluka came to be worshipped under the name of Gautama

ill. 31 : Idol of Gautam Buddha (without head) of Rivona, Sanguem Taluka, presently kept in Panaji Museum.

by the Hindus, while at Rivona the idol of Buddha was abandoned *(ill. 31)*.

From the time of Kirtivarman I, the kings and queens of the Chalukya dynasty of Badami, we observe the patronage of the Vaidic religion, and it is natural that close relatives of the Sendraka dynasty from Vantu-valabha proceeded in the same form. I have referred to such patronage of Vantu-vallabha, and this state continued up to the advent of Kadamba power in Goa.

Architecture of Shiva temples at Curdi and Nundem

We have seen that even in the times of the Bhojas a sect of sages of Shaivism, possibly 'Pashupata Panth', existed in Goa and also in the adjacent area of South and North Konkan under the Shilahars. Those sages had the epithet of 'Shambhu' and this is designated in the copper-plates of the Shilahars as 'Acharyas'. Presumably there was a bi-directional movement of those sages. In the ancient period, they lived in artificial caves as at Harvalem and Lamgaon (Bicholim taluka), and temples were constructed with timber with walls made of laterite stone, rubble and clay mortar. The roofs in relatively modern times were also constructed with timber with two or four sides in inclined form covered with the leaves of coconut, areca or jungle palm trees to preserve the timber-roof from rains. We find at Kurdi and Nundem of Astagrahar division of Sanguem taluka, two temples. The one existing in Curdi is of the Shilahar style, with huge frontal pillars of granite, the remaining part being of well-cut laterite stone without any cementing. The roof is a pyramidical tower (*Shikara*). There is no idol in that temple, however the black portion of the Nandi is seen in the pavillion. So, it is sure that the temple was constructed in about the 7th or 8th century A.D. by the Sendrakas, on the suggestion of those sages of Pashupata Pantha.

The other temple existing in Nundem village is of Shree Mahamaya and also belongs to this early period (6th or 7th century A.D.). It has a pyramidal type of tower and is constructed with well-cut laterite stone. A stone inscription in the Brahmi script (southern characters) was discovered near the temple and is supposed to belong to the 5th or 6th century A.D. [112] p.287.

I remember well, a little distance from this temple, the remains of a wall, quite high, of well-cut laterite stone. Villagers informed me that it was locally named '*Kilyant*' (fortress) and that it was constructed by Havig Brahmins.

The architecture of Curdi temple

I visited the temple of Curdi and surrounding areas in 1932, and later on, in about1951-52, while working to re-establish the boundary marks of mining claims near those sites, I revisited the temple (*ill. 32*) and that one at Nundem.

On my first visit in 1932, I was very impressed by the temple and it was one of the chief reasons which impelled me to study the ancient culture of Goa. The architecture

ill. 32 : Temple of Curdi, Sanguem Taluka.

of that temple, taking into consideration the time and place where it was constructed, is astonishing. The same kind of impression was produced in 1935 when I visited the temple of Shree Mahadeva of Tamdi-Surla of Hemadbarcem division in Sanguem taluka. Both the temples are situated in the jungle and there is no evidence of human existence nearby. The silence is awe-inspiring.

As the temple of Curdi is one of the two relics of ancient architecture, it deserves a full description. I quote Dr.Gune in the Goa Gazetteer pp 61-62[18].

"The shrine of Curdi is built of laterite and granite stones and is approachable only through heavy wild growth of banyan trees and bamboo groves all around it. The plan of the temple is simple, rectangular. It has two parts: the Garbhagraha or sanctum sanctorum with a pyramidical tower or Shikhara on it and an open entrance Pavillion or Sukhanasi which is wider than the Garbhagriha. The exterior walls are made of well-cut laterite stones which are piled up in a vertical position without any cementing in between. The walls are adorned with pilasters and some conical designs in the niches between them. The tower on shikhara is a perfect pyramid marked with horizontal stage that has the appearence of steps and can be compared to early Viman or Shikhara of the Kadamba style (about 7th, 8th century A.D.). The pavillion is raised on the front side by pillars of granite stone with a ceiling of a pendant lotus design which links it with the doorway to the Garbhagriha on the back side. The pillars are supported at the top by capitals and are adorned with circular rings. Some beautiful designs are noticed on them at the girdle.

"The black portion of the image of Nandi is seen in the pavillion. The doorway to the main shrine is also made of granite stone. It is ornamented by beautiful creepers and flowers designs on its two sides. The dedicatory block of the image of Ganesh is seen in the middle of its top. A special panel of some images is further raised on it. From its *Shikhar* and plan of the outlay, the temples seem to be of more than 1,200 years old and might have been constructed when the Shilaharas ruled over Goa (750-1010A.D.). A broken slab of stone inscription found at the site and written in the Nagari script also supported the period".

A two images of Umasahita alingana murti of God Shiva were collected from the caves existing nearby. God Shiva is seen here sitting on his vehicle Nandi and embracing his spouse Parvati or Uma, his sons, Kartikeya and Ganesh are seen on either side of the panel. The less ornamented image probably belongs to the same period when the temple might have been constructed while the others seem to be its later imitation during the 12th or 13th century A.D."

Dr. Gune gives three datings for the construction of the temple of Curdi, differing by up to seven centuries from one another. This form of indication of the datings cannot be excused. Dr. Gune cites the book 'Epigraphica Indica' in respect of the reading of the inscription found near the temple of Nundem in the Brahmi script,but does not give the context. However, according to recent information of the Department of Archelogy, Government of Goa, the inscription is placed in the 6th century A.D. So I have mentioned these two temples as of the period of the Sendrakas. But here a further point needs to be made: an inscription dated 785A.D. says that the Chalukya king Vijayaditya had granted the village Colamba to eight Brahmins, and their gotras were Bharadwaja, Kaushika, Kaudinya, Maudagalya, Atreya, Kasyapa and Vatsa. It is to be noted that the name of the Brahmin of the Vatsa gotra was Desaverma (and not Sharma) [84] pp.179-180. One of the idols of Brahmadeva installed by Vantudeva is found even today under worship at Colamba, as this village is situated in Astagrahar division of Sanguem taluka and was on the commercial route passing then from Curdi to Rivona. It is unknown where from and of what subcaste those Brahmins were and how they disappeared from the village. There are no signs of settlements in that village, so this point is open to further investigation. However, those Brahmins cannot have links with those temples and idols as there is no similar temple or idol in Colamba proper. The idol in the simple form of Umasahita alingana murti of god Shiva found in a cave near the temple of Curdi is surely of the 5th or 6th century A.D. established by the sages of Pashupata Pantha.With similar significance we find at Cudnem an idol of that period or earlier period as mentioned before.

In this Sendraka period, the sculpture of Hindu deities in different forms and style as well as of temples and shrines made great headway and this continued in the later period.

Education

As I have mentioned before, the system of training in writing, reading and counting was begun in the Sumerian fashion. A room was constructed adjacent to the temple, and the same system continued with the modification that with the residential houses of the priests being spacious, the training was conducted there by the priest. The students were naturally male offspring of Paddye Bhats, Saraswat Brahmins, the Kshatriyas, the Smiths entrusted with the making of jewellery, weapons and agriculture implements and the Vaishyas or Vanis, a merchant caste. At the time of Sendraka rule, the caste system was rigid as can be observed from the accounts of that period by historians of the Chalukyas of Badami.

The next step was of higher studies in Medicine, Astronomy, Astrology etc. And such study was done by the offspring of Bhats, Brahmins and Goldsmiths (who now name themselves as Daivadnya Brahmins). Advanced courses on the Vedas and Vedanta Nirukta and religious rituals was the specilization of the Bhats in general and of the Saraswat Brahmins who had devoted themselves exclusively to the priesthood through generations. The Saraswat Brahmins also received training in the preliminary stage and were designated as 'Senawayi', as we find in the copper-plate of the Konkan Shilahars.

**RELIGIOUS   SECTS   IN   GOA   DURING
THE   PRE-KADAMBA   PERIOD**

Shaivism in Goa

Branches

In Goa we find the male and female signs of lingas in separate as well as in conjugation form in the later period. There are many lingas (phalli) without the circular pindika (female element) like at Nagueshim at Bandodem. At the same time there is the female element in the vulva form named Mhatari at Savoi-Verem in Ponda taluka. However, the time of sublimation of those male and female signs into idols of Betal and Vanadevi respectively, occurred probably in the period of Vantu-vallabha of the Sendraka dynasty. As it was not found in any other period before that, the tradition of separation continued.

Prof. Gosavi's account

In this way, Hindu religious faith—some of its sects or system —which appeared in Goa, are branches of Shaivism which had its origin long before the compositions of the Rigveda. Prof.R.R.Gosawi gives a fine account of these sects in his book in Marathi called "Panch-Upasana Pantha" (Five Systems of Worship). He gives an account of worship of Sun, Shiva, Shakti, Vishnu and Ganapati. That all the sects took root in Goa is proved by the idols which were in worship. After Shankaracharya's unification, the worshipper's idol was put as the principal and this form of five idols together is named Panchayatan and their worship, Panchayatana-puja. Besides these, Puranic deities were also

ill. 33 : Idol of Patur-dey (Padyanchi-devi) found in an excavation at Zuno-Bazar (Old Bazar) at Madgaon and kept in Panaji Museum.

worshipped. The deities of Paddya Bhats, one of which was found in the excavations at *Madgaon* and is named in the Portuguese records as 'Paturdey' (Paddyanlidevi) *(ill. 33)* along with the remains of Surya-Narayana as well as non- Aryans deities like Gana -Rouduro and Kamin-Ronduro at Savoi-Verem, are examples. In the present case, we have to take note of Shaivism and Shaktism elaborated on by Dr. Gosavi. I quote from him only what is absolutely needed for this dissertation, and I have made notes wherever necessary. He says [113] pp.37-152:

"In Rigveda (1-114, 2-33, 7-46, 1-43, 6-74, etc.) we find hymns related to the God Rudra but he is of second rank. From the hymn 1-114-8 it is seen that he is destroyer of human being as well as of animals. He is of red complexion". Here my note is that we find Kamin-Runduro and Gana-Rouduro of aboriginal and non-Aryan tribes which have the epithet 'Rouduro' with identical factions of destruction. Rev. Haffmann in his Encyclopedia Mundarika, drawing up a chart of Mundari words and those of Indo-European languages with identical pronounciation and meaning says that this similarity proves that this tribe and the Indo-Europeans, must have lived in the neighbourhood some time or the other. He does not refer to the deities mentioned above.

"It is very important to note that in the fifteenth Mandala of Atharvaveda Rudra is designated as 'Vratya'. Its age however cannot very well be fixed. However in the later Brahmanas and Suktas, there is a rite to incorporate non-Aryans into Aryan society, and this rite is named 'Vratyastoma'. These Vratyas were non-Aryans. They did not accept Vedic rituals. Their religion was based on 'Yoga' and 'Dhyana'(contemplation, profound meditation). They were civilized and well advanced in the art of living, and their help was procured for defeating wild human beings who are designated as rakshasas. Besides, the Aryans were impressed by their religious rites of 'Yoga'and 'Dhyana'. In turn the Vratyas also were impressed by the worship of some Aryans deities (probably worship of the Sun).

"After Atharvaveda, following a long interval of time, the hymns of Yajurveda were composed and in those Rudra is named as 'Trambakahoma' and 'Shatarudriya' is designated for the first time as 'Shiva' and 'Shivatara in addition to his previous names".

Now Shiva- Rudra had the right, like other Gods, to have the 'Avirbhaga' (parcel of food given in his name) offered in the 'Homa' (sacrificial fire). Indeed there are prayers asking him to take this 'Avirbhagh'. In these hymns he continued to be named as 'Pashupati' besides the new names 'Girish', 'Vratapati'and 'Ganapati'in addition to exquisite names like 'Stenanampati' and 'Taskaranampati'. He is described as having a 'Mushaka' (rat) as his vehicle and a sister named 'Ambika' (Note :Ambika is an unmarried mother goddess while Uma or Parvati is the wife of Shankara or Mahesha—other names of Shiva).

In the time of Brahmanas, Vishnu came to have a prominent place in worship. Some Aryan and non-Aryan tribes who were absolutely biased in favour of the rites of 'Yoga' and 'Dhyana' continued to worship Rudra- shiva. The people of the Indus Valley—non-Aryan—were of this type.

Even the worship of Rudra-Shiva in the form of a phallus was adopted by the Aryans. It is worth noting that the Brahmins do not eat the food offered to him (Note: amongst Saraswat Brahmins of Goa, the cooked food offered to Mahadeva (name of Rudra- Shiva) on the day of Ganesh Chaturthi is offered to a person of the non- Brahmin caste).

In the time of the Upanishads, especially 'Shivetashwantara', the worship of male and female elements symbolized by Rudra- Shiva and Ambika respectively, was metaphysically sublimized and so the Shaivism and Shaktism sects originated.

Panini, 8th century B.C.(according to some historians 4th century B.C.) prepared a grammar of the Sanskrit language named 'Astadhyayi'. It mentioned Rudra with the epithets 'Bhava' and 'Sharva', and in section and Suktas (6-68 and 4-10) the words 'bhakti' and 'Bhakta' appear twice. From these words it is proved that in that period, the Bhakti procedure of rites (like puja - as differentiated from Yoga and Dhyana) of Shiva or Maheswar was already in vogue. Some of Panini's grammar Suktas in the Malayalam script and Sanskrit language carved on a bark of a tree were found a Thanem, Sattari taluka *(ill.34)*.

"In the Ramayana and Mahabharata we find references to the Bhakti system of Rudra or Shiva. So at the time of the last edition of these epics the Bhakti system of Shiva was highly developed. He was considered as destroyer as well as creator of all things existing in the world. Ramayan narrates the marriage of Shiva with Uma, daughter of Hemvant (Balakand 35-13 to 20). Nandi, the bull as his vehicle, describes the episode of the birth of his son Skanda (Balakand, 37 to 25), but does not refer to the worship of Shivalinga (phallus). From this fact we can conclude that the present form of worship of Shiva in idol form might have originated in the Ramayana period.

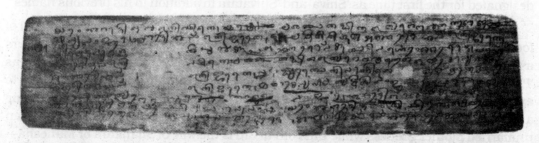

ll No. 34: Panini's grammar Suktas in Malayalam script and Sanskrit language carved on a bark of a tree found in the Archives of Bivam Rau Dessai, at Thane, Sattary Taluka.

"In Mahabharata time, both the systems, namely 'Yoga and Dhyana' was in use at a high level amongst the ascetics, while the popular way was of the Bhakti system of Shiva. The latter system was preferred by the writer of the Mahabharata (Dronaparva 41-15, 74-62, Anushasanaparva 112-19). Shiva was worshipped along with his consort Parvati. It is worth noting here that at that time the Kapalika sect also existed. It is narrated that Jarasandha, king of Magadha, used to make a sacrifice of the captured warriors before the idol of Shiva and Ashvathama - son of Dronacharya, worshipped Shiva in the form of Kapalika.

"Now we shall pass to the Puranic period, the period of composition of the Myths. Some books of myths, according to some scholars were being composed from the time of Atharvaveda onwards, but here, we will consider the period from the 1st to the 6th centuries A.D. Manusmriti (1st or 2nd century A.D.), the plays of Kalidas (5th century A.D.), the play 'Mritcchakatika' of Shudraka (1st or 2nd century A.D.) and some Puranas.

"Manu-Smriti refers to the worship of different deities, but does not refer to the worship of Shiva. On the contrary, it says that the food (Neivedya) offered to Shiva should not be eaten, so it appears that even at that time in certain areas the concept that the deity Shiva was non-Aryan (Aveidic) held sway. In the plays of Kalidas (5th century A.D.) they start with prayers to Shiva, and one play is based on the myth of the marriage of Shiva with Parvati named "Shiva-Parvati Parinaya", and another one named 'Kumara Sambhav' is based on the myth of the birth of Kumara (the other name of Skanda). But it is noticeable that up to that time the reference to 'Ganapati', second son of Shiva-Parvati, does not appear. So it appears that the god 'Ganapati' (Siddhi-Vinayeka) entered into worship after the 5th century A. D.

"During the Gupta Age (300-600 A.D.) different sects like Shaivism, Shaktism, Vishnuism, Soura (refers to Sun worship) were prosperous. There is a rock-inscription in an artificially carved cave at the time of Chandragupta II (380 – 414 A. D.) From that inscription it is learnt that a worshipper of Shiva was caused to carve that cave which is situated at Udayagiri mountain and offered it to a Shaiv ascetic.

"In the Puranas like Vayu (25-21), Vishnu (8-21) and Varaha (25-4, 25-19) reference has been made to the worship of Shiva. In the Matsyapurana (260) the worship of Shiva with Parvati has been recognized as symbolizing the unity of Shiva with his Shakti, or in other words, the metaphysical concept of unity of Purusha (reason of being) and Prakriti (the manifestation of this reason). Kshhetradnya and Kshetra, corresponding to the ancient male and female elements respectively, also admit at the time of that Matysapurana the worship of Shiva-linga in the joint-form of phallus and vulva. The Matsya-Purana and Pashupata sect of Shaivism appears to be referred to in Maharashtra. But it is a moot point as to when the composition of the Mahabharata was concluded."

Panini, in his cited grammar, mentions Vasudeva, Arjuna and Yudhistira, and its age is defined between the 8th and 4th century B.C. So, we can surely conclude that the worship of Shiva with his consort Parvati in human figures, as well as in the form of Shiva-linga with pindika, which is our subject matter, existed at least before 4th century B. C. In the same way we can say about the existence of the Kapalika system as Jarasandha and Aswatthama are referred to in the Mahabharata as of that sect. This is the position of both the sects in Northern Indian. Now, we have to find out when the same sects passed on to Southern India. In this respect Prof. Gosavi further says:

"From the stone inscription of Vikram Savant 1928 (821 A. D.) existing in front of the temple of Ekalingaji, 14 miles away on the North of Udaipur of Rajputana it is seen that a person named Lakulisha instituted the Pashupata sect of Shaivism".

In this respect Dr. R. Bhandarkar says:

"From all this it appears that there lived a certain person of the name of Lukulin (the holder of Lakuta or Laguda or Lakula i.e. a club) who founded the Pashupat system. Four schools sprung out of it and their reputed founders, whether historical or legendary, were considered his pupils. Lakulin is the same as Nakulin, and the fact that his rise has been represented by the Puranas to be contemporaneous with Vasudeva-Krishna points to the inference that traditionally the system was intended to take the same place in the Rudra-Shiva cult. We may, therefore, place the rise of the Pashupata school mentioned in the Narayaniya about a century after that of the Pancharatra system, that is, about the second century B. C. (Vaishnavism and Shaivism)".

The four schools of Shaivism

The four schools of Shaivism are: (1) Shaiva proper (known also as Kashmiri Shaiva), Pashupata, Karuka or Karunika and Kapalika.

The Kashmiri Shaiva school performed the worship of Shiva as well as of Shiva with his consort Uma in all the rites and rituals like Astopachara puja, japa etc., which are generally in common use by the Hindus. The Pashupatas also used to worship like the Kashmiri Shaiva; however, they did not accept Varnashrama-Dharma recognized in Hinduism. The Karanikas were probably those who worshipped Shiva in the form of Dhyana and Yoga and popularly known as 'Siddhas'. And the Kapalikas were generally named as 'Vamacharis', meaning practitioners of bad customs, like eating flesh and fish, drinking liquor and having illicit conjugal relationships among the male and female members of the same school; moreover, they performed sacrifices not only of birds and animals but also of human beings.

The names of Kashmiri Shaivas used to terminate in the word 'Shiva' and 'Shambhu' while those of Pashupatas by 'Rari'. The Shilahars of the North as well as of South

Konkana adored Shiva and there are some inscriptions of them making grants even of the villages to those sages [105] p. 81.

The evidence of Shaivite schools in Goa

In Goa we find three places, namely Harvalem and Bicholim in Bicholim taluka and a place at Kurdi of Sanguem taluka–all the places are caves, but we cannot say whether the sages were of the Kashmiri Shaiva or Pashupati school due to lack of their names. At Aihole an idol of Umasahita Shiva was found. It was established at the time of the Chalukyas of Badami, so it is certain that similar idols found at Harvalem and Kurdi were established at the same time of Vantuvallabh Sendraka.

Now in respect of the Karnaika school. We found on a mountain named 'Siddha' at Bhati village, Astagrahara division, Sanguem taluka, a Samadhi (a small construction for self immolation) of a Siddha named Karana-Siddha. The construction is of laterite cut stone, without mortar, in rectangular block form (0.7 x 0.6), 0.6 m height, and with a small black-stone 'linga' of height about 0.1 m. It is protected by a small laterite temple covered with tiles. Siddha appears with the word Karana, obviously because there were also Siddhas of other schools who were Natha-Siddhas. On the top of the mountain there is a triangular station (topographical mark) at 452.96 altitude and the Samadhi lies about 30 m. below the station.

Another place of Siddha is Bakhal hamlet of Dongurli village, Sattari taluka and is named Askin-Siddha, 'Askin' being the ancient name of that area. The Samadhi of the Siddha is below the ground level, so its location is fixed by the linga erected on the place, and is protected by a construction of laterite columns covered by country tiles.

In Borim village, Ponda taluka, there is a mountain named Siddhanath, and near the top of that mountain lies a temple with a Shiva-linga. One can see no Samadhi, but according to some persons, the Samadhi is below the ground level of that linga, like the Askin-Siddha.

A few kilometers from the Samadhi of Karana-Siddha, there is one more Samadhi in Curpem village of a Siddha named Madhava-nath, and he is considered to be the disciple of Karana-Siddha. The annual festival named 'Kalo' cannot be started at the Samadhi of Madhav-nath unless the 'Trishula' (trident) of Karana-Siddha is brought by Gosaya (Gosavi), named also as 'Mathkar', who performs the worship of Karana-Siddha. The worship of Madhavanath is performed by another family of Mathkars established in that village. The Samadhi of Madhava-nath lies at a low-land area at a little distance from the residential area. So the daily worship of it is possible, but the Samadhi of Karana-Siddha is situated on the top of the mountain, so particularly in the rainy season, daily worship is impracticable. Hence in the hamlet named Bamanvadi of Bhati there is a small temple dedicated to that Siddha and a small copper-plate with water was installed as his symbol and near by there is a trident. Only on the day of Mahashivaratra, the worship is made of that Samadhi. Sometimes sacrifices of cocks are made in front of a planted black stone not far from the Samadhi by people in fulfillment of their vows. It is said that the sacrifices are not received by Siddha but by his servant, a spirit (devchar) named 'Fatarsarvo', symbolized by that black-stone, who protects the village. On other days the sacrifices are offered near that temple with the same interpretation. The Moraskar family of the Vani caste, who established themselves there having come from Morgi of Pednem taluka, offer annually a goat. Other people offer cocks, and the sacrifice is performed by a person of the Velip caste, but he as well as all the members of that family and Gaonkars do not eat the flesh of the sacrificed goat and fowl. The flesh after proper cooking is eaten by the members of the Moraskar family, by village-servants of the Naik caste, those of the Mathkar family and others of similar caste who were present at the sacrifice.

Shaivite rituals

One important ritual should be noted here. At the great annual festival of Chaitra-pournima, the Mathkar at Karana-Siddha brings the trident in the morning and keeps it in front and at the side of the temple of Bhuta-nath. After the festival is over the next day, he takes the trident back. It is curious that at the side of Bhuta-nath, there is an oblong flat stone erected on a plinth, and outside the temple there is a black stone planted erect and named with the epithet 'sorvo' which is considered to be a spirit (*devchar*, like at Bhati). The distance between these two places cannot be less than 35 kms. The environment are different—while Bhutnath lies atop the Chandranath mountain (generally named as 'Parvat') and is surrounded by a relatively dense population or say semi-urban area, Bhati village lies in a jungle area and up to the beginning of the era of mining exploration, that is upto 1950, it was sparsely populated.

In these rituals, one finds an almost homogenous mixture of rites and rituals of the Kashmiri Shaiva, Pashupata, Karnaik and Kapalika schools of the Shaiva system, and also the Nath system. When and in which form did the amalgamation of different sects take place is what we should try to answer at this stage.

Bhairava worship

In the Skandapurana there is a section called 'Sahyadrikand' in which contains a chapter titled 'Chandrachudamahatmyam' with eight subchapters. In one chapter there is a reference to a holy water pond (tirtha) named Kapilathirth and in this respect the history of a king named Kapila (who is surely Kapalivarman Bhoja of the 6th century A.D.) is narrated. In another chapter mention has been made of the Madhava Math—sect of Vaishnavism—which was introduced from Udipi in the beginning of the

13th century in Karnataka and later spread in Goa in the 15th century A.D. So, exclusing some chapters concerning the myths of Shri Parashurama and his mother Renuka, we may accept its historical ground from the 6th to the 13th century A.D. So, it must have been composed more or less in the middle of the 13th century A.D.

The place referred to "Chandrachuda" in the Sikandapurana is located at the mountain commonly known as 'Parvat' at Paroda village, Quepem taluka.

To climb the mountain there are steps made of black stone from the bottom up to about the middle of the slope where residential houses are situated and this place is named 'Shtala'. From this place to reach the plateau of the mountain where the temples of Shri Chandrachuda or Chandreshvar and Bhutnath are situated, the steps are of laterite stone, constructed in the 19th century A.D. The staircase of black stone at the bottom was probably constructed at the time of the kings of the Bhoja dynasty.

In the north-east direction from the main temple of Shree Chandreshvar, on a gentle slope and about 40 to 60 m. away, there is a natural cave approx. 2 m. wide at the mouth but narrowing further. Immediately beyond the entrance there appears a 'linga' and nearby are '*Padukas*' (slippers). These are considered as symbols of a Jain sage while others consider them to be of a Siddha. The Sahyadri khand mentions Siddhas but not Jains. So the 'linga' may be a symbol of a Siddha while the slippers may be of the Jain sage or of the Siddha, but evidently installed there in a recent period. Both are not worshipped. There are four 'Bhairavas' (in the form of simple black stones) on the mountain: one is named "Shanka-Bhairava" and is installed in a small temple at the base of the mountain where the steps begin and this place is named 'Mulsant', meaning 'at the base'. Near the residential houses there are two: one named 'Siddha-Bhairava' and the other 'Kala-Bhairava'. The fourth Bhairava is Bhutnath who is considered to be the head of all the Bhairavas.

According to the doctrine of the Shaiva sect the Bhairavas are 64 in number headed by eight Bhairavas namely, Astianga, San, Ruru, Kala, Krodha, Tamrachuda, Chandrachuda and Mahabhairava and all these Bhairavas are considered to be servants of Shiva (Bhutagana). In this list we find Chandrachuda as a Bhairava and not as Shiva. Kala-Bhairava also appears but we do not find the names Bhutanath, Siddha-Bhairava nor Shankha Bhairava, so we have to reason why these names exist. In Gujarat, from which side the sects entered Goa, there are Bhairavas in each village, but with the simple name of Bhairava. In Maharashtra we find a corrupted form, as Bahiroba for Bhairavas, and like in Gujarat they are represented by a stone in each village. This type of symbolic form of the male element represents nothing but a phallus installed for worship thousands of years ago like it was done in Goa by the pastoral tribes. However, here we will limit the subject to the adoption of names according to the doctrine of Shaivism. Incidentally, it is only in the Punjab that we find the worship of Bhutanath as the principal of the Bhairavism of Shiva.

The point is, how did this name come directly from the Punjab to Goa. Swami Dayananda Saraswati (1824-1883 A.D.) founder of Aryasamaj, published two books titled Vedabhaishya and Satyarth-Prakasha. In the second book, while criticising the rituals of different schools of Shaivism and Saktism, he mentions the existing worship of Bhutanath in Punjab involving sacrifices of animals. And this name must have been adopted by the people of the second wave of Aryans who migrated at the time of the invasion of Jarasandha and who after camping at some resting stations, settled finally in the area which they named Chandravadi. That part of history is familiar to readers by now. Shiva is symbolized as the Moon in the form of a quarter crescent on the head-dress, and the symbol of linga appears in bas-relief on the stone-slab which represents Chandreshvar. It is said that during some days before and after the full-moon the slab at night is covered with humidity on the surface and sometimes even water accumulates at the base of that slab. Credulous people believe that humidity flows from the Moon, existing on the top though invisible. Based on this concept, the compositor of the Chandrachud Mahatmya mentioned the name 'Chandrachud' instead of 'Chandreshvar' or 'Chandranath'. We find the names of Shiva for the icons and idols which existed in the temples of Salcete taluka, just as we find those names in the Portuguese records.

The Siddha Bhairavas

Siddha-Bhairavas is a very interesting name which throws light on the amalgamation of the two schools of Shaivism, namely the Kashmiri Shaiva and the Karanika. The name Shankha-Bhairava suggests the amalgamation of the Kashmiri Shaiva school with the Nath sect, since the shankha (conch) is the principal item always maintained by the Jogis. This name is given to a branch of the Nath sect, who blow the conch while asking for alms in front of residential houses, thus announcing their presence. The trident is another item which is kept by the Jogis, but there is no such item near the icons of all the four Bhairavas. As seen before, the trident is brought from the temple of Karan-Siddha at Bhati and kept near Bhutnath at the time of the great festival, which demonstrates that this symbol of Karana-Siddha was adopted when the Jogis or perhaps the successors of that system —Mathkar— took over from them the performance of the worship of the same Siddha. It is worth noting here that on the Samadhi of Madhavanath there is no 'linga' like that of on Karana-Siddha which clearly shows that Madhavanath was a Siddha of the Nath sect.

tained by the Jogis. This name is given to a branch of the Nath sect, who blow the conch while asking for alms in front of residential houses, thus announcing their presence. The trident is another item which is kept by the Jogis, but there is no such item near the icons of all the four Bhairavas. As seen before, the trident is brought from the temple of Karan-Siddha at Bhati and kept near Bhutnath at the time of the great festival, which demonstrates that this symbol of Karana-Siddha was adopted when the Jogis or perhaps the successors of that system —Mathkar— took over from them the performance of the worship of the same Siddha. It is worth noting here that on the Samadhi of Madhavanath there is no 'linga' like that of on Karana-Siddha which clearly shows that Madhavanath was a Siddha of the Nath sect.

The Nath sect in Goa

The Nath sect was founded by Gorakhnath (Cf. 1000-1050 A.D.) with their head-quarters at Shree Sheila mountain, to arrest the indecent practices of the Shakti sect who earlier had their headquarters on the same mountain which lies in Nandikotakur taluka of Karnool district, Andhra Pradesh. Gorakhnath spread his doctrine through-out India and he must have visited Goa, since we find a pond on the top of a hill at Ela village, Tiswadi taluka, named after him —'*Gorkhi-talem*' (tank of Gorakha). But this sect after centuries split into different branches, one of them named '*Kanfate*'. The Mathkar or *Gosay* (Gosawo) are of this branch.

The Kashmiri Shaiva and Karanika schools of the Shaiva sect and the Nath sect were against sacrifices of any kind. However, we notice even today sacrifices of a goat and fowl in the name of Bhutanath and Karana-Siddha, the reasons, however, being different.

As I mentioned before, the slabs representing Chandreshvar and Bhutanath were originally deities of Kol, Mundari and other non-Aryan tribes whose descendants un-der different names of castes survive even today in those areas. Inspite of what has been adopted and sublimated, the idea of a high spirit, in respect of Bhutanath as the master of (Bhutas) spirits cannot be wiped out of their minds. So, the institutions of those three systems had to tolerate the practice of sacrifice of those people. Moreover, these kinds of offerings were being made by the people routinely. The practice had originated from the system of offerings which mankind throughout the world contin-ued to do—of what he ate with utmost relish. Whenever this was not acceptable, as in respect of worship of Karana-Siddha, they engendered the form whereby offerings was made to 'Fatarsarvo', his spirit-servant! So, in this procedure there is no interference in the practice of the Kapalika school which did not exist in Goa. But in the same period, that means before the existence of the Natha sect, a similar type of Shakti sect existed in Goa. Shaktism like Shaivism had three schools, excluding the Pashupata established at Savoi-Verem, Ponda taluka, in the 7th century A.D. However, the idol of Devaki-Krishna originally of Choraon (*Chodan*) island, Tiswadi taluka, transferred at the time of persecution by the Christian missionaries, to *Mashel* (Marcela in Portuguese) hamlet of Orgaon village, Ponda taluka is interesting. The idol is Devaki in a standing posture holding on her left arm the image of child Krishna. History says that Vasco da Gama was appointed Viceroy of all the colonies of the Far East as a gesture of honour. One day he visited Chodan island, and when he saw the idol through the main doorway, he immediately went on his knees, believing the image to be of Mother Mary with baby Jesus, but his companions brought to his notice the illusion and Vasco da Gama was mortified by his mistake.

Who might have first installed this type of idol with its prototype not to be found elsewhere in India? Surely they were Vrishnis, the people from Mathura, who migrated first due to the invasions of Jarasandha and came to Goa acccompnied by the Bhojas and Chedyas. Some families of that clan occupied Chodan village. Shree Krishna was the hero of the Vrishni clan to which he belonged. He was born at Mathura. The childhood of Shree Krishna was spent in Gokul on the other bank of the river Yamuna. He was brought up by Yashoda, wife of Nanda, though his real mother was Devaki, wife of Vasudeva. So, in the mind of the Vrishnis, the period of Shree Krishna was etched indelibly. Hence they installed an idol of Devki-Krishna in a mud-house and later on in a temple of laterite stone. The waters of the river were also sacred to them because the river Yamuna had allowed Vassudeva to pass across to the other bank. Hence, on the day of the birth of Shree Krishna—Gokulastmi— devotees have a bath at the banks of Marcela river, a tributary of river Mandovi, as a part of the festival. Moreover, the water of the river Mandovi at that time had less salinity due to the rains.

Later on, during the time of Kadamba Jayakeshi I (1050/52-1080 A.D.) a temple dedicated to Saptakoteshwar was constructed in Narvem of Divar island (*Divadi*), (Tiswadi taluka) and the king venerated Him as his family-god. This was a Shiva-linga; hence, according to Hindu rituals, bathing in the holy waters of rivers on each Monday during the month of Shravana near the place of a Shiva-linga showers merits on the devotee. The same is true also for Gokulastami which also falls in the month of Sravana. The waters of the river on the banks of Narvem were sweeter than *Chodan* island. So, bathing at Gokulastami was moved to the banks of Narvem, and the images of gods from different villages were transported in *palankins*, obviously as a token of homage to the god of the king. In the Portuguese time, the temple of Saptakotesvar was destroyed and holy bathing was prohibited. The Shiva-linga of Saptakoteshvar was transferred to Naroa village (Bicholim taluka) which was situated then in Sawantwadkar Bhonsle's kingdom. At the time of the fervour of Christianity, the idol of Devki-Krishna was transferred from *Chodan* to Maem village of Bicholim taluka and later to *Mashel* where it is currently situated.

Vaishnava Math at Partagal

Worship of Devki-Krishna does not mean that Vaishnavaism existed in Goa from that time. Upto 1476 A.D. there was no proper Vaishnavaism in Goa. There were many deities of different designations and forms of Shiva, Shiva-Shakti, Vishnu, Ganesh as well as of the original settlers under worship, but around that year Vaishnavism entered Goa. The reason is as follows: Madhvacharya at Udupi in South India established the centre of the Vaishnava sect by constructing a Math. The tenth Acharya of his order started his pilgrimage to Kashi. Half-way, he suffered from dysentery and fearing that death was imminent, he prepared the proper records and nominated his successor in the order—a Gaud-Saraswat Brahmin, his disciple, who was accompanying him. However, the Acharya recovered from the disease and after completing his pilgrimage returned to Udupi. The Vaishnavas of that area did not accept the disciple as their future Acharya because he was not a Dravida Brahmin. The Acharya then, to placate his followers, instituted a Dravida Brahmin to continue the order there, and ordered the Gaud-Saraswat to preach the dogmas of his sect in his native country [114] p. 9. It is said that according to the order of his teacher (*guru*), the disciple established his permanent residence in Benaulim (*Banavali*) village, Salcete taluka, and later on at the time of the propagation of Christianity, the 'Math' was shifted to Partagal in Canacona taluka, where it lies presently.

The Smartha Math at Kavle and its traditions

But before the establishment of this Vaishnava Math, a Smartha Math existed in Goa at *Kutthal* (Cortalim in Portuguese) village in the same Salcete taluka, established in about the 8th century A.D. in the time of the Sendraka dynasty. This was destroyed by the Christian Missionaries and after the lapse of a century it was established at *Kavle* (Ponda taluka) where it exists today. The reason for establishing this Math in Goa was the same which induced the Shankaracharya (ending of the 7th or beginning of the 8th century A.D.) to establish four main Maths in the four corners of India. Vidyaranacharya and Shankaracharya were both disciples of Govinda-Yati who, according to some writers, was a disciple of Shree Gaudapadacharya, while according to others, he was fifth in order from this Acharya. Shankaracharya was a Nambutiri Brahmin from Kerala and was born about 788 A.D. and at his time the Vedic religion in Southern India had deteriorated through the appearance of different sects like the Shaiva, Shaktas Vaishnava, and Kapalika. This was harmful to Hindu society. Besides, there was inertia created by practices introduced by Buddhist and Jainist monks involving wrong interpretations of the fundamental principles of their religion. Shankaracharya defeated the Jain monks in public debate and tried to put an end to the aberations of the Hindu sects. Besides this, Shankaracharya amalgamated all the

Hindu sects, preaching the system of worship called 'Panchayatana-puja'. This system was practical and followed from the basic principles of the Vedas and Upanishads and which the Bhagavd-Gita has thus summarized:[115] p. 34

> *Whatever may be the form in which each devotees seeks worship faith - in that form alone do I make his faith steadfast.* ॥
>
> *Possessed of faith, he worships that form, and his desires fulfilled, granted, in fact, by me alone* ॥
>
> *But infinite is the result gained by these men of small minds. Those who sacrifice to the gods go to the gods, those who worship me come to me* ॥
>
> *Not knowing my supreme nature immutable and transcendent, ignorant men think that I, the unmanifest, am endowed with a manifest form* ॥
>
> *Veiled by my divine power I am not revealed to all. This deluded world knows me not as the unborn and the eternal.* ॥ (116) p. 34.

The name of the Saraswat Brahmin disciple is unknown, since the records maintained in the Math at *Kutthal* were set on fire by Christian missionaries. According to tradition, the names of 53 swamis (high-priests) of this order who had settled in that Math should have been preserved but we do not find them. These swamis who had their names suffixed with 'Ananda' and used the epithet Gaudapadacharya to denote their order had originated from Shree Gaudapadacharya, and this continues even today.

The form of 'Panchayatan-puja' introduced by Shankaracharya, and 'Vidyaranacharya, induced a three-fold Bhakti (deep devotion) system consisting of Bhajana (singing in praise of God), Pujana (proper worship) and Namasankirtana (celebrating the name). Shankaracharya did not camp at one place teaching his doctrine. He went on excursions through the whole of India trying through his preachings to bring about unity in diversity. And for this purpose, he installed four Maths at the four corners of India.. These places are: *Shringeri* in South India, *Dwarka* in Kutch, *Jaganathapuri* in Orissa and *Badrikedara* in the Himalayas. He tried also to amalgamate the subcastes, and out of ten of them he maintained only two castes of Brahmins named Pancha-Gauda and Pancha-Dravida. He took samadhi (self -immolation) at 33 years of age [116] p. 87.

Muslim settlements in Goa

It is generally considered, though incorrectly, that Muslim families settled here from the time of Kadamba Jayakeshi I (1050/52-1080 A.D.). In order to help them to maintain a Masjid, he gifted them the custom sur-tax (toll) on vessels coming to Sindapur post, issuing an order to this effect (copper-plate dated 1053 A.D.) at the request of his

Muslim Arab minister. But the real fact is that from the time of Vantudeva or from the beginning of the 7th century A.D., Muslim colonies were being established in Goa. The horses were brought by Muslim Arab merchants and sold to Vantudeva and to his successors. The mediators were agents of those Arabs who were staying temporarily at Sindapur to sell horses and to buy local goods. They ran their commence sitting at the port-side. Though the general procedure of care of those horses might have posed no problem, their peculiar diseases and its treatment was unknown to the local people, and the merchants as well as their agents never gave information about it nor did they bring mares to sell to prevent breeding. The agents and merchants wanted the horses to perish quickly, so that the kings would be forced to buy more horses. Vantudeva and his successors saw through this trick. To take care of horses in the ships there were some slaves. The kings or their agents secretly might have contacted these slaves and taken them away from Sindapur to Sattari. The Arab merchants could not find their new habitat. Moreover, they could never capture them against the wish of the kings. For the slave, the position was better because they received good treatment. They were married to the local girls of lower caste and lived happily and their descendants continued there. They settled in Thanem hamlet of Dongurli village since it was the centre of seven villages. About four centuries ago many families of that community migrated to Valpoi, some embracing agriculture and others transporting goods, timber and firewood on bullock-carts. At the time of Babu Bivam Rau Desai, grandfather of Shree Baburau Desai of Thane, a Muslim family was residing in Desai's house to look after a horse that Baburau Desai had. That family continued to live there till his death, and later migrated to Valpoi.

Muslim families of Valpoi

The Muslim families of Valpoi consider by tradition that their forefathers were servants of the Desai family, and that they have their Pir in that area. In fact, on the boundary between Thanem hamlet (Dongurli village) and Chóraunem village, there is a black stone erected and named '*Lafadarcho-gundo*'—'Lafadar' in Marathi means a scarf with a golden border and the villagers believe that a spirit watches the boundaries of the village and protects the families. On the day of Ashadha shuddha dvadashi, at sunset, a goat is sacrificed every year. On that day the Mhar of Thanem village, early in the morning, announces the sacrifice by beating his drums. In the evening the procession begins from the main Santeri temple of Thanem hamlet. The Mhar heads the procession, beating a small drum. Behind him runs the sacrificial goat. The villagers follow. After taking a round of the temple, the procession moves to the black stone, where the goat is sacrificed, its meat dish is prepared and distributed among the villagers present who are supposed to eat there. There is a ban on taking the meat out of the place. There is also a ban disallowing children less than seven or eight years old as well as pregnant women from watching the procession. It is remarkable that the Muslims do not participate in the procession, perhaps because the sacrifice is performed by a Hindu Gaonkar. Besides, according to the Muslim canon, a Muslim should not eat the meat of an animal which is slayed without the performance of certain rituals named 'Halal', and once he takes part in the procession he should not leave the place without eating the meat of the sacrificed animal.

Horse trade in Goa

Mares were not brought by the Arab merchants, but to resolve the problem of breeding, the Sendrakas of both branches might have brought mares from Kathiyawar by the sea-route and bought about cross-breeding. So, besides the Muslim colonies existing in Valpoi and Bicholim we find some Muslim families sporadically in Pednem taluka. We know from history that from about the 6th century, Arab and Irani merchants began their settlement on the Malabar coast and married native girls and their offspring were named Nayates. The main profession was as agents or mediators for Arab and Irani merchants. They were centralized more on the Kerala coast and even though they were in a foreign country, they sold horses to the enemies of the kings because they were getting a high price. So the kings naturally harassed them, driving them away to migration to another country. Hence some families established themselves on the shores of the Mandovi river in Tiswadi taluka at Ela village. This is the Muslim community which is referred to by Ibn Batuta in his cited book. Besides these, in the first period of Bahamani rule in Goa (1352-1377 A.D.), the second king of this dynasty had converted some Hindu families to Islam. Some Muslim families of his servants and troops had also settled in Tiswadi taluka. At the time of the conquest of this island by the Portuguese, in 1510 A.D., Afonso the Albuquerque killed male members of the Muslim colony as well as old women. The young ones were married to the Portuguese soldiers. At this time some Muslim families fled and settled in Marcel (*Mashel*) and in Bhoma village, both in Ponda taluka. During the time of the Moghul kingdom, some Muslim families settled in Ponda town, and some from this town migrated to Sanguem, town performing the duties of messengers of the Nadkarnis of that area. Thus the Muslim colonies found in Goa have different origins.

The Muslim settlement in Pednem taluka

In Pednem taluka also we find signs of Muslim settlements in the villages of Morji, Mandrem, Chandel, Varkhand, Harmal, Palyem as well as the tombs of 'Pirs' (Muslim saints). At Morji Muslims from different parts assemble and celebrate the festival of 'Urus'. In Mandrem village also they have such a festival in commemoration of the local 'Pirs'. There are some villages named Ibrampur, Hasanpur (Hansapur), Nanus (we find also Nanuz hamlet near Valpoi in Sattari, and a Nanuz in Usgaon in Ponda taluka) etc. There are properties also with Muslim names like Eklaskhan, Pashkhan, Hassan, Inasbag, Madhla-maj, Udik, Ramjan, Allikhan (Alkand), Bindurbag, Dandos and Pineachi-Bhati in Mandrem village. In the Udik property, there is a well named '*Ghodebain*' (waterpond serving horses). Nearby there are two places, one named '*Khajina*' (treasury) and adjacent to it, '*Mahal*' (Palace). On the route from the property named Allikhan (Alikant) to Pednem town, there is a water-tank named '*Hussein-tali*' made by carving a rock.

Based on these signs, some persons consider Pednem taluka to have been under Muslim dominion in ancient times. In fact, the origin of the Muslims of Pednem taluka is the same as those of Valpoi, which I have mentioned earlier. The Junior branch of the Sendraka dynasty brought some Muslim Arab slaves engaged in the maintenance of horses at the end of the 6th and at the beginning of 7th century A.D. They were married to the native girls, and their offspring are the present Muslims of that area. When the kingdom of the Sendrakas and their successors declined, the maintenance of horses suffered and the Muslims had to take to agriculture. So, they started culti-vating forest land. This is why some villages bear Muslim names like Ibrampur, Hasanpur, etc. Many families migrated elsewhere.

FROM SHILAHARAS TO THE GOLDEN AGE OF THE KADAMBAS

Shilahara dynasty—evidence of partial rule in Goa

The Shilahars politically had very little influence in the territory of Goa, as I have explained earlier. The South Konkan Shilahars ruled from Chandrapur through their Governor from c. 945 to 980 A.D. only, while the North Konkan Shilahars held sway in Gopakpura or Govapuri in Tiswadi island where that town was situated from c. 983 A.D. to c. 1020/25 A.D. Here I must add a note: The Janjira inscription of Aparajit, on the North Konkan Shilahar says that his kingdom extended to the South up to Chandrapuravam—'puram', which means that the Southern boundary of his kingdom did not include Chandrapura. This inscription is dated 993 A.D. [106] p. 21, while the inscription of a grant issued by Gandaraditya and Jatiga I, rulers of the Kolhapur Shilahars, in the middle of the 10th century A.D., refers to a place named Gomanta-durga or say fort of Gomanta, which surely refers to the Gopakapattan area [18] p. 33.

Thus, here there is a conflict between two inscriptions— whether Aparajit, ruler of the North Konkan Shilahar, conquered Gopakapattan or Gandaraditya of the Kolhapur branch of Shilahar did. I presume that this problem may be resolved as follows: Aparajit conquered Gopakapattan and the ruler of the Junior branch of Sendrakas had to leave the town as well as Tiswadi island wherein that town was situated. He went to Bardez taluka. Meanwhile Gandaraditya, being a close relative of the defeated ruler, might have come to help him but noting that he was incapable of accompanying him with the troops, Gandaraditya might have taken revenge for his relative's defeat by capturing the town with his own troops. However, due to constant attacks from Aparajit, maintenance of his sway on the town might have been difficult because he had to be present there personally while his own domain in Maharashtra was open to the threat of invasion by his enemies at any time. So, after the last attack of Aparajit he might have left the town and returned to his own dominion, and Aparajit thus regained powers on Tiswadi island. But in about 1020/25 A.D. Shashthadeva I, ruler of the Kadamba dynasty, conquered it forever, so the dominion of both the houses of the Konkan Shilahars ended in Goa very soon. That brings us to another point. Dr. Gune has identified 'Gomantadurga', mentioned in the inscription of Gandaraditya, with Tiswadi taluka, but the inscription does not make any reference to his having conquered it—a reference which was absolutely necessary. It is probable that 'Gomantadurga' existed in the area of Kolhapur. Had it been discovered there, it would have resolved a great question mark in respect of the mountain 'Gomanta', referred to in 'Harivamsha' as the place of the battle between Jarasandha and Shree Krishna.

From the above account, it is clear that the Southern Konkan Shilahars ruled for about 35 years and those of the North Konkan 42 years or less, in different parts of Goa with Chandrapura and Gopakapattan as capitals respectively. No influence of their dominion is noticed as compared to the preceding period. Dr. Gune in the Goa Gazetteer says that the temple of Curdi is of Shilahar style and that the Mahalaximi temple had been constructed in the Shilahar period, with an incorrect conception in respect of the dominant ruling dynasty of that period, as no shadow of the Shilahars appeared in that area during those periods.

Influence of short-lived Shilahara rule

However, from the inscriptions of the Konkan Shilahars we find indirect information of some importance connected to the people from Goa. Even though politically Goa was separated from the rest of the Konkan, it is obvious that some commercial transactions as well as change of settlement from Goa to the Konkan and vice-versa existed during the period. In one of the three Balipattan copper-plates of Rattaraja, the Southern Konkan Shilahar, dated 24th December, 1010 A.D., it is recorded that the grant of a plot named Kalvala from the village of Bhaktagrana and a grove of betelnut near the agrahara of village Palaure was made to Sankamaiya, son of the Brahmin Senavai Nagamaiya. This is probably the earliest reference to the Shenavi Brahmins of Goa. The composition of the inscription was made by a Kayastha and he does not carry the epithet Shenavai. So this proves that at the time of this inscription the epithet Shenavai used was of a later period and so the 'Senavai' mentioned in the inscription is surely a Saraswat Brahmin from Goa, originally from *Kelshi* and *Kutthal* villages. In ancient times they were merchants involved in commerce by the sea-route, being members of the group, 'Shreni', and so the members were considered as Shrenipatis. The Sanskrit word 'Shrenipatis' deteriorated in Prakrit form to Senavai, through this form of mutation: Shrenipati- Senivai-Senavai-Shenavi (Shenoy in Konkani and Sinai in Portuguese). As merchants by profession through generations, the male generation obviously had to be proficient in writing and counting. So that word came to be employed after that date of the inscription by the Kayasthas and, rarely, by Vaishas also.

However, Saraswat Brahmins were considered to be exceptionally versatile in the art of writing. Hemadpanta, chief minister of Ramachandra Yadava of Devgiri prepared drafts of letters addressed according to social or official categories and those forms were named as "Shenavai Mestikem". He probably adopted those which were in use among Saraswat Brahmins. It is also said that Hemadapanta introduced the 'Modi' script in official records and this script was brought by him from Lanka. In fact, the 'Modi' script might have been employed by the Shenavi Saraswat Brahmins, originally of Salcete taluka, and later the spread also to Tiswadi taluka, where some Gujarati type of alphabets were introduced in the Marathi script to facilitate the entry of running alphabets in the writing. Tiswadi, being an island, was named in figurative language as Lanka; otherwise there is no documentary evidence in history naming Tiswadi as Lanka.

It appears that the ministers of the Southern Konkan Shilahars were mostly Saraswat Brahmins originally from Goa. Hence they always tried to maintain good relations between this house and the Sendraka rulers of Goa. If Bhima, Southern Shilahar annexed Chandrapura to his dominion, the reason may be that the Senior branch of the Sendrakas who ruled in the area with their capital at Chandrapura were incapable of stopping the expansion of Kadamba power up to the doorstep of their own kingdom. However, these efforts were in vain as we have seen from history.

KADAMBAS

The Goa Kadambas

From Shashthadeva I to Kamadeva (?)

The Kadamba dynasty ruled in Goa from c. 980 to c. 1352 A.D., sometimes independently and at other times as feudatories of the Chalukyas of Kalyani and Yadavas of Deugiri. Meanwhile, Jaykeshi II (1125-1148 A.D.) tried to be independent and adopted for himself the title 'Konkan Chakravarti', as a mark of merit. But Vikramaditya VI, Chalukya of Kalyani, then the overlord, sent his feudatory Achhugi, a king of the Sind family to invade and burn Govapuri. He forced Jaykeshi II to accept the supremacy and re-establishment of the overlordship of Virkamaditya IV. However, noting his qualities, Vikramaditya offered him his daughter Maylayadevi in marriage. After the death of Vikramaditya, Jayakeshi revived his ambition for independence but his brother-in-law, Someshwar, son of Vikramaditya, sent Permadi I, son of Achhugi, who subdued Jaykesi II. The latter, thus, was obliged to accept the overlordship of the Chalukyas for the second time. After Jaykeshi III (1185-1225 A.D.), his second son Soyedeva or Tribhuvanamalla (1216-1238 A.D.) appeared as his successor as his elder brother, Shivachitta Vajredeva had died when his father was alive. At the time the Yadavas of Deugiri had subdued the Chalukyas of Kalyani. Vichanna, commander of the troops of the Yadavas, had defeated Soyedeva, who must have been slain in the battle, and the Kadamba kingdom thus came under the sway of the Yadavas. During those ten years, Shashthadeva III, son of Soyedeva lived in exile. At the time of Soyedeva Kadamba, a Saraswat Brahmin named Mayimdeva held the highest post among the Singhana Yadavas. His ancestor Devasharma had established himself in Hindule village of Sawantwadi in the time of Shivachita and the Vishnuchitta Kadambas (c. 1146 A.D.) and was honoured by them by offering him a high posts. His successors continued to have such high posts. Mayimdeva, impressed by the favours of the Kadambas intended to re-establish Shashthandeva III on the throne, releasing for that purpose from direct domination the area under the Kadambas since ancient times. At that time, Singhana Yadava was deceased, and many feudatories wanted to re-establish their own sway. Under these circumstances, obviously the successor accepted the proposal of Mayimdeva. Moreover, this person who had been faithful to the Yadavas, being chief-minister of the Kadamba, faced no obstacles from this side of the Kadamba kingdom. The copper-plate known as Nagadeva (successor of Mayindeva [117]) refers to it.In the reinstallation to the throne in 1246 A.D., Kamadeva, a Konkan Chalukya, brother-in-law (husband of sister) of Shasthadeva III also helped him [117]. After re-establishing the sway of the Kadamba king on Goa, Kamadeva turned his eye to the area of the previous dominion in North Kanara, where there was anarchy. He established his sway in that area too. After the death of Shashthadeva III, Kamadeva succeeded as Shashthadeva had no progeny.

The dating of the rule of Kamadeva is uncertain. Different historian provide varying dates and without evidence. Moreover, recent historians, like Dr. Gune and B. D. Satoskar despite the availability of new evidence through the Corgaon coper-plate of Bhima Bhupala, have taken no notice of it while studying the history of that period.

Malik Kafur's invasion

About the year 1310 A.D., Malik Kafur, envoy of Alla-ud-din Khelji of the Delhi Sultanate, invaded Gopakapattan and destroyed it. Mahamud-Bin-Tughluk, of the Sultanate of Delhi in about 1327 A.D. had come to South India with the intention of establishing his capital at Devgiri (named later as Daulatabad) but he had to change his plans and return to Delhi. But during this period he looted Gopakapattan and perhaps Chandrapura. Fr. Heras has found a copper coin of Mohamud-Bin-Tughluk in the debris of the temple of Basaveshwar destroyed by his soldiers. During both times the ruling dynasty surely was of the ancestors of the Bhima Bhupala, and a 'Viragal' found and kept in Old Goa Museum commemorates the death of Viravarma's feudatory chief (Samanta) who died in a sea-battle. Fr. Heras has dated it as 1294 or 1354 A.D. But the fact is that the 'Viragal' refers to the sea-battle which took place in 1342 A.D. when the nabab of Honawar assaulted Sindapura. I have referred to this before. So, Viravarma should be an ancestor of the Bhima Bhupal. But we do not know who was ruling Chandrapura at that time. The same problem arises in respect of the time of invasion of the Nabab of Honawar in 1342. What was the name of the king who had been killed, and what were the names of his descendants? We do not have any idea so far of the rulers in Chandrapur at that time. We may assume that about 1352 A.D., the Kadamba dynasty ended and Bahamani Muslim rule began in Goa territory.

The history of King Vira Kavana

When we say that the Kadamba dominated Goa territory it does not mean that the whole territory of Goa was under their sway. It has been observed that a king named Vira Kavana with a mark of merit, 'Vallabharaja Maharaja', ruled in the year 1380 A.D. He was surely a descendant of the Senior branch of the Sendraka family, continuously ruling over a part of Goa territory. So, that dynasty was ruled for eight centuries. On the other hand, we find that in the year 1391 A.D. a feudatory of Harihara II of Vijayanagar had gifted land in the name of his overlord in Pednem area [118] p. 31. From an inscription of the Yadavas it is seen that Bahanna was nominated as governor of Sashti (Salcete taluka), and not of entire Goa. This means that the Kadambas at that time ruled only over Salcete taluka, and the other talukas of Goa were under other feudatories or independent kings. The Yadavas had recognized their rights, as practically there was no material advantage in subduing them as the area ruled by them was jungle terrain.

I have referred to some inscriptions of the Kadamba kings wherever this was necessary to depict an overall picture of the rule of the Sendraka family and the history of this dynasty which was divided into two branches.

Jainism prospers during Kadamba period

We find some idols of Jain Thirtakaras in some villages in Goa. There is a life-size idol in *Cothambi* village (Bicholim taluka), and another in a property named *Konar* in Bandodem village (Ponda taluka) named Neminath (?). In Chandor village (Salcete taluka), adjacent to *Kawadi* (Cavorim in Portuguese) village at a place named Jainacho-Math, an idol has been discovered about 30 cms in height, in a standing posture, with the left hand bent at the elbow and the forearm entwined by a serpent. This idol at present is in the possession of a Christian person living in the area. The name of the idol is surely Naganath and in the Portuguese records of the destruction of temples, this name is assigned to Cavorim village. In a stone-inscription dated 1103 A.D. it is found that a person named Bomisetti constructed a '*Basati*' (residence for Jainist monks) in a place named Malakarnakona. This place is surely the village named Melcapona of Quepem taluka, but at present there are no remnants of such a '*Basati*' [119] p. 240. However, on top of a hill near that village there is an idol of a person in standing posture in a jungle and he is named "*Ranantlo-Dev*" (the god of the jungle). The said Setti must be a person of the Vaishya caste and his profession probably that of a merchant. In fact we note that families of the Vaishya caste had embraced Jainism, perhaps because despite their riches they, on the social ladder, could not scale high positions. But these families abandoned Jainism and embraced Hinduism and the priests came to be named Gurav.

In the temple of Shree Devaki-Krishna at *Mashel* (Marcela in Portuguese) in Ponda taluka, a wooden column is kept named '*Jainacho-Khamb*'; and at the time of the procession of Shree Devaki-Krishna, a Gurav adorns the column with clothes and flowers, like the tarangas of other minor deities like Ravalnath and takes part in the procession. The priest of Chandranath-Bhuthnath temple existing on the top of Chandranath-Parvat at Paroda village (Salcete taluka) was a Gurav. It is said that his family got reconverted to Hinduism. But the family was considered as a weaker Bhat, and so came to be treated as of the Vaishya caste. About sixty years ago, a person of that family claimed rights to lands in the Civil Court. So the Mahajanas released him from his duty, admitting a person of Bhat family as his substitute. In Ramnath temple of Bandodem village the priest was also a Gurav. The Guravs of Goa make all the rituals just like genuine Brahmins, however they are considered as of the Vani caste (Vaishas considered to be superior to the Vanis). In a temple of Pednem taluka, there are two idols installed—one named '*Gurav Purusha*' and the other '*Jaina Gurav-Purusha*'. This shows that the Gurav was a caste of priests of the deities of non-Aryan tribes, like Bhagats. In Maharashtra and Karnataka also Guravas are found. They are of a separate caste, with their own subcastes. Some are Hindus whose rituals are like the Brahmins, some are Lingayat, some wear the holy thread (Yadnopavita) as well as the linga on the chest, and others are Jains. Originally they were all Shaivaites.

Some historians postulate that Jainism appeared in Goa before the Ashoka period, while others believe that it was introduced by the Rattas who came from the South, at the time of Kamadeva, brother-in-law of Shashthadeva III. Later writers consider that some Brahmin families due to persecution migrated to Ratnagiri side (South Konkana). But both parties are mistaken because history shows that the Kadambas introduced Jainism in Goa at the beginning of their rise. The copper-plate inscription dated 1094

A.D. issued by Anantadeva or Anantapala, nephew of Mammuni, North Konkan Shilahar, says that he expels those who practised sin and inflicted persecution on the gods (Hindu deities) and Brahmins. His fame spread up to 'Chandra-bimba' (Chandramandala meaning Chandravadi) that is up to to Chandrapura [60] p. 44. In this year, Guhaladeva III or Tribhuvanamalla (1080-1125 A.D.), elder son of Jayskeshi I, was on the Kadamba throne. From the beginning, the Kadambas were Jains. Sashthadeva I, founder of the Kadamba dynasty was obviously a zealous Jain and his other name was Kantakacharya—a name with the epithet 'Acharya'. A Jain Acharya named Hemachandra in his book titled 'Dwadhashrayakavya' composed in the second half of the 12th century, glorifies Shasthadeva; and this is the same Acharya who induced a king of Anhilwad in Gujarat, Kumarapala of the Solanki dynasty, a close relative of the Kadambas to accept Jainism. That king became such a Jain fanatic, that he removed the idols of Hindu deities in worship in his own palace and started persecuting Brahmins [61] p. 45. Due to the injuries inflicted by the Kadambas, the Brahmins migrated from Goa to the Konkan up to North Konkan. There, they obtained higher posts in administration like those of chief-minister, minister of defence, minister or vice-minister of the treasury, as well as King's priest, astrologer and palace poets. They had surnames like Pay, Pay Prabhu, Prabhu and Nayaka.

Goans rebel against the Kadambas

The dominion of Kadambas was not willingly accepted by the population under their sway in Goa due to their Jain religion. Guhaladeva I firmly established his sway on Chandrapura. He might have visited Someshwar (Somanath) at Dwarka but probably he continued as a Jain. His son Shashthadeva made a pilgrimage to Dwarka, Mahalaxmi of Kolhapur and Gokarn-Mahabaleshwar. And the second time he revisited Dwarka he was accompanied by the people from Goa to show that he was faithful to Hinduism. But it appears that the people always considered the Kadambas as strangers. It is seen that Jayakesi I, son of Shashthadeva appointed a Muslim Arab as his chief minister, only because he had no confidence in any Goan person. It is said that Jayakeshi I was a devotee of Saptakoteshwar, but I did not find any evidence to that effect. There was a coin of his time named 'Bairava' in which the name 'Math Bhairava' was carved, but at that time Jainism had already admitted Hindu deities like Bhairavas and Yoginis in their pantheon. So, there is no certainty about his devotion to Saptakotishwar. Only from the time of Jayakeshi III (1187/88-211/12 A.D.) we find engraved on a gold coin called 'Padmatanka' the words "Shree Saptakotishalabdhawara Virajayakeshideva". The name of the year 'Pramola Sanvatsara' corresponds to 1211 A.D. So we can surely admit that from that year the Kadambas were genuine Hindus. However, I do not know, the reason for the acrimony between them over the generations. It may be that Guhaladeva I Kadamba had taken Chandrapura by treachery without giving time to the king of the Sendraka dynasty who was lying peacefully in his palace, the king who was highly loved by his people. The tradition was so strong that after the death of Soyedeva, his son Shashthadeva III was in exile for ten or twelve years. His brother-in-law Kamadeva came and put him on the throne, but he could not keep him there, so he sought the help of a Saraswat Brahmin Mayindeva who came to be the chief minister. Thus peace and order was maintained. Kamadeva came to rule the portion of North Karnataka of the Kadamba kingdom. After the death of the issue-less Shashthadeva III Kamadeva occupied the throne, and because Mayindeva continued as chief minister the people remained calm, but after the death of Mayindeva they renewed their protests. However, Kamadeva continued, and after his death probably his son came to the throne but his name is not known.

Cansarpal copper-plates of Nagadeva

It is known from the copper-plates of Nagadeva that a rebellion was provoked by the Maratha people after the death of Soyedeva. The revolt lasted about twelve years and finally Mayindeva subdued that revolt and brought Sashthadeva III to the throne [60] p. 65. The phrase "devadashavarsha akrantavato maharashtran chhamulya" of that copper-plate is considered wrongly by the writer Valaulikar to refer to the Yadavas of Devgiri. This praise in reality refers to the revolt of the local people of the Chadde caste who are mentioned as Marathes by the compositor, because at the time of composition, they mixed with the Marathas who had settled around Cuncolim (*Kunkalli*). About ten years ago, a stone-carving in Marathi script was found during excavations for a road and Dr. Morais, the writer of 'Kadamba-Kula', then Professor of History in the Post-Graduate Centre, told me that up to that time he had considered himself to be of the Chaddo caste, but the inscription showed that he was of the Maratha caste, which was inferior to the Chaddo caste. Some of the people of that caste were converted to Christianity but some reverted to Hinduism and now families of both religions consider themselves as Gaonkars of Cuncolim (*Kunkalli*) village. The Shaka number carved on the copper-plate is confusing. Valaulikar considered it to be 1234; hence it corresponds to 1352 A.D. On the other hand, it is to be noticed that from that copper-plate, Nagadeya granted a village named '*Varande*' (present Kansarvarnem) of Pednem taluka to a copper-smith named Lashhumasethi from Kasarpal village of Bicholim taluka. We note from the Korgaon copper-plate of 1351 that Bhima Bhupala granted land situated in Pednem town of Pednem taluka. That means the year considered as Shaka 1234 (1352 AD) by V. V. Valaulikar was an error. Another expert reads that number as 1354 Shaka instead of 1234. This corresponds to 1452 A.D. and it appears to be more probable.

The copper-plate was issued from the temples of Shree Kalika of Kansarpale which probably was under the direct sway of the donor Nagadeva. Kansarvanem was practically in possession of the copper-smiths who had their temple and relatives in

Kansarpale. Nagadeva had good relations with the descendants of the Bhima Bhupal, ancestor of Parmekar and the Usapkar Desais, and thus the grant was made with their consent. Except for the dating, the other conclusion made by V. V. Valaulikar must have been correct. So the place name Indule must be that which is situated in Narvem village of Bicholim taluka. The Desais with the title of Jasvantrao, Viswasrao, Suryarao, and Amonkar and Nerurkar families are the descendants of Nagadeva. Nagadeva was the son of the grandson or the grandson of the grandson of Mayindeva, and so the lapse of time of about a hundred years is justifiable.

Shashthadeva I or Kantakacharya, founder of the Goa Kadamba dynasty was its patron. Otherwise the whole family of Kadambas, despite the grants made to the Brahmin priest (Bhats) from the time of Jaikeshi I onwards, was always hated by the Saraswat Brahmins and the Chaddes of high caste. These kings also never trusted the Saraswat Brahmins. It is correct that from Jayakeshi I onwards, the kings changed their minds as far as religion was concerned, but it was too late. From this fact it is evident that people may tolerate any kind of harassment except in the matter of religion.

The influence of Jainism on Nath-Sampradaya

Now we will turn to the other issue. I have already referred to the expansion of Nathasampradaya (Natha-wing) started by Gorakhnath (1000-1150 A.D.). The remnants of the existence of this wing in Goa is testified to the temples existing in Usgaon village of Ponda taluka and its surroundings. In Usgaon the main village temple is considered to be of Shree Adinatha. At Tisk in Usgaon there is a temple of Gananath belonging to by the Parkar family vani caste. There are also two small temples of the Nath epithet in the same village and the idols installed are worshipped. The epithet Nath is found also in Jainist idols, an the name Adinath is also given to Rhishabhanath, the founder of Jainism. We find at *Mashel* (Marcela in Portuguese) in Orgaon village of Ponda taluka a temple of Mallinath which was transferred from Chodan (Chorão) island of Tiswadi taluka, which has been mentioned before. In Ela village of Old Goa, atop a hill, we find a lake named '*Gorkhitalem*' (tank of Gorakha).

The difference between the idols of the two religions is clear. The idols of Jainist thirthkaras when it appears in a standing position is in nude form (Rhishabhanath) or with a serpent (Naganath) or connected to a 'Basati' (*Ranantlodev*, at Malkapon), or in a seated posture with legs crossed in Padmasana (Neminath at *Kothambi* of Bicholim taluka). Adinath and Gananath are both dressed and in the standing position, but without the bull (Nandi-vehicle of Shiva). Mallinath is in fact a woman but her idol is styled like a man. The Natha-Sampradaya spread out of Goa to the vicinity of Savantwadi, and Kamadeva, the Konkana Chalukya, brother-in-law of Shahthadeva III Kadamba was a devotee of Mallinath. In Parulem village in the vicinity of Sawantwadi we find a temple of Adinath, who is also named as "Kanakalya", the later name probably being of the Chalukya king who might have established himself there. In South Konkan and in Pednem we find even in recent periods adherents of Jainism, like Saint Sairoba Ambie of the time of Jiubadada Kerkar, commander of the troops of Mahadaji Shinde of Gwalior state, Goraksha Valaulikar, Portuguese envoy in the Peshwa period at Pune. But at present we rarely find anybody in Goa practising the rites of that wing.

Havig Brahmins in Goa

It is said that Mayurvarma, founder of the Kadamba-kula in Karnataka (345-360 A.D.) brought from Ahikshetra (from Gujarat) three hundred families to perform Yadnas at Gokarna.

Later they spread in the area named Gorastra which extended from Gokarna up to the river Sharavati which crosses Honawar district. They all desired to go back but Mauravarma prevented them and to distinguish them from other people he obliged them to maintain their hair with a frontal knot on top of the head. They are found in Shimoga district of Karnataka and are perhaps more concentrated in Shirshi taluka. Some are engaged in the priesthood and some work in their own areca-nut gardens. They belong to seven gotras with four subdivisions [120]. Earlier, while referring to the rule of the Senior branch of the Sendraka dyanasty, I had pointed out the grant of Colamba village of Astagrahar division of Sanguem taluka to eight Brahmins. Those Brahmins were surely invited by a king of the Senior branch of the Sendraka dynasty from North Karnataka. The invitation was made to them obviously because they were skillful agriculturists. The advent of Havig Brahmins from Shirshi is proved by the name of a variety of betel-plant named '*Shrishi-khauchipanam*'. It's juice has a soft taste while the local variety of betel-plant is named '*Kalim Khauchipanam*' and its juice is bitter. The colour of the leaves is also darker. In the Astagrahara area the families introduced areca-nut and coconut gardens. More important is the work of artificial channels, like that of '*Ramanathacho-pat*', mentioned before, that begins at Curpem village. These Brahmins were accompanied by families involved in cultivation named in that area as Velip. It is probable that more families of Havig Brahmins might have come from North Karnataka at the time of the Kadambas, especially at the time of Shivachitta Kadamba (1147/48-1176/77 A.D.) The poem 'Konkana-Akhyana' composed in Shaka 1589 (1667 A.D.) mentions in the second part, chapter V, stanza 124, the existence of a copper-plate referring to the villages Curpem and Vichundrem (of Astagrahar division in Sangem taluka), but we have not found that copper-plate which might surely have thrown light on the history of the development of that area.

At Shree Sheila Parvat, on top of the hill in South India, the Shakta-Sampradaya (Shakta-wing) had established a temple of Uma-Mahesha named Mallikarjuna. After the wing was suppressed by the Natha-Sampradaya (Natha-wing), the idol was worshipped by Hindus of the Shaivaite sect in the form of a shivalinga. So the Havigs who had adopted that name established the temples of Mallikarjuna in Canacona (*Kankon*) and in Astagrahar. Thus, we find shivalingas with the name Mallikarjuna in the following villages: at Shristhal of Kankon village, in Gaondongrem and Angodem villages of Canacona taluka, in Bhati and Kunbhari villages of Astagrahar of Sanguem talukas, in Molcornem (*Malkarnem*) village of Quepem taluka, in Cundaim (*Kundai*) and Marcaim (*Madkai*) village of Ponda taluka and in Pali village of Bicholim taluka. From Portuguese records it is noted that in Assagaon and Pomburpa, villages of Bardez taluka, temples of Shree Mallikarjuna existed which denotes their settlements in those villages.

It is remarkable that the Shivalinga established at Viliena village, adjacent to Kumbhari village is named Shiveswar, while Shiveshwar is also the ancient name of the area constituting Karwar and Kankon (*Advat*) together. The annual procession of the insignia (*tarangas*) of Mallikarjuna crosses the Kankon-Karwar boundary and goes up to the bank of Gangavali river. This is significant indicating the hegemony of the Havigs in an ancient period up to that boundary.

They also established Shivalingas with the name of Saptakoteshwara, this name meaning the creator of seven types of livestock classified through the mode of birth and named as Jaraja (from copulation), Andaja (from eggs), Swedaja (from perspiration like a louse), Udbhija (born without seed like a bamboo), etc. We find a temple of Saptakoteshwar installed at the top of Morpirla mountain at Bali in Quepem taluka, another with the same name at Old Narvem village of Divar (*Divadi*) island in Tiswadi taluka, shifted in Portuguese times to *Narvem* village of Bicholim taluka, and there is yet another under the name of Saptokotesha in a village in Pednem taluka.

Shiva-chitta Kadamba and his wife were both pious and this is proved by some grants (recorded on stone and copper-plate inscriptions) made to Brahmins (Agrahars). During the period of the reign of Shiva-chitta, a famine occurred in Karhad and many Brahmins from there came and settled in Goa. From that time there were marriage links, so some Paddye bhats migrated to Karhad after the famine. The Paddye community compared to that of the Karhads was small, so from that time the Paddye community came to be considered as a branch of the Karhade brahmins. On the other hand, the Karhade Brahmins who settled in Goa took up professions which were handed down through the generations. Accordingly, some are named *Kirwant* (those who perform the rituals of incineration), *Ghaisass* (who perform duties in temples), *Kramavant Joshi* (astrologers as well as performers of rituals of incineration) and *Joshis* (astrologers).

Due to the pious action of Shiva-chitta Kadamba whose original name was Permadi (Pronounced as Hemadi) Deva, his idol is installed in a temple at Uguem village of Sanguem taluka. This installed idol is named *Hemad-Deva*, and his festival (*Kalo*) is performed annually with great pomp. Uguem village was the capital of Sanguem taluka before the Portuguese regime.

In Bhati village there is a place named '*Kankona*', where a stone named '*Kanadi Purush*' was found. In the year 1971 during excavations a shivalinga was found there but its plinth was square while that of Mallikarjuna is circular. It appears that the Havig Brahmins, perhaps the second wave of the time of Shiva-Kadamba, who came from *Kankona* established themselves first in that area and named it so after their original settlement. In a hamlet named '*Bend*' in Sangem town we found a stone named as in a very small isolated temple (*devli*). In Bhati village in a place named '*Kota*' where we came across signs of a fortress formed of a mud wall with two tombs at one side, and a well in the middle. About twelve years ago, a man discovered some vessels in that well, but he never disclosed the type and nature of the metal. It is known that due to an epidemic all the people of Astagrahar division quickly dispersed elsewhere. The Havig Brahmin families of Neturli village went to Pali village of Bicholim taluka, and came back and reestablished themselves after at least one generation. These families adopted themselves as 'Desai', being of the said Astagrahar. Some families of Velips also returned like those Brahmins. I have already referred to the Velip gaonkars found in Astagrahar (part of Sanguem taluka), Canacona and Quepem talukas.

Even though we find only a copper-plate of a grant of Colamba village, it is certain that Shiva-Chitta Kadamba must have made a gift of this area to the Havig Brahmins. This area of Astagrahar is found mentioned in the Konkanakhyana, chapter V, stanza 51, as third in order of primary of talukas, probably marked in the Kadamba period, representing each tribe contributing to developing the village communes. The first was considered of the Saraswat Brahmin whose first settlement was established in Salcete taluka and this taluka was of the first order. The second order was Antruz represented by the Paddye Bhats, and the third was Astagrahar, represented by the Havig Brahmins.

The Astagrahar division was subdivided into eight gramas with each grama constituting several villages. These gramas in the time of Muslim dominion were called tarafa. So the eight tarafas are constituted in the following form: tarafa Rivona consists of Rivona and Zambaulim; tarafa Colamba consists of only one village, tarafa Curdi consists of Curd Curpem, Pottem, Zhamodem, Hatiyanem and Angad villages; tarafa Netravali or Neturli consists of only one village, so also tarafa Vichindrem, tarafa Jekem-Nundem and tarafa Vetlem; tarafa Bhati consists of Bhati, Talauli, Viliena, Kumbhari Dongor, Shigonem, Pangarem, and Naiquinim villages. The last village Naiquinim consisted of large hamlets named Mayda, Galiem and Valshem.

Ancient schools of the Kadamba period

The Brahmapuris

We have already seen that artisans were instructed in the job by their fathers. Those who were not artisans were instructed by the priests or by the Shenavis named as *Sheneimam*. The balcony at the entrance of the main temple of the village was used for teaching. At times the teaching was conducted in a big hall of a renowned teacher's residence. But in the time of the Kadambas, a vast area named 'Brahmapuri' was established for this purpose in the capital of the kingdom. This type of place were installed first in Karnataka. A copper-plate inscription was found in a Keni family of *Kunkalli* (Salcete taluka) and was diciphered by G. H. Kare, who has designated it as 'Copper-plate of Shaka 1028 of the time of Tribhuvanamalla amba' [121]. This date tallies with the history of the Kadambas. The Shaka corresponds to 1106 A.D., and that copper-plate says as follows: in short, Gandagopala Keni of Panjar Khani, who, through three generations, served the Kadamba king, constructed a tank and installed a Brahmapuri, constructing three houses and a temple. In these three houses, twelve families of Brahmins were established. The temple has an idol of Saraswati under the name 'Bharati'. He purchased a rice-field named 'Sheilendhri' situated in *Madgaon* (Margāo of Salcete taluka) and from the income of that field the expenses of daily worship of that idol as well as daily reciting of holy books (Puranas) were to be done by those Brahmins. Besides this rice-field, he purchased Khajan land measuring about ten hectares in Marcaim (*Madkai*) village, and many others in different villages. The copper-plate mentions the name of each property and its location. The name of a rice field in *Madkai* for example is Naga Paiya. Today we find the surname of all Gaonkars of that village as 'Kamat' while their gotras and family-deities are different, which shows that in ancient times those families had the surname Paiye, later changed to 'Kamat'. They were entrusted with the maintenance of the embarkment of khajan lands, hamletwise, and this profession was called '*Kamatpan*'. There are six conditions mentioned in the copper-plate to the effect that the Brahmins must continue there with their duty of teaching. The teaching in a Brahmapuri was of secondary, and not primary school, as this latter kind existed in the villages in general. The teaching in a Brahmapuri consisted of Vedas, Vedanga, Astronomy, Astrology, and Medicine. The teaching of all subjects, except the Vedas and Vedangas, was ministered also to Chaddes and Deivadnya Brahmins (gold-smiths). The system was the same as in Karnataka.

At the time of installation of Brahmapuri the ruling Kadamba king was Guhaladeva II, known also as Tribhuvanamalla as well as Shiva-chitta-Vira-Permadi (1080/81—1125/26 A.D.) His name Tribhuvanamalla is recorded in the copper-plate, but it is remarkable that all the expenses for the construction of the water-tank, houses, temples and lands gifted were totally from the pocket of Gangagopala Keni. We also find some copper-plates from the time of Jayakeshi I. This king made a gift of a village named

Kuppatgiri to the temple of Shivalinga named Galgeshwar situated on the banks of the Malaprabha river, in Halshi area (Karnataka). The copper-plate is dated Shaka 1055 (1133 A.D.). After this time we find some inscriptions proving that grants were endowed to the Brahmins in North Karnataka and Goa, but they never tried to establish another Brahmapuri.

The existence of the Brahmapuri at *Vodlem Goen* (present Goa Velha) is proved by the remnant of the tank of *Gandagopala* (*Gandagopalachem talem*) at the side of nearby Ganci village, with an embankment of mud about one kilometre long and two metres high. At present that tank is silted.

In about 1310 A.D. Malik Kafur, commander of Alla-uddin-Khilji, invaded Govapuri. Later the Sultan of Delhi, Mahamad-bin-Tughlak did the same in about 1327 A.D. He was a zealous Muslim. So, if not in the time of Malik Kafur then at least in the time of Tughlak, the idol of Bharati in the form of Sharada might have been transferred to *Madkai* village. Now we find there a separate temple dedicated to that idol. It is interesting that an idol of Ganapati under the name of 'Nyanesha Ganapati' also stands there. This means that even though in the copper-plate we do not find the name of Ganapati, it is certain that the Brahmins of Brahmapuri also established the idol of Ganapati.

After the eclipse of Brahmapuri, a member of the Sarjotishi family obtained a *Farman* (gift-document) from the Mughal Subhedar in the year corresponding to 1667 A.D. From then the lands previously belonging to the said Brahmapuri were granted to him. There were a few rice-fields situated in *Madkai* village, but the Brahmin Gaonkars did not permit him to acquire them, and so they were incorporated in the properties of the village commune. Those lands are recorded in the inventory of properties of the commune. It is interesting that the same names of properties have continued through eight centuries according to the general procedure of village-communes of all the talukas. This excellent system helps to acquire clear historical proof. A large area of a rice-field measuring about ten hectares is recorded in the inventory as "Khazana of Brahmapuri".

Origin and importance of Brahmapuris

The most ancient of Brahmapuris we find established in North Karnataka. The first of them was established in 1010 A.D. at Balligave named Keshvapura, so named after its founder, Dandanayaka (Governor) Keshimayya of Banavasi where the village was situated. It is interesting to see how a person is led by others to establish such important institutions.

"Before proceeding to study the economic aspects of life in the agraharas, it is necessary to differentiate them from the Brahmapuris, or quarters for Brahmans in agraharas which were also known as Brahmapuris. The similarities between them were that both were educational centres and both were under the control of the mahajanas. But one major difference between them was that, while the agrahara was a village, the Brahmapuri was a part of a town or city. The Brahmapuris flourished in capitals like Balligave, Vikramapura, Sudi and Anniger. Of these, Annigere had five Brahmapuris and Balligave seven.

"The best example of how a Brahmapuri came into existence is to be seen in the foundation of Keshavapura in Balligave. When Dandanayaka Keshimayya was governor of Banavasi, his assistant Recharasa told him, 'This city (Balligave) ... Has become known in all the world for the Satras, (gift of cooked food daily for the poor) pleasure-gardens, temples, large tanks and lines of water-sheds established by the former early dandadhipas (governors) ... where a Keshavapura founded here, named after your lordship, and in it a temple erected to the God Virakeshava - you will obtain in the present world unspotted fame....' Dandadhipa Keshiraja agreed and built for the God Keshava an abode filled with beauty and a joy to the sight. And on a large piece of land in front of that temple, he built a town named Virakeshavapura and gave that town, filled with commodious houses, having cots in each chamber, containing the softest beds and all manner of vessels, to a band of Brahmins. And for the purpose of granting shares (vritti) for that puri, he obtained the consent of the authorities of Jiddligenad and acquired from them the village of Belvani.

"A Brahmapuri got its revenues in various ways. This will become clear from the examples of Brahmapuris at Sudi and Vikramapura. In 1010 A.D. the six Gavundas and eight Settis of Sundi, representing the secular administration, leased out to the Mahajanas of the local Brahmapuri certain specified estates with the stipulation that they should take due care of the estates and not alienate the land or a single street in which they resided under any pressure. The Brahmapuri at Vikramapura (modern Arisibidy, Bijapur district) was more fortunate. In 1053 A.D., Akkadevi made a land gift to its forty-two learned Brahmins. In 1061 A.D. Chattimayya, manager of the Vaddaravula revenue, made with the sanction of the emperor a gift of a palm and 100 areca nuts on every areca-palm garden to the forty-two Brahmins of the Brahmapuri at Vikramapura. In 1087 A.D., with the consent of the king, Varasa governor of Kisukadu Seventy made a gift of land and house-sites to the forty-two Brahmins. Thus they as a body, received land, income from taxes, etc., and hence like the mahajanas of the agraharas, they had to manage estates but their part in the administration of their own was much less than the part of the mahajarnas in the administration of their agraharas, because there were other agencies also in the former to look after the municipal administration. In Balligave, there was as superintendent of Brahmapuris; and for the administration of the town there were Mayors (Pattanaswamis) and various other bodies to help them".

The Agraharas of Havig Brahmins

The Haviga's irrigation system

From what has been mentioned above the difference between Brahmapuri and Agrahara is clear. The word 'Agrahara' appears in Goa for the first time in the Sahyadrikhand of Skandapurana, which include also legends of the time of the Kadambas, composed with an addenda after Kadamba rule ended. It is said in that book that Shree Parashurama brought Brahmins from Trihotrapur for performing yadnyas, gifting them agraharas for their settlements. I have already discussed this subject in a previous chapter at length. Later on, it is known that "Kushasthali" (*Kutthal*) Cortalim and *Kelshi* (Quelossim) were designated as agraharas in the 17th century A.D., in the village-commune records, areas which were granted to the Brahmins of the second wave of Aryans. The Brahmins of some families of that wave of migration continued to teach. The Havig Brahmins were also gifted lands under the designation of agraharas. The population was scarce, hence those agraharas could not constitute educational centres. However, the children were taught by their fathers or grandfathers. These Brahmins had sufficient time to improve cultivation. They were skilled in setting up irrigation systems, as I have proved on the basis of a channel named 'Ramnathacho-pat' at Curdi village. I cannot go further without mentioning their engineerig skills on the levelling of land. I have mentioned before that the Havig Brahmins lived in Old Narvem of *Divadi* island in Tiswadi taluka.

On the bank of the river Mandavi they engineered khajan land which produced 2,000 khandis (1 khandi=160 litres) of paddy annually in the rainy season. It is known that if prior to ripening of the crop there is no rain, the grain cannot be formed and the produce is ruined. The Havig Brahmins overcame this by using their skill. After the end of Ashadha month, the water of the river Mandavi becomes sweet and continues in this form at least during three months of the rainy season. They first did levelling work in a crude form, and constructed a high level ditch throughout the field. The sluice-gate was fixed firmly with laterite stone at the base. So also the line of the ditch was built firmly of a laterite stone base about 30 cm. in length, and about forty-five metres in height. Such stone was also used at each change of direction of the ditch. Those laterite signs are named '*sannams*' (*sannam* is a Konkani word meaning a sweet prepared of rice-flour, a spongy-like cake which is divided into cubes, and their taste is like the idlis of Karnataka cuisine). These laterite stones were shown on the cadastral survey map prepared in the year 1905, and also in the large-scale map of the inventory of that village commune. I, as a survey-officer, had inspected and prepared my report because a private owner had raised objections about the entry of water against the village-commune which owned that khajan-land. The Portuguese Governor General Vassalo de Silva, who was also a civil engineer, took a joint meeting in his chamber at Government Palace at Panaji. I showed him the maps and told him that the work had been done by Havig Brahmins in the12th century A.D. He was not convinced because he always thought that like the use of lime and country tiles, the irrigation work was also introduced into Goa by the Portuguese. Moreover, in the 12th century A.D., the Portuguese were in the dark about this science which otherwise requires levelling instrument of great accuracy. The slope of a ditch of irrigation of this type cannot fall more than 20 cms. in 100 metres. The Havig Brahmins had achieved that level of expertise. One may understand how these Havig Brahmins helped agricultural growth in Goa.

Genocide of Havig Brahmins in *Kankon* (Canacona)

In Kankon talukas, the Havig Brahmins had settled in Shristhal of Kankon village. But the Marathas who came later were anxious to take possession of all they had done. They attacked during the night and killed all the male members of their families which resided there in separate houses. The promoter of the Marathes had committed a sin, and for this reason he made a pilgrimage to Kashi. When he died, his image, named 'kashi-purush' was established near the temple and he is annually worshipped as the destroyer of Havigs.

At present, as I said before, there are only ten families of Havig Brahmins in Astagrahar—namely in Netorli and Vichudrem. In Netorli, there is also a family of a Paddye-Brahmin with the surname 'Dhume'. I was surprised by his using a surname identical to mine. His gotra as well as his family deity are different, and he informed me that his forefathers had migrated from Khanapur-Supe side. There are surnames like Desai, Kumar etc. which denote a profession, official or non-official, but my surname is not among them, and even today I don't know how this occurrence of identical surnames took place.

Other grants

Besides the establishment of a Brahmapuri and gifts made by the Kadamba kings, we find grants made by village-communes to the families of servants of village-deities, and to those serving the village population, like the barber, washerman, blacksmith etc. These properties were named as '*Namashis*'. The word 'Namashi' is a Prakrit one derived from the Sanskrit 'Namasya', meaning 'handed over perpetually'. The donees occupy these lands through the generations in return for the service rendered by them but the lands could not be sold or given in guarantee against a loan. If any person or family was released from services of the deity, the land was given to another person or family entrusted with the same work. These were named as '*Mhalea-nomos*', '*Mesta-nomos*', or '*Kamra-nomos*' and '*Madvala-nomos*', meaning respectively 'Namas of barber', 'Namas of blacksmith', 'Namas of washerman' etc. These words were translated into Portuguese as "Nomoxim dos Barbeiros', 'Nomoxim dos Ferreiros', 'Nomoxim dos

Mainatos', etc. In some villages in the New Conquests, we find also '*Ghaadiyam-no-mos*', meaning 'Namas of witchcraft'. These were also lands the produce of which was destined to the worship of the deities and they were named '*Dulau-nomos*'. Instead of the designation 'Namas', in *Kumbharjuvem* (Cumbarjua) island of Tiswadi taluka they adopted the word '*Hakka*'. It appears that this word was adopted in the Muslim kingdom. So, we find there, '*Bhavnicho-Hakk*', '*Sarangueacho-Hakk*', '*Mridangeacho-Hakk*', etc. meaning respectively 'gift of Bhavina' (a non-married woman, servant of a deity), 'gift of player of sarang' (a fiddle-like musical instrument), 'gift of player of mridanga' (a type of tambor), etc. At the time of the Inquisition all these properties were confiscated and we find Portuguese records of these properties, generally rice-fields and rarely areca-nut or coconut gardens, taluka and village-wise. These records are valuable to those interested in studying the ancient history of lands. The confiscated lands were gifted to the Christian Missions, but in about the year 1759, the lands were taken back from the Jesuits because the missionary order was against D. Jose I, king of Portugal. The expulsion was ordered by the Marquise of Pombal, his chief-minister. Later, on all these lands were sold at public auctions to private purchasers. Calculating the area of these lands, it is seen that about one third of the total area of rice-fields of the talukas in the Old Conquests were granted by the village-communes during the time of the Kadambas.

In Sattari taluka where village-communes existed in a rudimentary form, there are some lands under the epithet '*Namas*', and some under the name of '*Devasu*', a Prakrit word derived from the Sanskrit 'Devasvam', meaning 'dedicated to the deity'.

Literature during the Kadamba period

We have seen that many grants of lands were awarded to the Brahmins, and also the Brahmapuri was created. Surprisingly, we do not have even a single written record which can be considered of that time. It is seen that from the Northern Konkan, Shilahars, Aparaka (c.1110—C.1140 A.D.) compiled a commentary of Yadnyavalka-smriti—poetic art. It is improbable that no library or book existed in the Brahmapuri. Certainly, at least some of the twelve Brahmins or their descendants had creative minds. It is certain that at the time of the invasion of Malik-kafur, or most probably at the time of Muhamad-bin-Tughlak these books were reduced to ashes. Also, the Portuguese missionaries, who went even into the area then under Vijapur kingdom at *Mashel* (Marcela in Portuguese), Ponda taluka at night with Portuguese soldiers and collected and took all the books, while searching the houses of priests. So, today we do not find any evidence, especially of books, which might have been available in the villages of the New Conquests. Some were surely destroyed by white ants due to negligence on the part of the owners. So, to gauge the creativity of the people of that time, we have to go by their work in the fields of irrigation, architecture and sculpture.

Architecture and sculpture during the Kadamba period

We have already observed that in the time of the Bhojas and Sendrakas architecture could not develop as the art of carving of blocks of laterite stone was not known. Moreover, the laterite stone known locally as *Mirio* available in the coastal zone was very porous. During the Kadamba times, a hard laterite known locally as *khadpo* was found in the area and the masons also were skillful in cutting regular blocks of different sizes. They also knew the art of joining them together without lime. The use of lime as mortar came to be known only with the advent of the Portuguese. So, we find the temple of Mahamaya of Nundem and a temple in Curdi built with this stone. For the temple of Curdi, cylindrical columns of granite rock were used. An inscription is found at the temple of Mahamaya, which is erroneously considered to be of the 6th century p. [119]. The inscription says that Sinharaja gifted a door to the Parvati-Swami and also a garden of jackfruit trees to a Brahmin named Ellaswami. We do not find any king named 'Sinha' in all those dynasties; but there was a person named 'Sinha' who was a minister and dandanayaka (Commander of troops) of the Kadamba king Jaykeshi II (1126-1147/48 A.D.) Sinha was the second son of Lakshmana or Lakshmanaraya who accompanied the wife of Jaykeshi II, Meilaladevi, daughter of Vikramaditya Chalukya p. [119]. Thus it can be seen that the Sinharaja mentioned in the inscription is the same person referred to above, who in the Narendra inscription is described as 'perspicacious and an ornament among commanders of troops.'

Mahadeva Temple at Tamdi Surla

An important temple is of Shree Mahadeva of Tamdi-Surla in Hemadbarcem division of Sanguem taluka *(ill. 35)*. Unfortunately, Dr. Gune forgot to mention this temple in his article published in the Goa Gazetteer, But in his book 'Ancient Shrines of Goa', referring to the temple he says [98] pp. 15-16: "The structural stone temple at Tamdi Surla, now enshrining a Shivalinga in its garbhagriha, is situated on the bank of a small river, surrounded by the hills on the south-west and a thick forest allround. It is by far the only ancient and best preserved stone structural 'temple of Goa'.

"The temple facing east is raised on a plainly-moulded plinth and is constituted with a Sabhamandapa (main hall), antra-laya (middle hall) and garbhagriha (sanctuary), each following the other and all in the same principal axis. The sabhamandapa has three projected entrances facing north, east and south; each approached by a flight of steps in front. In all, there are ten plain pillars on the sides and four well-carved pillars in the central bay of the sabhamandapa. It is provided with four devakoshthas in the rear wall and kakshasanas on the sides. The ceiling is made up of large slabs throughout on the side bays and fashioned with kapotas over the entrance

ill. 35 : Temple of Shree Mahadeva at Tamdi-Surla,
Sanguem Taluka, dated c. 13th Century A.D.

and reducing tiers finally covered by a rectangular slab embossed with lotus reliefs
over the central bay *(ill. 36)*.

"The doorway of the antralaya is flanked by perforated grills and that of the

ill. 36 : Ceiling of the temple of Shree Mahadeva of Tamdi-Surla, Sanguem Taluka, dated c. 13th
Century A.D.

garbhagriha has Gajanana in the lalatabimba or the lintel. The exterior walls are throughout plain, excepting the portion below the back of the Rakshasanas which is carved with bold reliefs of rosettes. On the ceiling of the garbhagriha rises the Shikhara with its dilapidated shikhanasi in the Dravida style. The riches of the Shikhara are filled with bas reliefs of superb workmanship of Brahma, Vishnu, Shiva, Parvati, Kalabhairava and the devakoshthas with Mahishasuramardani, Naga etc. Of them the Shiva-Parvati bas relief is rather interesting as Parvati also is shown to have won kiritamukuta, an unusual feature in the region and both are seated on their vahana, i.e. Nandi. Another curious bas relief, probably of some significance is an 'elephant trampling a horse'.

"The ground plan padavinyasa, the style of the pillars and Shikhara, the elaborate and minute, ornamental carvings, the proportionate and graceful delineation of the physical features of the bas relief and other decorative motives have a close resemblance to those of the medieval temples of the Western Chalukyas of Kalyani and their successors the Yadavas of Devgiri. The sculpture of this temple has a close resemblance to that of Shri Vithal (temple at Pandarpur which is considered as a specimen of the mixed Hoysala-Yadava style). The Goa Kadambas were the feudatories of the Chalukyas and the Yadavas for some time. The temple may therefore be dated to the 12-13th century A.D."

Dr. Gune does not give importance to the existence of an idol of Subrahmanyanam—Serpent—at the entrance of the middle hall. He also ignored the construction of exterior walls and a stairway existing nearby, which is made of granite steps about 2 m. long and about 15 cm. wide and 30 cm. broad which takes us to the top of the mountains. It is named 'Ranichi-paj' (stairway of the queen). Had he seen these features. Dr. Gune perhaps might have changed his mind in respect of dating of the construction of this temple, of placing it in the period of 11th-12th century A.D.

Personal investigations of the temple

In April,1935, I had the opportunity to visit the temple for the first time. At that time, as an ancillary expert of on a batch of road constructions of the Executive Committee of Sanguem taluka, I was entrusted with the layout of roads, and as such I was making a reconnaissance for a suitable site to construct a bridge on the river 'Ragado', which passes between Sancordem and Surla village. In Surla village I heard that at a place named Tamdi situated about four kms away there was a beautiful temple of black stone. Fond of visiting such places as a hobby, I went to the temple accompanied by a guide. I was surprised by the construction of the exterior walls. At the right side, from the entrance near the junction of the main hall and the middle hall, were two slabs at a metre's distance from the plinth. They were not in an erect position and were inclined forward. One could see rounded granite pebbles of filling up the open space between the two slabs, one on the outer and the other on the inner side. Each face of wall consisted of small granite slabs (or basalt slabs?) with straight borders but forming irregular geometric forms, generally quadrangular. They were joined with adjacent slabs by the system known as the 'male-female system'. The talent of the architect was admirable because to obtain stability in the work required knowledge of mechanical techniques. Each slab had to support the weight of the slabs on one hand as well as the lateral pressures of the pebbles poured in the open space. It is pertinent to mention here that the staff of the Central Directorate of Archaeology had planned reconstruction work after liberation, but not only did they not rebuild it, but pulled down completely the portion of the wall which was partially damaged!

We do not find this type of construction anywhere else in Goa. It is interesting to note that at one side of the open yard in front of the Convent of S. Caetano there was a doorway of granite like that of the temple of Tamdi-Surla. A picture of this was published in the article 'Os Hindus de Goa e a Republica Portuguesa' ('Hindus of Goa and the Portuguese Republic') by Judge Dr. Antonio de Noronha. This doorway was considered to be part of a Muslim palace which existed there. Some consider it to be part of the temple of Mahadeva which existed there before the Muslim period. Others are of the opinion that the doorway was brought from the temple of Shri Mhalsa of Verna by the Portuguese. At present we find pieces of round granite pillars lying around the plinth of the ancient temple at Verna. We have no other architectural work of the type found in the temple of Tamdi-Surla in Goa, so this edifice needs to be well preserved. It is situated in a jungle area. After visiting the temple and *Ranichi paj* (the stairway of the queen), I was taken by the guide to about six metres to the right where there was a black stone with an inscription in Kanadi-type script.

At the first opportunity I met my maternal uncle Dr. P. S. Pissurlekar and told him about the temple. Dr. Pissurlekar, with keen interest in such matters, recommended Eng. Arthur Dias to take the photographs. He shot about five pictures of the temple. At that time Dr. Pissurlekar worked as an archivist in the Office of the Government Chamber, and Major Hygino Craveiro Lopes (later the President of the Portuguese Republic) was head of the Department. Dr. Pissurlekar showed him the photographs, and Major Lopes went on horseback to visit the temple. He was so impressed that he proposed to his father, General Craveiro Lopes, the then Governor-General, to classify it as national monument and to make necessary improvements on it with funds from the Government treasury. As such, the order was published in the Government Gazette.

The last Portuguese Governor Vassalo de Silva also visited the temple and posted two watchmen, Gaonkars of Tamdi, to look after it, paying them a monthly salary of forty rupees each.

Some new light on dating of the temple construction

Who might have constructed that temple? And when? These questions have not been resolved so far. Surely the Kadambas did not construct it. In the 13th century they were so weak they could not sustain their own kingdom. In the 12th century also it was not possible because the Kadambas never entered the area of Goa very far from their capital, especially when it was covered with dense forests and when there was no practical economic advantage to them. We have seen that in the year 1380 A.D., a king named Virakawana Vallabharaja Rajadhiraja ruled a part of Goa. So, it is probable that a queen of that dynasty ordered the construction of the temple. I emphasize that the construction must have been on account of the queen, not only because the stair-way named *Ranichi-paj*, but also because the image of Parvati is styled as seated on the Nandi, separate from Shiva, which indicates that the sculptor showed the person-ality of the queen as distinct from that of her husband, the king. It is likely that she was the daughter of a king of the Badami Chalukya dynasty. Here, another point raises its head. As the temple was constructed at Tamdi, the capital of the concerned kingdom must have been nearby. If I remember well, at a short distance from the temple, the guide had showed me a place named '*Kotant*' (a fortress), but there was no sign of the fortress. The land was plain; the fortress was probably constructed of mud walls, and so could not be distinguished. I have mentioned this only to provide a direc-tion to historians for future study.

In the year 1963, Von Mitterwallner, professor of Indology of Munich University, Germany visited Goa and stayed here for nearly two years to study the sculpture of Goa. I was then the Director of the Land Survey Department of Goa and on many occasions she happened to visit my office to acquire plans of specific areas. While discussing Goan temple sculpture, I informed her about the sculpture of Tamdi-Surla with specific reference to the peculiar technique (joining of bolders) used for the con-struction of the temple walls. Later on she informed me that she had visited the temple twice before proceeding to Hampi, Haliebid and other places in India to check whether such type of construction technique existed elsewhere. She confirmed that this was a unique system which gives a clear picture of the skill of the sculptor in using the principle of stability to raise the walls of the Tamdi-Surla temple.

From the photos of the temple we get a clear picture of the advances made in the sculpture of idols along with architecture in the Sendraka Kadamba period. But more interesting were the idols of Rama, Sita and Laxman of about 30 cms. height, of granite which existed on the side of Curpem village, near the site where an embarkment is constructed annually for irrigation, locally named '*Kandevacho-pantho*'. I had seen those idols in the year 1932, but according to my information those idols are no longer there but the beautifully carved granite niche still remains. This work probably was of the time of the Havig Brahmins.

Use of mud-bricks for temple at Chandor :

Finally I must refer to the use of mud bricks in construction because this does not appear anywhere else in India during the Kadamba period. This construction is of a temple of Basaveshwar at Chandor and is of the time of the Kadambas. The area is known as *Kotant* (fortress) and the surroundings of the temple was covered by forests. After the liberation of Goa an agency of the Central Archaeological Department worked there, and now we can see clearly the base of that temple. The temple faces east like that of Tamdi-Surla. From the appearance, it is clear that the main construction was based on a timber frame-work, the pillars were square in form, fixed on a base of granite square stone. The roof was of two slopes and totally covered by timber planks closely set. The open space between the pillars was filled with clay bricks measuring about 33.5 x 22.0 x 6.0 cms. The roof also was covered by clay bricks but of different dimensions, generally, about 1.50 x 9.5 x 1.0 cms. The joints of these bricks were covered by mud (half-tube type) but this was not sufficient for protection from the rains. So an annual supplementary covering with coconut-leaves was necessary. The bricks of the wall were joined with clay only.

It should be noted that at the request of the Jesuit Fathers, the Viceroy by the orders dated 20 December, 1565, and 27 February, 1566, prohibited in Salcete and Bardez talukas, the construction, reconstruction or repairing of Hindu temples, as well as the annual coverage of roofs with palm-leaves or grass. But a commission of Hindu Brahmins implored the Viceroy not to execute the orders. The Viceroy vacillated but the Archbishop insisted upon the execution of the orders because with this Draconian measure, all the Hindu temples would have crumbled in a short period. The Tribunal of the Inquisition had already been established in 1560, but its jurisdiction was limited to the Hindus converted to Christianity, named Neo-Christians. But it soon expanded its authority step by step after the year 1566, with the Portuguese always suspecting an invasion from Vijayanagar, through this kingdom ended in 1565. The Portuguese thus had the liberty to propagate Christianity. History says that a Portuguese named Rodrigues, Captain of the fortress of *Raitur* (Rachol in Portuguese) set on fire about 300 Hindu temples situated in Salcete taluka (including the present Mormugaon taluka) in a single day. And it was easily accomplished because the frame-work as well as the roof of the temples was of timber and the roofs were covered with grass and palm-leaves.

The administrative set-up of the Kadambas

The administrative set-up did not change as compared to that the Sendrakas and Shilahars. Only the designations changed, with Kanadi names sometimes mixed with Konkani words.

Village communes and Gaonkars

The taluka (mahal) committee consisted of the representatives of the principal villages (village-communes) named '*Mhalgades*'. They fixed the revenue payable by each village. The revenue was of two categories. The first was named *Khushi-varad* (willingly accepted tax) and the second *Ghoda-varad* (the expenses of the horseback warriors). The committee of each village-commune collected the revenue, fixed proportionately on each property in possession of the respective holder. The village-commune was entitled to give the base of uncultivated lands and the system was named as '*Shiristo*' (meaning according to the customs). Those lands were suitable for coconut, areca-nut gardens and rarely rice plantations. This cultivation was done by the village-commune itself. The time given to bring the land under cultivation was fixed at twenty years, and the grant of land was made on the basis of the number of trees which might be grown in that area. The rate of rent was already fixed, based on the number of fruit-bearing trees. After 20 years the rent was determined and so the land was named as *Cutumbana*. The necessity of green manure as well as of mud needed to grow and increase the productivity of the trees was also factored in. The area adjacent to the cultivated land was named '*Antod*', and that of green manure '*Visoi*' or '*Visolem*'. When the adjacent land was a rocky area, then land from another village could be granted. This was called '*Antod-Visol*'.

The land could be granted only to the Gaonkars of the respective village. The property was heritable but not transferable except with the consent of all the members of the village commune-committee, which consisted of the elders of each branch (*vangad*) with its rank in voting. These elders were named '*Naikbares*'. The president of this committee as well as of the Mhal committee were representatives of the first rank, and the record keeper-cum-accountant (now named 'Kulkarni') was a paid person but his profession continued through the generations. A single vote '*Naka*' (No) was sufficient to reject the proposal. The annual rent payable on the granted land was named as '*pangas*' from the time of the Bhojas. Now this word was changed to '*Shidav*', derived from the Kanadi word 'Siddaya', the other Kanadi word which was utilized and continues to be used in respect of any tax of any type to be paid on the expenses of the village (grama-Kharcha) or in respect of the festival of the God or Goddess of the respective village. The village-commune committee had economic, religious as well as judicial powers. One could appeal to the Mhal-committee, and the representative of the government named from the Muslim period as Thanedar was responsible for execution of the resolution taken by the Mhal-committee. During the village-festivals like Shigmo, the singer-girls with their ancillary staff visited each house of the Gaonkar-Naikbars, according to their rank.

The profit or loss of the village—commune was shared (share known as *jan*, jono in Portuguese) among the Gaonkar members according to custom, which means by capita and for this purpose only male members with the minimum fixed age in each village were counted. In some village communes widows without children had the right to half share ('jan'), and the same was the case with unmarried girls of the Gaonkars.

Besides Gaonkars, there were other interested parties called '*Kulacharis*' and '*Khuntkars*'. The word '*Kulachari*' is derived from the word 'Kul' meaning land, so the Kulacharis are those persons who brought under cultivation the lands which were not granted previously. They were of Brahmin or other castes. The *Kuntkars* also were of the same category but their caste was different from that of the Brahmins. People of these categories could not obtain land according to the village-commune rules. However, they were allowed to cultivate uncultivated lands. All these areas were incorporated into village-commune land and they were given the right corresponding to one 'jan' or generally 'half jan'. They had no right to vote, nor were they obliged to contribute when the village-commune was at a loss, as they were not members of the village-commune. However, their right to 'jan' or 'half jan' was hereditary.

When any village went into a loss and could not pay the revenue, then the head village to which the Gaonkars originally belonged, would take over the administration, and make the necessary improvements. And the Gaonkars of that village, noting the improvement, could take back its administration on the condition that the expenses incurred would be paid back to the head village in instalments.

In the year 1526, Afonso Mexia, the Portuguese Superintendent of Revenue and Taxes, published an order known as 'Charter of Uses and Customs of Gaonkars and Cultivators of Goa Island'. This order is enough to give us a picture of the economic administration of the area. To lay down these rules, Mexia had to take the help of persons with full knowledge of Hindu law. Now the point is, which smriti was in use at that time—Manu-smriti or Yadnyavalka-smriti? It is known that the Northern Konkan Shilahar Apararka had compiled a commentary on Yadnyavalka-smriti. But it is to be noted that Yadyavalka does not admit adoption because he thinks that this ultimately constitutes purchase of a child which is not acceptable according to the Shastras. However, he accepts 'Niyoga' which allows a married woman to give birth to a child from a person other than her husband. But neither in Goa nor in the whole Konkan, was this custom accepted. In fact, there is a saying, "Shasrad rudhi baliyasi", meaning customs prevals over socio-religious rules. It is also seen from that Chart of Afonso Mexia that when a person died without adoption or a collateral heir, the land reverted to the crown and not to the village-commune which had granted that land. This custom is also contrary to socio-economic principles.

There were some villages which had no such communes, as for example Kumbharjuve village. In Portuguese records of the village in Tiswadi taluka, there is no mention of Khumbharjuve, because it was linked by a tongue-like isthmus to the main land of Corlim village. At that time it consisted only of a small area which at present is known as 'Gawant'.

About the titles Uridiye and Malilige

Earlier, the Northern area of Sindapura (present Goa Velha) was occupied by fish-ermen families. Later, a Saraswat Brahmin family came and settled there. Their previ-ous name is not known but they were named, in the Kadamba period, as 'Urudiye' meaning headman of the village. He was the representative of the resident people and not the official of the crown. He had no Kulkarni, and the collection of revenue to the crown was his own duty. He was also responsible for maintenance of peace and order in the village, and had the right to issue the order when he deemed it fit. He was the only person who punished defaulters. Before the issue of the order and the finalising of the punishment, he took the advice of the elders of the families. His post was heredi-tary. Besides the 'Urudiye', there was a person nominated by the Crown and named 'Malilige' whose duty was to inform the government about the peace and order situa-tion and to send the revenue passed to him by the 'Urudiye' to the Crown's treasury. This post was also hereditary. These designations now appear modified. 'Urudiye' has changed to 'Wadiye', and 'Malilige' to 'Maliye'. Presently the descendants of both fami-lies reside in *Madgaon* (Margão) town but they worship every year the village-deity, the procession of which takes place at the beginning of Chaitra. The procession first visits the house of the 'Wadiye'. At present there is no house but only a well but the place of the household is well defined. Next, the palkhi of the deity visits the house of the Maliye, a practice which continues to exist. I have narrated this only to show how ancient customs continue even today, irrespective of the riches of that person. The honour was given to the house and not to the person.

Influence of Yadavas

As noted, the direct administration of the Yadavas on Goa was for a very short period of eight years during the period of the exile of the Kadamba Shashthadeva III. Bichanna, dandanayaka of the Yadava Singhana II (1209-1247 A.D.) ruled Goa during this period. In the period of the Yadavas many members of Saraswat families of *Kutthal* village in Salcete taluka occupied high posts in the government. We find on two slabs of black stone at Pandharpur, the names of the principal doners who had assisted in the reconstruction of the temple of Shri Vithhal. Thereafter, we find the name of Ramadev Yadava on the top and further, we find some surnames like Lada, Dalvi, etc. We also find a surname Singhana Dalvi recorded in the list of the Mahajanas of Shri Manguesh of *Kutthal* now established at Priol, and this surname belong to the families who are now known as 'Shingbal'. Thus, we can say that from the time of Singhana at least, persons from these families occupied high posts. However, *Kutthal* and *Kelshi* villages had no right to send their representatives (*Mhalgado*) in the Mhal-committee. The

Konkanakhyhan gives a detailed account. From the second part, chapter VI, it is seen that during the time of the Kadambas, around the beginning of their rule in Goa (and not in the period of the Yadavas) the other four villages could also send their representatives (*Mhalgades*) in the Mhal committee, in the following order: *Kutthal* village had the 9th rank, *Kelshi* the 10th, *Betalbhati* 11th, and *Kolwem* 12th. Thus they had a total of 12 votes in the Mhal-committee, instead of 8 votes as before. The Gaonkars of *Kuthal* and *Kelshi* villages were Saraswat Brahmins, while those of *Betalbhatim* and *Colva* villages were of the Vaishya caste. I have referred to this to show that a person of high status even recommended the names of the Vaishya caste, and in this way they tried to give equal rights to the minority in Aryan society. On all occasion, whenever necessary, all the male adult members of Gaonkars assembled in the village to take resolutions. That assembly was named simply as 'Gaon' and its function as '*Gaonpon*', and the resolutions were recorded.

In about 1352 A.D. the sway of the Bahamani kingdom begins in Goa. They introduced the Muslim system of administration. The main feature of this system was revenue farming. The collection of revenue was entrusted taluka-wise to persons named Desai and Sardesai - an intermediary between the people and the crown. The same type of system was employed, irrespective of the collection of customs duties by appointing a private person. The amount of revenue as well as of customs duty was already fixed and paid by the Desai and the Sardesai at the treasury of the Crown. They collected the revenue from village-communes and private parties according to the rates already fixed by the Crown. When payment was stopped, as well as when a private owner died without issue or heir, the property passed to the Desai or Sardesai. They maintained troops not only to collect Government dues, but also to help the Crown when ordered to do so. This system continued even in the time of Vijayanagar.

The advent of the Bahamani kingdom in Goa (1352 A.D.) began with the Muslim invasion and that brings us to the end of the ancient period of Goa's history.

SUMMARY

Based on the inscriptions of the twelve copper-plate and stone records of the Chalukyas, Shilaharas and Kadambas periods and taking into consideration the dates scrutinized from these inscriptions, the following events are described in chronological order:

As mentioned in the previous chapter, Vantudeva Senanandaraja (maternal uncle of Pulakeshi II of Chalukya Dynasty) was a feudatory of Pulakeshi II who subsequently founded the Sendraka Dynasty in Goa.

Vantuwallabha transferred his capital from Ponda to Chandrapura (Chandor). About a century after him, the Rastrakutas established a dynasty of Shilahars of Southern

Konkana. Later, another branch of the Shilahars appeared from Kolhapur side and occupied North Konkan. They are known as the Northern Shilahars. Both these families had good relations with the Sendraka branches and probably due to the close kingship through marriage they always acted as mediators whenever there was any internal litigation. The Junior branch did not have a good sea-port, so a Southern king forced a king of the Senior branch to cede Sindapur and the surrounding area in favour of the Junior branch. After the advent of the Kadambas, and sensing the weakness of the Senior branch, a southern Shilahar king occupied some area but his efforts went in vain. The Kadamba king occupied the area and the Shilahars or say their baron, had to retreat and return to Southern Konkan. So the Kadambas held sway on the area originally occupied by the Senior branch of the Sendrakas—the Hemadarcem division of Sanguem taluka. In the eight century A.D., during the period of the Sendrakas, some families of the Konkan Shilahars attempted to check the Kadambas, but in vain. The Kadambas took the port and the surrounding area.

During the Kadamba period, Natha-Sampradaya was introduced by Gorakshanath and it spread in Goa. As a result, Shakti-Sampradaya which was growing sporadically, was transformed into Bhakti Namasankirtana, a soft form of worship in Goa. The Vedic and Puranic systems were strengthened by Vidyaranacharya Gaudapadachaya and this inhibited Shaktism.

In this chapter, the overall system of administration of the rulers has been discussed. The revised form of maintenance of the village-communes, the mode of collection of taxes (revenue), the rights and obligations of Gaonkars towards the village-communes are described at length. The impact of the rulers on traditional customs and old festivals that have continued through the generations, their historical significance such as that of Ghodemanni are described in detail. The establishment of the ancient school—the Brahmapuris—had its roots during the Kadamba dynasty. Also, mention is made about the advent of the Havig Brahmins and their art of cultivation and irrigation of fields.

The cultural evolution reflected through sculptures and the architecture of the different temples has been emphasized, with special reference to the Mahadeva Temple at Tambdi-Surla, discovered by the author in the year 1935 during his field work in that area.

The Kadambas, for the people of Goa, were outsiders. Moreover they were Jains and tried to introduced this religion into Goa, perhaps with the intention that the people of low status might readily embrace that religion and go against the people of high status. But the result was infructuous. Some Saraswat Brahmin families migrated to the Konkan area due to harassment by the Kadambas, but the Kadambas never gained popularity. They got converted to Hinduism and ostentatiously made pilgrimage taking with them people from Goa, but this did not produce. Only when a Saraswat Brahmin like Mayimdeva took the government in his hand was there peace. But after his death, the previous state of affairs recurred. After the death of Kadamba Shasthadeva III, the Kadamba kingdom weakened and finally with the advent of the Bahamani rulers, the Kadamba dynasty came to an end in 1352, if not earlier.

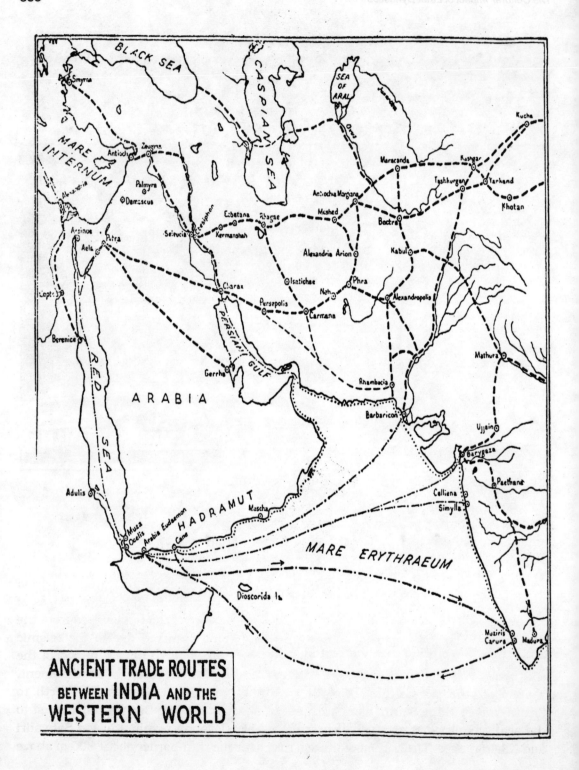

ANCIENT TRADE ROUTES
BETWEEN INDIA AND THE
WESTERN WORLD

Chapter - 8
THE CULTURAL SYNTHESIS AND HERITAGE OF GOA
[Epilogue]

Settlers and rulers contribute to cultural synthesis

THE GENESIS OF GOAN LAND

We have wandered through a chronological runway, covering in our path a period of about twelve thousand years which constitutes the ancient and medieval ages of the cultural history of Goa. It begins from the appearance of the land of Goa from the depths of the saline waters of the Arabian Sea which occurred due to the seismic movement of Earth which took place at the end of the fourth pluvial period of the southern terrestrial globe in about 10,000 B.C. As a result of this seismic movement, a strip of the sea-bottom from the mouth of the Tapti river in the North to Kanyakumari in the South, along with the adjacent area of the Deccan trap closest to the sea, was elevated above the sea waters. This elevation resulted in the Sahyadri and Nilgiri ranges. The bottom of the sea rose near the trap-border about 600 m above the mean sea-level. In the year 1943, I had come across a marine-conch with its outer layer already fossilized in Ambeacho-Gor village adjacent to Surla village of Sattari taluka. This constituted clean proof. Besides, even today one can visualize the effect of the seismic movement, its intensity declining towards the present sea-shore. The massive laterite produced by metamorphic form on the top of basaltic rocks was broken into large blocks and hurled over long distances as a result of this tectonic movement. So, we find in the bottom of rivers as well as in the sub-aerial area, large blocks of such massive laterite at different places even to a depth of about 15 metres. This rock is locally named 'Khodpo.' The Pluvial-rains continued, though with diminishing intensity, for one thousand years. During this period mud and salt of marine origin continued to be de-salted and the process of cohesion started and continued slowly. This movement resulted in the origin of another type of laterite of great porosity which is locally called 'Miryo'. We often find the two types of laterite on the same area at a little distance from one another. Dr. Oldham classified these types of laterite as high level and low level laterite, putting the boundary arbitrarily and unscientifically at an altitude of 600 metres. Even today the Geological Survey has not done any investigative work in this regard. It is understood that this Department commenced its study in the Konkan, but not a single report has been published so far.

c. 9,000 B.C., the pluvial rains suddenly stopped and the climate became very hot and completely dry. Soon after came the high winds from the West to the East. The influence of these cyclones impacted some areas of the west coast from Britain to India, and even in Iran and other countries of the terrestrial globe, except China. Due to these cyclones, trees were uprooted and large areas were inundated with hot silt and sand, sometimes remaining on basalt rock covered with the powder of basalt-schist, under pressure, and thus were fossilized in caverns. In respect of settled tribes in Goa or even elsewhere we can refer to them by the general designation in use and not by any specific species of mankind because the races were mixed.

SETTLERS OF GOAN LAND

a) Mhars

With habitats disrupted by the sudden environmental impacts, people had to search for a safe shelter. The cyclones generally damaged the tops of mountains, but even low lying areas suffered with the deposits of hot silt and sand upto a great height. This situation probably continued for about 500 years in the west coast of India. And after the cessation of this calamity, and with regular seasonal rains, the surviving population continued their migration through the foot of mountains as well as by spreading out to the west up to the sea-shore. From around 5000 B.C. security among settlements in Goa was more or less assured.

During the period when man dwelled in caverns, there was scarcity of food and so there was increased mortality. Now the conditions changed. The population gradually increased and people wandered here and there in small groups in search of food and sweet water. Even these groups did not try to settle permanently. They were forced to frequently change their dwellings in search of edible roots, wild fruit and gram. The population grew, and as such new sites were selected for settlements. Simultaneously, by natural instinct especially among the women folk, they practised rudimentary agriculture, cultivating wild grain and fruit and preparing mud-vessels for storing the grain. This primordial phase of the Neolithic stage occurred in all parts of the world, differing only in respect of time. The use of fire was known in India in the Neolithic Age, and this is proved by the remnants of fire in Karnool cave in South India.

The people from North as well as the South came to occupy the new-born area starting from the western foot of the Sahyadri and Nilgiri ranges. The human folk which first established themselves in Goa are those that came from the foothills of the Sahyadri range. They were named by the newcomers (in the Mundari language) from North India as Mhars, meaning "of the eldest house" or say the most ancient settlers. The Mhars did not hunt because they had no implements. So their food was only that which was produced spontaneously. They ate flesh but only of the beasts already dead. Kills with stone were rare. They worshipped only the dead ancestors, believing in the existence of spirits. Such worship has been noted in all the ancient tribes throughout the world, from the time of the Neanderthals.

b) Pastoral tribe

Next, in about 4,000 B.C. i.e. six thousand years ago, a wave of buffalo-rearing people appeared in Goa, having migrated from South India. They were a pastoral tribe and had knowledge of domestication of animals. This tribe, after centuries, was divided into two groups, namely the Naik caste and a second group of the matriarchal system consisting of Chedvans, Bhavins and Kalavants and their brothers. This tribe initiated the worship of female and male elements symbolized by stones.

c) Asuras

Later on, probably around, 3,500 B.C., a tribe named 'Asura' appeared from the Northern area around Chota-Nagpur of Madhya Pradesh. They probably had a crude notion of the use of copper and iron in spongy form and utilized their knowledge in producing ornaments and small tools for shaping stone implements. They started agriculture by the cut-and-burn method, locally known as the '*Kumeri*' system and produced cereals. They installed deities like '*Khaman-Rouduro*', '*Gana-*

Rouduro', and 'Dhawaj-Rouduro'. Some deities installed by them later were changed by sublimation. This tribe was subdued by the subsequent Kol tribe who dispossessed them from the land. So, the members of this Asura tribe had to adopt certain professions. Some became black-smiths and potters, some labourers and others formed part of the Vani caste. The Bharvankar caste in the Christian community is of this stock.

d) Kols, Mundaris and Kharwas

Next, around 5,000 years ago (3,000 B.C.), Kols as well as Mundaris and Kharwas came from the same area as the Asuras.

The Kols occupied the lands, cultivated paddy-fields and organised a village-socio-economic administration, establishing a 'Barazan', that is a group generally formed of twelve hamlets of villages. Paddy-fields were subdivided into 'Bandis' and were cultivated by a rotation system. Probably later, this might have led to permanent ownership by various families. It is in this tribe that we note for the first time the roots of primitive communes. Their main goddess was 'Ro-en' (ant-hill) named later by the Aryans as Santer and Bhumika. These words, Santer and Bhumika, are derived respectively from the words 'Santera' and 'Bhumika' meaning 'with the holes', and 'the child of the Earth'. This tribe, now constituting a caste named Satarkar, has derived its name probably from their main deity, Santer.

The Mundaris who probably came after the Kols worked under their hegemony. They had no special cultural trends, except the worship of a forest-tree named Kel. The Konkani word 'Mundkar', meaning 'protectee' is derived from this Mundari word.

The Kharwis came probably along with the Mundaris, but there is no proof for their independent settlement in village form. They took to the profession of fishing and boating and form the present Kharwis (fishermen) caste.

The religious customs of all these three tribes who came from the same northern area were uniform.

e) First wave of Aryans

Next around 2,400 B.C., came the first wave of Aryans.

The advent of the first wave of Aryans has been referred to in the first Chapter. The chronological order of the settlement was set aside because we had to debate in the first place on the designation given to the Malabar coast as 'Parashurama Kshetra' in the legendary history of India. Some writers were of the opinion that the land of the Malabar coast emerged from the waters in the time of Shri Parashurama while others consider Shri Parashurama as a legendary character. Since physical geology had to be discussed in the beginning, I had to examine the legend and prove through the finds and other evidence that the Malabar coast surfaced from the sea-waters about 12,000 years ago and that Shri Parashurama was not a mythical figure but a real person. I have mentioned the families that accompanied him on the excursion and who settled here. That wave, however, did not introduce any change in the existing order which had evolved slowly as a result of a give-and-take policy.

f) Sumerians in Goa

In about 2,000 B.C., the people from Sumer, now part of Iraq, came and settled in Goa. Their advent produced changes in the thinking process of the first wave of Aryans and, gradually, their customs were modified. 'Land belonged to the king' was the Aryan concept. It gave place to the Sumerian view that the village-land belonged to the village-god or goddess, and as such the land within the boundaries was indivisible. The gods as well as goddesses came to be worshipped in special constructions of a permanent nature. Besides the priests, singer-girls made their debut. The administration and the resolution of all manner of problems passed to the hands of a committee constituted from the elders of each family, thus substituting the 'Barazan' system by the village-commune system. The fourth chapter deals with the advent of Sumerians.

g) Second wave of Aryans

Next came the second wave of Aryans accompanied by the non-Aryan tribe in the period between 1,400 to 700 B.C. Now, the contact between Aryans and Sumerians became more intense and marriage links were established. Thus, the Saraswats have a titulary deity (*Palavi-devata*) besides the family-deity (*Kula-devata*)—the consultation of oracles, the idol of *Grama purasha* (the builder of the temple) before the face of the deity. For example, at Shri Mangeshi, Priol, the construction of a tower (*dipa-stambha* - tower with lamps) in front of the temple in substitution of a huge bamboo and water-tank are characteristics of the acceptance of the Sumerian system, besides the existence of dancing girls in the precincts of the temple.

The system of construction of residential houses also shows the Sumerian influence. For example: at the entrance a pot of water for washing feet and hands, a room at the right side for a guest, an inner open yard just after the entrance, a room on each side of this yard with the entrance door from the bordering upper plinth (*padvi* in Konkni), rooms used generally as residences of servants, ware-room, cuisine, dining room and sanctuary etc.—all reflect the Sumerian influence. The staircase from the plinth to the first floor, where rooms were constructed for sleeping is also of Sumerian influence.

Thus, from the second to the fifth chapters, I have referred to the remnants of antiquity in the form of deities, customs, mode of residential houses which denote the cultural trends of the different tribes.

THE KINGDOMS IN GOA

a) Earlier dynasties: Bhoja, Konkan Maurya, Badami Chalukya and Sendraka

The sixth and seventh chapter deal with the history of kingdoms to denote their influence on culture. It starts from the inscription that we have from the time of **Bhoja Devaraja**, c. 3rd century A.D. But it does not mean that before that king there was anarchy in other areas like Salcete, Tiswadi and Bardez talukas. The villages were administered by the committees of village-communes. One could appeal to the Mhal-committee (taluka-committee). All resolutions of importance, called '*Nems*', were recorded on a thick, regularly cut plank, and the usual records were recorded on leaves. The necessity of a person with powers of a king was felt for defence purposes when the Konkana Mauryas invaded the vicinity and the people of those talukas voluntarily accepted the kingship of the Bhojas. The head-man of each village was selected by the Gaonkars and was designated as *Bhojaka* whose post was hereditary, and the record-keeper-cum-accountant was named '*Ayuktak*'. He was nominated by the assembly of *gaonkari* whose post was also hereditary. Each village had to pay revenue known as '*Bhojika*', collected by Bhojaka and sent to the crown's treasury under the direct supervision of the *Bhoji Kamatya*. There were some private properties which paid a certain amount to the village-commune annually. This was named '*panga*'.

Next came the **Konkana Mauryas** who occupied Bardez taluka, but they did not bring about any changes in the system of administration.

At about the beginning of the Christian Era, people from Deccan Plateau entered through Rivem village of Sattari taluka under the leadership of a member of the **Sendraka** family, expelled Satarkars (of the Kol tribe) and occupied that area. The expansion of these people subsequently known as 'Marathas' continued in Hemadbarcem and part of *Dicholi* taluka.

The Golden age of Vantu-vallabha

Then **Badami Chalukya** Kiritivarman I subdued the Konkana Mauryas and the area of Goa was put by him under his brother-in-law Vantu-vallabha Senanandaraja—a nominal feudatory of town where he established his capital, constructed an excellent port near *Agshi* (Agaçaim) named Sindhapur (present Goa Velha) in Tiswadi taluka, so that foreign trade flourished. For defence purposes, he had an army as well as a navy, but he also needed horseback troops, so he purchased Arab horses, and tried to acquire some Arab slaves to maintain the horses in Sattari side. These Arab slaves married local girls, and their descendants continue to live in that area. Vantu-vallabha had to cede in favour of his nephew, the son of his brother, the northern portion of Goa. Thus the Sendraka family was divided into two branches, Senior and Junior. The Junior branch also purchased Arab horses and employed Arab Muslim slaves, and thus established an equine centre at *Morji* (Morjim). The Arab Muslim merchants had taken special care in not bringing mares to prevent procreation of the horses locally. But this was overcome by both the branches by importing mares from Kathiawar.

Vantu-vallabha also provided incentives for the construction of temples, and supplied even idols brought from North Karnataka. His period may be considered as the Golden era of Goa.

b) **The later dynasties: Shilaharas and Goan Kadambas**

The Rastrakutas had conquered some areas of South Konkana and Goa where they established the **Shilahars** as their feudatories. They are known in history as the Southern Konkan Shilaharas. Later on came another family of the Shilaharas from Kolhapur who established their sway over North Konkan. They are known in history as the Northern Konkan Shilahars. Both these families enjoyed the friendship and surely marriage ties with both branches of the Sendrakas. So, at a certain time a king of the Southern Shilahari dynasty persuaded a king of the Senior branch of the Sendraka to cede Sindapura as well as the surrounding area in favour of the king of the Junior branch.

Later on, in the 10th century A.D. appeared a new family—the **Kadambas** of North Karnataka, a threat to the Sendraka dynasty. A king of the southern Konkan Shilahar found a weakness in the Senior branch of the Sendrakas and to put a stop to the Kadambas, took control of Chandrapura and the surrounding area. And so the Senior branch of the Sendrakas had to retreat to Sattari. However these efforts were in vain as the Kadambas conquered Chandrapura and held under their sway the surrounding area as well. The destiny of the other branch of the Sendrakas was not very different. At that time, both the Junior branch of the Sendrakas and the Southern Konkan Shilahars were in a vulnerable position, so the Shilahars of the North conquered Sindapura, and in this way they tried to stop the march of the Kadambas, but in vain. The Kadambas conquered Sindapura along with the surrounding area of Tiswadi taluka. But the Kadambas were not well received by the people because from the beginning they were Jains and tried to impose their religion on the people. Some Saraswats migrated and settled in the Konkan and became their enemies over the generations. This is why the Northern Shilahars might have taken Sindapura to avoid their contact with their own kingdom, because at the time the North Konkan Shilahars had also occupied the South Konkan. To overcome the obstacle, the Kadamba kings embraced Hinduism and to convince the people, a Kadamba king accompanied by some citizens from his Goan kingdom made a pilgrimage to Dwaraka, Kolhapur and Gokarna. Shivachitta Kadamba and his queen Kamaladevi gave gifts to the Brahmins. As a result Shivachitta's standing idol was installed at Uguem village of Sanguem taluka, capital of the taluka at that time, in a temple which continues to be worshipped even today like that of Vantuvallabha whose two idols in different styles are under worship at Ponda town—one in a temple and the other in an open place. This type of worship had never existed before in Goa and even in India.

However, the people considered the Kadambas as strangers and their rule was always objected to. Even though at the time of Shashthadeva III, due to the dominant Mayindeva, a Saraswat Brahmin, the people were pacified. But after his death, the people, especially in the defence services, once again became restless. Chandrapura was conquered by the Nabab of Honawar, the king was killed and the queen immolated herself in the waters of the river. Since then, the Kadamba dynasty could never stage a come-back. In about 1352 A.D., the **Bahamani kingdom** rose in Goa. The period from the installation of the Bahamani kingdom and thereafter, witnessed changes in the administrative system, especially in revenue collection.

Treacherous end of later dynasties

Lessons are always learnt from history. To take revenge against his father, a Kadamba prince invited the Nabab of Honavar in 1342 A.D. From that time the Muslim Bahamani kings learnt the way to conquer Goa. Similar treacherous events were witnessed in the history of India. Jayachand Rathod, father-in-law of Prithviraj Chavan, in order to take revenge on his son-in-law, invited Muhamod Ghori who killed Prithviraj Chavan in battle in 1192 A.D. and conquered Ajmir and Delhi and established his Delhi Sultanate. Thus Muslim power as well as religion entered India. Afonso de Albuquerque in 1510 was helped by Mhalu Pay Sar Desai to conquer Goa from the Adilshahi of Vijapur. He believed that Albuquerque would pass the kingdom of Goa to Vijayanagar and so Pay Sar Desai would have a permanent source of revenue.

Pay was then under the impression that the Portuguese wanted only monopoly over commerce and had no interest in maintaining the state under their dominion.

But Albuquerque told him that he had written a letter to this effect to his king in Portugal, and without his permission he could not release Goa from his hands. But he never wrote such a letter to his king, as we can see from the letters recorded and published. Instead, he asked the king to send young boys of high status who might be married to beautiful native girls and he would give them lands which did not belong to anyone but the king. In this way, the domain of Portugal was perpetuated!

ETYMOLOGY OF GOA

In earlier chapters the origin of the place-name of Goa has been traced. Four thousand years ago, Gudea (2143-2124 B.C.), the ruler of the city-state Lagash (alias Sirlapur) of Sumer refers to Goa as Gubi in his records. The Greek geographer Ptolemy (c. 150 B.C.) mentioned Goa as Gouba whose corrupted version in the Greek language was Kouba. The city name Govapuri (present Goa Velha —Goa the Old) appears in the Suta-Samhita. The same designation Govapuri appears in the inscriptions of the Goa Kadambas.

B. D. Satoskar considers the place-name Goa to be derived from the Asami word 'Guwi', meaning areca-nut. This view is not admissible as there is no evidence that the Assamese people ever migrated to Goa. On the other hand, the cultivation of areca-nut as well as of coconuts was introduced first in South India with seeds brought by the people who migrated to South India from South-East Asia. In fact the word Goa is derived from the Mundari word 'Goen-Bab' meaning 'inclined ear of paddy'. The first agriculturists who migrated to Goa were the Kols. And this Kol tribe first introduced in Goa the cultivation of paddy. As the land was virgin, due to the weight of the grain the ears were inclined at one side. From this word Goen-Bab came the contracted word Goe-ba. This later changed to Goen from which arose the word Goen (Marathi—Gove).

GOAN EMIGRATIONS

The Goan people did not limit themselves to Goa. They migrated to South East Asia and propagated Hinduism. There is proof that the Bhojas as well as Saraswat Brahmins of the Kaudinya gotra migrated from Goa, and established their kingdom. The Sarawats first spread to the Coramandel coast of India. They started from Kanchi and established their kingdom in Cambodia in the first century A.D. These Kaudinyas used ships with four sails in their voyage. Each ship was capable of transporting up to seven hundred persons besides one thousand metric tonnes of material. In the fourth century A.D. a person of the Kaudinya family migrated to Funan, and the people voluntarily selected him as their king. They had constant contact with South India. They brought artisans from South India and carved sculptures—a testimony to splendour and prosperity. Obviously they married local girls and their offspring named Khmer came to govern different portions of those areas, forming separate states. These Khmers even went up to South America where they established their kingdom—the present Mexico. In Cambodia, we find stone inscriptions, the ancient ones in Sanskrit and those of the 7th century in Tamil. The names of kings mentioned in these inscriptions are Hindu, for example 'Jayavarma'. It is interesting that the epithet adopted by the Kshatriyas in India, according to Manusmriti, is 'Varma'.

After the domain of Muslim rulers the people were converted; however, they celebrated the rituals as well as worshipped Hindu gods. The male offspring wore the sacred thread. The marriage rituals also were celebrated, first in the Hindu form. At the time of monarchy, the Sultans were coronated by first performing the 'Abhisheka'.

Shri Parashurama started his expedition to South India in about 2,400 B.C. only with the aim of putting into practice 'Krinvanto Vishvam Aryam', 'civilise all mankind', and his successors continued this not only in India but also outside in South East Asia and South America, trying to develop brotherhood and peace wherever they went, working like missionaries, following the teachings of Kathopanishada.

THE CULTURAL HERITAGE OF SETTLERS AND RULLERS OF GOA

a) Garments—from bark to cotton

In India, mankind stepped out of caverns as habitats in about 10,000 B.C. There was absolute need for garments and the material at hand was the leather of game or of dead animals like elephants, deer, buffalo, bulls, as well as tigers. Probably strips of leather were used for sewing. After thousands of years, or say about 6,000 B.C., the people turned to the use of the inner bark of trees. They tried and were capable of making thread. They had found spontaneously growing silk-cotton trees.

The garments of the Kols, Mundaris and Kharwis were very simple. The male person of those tribes used only a loin-cloth worn in different fashion according to their caste. It was made of cotton or sometimes of silk, tied around the waist and used by Mhars and shoe-makers. The head-dress was of a drape of cotton or, rarely, of silk. The female folk of the Kol tribe wore their garments up to the knees. The Kalvants were dressed without the rear padded portion of a sari (*kas* in Konkani), and that portion varied from caste to caste. They never used a bodice. Women of other castes wore saris covering their back and breasts fully. In ancient times, a Kalavant used a skirt and bodice—Sumerian type of garments. Observe the photo of the deity discovered in the excavation at *Madgaon*, named Paturdey—as set down in the Portuguese records—meaning the deity of the Paddyes. Hair-dressing among women was in various styles and depended on the caste. Among the Kols the legend of Bali is narrated through song. It relates to the advent of Sumerians in that area on the river bank. All this has been described and discussed in Chapter 4.

In Goa, besides the garments, the people also needed protection from rains. So along with the making of garments of leather, the people prepared a shelter from sheets of leaves of the jungle-palm tree called *Bhillamad*. This shelter or 'rain-coat' was named *Santli* in the Konkani language. The original specimen was simple, without a handle, and later on it was made with a handle and both these kinds were under use 50 years ago. Even now the former specimen is in use in villages of Goa in the rainy season. Generally, bakers in villages use it on their distribution rounds.

The Sumerians came and settled in Goa in 2,000 B.C. In Sumer, they had a well developed industry in making cloth which was their main product of external commerce but the material used was wool. Here wool was not available and they never knew of the existence of cotton. Garments were a priority. So, very soon they started making cloth. Their weaving machinery was of an advanced type, so, we may say that the Sumerians introduced the art of weaving in Goa for the first time. With the help of the same weaving machinery they also made in Goa, again for the first time, coarse blankets from animal hair for protection from the rains. When external commerce started with the Deccan plateau the industry of blankets was abandoned, but cotton cloth continued at least for some centuries and later on this industry was limited to the making of thread and weaving. In about 1906, an Englishman obtained government land situated at Varquinim village of Hemarbarcem in Sanguem taluka and turned it into a large scale cotton-tree plantation. The land was therefore named *Capshini-mol.* After ten years the Englishman went into a loss, as he could not withstand the competition in the market and abandoned the land. I had seen the existence of cotton-trees at that time, in 1940, and even today one finds such trees growing spontaneously in Goa.

b) Shelters—from caves to clay bricks

Primitive shelter for humankind was the natural cave. Then man left the caves and settled in the plains in the open air. Families, once isolated in the caverns, now joined others in the plains. They formed clans, with the result that they remained in groups searching jointly for edible roots, fruits, game and fish. At the time those in the caverns had studied and improved the art of making implements.

The intensity of the rains had diminished. Rustic cottages were built with bamboo, twig and grass. These constructions were small and quasi-round. The walls were made of bamboo and twigs, covered with grass. The ceiling was also made of bamboos laid in criss-cross fashion, sloping in all directions. Similar cottages are found even today in Brazil, South America, in the region named Curizevo, Alto Xingus. These were the residential huts of Red Indians named Meinacus. They had no idea that the Portuguese had occupied and Christianized the people around them. The existence of this village was recognized when the Brazilian government resolved to map the area by aerial photography. Humankind continued in this form for five centuries [122].

The pastoral tribe knew how to domesticate buffaloes and goats. They continued to live in cottages but they were now building walls of stone and mud. Sometimes the walls were made of plants named 'karvam', a plant with an odour that kept away white-ants. These plants were plastered on both sides with clay.

After about 1,500 years or say, in about 2,500 B.C. a wave of the Aryan-Bhargavas and Angirasas appeared and settled in Goa, but they did not alter the construction of huts.

In about 2,000 B.C. the Sumerians came from Sumer, but no changes were brought about in the construction of huts. However, they improved on the making of iron, converting it to pig iron, a more solid product. It was utilized for shaping plough shares of the wooden plough, axes, hoes and other implements of black stone like daggers. They introduced a type of house with a middle rectangular court-yard named 'Rajangan', flanked on all four sides by open passages. These houses also had a first floor with wooden stairs at one corner of the passage. However, the walls were built of dressed stone fixed with and plastered on both faces with clay. Generally, like in Sumer, a big pot with sweet water was permanently maintained at the entrance of the house, according to the custom that people should enter the house only after washing their feet. In Savoi-Verem village, in the area of 'Silcum-Inam Thican', I found a big pit of about 1.5 metres depth and one metre in diameter dug in laterite, which was probably maintained for this kind of use.

In the 6th century A.D., in the time of Vantudeva of the Sendraka family, regularly cut laterite stones were used in the construction of temples. Rounded black stone pillars sustained the weight of the ceiling. We have laterite plinths in the temple of Mhalsa at *Pornem-Mhaddol* at Verna village, Salcete taluka, the Mahamaya temple at Nundem of Sanguem and a temple without any shrine, but probably of Uma-Mahesha, at Colomba in Quepem taluka.

At the time of the Kadambas, or say in about 1,000 A.D., the temple of Basaweshvara was constructed with clay-bricks while the main structure, columns and ceiling were made of timber. The ceiling was constructed with timber planks fixed with nails of copper on the timber rafter, and sloping in all directions for drainage of rain waters. It was covered with small clay-bricks, the joints being covered with semi-tubular pieces made also of clay and covered with grass or palm-leaves. Every year after the rainy season, the grass and palm leaves were removed. This is the reason why, within a day, about three hundred temples could be set on fire at the time of the advent of the Christian missionaries. The art of making mortar and plaster with lime prepared by burning marine shells as well as the production of country tiles was introduced by the Portuguese in Goa.

c) Material improvements

The development of the irrigation system made very good progress due to the advent of the Havig Brahmins during the time of the Sendrakas and Kadambas. Architecture also improved, Mud-bricks were used as we see in the temple of Basaweshwar of Chandor. The most important evidence in this regard is the temple of Shri Mahadev at Tamdi Surla, not only in terms of its architecture but also its sculpture. However, it is not proved who built that temple and when.

The Havig Brahmin Kanadeva introduced a running style of writing and named it Kanadevi or Goe-Kandi script. Another running style in Devanagari named the 'Modi script' was introduced by Saraswat merchants of Goa, and Hemadpanta, the Chief Minister of the Yadavas of Devgiri adopted it as the official script for correspondence. It was also adopted by the Muslim Adilshahi kings for passing titles and orders in Goa.

Like the present university, in the Kadamba period, an institution of learning was established and was designated as Brahmapuri. It was established at Govapuri (present Goa-Velha) with all the facilities for higher education and development of literature, science, medicine and astrology. It is remarkable that the institution was installed by a private person at his own expense.

There are still some influences of the time of the Kadambas on Goan society. They introduced Jainism which declined later, but some customs continued. For example, the word "Shivrak", was derived from the word "'Shravaka", named after a Jain monk for his vegetarian diet.

d) Religion—from primitive paganism to temple worship

i) Religion of the Mhars and the pastoral tribe

The religion of the **Mhars** consisted of annual worship named 'Mhal' and the worship of the spirits of their ancestors. The pastoral tribe, which settled next, worshipped male and female elements. They worshipped the banana tree in the form of its sprout—'*Makho*', and also the mother goddess in the form of a vulva. The worship of ancestors is noticed from the time of Neanderthal man, between forty to twenty thousand years ago, and the worship of the mother-goddess is noticed in the primitive people of the ancient world in the form of a headless nude woman. This is represented by a clay figurine in Tepe Sarab, Jericho, North Iran, of about 6,500 B.C. Similarly, a clay figurine named Lajja-Gouri was found in the Deccan plateau. Perhaps more important is the carving of a vulva found on a rock in Kerala where matrilocal and matrilineal people lived. This shows a link between the pastoral tribe and the people who came from that side.

ii) Religion of the Asuras

The principal god of the Asuras was Sing-Bonga, Sun, a benevolent god and *Gana-Rouduro* (destroyer of animals) and *Khaman-Rouduro* (destroyer of human kind), malevolent semi-gods and spirits, who were worshipped by sacrificing hens. Sing-Bonga was generally worshipped by looking at the Sun in the early morning, muttering some words, while the other two semi-gods received the sacrifice of hens and cocks of colours other than white. Besides these, they also had goddesses without a symbol, named Nagiera and Bindiera, both sisters and virgins. They were worshipped like the Sing-Bonga and the other two semi-gods, and they were considered as malevolent spirits living near ponds.

At the temple of Nagesh at Bandodem village, Nagiera was supposed to exist near the tank and it was considered that she lived there as a serpent. Lest people should drink water from that tank, it was maintained without purifying it. The name of the village Bandodem was derived from the word Bindiera, but we do not know the whereabouts of the pond where she was considered to be living. The superstition of the worship of the cobra was probably derived from this concept. Besides *Gana-Rouduro* and *Khaman-Rouduro* at Savoi-Verem, those semi-gods were esstablished in the form of two stones at Zormem village, Sattari taluka and they are considered now as gods of Hebars (Shabars). The same gods also existed on the top of the hill of Chandranath of Paroda and were sublimated in the time of the Bhojas as Chandreshwar and Bhutnath. Both are in stone form and the latter is considered to be the head of the servants— Bhairavas—of the former Shiva.

iii) Religion of the Kols

Next appeared the Kols. They worshipped the anthill which later on the Aryans named as 'Bhumika' (child of Earth) or *Santer* which is the corruption of the Sanskrit word 'Santara' meaning 'with holes', while in the Mundari language the word is 'ro-en', again meaning 'with holes'. In Chota Nagpur from where they came, the anthill was also worshipped but it was of secondary value, its worship being limited to spreading leaves on anthills existing in the forest. The forest grove was always maintained intact, without cutting, which in Sattari and the adjacent area is named '*Rae*' while in the Astagrahar division of Sanguem taluka it is known as '*Panna*'. In Rivem village of Sattari taluka, there once existed the outline of a female figure up to the knees, carved on an oval and larger basaltic schist. The figure was named '*Shambradevi*' and was worshipped by the Kols but that slab was destroyed by Portuguese soldiers. The Kols also worshipped a jungle-tree known as '*Kel*' which has aerial roots, the symbol of opulence.

There was a peculiar custom whereby in fulfilment of a vow, a person hung himself by an iron hook, perforating the skin of his neck. This custom which was in vogue at Cundaim village was introduced by the Asura tribe and was prohibited by the order of the Governor General dated December 6, 1844. However, at *Painguin* (Poinguinim) village, *Kankon* (Canacona) taluka, during '*Gadeanchi-jatra*', celebrated triennally, some members of a family tie themselves on the surface of a large wooden wheel which is rotated violently on an axis till a member of the Gaonkar of the first rank orders otherwise. That family, for the performance of this ritual, was given a rice-field, kept with them through the generations.

iv) Religion of the first wave of Aryans

The Aryans of the first wave continued their custom of worship of the holy fire—*homma*—and did not interfere in the rituals of the primitive settlers.

v) Religion of the Sumerians

Then appeared the Sumerians who came with their deities. At Savoi-Verem of Ponda taluka I had seen an idol of the god Anu. They worshipped this god as well as the goddess Inanna, a goddess in nude form though with a short pantaloon (see ill. 19 on page 161 ch. 4). While the worship of gods of other tribes was performed in the open air, the Sumerians worshipped their gods installed in temples, which had, at the frontal left corner, a tank of water of which was used to wash the feet before entering the temple. [65]

vi) Impact of the second wave of Aryans

Next, in about 700 B.C., the second wave of Aryans emerged with the non-Aryans. The Vaishya clan established itself in *Chodan* (Chorão) island of Tiswadi taluka. Before them, the Padye Bhats-Sumerians of the priesthood had already settled there. As a result of the contact, they established the temple of their hero 'Devaki-Krishna'. It was built of clay and worship was performed in the Sumerian style but without sacrifices of any kind. We may consider this temple as the first symbol of Hinduism established in Goa. Next comes the temple of Mhalsa at Verna, Salcete taluka, where worship was an open air affair in a flat place—mal—since she was 'Malavya', goddess of the open air. During the time of Vantudeva, in the 6th century A.D., the temple of god Anu was re-established but the idol of Anu was replaced by an idol of Seshashayi-Vishnu (Ananta), made and transported from the South of Goa. But Inanna could not be transformed into a Hindu deity, hence its bust, moulded of silver, was maintained separately in the temple of Ananta. It was worshipped separately at the time of the great festival. The construction of temples as well as the worship of Hindu deities in Sumerian style started from that time onwards. Vantudeva, besides helping in establishing the temple of Anu, had six idols of the god Brahma made, and established them in different places, as mentioned before—more or less on the boundaries of his domain. Besides this, he established the idols of Santer, Kelbai (in the form of Gaja-Laxmi) and Brahmani at Naneli village of Sattari taluka.

vii) Religion during the Bhoja kingdom

During the times of the Bhojas, in about the third century A.D., Buddhist monks had established themselves at Colvale of Bardez and Lamgaon of Bicholim taluka, but their religion did not spread throughout Goa. Next, Shaivism was propagated during which period Uma-Mahesha idols were set up at Harvalem of Bicholim taluka, Colamba in Quepem taluka as well as at Chandranath Parvat, Salcete taluka. The Kadambas brought Jainism and we find that a merchant established a Jain Basti in a village of Astagrahar division in Sanguem taluka with an image of Jain Thirtakar on the top of a hill of the same village. In Chandor village, the capital of the Kadambas, a Jain Basti was also established—known at present as '*Jainacho Math*'. At this place an idol of Naganath (an image with a serpent in the left hand) was found. This is referred to in the Portuguese records of temples destroyed by them as Nagunata.

Meanwhile, a sect of Sidhas also appeared in Goa, but the dating of their arrival is not known. It was a sect which believed in the ascetic way of life. It was not a religion proper, but purely an individual way of life. About 1,000 A.D., the Natha sect, established by Gorakhnath, made its appearance and we find the evidence in the form of Mallinath now worshipped at Marcela and Chouranganath at Hadphadem (Arpora) of Bardez taluka. The saint Soiroba Ambiye was of that sect. The sect also spread to Sawantwadi. A separate branch of the same sect were the '*Mathkars*' who are linked to the worship of Sidhas.

viii) Influence of Sumerian system of worship on Hinduism

The Sumerian system of worship influenced Hinduism to a great deal. The temples were styled with the garbha-griha (womb form) where the deities were put. There were *Bhavnis*, unmarried women with their brothers known as '*Deulis*', who were engaged in the cleaning of vessels and lighting of torches respectively. Now singing and dancing girls like the '*Salmes*' of the Sumerians were introduced in the service of the temple. They were also unmarried women named '*kalavantans*'. Their brothers were known as *Ganas*. They were in charge of playing harps—a musical instrument of Sumerian origin—besides the *Ghumata, Mrudangas, Shenai, Sura* and *Tabla*, which were of Indian origin. From the pastoral tribe some families went their divergent way. Some families adopted the profession of *Bhavins*, others of *Kalavantas*. Some became *Chedvans* with their brothers named *Bandes* and both were bonded to the families of their lords. The remaining stock was of the Naik caste, involved in agricultural work as tenants but were not considered as Mundkars. The deities of this pastoral tribe, *Mokho* and *Baukadevi* were styled in the human form. Probably '*Mokho*' was a transformed form of Betal or say, Bel talal, the fighter deity representing virility in the Sumerian style and Baukadevi in nude form substituting the symbolic form of vulva. The latter was worshipped by the village *Bhavina* as the deity of her family. The Sumerians of Savoi-Verem, however, while symbolizing the monument of the sepulchre of the dead Ne-an, the high priestess who had accompanied the people when they came from Sumer, adopted the symbol of the vulva with a niche prepared of slabs of basaltic schist since they had no symbol in their religion to symbolise such a monument. They named it '*Mhatari*', meaning 'the old woman'. After the death of Ne-an, the high priestess of god Anu, that practice was discontinued as the woman had to be of the Padye family, and would have to stay unmarried, contact with man being punishable by death. This practice was rejected vehemently by the Aryans with whom they had by now marriage links. However '*salmes*', girls of other castes, were admitted to the temple as dancing and singing girls.

ROOTS OF GOAN FOLK-ART

Entertainment started in Goa from the time of the settlement of the Asuras. They danced to the beat of the drum like the *Ghumat* on festival days. In the month of Poush, there was a festival of *Mage Parab*, when the men and women danced together to the rhythm of the *Ghumat*, and the rhythms were various, notations of which are given in the Encyclopedia Mundarica by Haffman. But in Goa this festival was celebrated only by women-folk in the month of Poush. The festival of *Sigmo* is celebrated in the month of Poush in Savoi-Verem village together with *Dhalo*, while in other villages the *Dhalo* is played in the month of Poush without the accompaniment of other musical instruments. The festival of *Sigmo* is celebrated in the month of Falgun by the menfolk accompanied by the *Dhol* and *Ghumat*.

This *Dhalo* programme lasts for a week and dancing takes place at night. The nights are cold and during the night, after dinner in their house, the women gather in an open place known as 'manda'. An old woman sings a song and others repeat it with certain movements of their body, moving the body in front as well as at the rear like a flower which moves with the breeze. In Konkani this is called *dholap*, from which is derived the designation 'Dhalo'. During these dances, sometimes some women fall motionless and people say that the spirit of Nagiera and Bridiera had possessed their body. These women are known as 'Rambha'. After the dance, the old woman sprays water on the women to revive them.

At the end of the dancing period, in the early morning, the next day, an old woman selects a young daughter-in-law among the gathered women and enacts a hunting scene. The young woman falls down and the old woman simulates acts of cutting and of offering different parts of the body, invoking at each time the name of the village god and goddess and sometimes of the god linga also. The ritual is named 'savaj-marap', meaning hunting of game, and only after the performance of this ritual, does the 'Dhalo' festival end.

In ancient times, among the Kols and Mundari there were similar rituals. On the last day they hunted for game and the lard of the hunted animal was offered to the different village-deities and godlinks. Now this last ritual is performed by women-folk in a symbolic form. In Sattari taluka, in the absence of Asuras, Kols or Mundaris (the Marathi people having expelled them from that taluka) there is no such festival of *Dhalo*. However the Gaonkars of Zarmem village perform such rituals, arranging a raid named 'Devachi-Bhoundi'. The lard of the game caught is offered to all the deities, except to Brahmani, because they consider it to be the deity of the Brahmin caste.

The Sumerians brought the harp with them (*sarangi*) and the game called 'tabulfalem'. A game, 'lion and lambs' was introduced by them after renaming it representatively as 'tiger and goats'. The Aryans of the second wave brought with them the game of 'Dhoota', known in Goa as 'Pagam'.

Appendix

List of names of villages of Goa district similar to those of Ratnagiri and Kolaba districts (Southern and Northern Konkans respectively). Abreviations of the names of Talukas are indicated at the end of the list.

S. No.	Goa Districts	Ratnagiri District	Kolaba District
1.	Odli Sl.	Adeli, VGR	
2.	Ambed, St.	Ambadganv, SWT	
		Ambadve, MDG	
		Ambadpal, KDL	
		Ambadve, MDG	
3.	Ambali, St.	Ambere Budruk, CLN	
4.	Ambeli, St.	Ambere Khurd, Ghar	
		Ambeli, SWT	
		Amberi, MMVN	
		Amber, KDL	
5.	Assolda, Q	Asolde, KVL	
	Asode, St.	Asode, LNG	
6.	Asore, St.	Asore, GHR	
7.	Bombode, St.	Bombarde Taraf	
		Kalasuli, KDL	
8.	Bamboli, T.	Bambouli Tarf	
		Haveli, KDL	
9.	Tivere, Po.	Tivare,	Tivare, Krt.
		Tivare, RJP	Tivare, Krt.
		Tivare, CLN	Tivare, Sgd.
		Tivare, Tarf	
		Devale, SGR	
		Tivare Chera	
		Prachitgad, SGR	
		Babtievre DPL	
		Kond Tivre, RJP.	
10.	Bandivade, Po.	Bandivade, RJP	
		Bandivade Budruk, MVN	
		Bandivade Khurad, MVN	
11.	Barde D.	Bharate (hamlet) RJP	
12.	Borda (hamlet) St.		
13.	Bhironde, St.	Bhirvande, KVL	
14.	Bhoma, Po.	Bhoma, CLN	Bhoma, Urn.
15.	Bhoma Sg.		

S. No.	Goa Districts	Ratnagiri District	Kolaba District
16.	Bombade (hamlet) St.	Bhombadi, DPL	
17.	Bori, Po.	Borivali, LNJ	Bori Pn.
			Bori Budruk, Urn.
		Borivali, DPL	Bori Khurd, Urn.
			Borivali, Krt.
18.	Chikli, Mor.	Chikhali, GHR.	Chikhli, Alg.
19.	Chikhli, B.	Chikhli, SGR	Chikhli, Pld.
			Chikhli, Bhoma Urn.
20.	Dhavkond, Sg.	Davakhol, SGR	
21.	Dhavli (hamlet), Po.	Davali, DPL.	
22.	Deusa, Mor.	Devasu, SWT	
23.	Dharmapur, Sl.	Dhamapur, MVN	
		Dhamapur, Tarf	
		Devrukh, SGR	
		Dhamapur Tarf, SGR	
	Dighi, K.		
24.	Dighi mountain Sg.	Dighi, MDG	
25.	Dingane, St.	Dingane, SWT	
26.	Dongar, Sg.	Dongar, RJP	
		Dongarpal, SWT	
27.	Durgavadi T	Durgavadi, MDG	
28.	Gavane, St.	Gavane, DGD	Gavhana, Pnl.
29.	Gavane (hamlet) Po.	Gavane, LNJ	
30.	Verne, Sl.		
31.	Verne, B.	Harnai, DPL	
32.	Juve, T.	Juve Rajapur, DJP	
		Juve, RTN	
33.	Kumarjuve, T.	Juva-Koil, MVN	
34.	Juve, B.	Juva, Anjanach, MVN	
		Juva Dhanaji, MVN	
35.	Khandepar, Po.		Kandalganv
36.	Khandoli, B.	Kanduli, KDL	Khandale, Alg.
37.	Khandole, Po.		Khandepale, Mgn.
38.	Khorjuve, B.	Karjuve, SGR	
39.	Karambali, T.	Karambeli, SGR	Karambali, Klr.
40.	Karambali (Brahma) St.	Karambele Tarf	Karambeli
		Devle, SGR	Chatishi, Pn.
			Karambeli Tarf
			Taloja, Pnl.
41.	Karambali Budruk St.		Karambali Buduruk Mgn.
			Karambali Khurd, Mgn.
			Karambali Tarf -
			-Boreti, Klr.

S. No.	Goa Districts	Ratnagiri District	Kolaba District
42.	Karanzol, St.	Karanjali, DPL	
43.	Karanzol		
44.	Karanzalem hamlet, Po.		
45.	Karanzalem hamlet, T.		
46.	Kamurli, Pn.		Karmeli Tarf Vaje, Pnl
			Kamarli, Arg.
			Kamarli, Pn.
47.	Kava, St.	Kavadoli, DPL	
48.	Kavale hamlet Po.		
49.	Kelsai, St.	Kelshi, DPL	Kelshi, Mgn.
	Kelsai, St.	Kelshi, Mor.	
50.	Kelshi (Shudra) St.		
51.	Kelavade, St.	Kelavade, RJP	
52.	Khadpal, D.	Khadpoli CLN	
53.	Khadpal, K.		
54.	Karangini, Sg.	Khinagini, RJP	
55.	Kodli, Sg.	Kodavali, RJP	
		Kudli, GHR	Kudli, RH.
56.	Kule, Sg.	Kule, SGR	
57.	Kolamba Sg.	Kolamba, RJP	
58.	Kule, Sg.	Kule, SGR	
59.	Kumarkhana, Sg.	Kumbharkhani Budruk, SGR	
60.	Kumarkhana, St.	Dumbharkhani Khurd, SGR	
61.	Kudne, D.	Kurne, LNJ	
62.	Maulinge, D.	Mahalunge, DPL	
63.	Maulinge, St.	Maulange, KD.	Mahalunga Pn
		Maulange, SGR	Mahalunge, Rh
64.	Maulinge, Sg.	Mahalunge, DGD	Mahalunge Budruk Mrd.
65.	Maina, Q.	Maina, KVL	Mahalung Khurd Mrg.
66.	Makazana, SP.	Makhanjan, SGR	Mahalunge, Pnl.
67.	Morle, St.	Mirle, KD.	
68.	Nurdi (hamlet) D.	Murdi, DPL	
69.	Nakari, Q.	Nakhare, RTN	
70.	Nagave, B.	Nagave, KVL	
71.	Nagave Sl.	Niveli, RJP	
72.	Neturli, Sg.	Netarde, SWT	
73.	Nevare (Vodle) T.	Nevare, RTN	
		Niven Budruk, SGR	

S. No.	Goa Districts	Ratnagiri District	Kolaba District
74.	Neure (Dhakti) T.		
75.	Nhaveli, Sl.	Nhaveli, SWT	
76.	Naveli, D.		
77.	Nuve, Sl.	Nuve, KD.	
		Nuve, Khurd SGR	
78.	Onvolie, St.	Ovaliye, SWT.	Ovale Mhd.
		Ovaliye, MVN.	Ovale, Pnl.
79.	Ozari, Pn.	Ozar, RJP.	
		Vazare, SWT	
		Ozare, Budruk, SGR	
		Ozare, Khurd, SGR.	
80.	Pale, Po.	Pali, GHR	Pali, Sgd.,
		Pal SWT.	Pale Mhd.,
		Pali, RTN.	Pale Urn.,
			Pale Khura, Rh.,
			Pale Tarf Ashtami,
			Rh., Pali Budruk, Klr.
81.	Pali, St.	Pal. KD.	Pali Budruk, Pnl.
		Pali, CLN.	Pali Devad, Pnl.,
			Pali Khurd Klr.
82.	Palie, Pn.	Palye, SWT	Pali Khurd, Pnl.
			Pali Tarf Kothal
			Khalati, Krt.,
			Pali Tarf Varedi,
			Krt., Pali Tarf
			Vasare, Krt.
83.	Phonda, Po.	Phonda, KVL.	
84.	Pirna, B.	Piranadavane, SGR.	
85.	Pomurpe, B.	Pomurle, BGD.	
86.	Parye, St.	Purye Taraf Devle, SGR	
		Purye Tarf Savarde, SGR.	
87.	Sankhli, D.	Sakhalkond, SGR.	
		Sakhloi, DPL.	
88.	Sancorde, Sg.	Sankurde, DPL.	
89.	Salgaon, B.	Salgaon, Kdl.	
90.	Sange, Sg.	Sangve, KVL	
		Sangve, SGR	
91.	Satre, St.	Santhare, RTN	
92.	Savarde, Sg.	Savarde, CLN	Savarde, Svn.
93.	Savarde, St.	Sharval, KD.	
		Shirval, SWT.	
94.	Shirvoi, Q.	Shiraval, KVL.	

S. No.	Goa Districts	Ratnagiri District	Kolaba District
95.	Shelpe, Sg.	Sherpe, KVL.	
96.	Shelap Budruco, St.		
97.	Shelap Curd, Sg.		
98.	Sirsode, St.	Sirsadi, DPL.	
99.	Sirvoi, Q	Shiravali, LNJ.	Shiravane, DPL.
	Sarvona, D.		
	Sigone, Sg.		
	Sigone, St.		
100.	Shirgaon, B.	Shirganv, KD.	Shirganv, Mhd.
		Shirganv, CLN	Shirganv, Mn.
		Shirganv, DGD.	
103.	Sirali, St.	Shiral, CLN.	
104.	Shirode, Po.	Shiravade, MLV	
		Shiroda, VGR	
105.	Soldade, Sl.	Solivade, RJP.	
106.	Sonal, Sg.	Sonaval, SWT.	
107.	Sonal, St.	Sonaval, DPL.	
108.	Surla, St.	Surla, GHR.	
		Surle, MDG	
109.	Talgaon, T.	Taleganv, RJP.	
		Taleganv, MLV.	
		Talganv, RJP.	
		Talganv, MLV.	
110.	Talvadi, Q.	Talvade, KVL.	
		Talvade, SWT	
		Talvade, LNJ.	
		Talvade, RJP.	
		Talvade, CLN.	
		Talavali, GHR.	Talavali Tarf-
111.	Talavali, P.		-Ghosale, Rh.
			Talavali Tarf.-
			-Khadale, Alg.
			Talsuli Tarf.
			-Umate, Alg.
112.	Tambadi, Sg.	Tambadi, SGR	Tambadi, Mgn.
			Tambadi, Rh.
113.	Usgaon, P.	Usganv, SGR.	
		Usaganv, DPL	
114.	Vadavali, D.	Vadavali, DPL	
		Vadavali, MDG.	

357

S. No.	Goa Districts	Ratnagiri District	Kolaba District
115.	Vade, Sg.	Vade, DGD.	
116.	Vadi, P.	Vadi Adhishthi, SGR.	
		Vadi Beladar, KD.	
		Vadi Khurd, RJP.	
		Vadi Limbu, LNJ.	
		Vadi Malde, KD.	
		Vadi Bid, KD.	
		Vadi Jaitapur, KD.	
		Vadi Phanasvadi, SWT	
		Vadi, KDL.	
117.	Vagheri (mountain) St.	Vagherim, KVL.	
118.	Vana, St.	Vanamule, LNJ.	
119.	Vaingini, D.	Vayangane, SGR.	
		Vayangani, RTN.	
		Vayangani, KVL.	
		Vayangani, MLV.	
120.	Velus, St.	Velas, MDG.	Velas, Qvn.
121.	Verle, B.	Verle, SWT	
122.	Verle, Sg.		
123.	Virdi, D.	Virdi, SWT.	
124.	Adosi, T.	Asoshi, Klr.	Ajosi, Klr.
			Andosi, Alg.
125.	Adulsha (hamlet) Sg.		Adulshe, Sgd.
126.	Agarvado, Pn.		Agarvada, Mslr.
127.	Agshi, T.		Akshi, Alg.
128.	Ambeli, Sl.		Ambivali, Kh.
			Ambeli, Mgn.
			Ambi Prudruk, Krt.
			Ambivali Khurta Krt.
			Ambivali Botati Klr.
			Ambivali Tarf.
			Kothal Khalati Krt.
			Ambole Sgd.
			Amboli, Mrd.
129.	Hanjuna, B.		Anjaruna, Klr.
130.	Hanjune, St.		
131.	Daboli (hamlet) Mor.		Dabhal, Mhd.
132.	Dongri, P.		
133.	Dongri, T.		Dongari, Urn
			Dongari, Mrd.
134.	Gaondongri, K.		
135.	Gandavali, T.		Gana Tarf

S. No.	Goa Districts	Ratnagiri District	Kolaba District
136.	Gana (hamlet), Po.		Shigaou, Alg.
			Gana Tarf
137.	Girvade, B.		Parthur, Alg.
138.	Hivare Budoruk, St.		Girvale, Pnl.
139.	Hivare Khurd, St.		Havare, Pld.
140.	Jambauli, Sg.		
			Jambivali, Krt.
			Jambivali, Pnl.
			Jambivali Tarf
			Chatishi Klr.
141.	Khodpi, St.		Khadpi, Pld.
142.	Khandepar, P.		Khandpale, Mgn.
143.	Korde, Q.		Khardi, Pld.
144.	Mulgaon, D.		Mulganv, Krt.
			Mulganv, Klr
			Mulganv, Khurd Klr.
145.	Nagzar, Pn.		Nagzari, Pld
146.	Naneli, St.		Nanavali, Svn.
			Nanavali, Sgd.
			Nanaevali, Klr.
147.	Nerul, B.		Neral, Krt.
148.	Padelist, St.		
149.	Padle, Pn.		
150.	Salauli, Sg.		Salav, Mrd.
151.	Shigone, St.		Shingnavat, Pn.
152.	Shigone, Sg.		
153.	Shirsai, B.		
154.	Shirdona, T.		Shirdhona, Pnl.
155.	Shiroli, St.		Shiravali, Pnl.
			Shiravali, Rlr.
			Shiravali Tarf
			Boreti, Klr.
			Shiravali Tarf
			Chateshi, Klr.
			Chiravali Tarf
			Nizampur, Mgn.
156.	Tamboshe, Pn.		Tambas, Krt.
157.	Tudou, Sg.		Tudal, Alg.
158.	Tudou, Sg.		Tudil, Mhd.
159.	Wadavali, D.		Vadavali, Krt.
			Vadavali, Khd.
			Vadavali, Mgn.
			Vadavali, Sgn.

S. No.	Goa Districts	Ratnagiri District	Kolaba District
160.	Velge, St.		Valanga, Klr.
161.	Valpai, Sl		Valavali, Alg.
			Vadavali, Sgn.
162.	Virode, Sl.		Varande, Alg.
163.	Verne, Sl.		Varane, Krt.
164.	Kansarvarne, Pn.		
165.	Varna, Q		Vashi, Pn
166.	Vanshi, T.		Vashi, R
			Vashi Havale, Mgn
			Vashi Mahaganv, Mgn
167.	Panvel, T.		Panvel, Pnl

Abbreviations of names of Talukas

Goa District : Pn - Pednem; B. - Bardez; D - Dicholi (Bicholim);
St. - Sattari; T. - Tiswadi; Mor. - Mormugaon;
Sl. - Salcete; Po. Ponda; Q. - Quepem;
Sg.- Sangem; and K. - Kankon.

Ratnagiri District : CLN - Chiplun; DPL. - Dapoli; DGD. - Devgad;
GHR. - Guhagar; KVL. - Kankavali; KD. - Khed;
KDL. - Kudal; LNL. - Lange; MVN. - Malvan;
MDG - Mandangad; RJP. - Rajapuri;
RTN. - Ratnagiri;
SGR. - Sangameshwar; SWT. - Sawantavadi;
VGR. Vengurla.

Kolaba District : Alg. - Alibag; Krt. - Karjat; Klr. - Khalapur; Mhd. - Mahad;
Mgn. - Mangaon; Msl. - Mhasla; Pnl.-Panvel;
Urn. - Urana.

Index

A

Achugi (King) of Goa, 268
Adityaraja - copper plate, 213, 214
Agri, 92
  mit agri, 92, 95
Agriculture (cumeri),41
Aiyapa 259, 263
Aiyapa (S. Konkan Shilaharas), 262, 263
Albuquerque, Afonso de,153, 301, 341
Allaudin, 272
Altinho cave, 15, 27
Amareshvara Sarvatantraddhikrita, 214
Ambeacho-Gor (Surla),13, 14, 17 ,18, 335
Ancient races & tribes, 32-34
Area (of Goa), 2
Aryans (first wave)
  arrival of, 11
  clothes, food, housing 174, 177
  first settlements in India, 172
  land system, 175
  mhal administration, 174
  rigvedic culture, 176, 199, 348
  village administration, 174
Aryans (second wave)
  administration, 177-179
  arrival of, 168
  culture, 191
  culture synthesis with sumerians, 348
  dating, 181
  development, 199
  dress, 199
  housing, 199
  religion, 169, 199
  science, 188
Asamkita Hirregutte, 215
Asankitavarman, 217, 228-230
Askin-Siddha, 39, 238, 292
Asura, 58-60, 91-99, 100, 336
Australoid, 32, 50, 81
Avasara II, son of Adityavarman, 259, 263-265

B

Balichi-Katha, 71, 92, 138
Balipratipada, 81
Banavasi, 5, 10, 315
Barazan (Place of village administration), 100-105
Bardez (origin), 233
Batik, 88
Bhagat, 79, 85
Bandari, Satwant, 187
Bharvankar, 94-96
Bhatikar clan (of Gavde), 69
Bhatta-Prabhu eykya-prakaran, 212
Bhavin, 84-88, 146
Bhill tribe, 73, 76
Bhima (S. Konkan Shilaharas), 265 304, 309
Bhimabhupala, 267-269
Bhojika, 205, 206, 211
Bhojikamatya (Revenue collector), 206, 211, 213
Bori (headquater of Antruz), 212
Brahmapuri (ancient school), 314, 315
Buddhism, 229
  decline of, 282
  idols, 282
Casts, 44-47, 70, 91
Chaddes, 178, 181, 202
Chalybes, 42
Chandor, 206, 271
Chandra-chuda, 206-207
Chandrapura, 247, 272
Chandraura, 206, 207
Chandravadi, 182, 194
Chandeshwar, 218, 294
Chandra-Ura, 55
Chardo, 67, 68
Chedo, 87
Chedum, 87
Copper plates and inscriptions, agra (of Kapardivarma), 222

Index of The Photographs

Photo No.	Description	Page

References

1. Sarkar, H. *Monuments of Kerala.* New Delhi: Archaeological Survey of India, 1973.

2. Mirashi, V. V. *Satavahana ani Pashchimi Kshatrapa: Yancha Itihas ani Koriv Lekha* [marathi]. Mumbai: Maharashtra State Board for Literature and Culture, 1979.

3. Sreenivasa Murthy, H. V., and R. A. Ramakrishnan. *History of Karnataka from the Earliest Times to the Present Day.* New Delhi: S. Chand, 1977.

4. Nilakanta Sastri, K. A. and G. Srinivasachari. *Advanced History of India.* New Delhi: Allied Publishers Ltd, 1980.

5. Ghurye, G. S. *Caste and Race India.* Mumbai: Popular Prakashan, 1979.

6. Deglurkar, G., M. K. Dhawalikar, and R. N. Gayakwad. *Prachin Bharatiya Itihas ani Sanskriti* [marathi]. Mumbai: Maharahtra Vidyapith Granthanirmiti, 1973.

7. Pissurlencar, P. (ed.). "Tombo das Rendas Que Sua Magestade Tem nas Terras de Salcete e Bardez e Nesta Ilha de Goa". In *Boletim do Instituto Vasco da Gama,* No. 68. Bastora (Goa): Instituto Vasco da Gama, 1952.

8. Gray, John. *Near Eastern Mythology.* London: Hamlyn, 1975.

9. Asthana, Shashi. *History and Archaeology of India's Contacts with Other Countries.* Delhi: B.R. Publishing Corporation, 1976.

10. Lamberg-Karlovsky, C. C., and Jeremy A. Sabloff. *Ancient Civilizations: The Near East and Mesoamerica.* New York: Benjamin/Cummings Publishing, 1979.

11. Dev, G. B. *Puratattva Vidya* [marathi]. [n/a], 1976.

12. Pusalkar, A., K. Munshi, and R. Majumdar. *History & Culture of Indian People, the Vedic Age.* Mumbai: Bharatiya Vidya Bhavan, 1971.

13. "Relatório da Comissão Encarregada de Demarcar os Terrenos da Província de Sattari – Aldeia Ambeacho-gor" [Part I]. In *Boletim Oficial.* Panaji (Goa): Governo de Goa, 1866.

14. See Parulekar's article. In *Navprabha* (marathi newspaper). Panaji (Goa): 27th July, 1978.

15. Letter of Dr. Parulekar, Scientist at the National Institute of Oceanography (Chemical Oceanography Division), Dona Paula, Goa.

16. Jordan, E. L., and P. S. Verma. *Invertebrate Zoology*. New Delhi: Sultan Chand and Company, 1976.

17. Oertel, Gerhard. "A Geologia do Distrito de Goa". In Assunção, C. F. Torre de, and A. V. T. Pinto Coelho. *Sobre a Petrografia do Distrito de Goa*. Lisboa: Junta de Investigação do Ultramar, 1960.

18. In *The Gazetteer of the Union Territory: Goa, Daman and Diu* (part I). Edited by V. T. Gune. Panaji (Goa): Government of the Union Territory of Goa, Daman and Diu, 1979.

19. Wadia, D. N. *Geology of India*. New Delhi: Tata-McGraw Hill, 1976.

20. Basham, A.L. (ed). *The Civilizations of Monsoon in Asia*. New Delhi: S. Chand and Company, 1974.

21. Hawkes, Jacquetta, and Leonard Woolley (eds.). *UNESCO History of Mankind: Prehistory and the Beginnings of Civilization* (vol. I). New Delhi: UNESCO, 1963.

22. Whitcomb Jr., John C., and Henry Madison Morris. *The Genesis Flood: The Biblical Record and Its Scientific Implications*. Madras (Chennai): India Bible League, 1980.

23. Ghirshman, R. *Iran*. New York: Penguin, 1978.

24. Lamberg-Karlovsky, C. C., and Jeremy A. Sabloff. *Ancient Civilizations: The Near East and Mesoamerica*. New York: Benjamin/Cummings Publishing, 1979.

25. Sankalia, H. D. *Prehistory and Protohistory in India and Pakistan*. Mumbai: Bombay University Press, 1963.

26. *The Gazetteer of the Union Territory: Goa , Daman and Diu* (part I, chap. I). Edited by V. T. Gune. Panaji (Goa): Government of the Union Territory of Goa, Daman and Diu, 1979.

27. *The Gazetteer of the Union Territory: Goa , Daman and Diu* (part I, chap. VI). Edited by V. T. Gune. Panaji (Goa): Government of the Union Territory of Goa, Daman and Diu, 1979.

28. Das, B.M. *Outlines of Physical Anthropology*. Allahabad: Kitab Mahal Agencies, 1980.

29. In *The Illustrated Weekly of India*. Mumbai, 26th August, 1981.

30. *Indian Archaeology: A Review*. Delhi: Archaeological Survey of India (1964-1965).

31. Childe, Gordon. *A Pré-História da Sociedade Europeia*. Lisboa: Europa-América, 1962.

32. Marshall, John. *Mohenjo-Daro and the Indus Civilization* (vol. I). Delhi: Indological Book House, 1973.

33. Hoffmann, J., and A. Van Emmelen, A.(eds.). *Encyclopaedia Mundarica*. Patna: Government Press, 1924.

34. Dikshitar, V. R. *Prehistoric South India*. Madras: N.S. Press, 1951.

35. Vasilyev, M. *Metals and Man*. Moscow: MIR Publishers, 1967.

36. Woolley, Charles Leonard. *The Sumerians*. Oxford: Clarendon Press, 1928.

37. Karve, Iravati. *Amachi Sanskriti* [marathi]. Pune: R J. Deshmukh & Company, 1960.

38. Kosambi, D. D. *Purankatha ani Vastavata* [marathi]. Mumbai: H. B. Ghanekar, 1962.

39. Nilakanta Sastri, K. A. *A History of South India*. New Delhi: Oxford University Press, 1975.

40. Mahajan, Vidya Dhar. *Ancient India*. New Delhi: Chand and Company, 1976.

41. Roy, Sarat Chandra. *The Mundas and their Country*. London: Asia Publishing House, 1970.

42. Dalton, Edward. *Descriptive Ethnology of Bengal*. Kolkata: Office of the Superintendent of Government Printing, 1872..

43. Names cited in the article on village and place named by P. P. Shirodkar. In *Sagar* [marathi periodical]. Panaji (Goa): 1982 (annual issue).

44. Satoskar, B. D. *Gomantak Prakriti va Sanskriti: Samaj Rachana ani Samaj Jivan* [marathi]. Pune: Shubhada Saraswat Publications, 1974.

45. Ghurye, G. S. *Gods and Men*. Mumbai: Popular Book Depot, 1962.

46. *Sahyadri Khanda (Skhanda Purana)* [marathi]. Translation from Sanskrit by V. D. Gaitonde. Mumbai: Katyayani Publications, 1972.

47. Gomes Pereira, R. *Hindu Temples and Deities.* Panaji (Goa): A. Gomes Pereira, 1981.

48. McEvedy, Colin & John Woodcock. *The Penguin Atlas of Ancient History.* Harmondsworth (U.K.): Penguin, 1967.

49. Rajwade, V. K. *Bharatiya Vivaha Samsthecha Itihas* [marathi]. Pune: Shrimati Shanta Rajwade, 1976.

50. Rajwade, V. K. *Rajwade Lekha Sangraha* [marathi]. Pune: Smt. Shanat Rajwade, 1976.

51. Dhere, R. C. *Lajja-Gauri* [marathi]. Pune: Shri Vidya Prakashan, 1978.

52. Pissurlencar, P. (ed.). "Tombo das Rendas Que Sua Magestade Tem nas Terras de Salcete e Bardes e Nesta Ilha de Goa". In *Boletim do Instituto Vasco da Gama,* No.68. Bastora (Goa): Instituto Vasco da Gama, 1952.

53. Fleet, John F. "Chiplun Copper-Plate Grant of Pulikeshin II (ca. 609-642 CE)". In *Epigraphia Indica* (vol. III). Calcutta: Office of the Superintendent of Government Printing, 1894-95.

54. Shastri Joshi, Mahadev (ed.). *Bharatiya Sanskriti Kosh: Asur ani Asurjamati.* [marathi]. Pune: Bharatiya Sanskriti Kosh Mandal, 1962.

55. Nadagonde, G. *Bharatiya Adivasi* [marathi]. Pune: Continental Prakashan, 1979.

56. Saldanha, J. A.. *The Indian Caste.* Mumbai: Siris, 1904.

57. Nilakanta Sastri, K.A. *Development of Religion in South India.* Madras (Chennai): Orient Longmans, 1963.

58. Pissurlekar, P. "Inscriçoes Pré-Portuguesas de Goa (Breves Notas)", in *O Oriente Português,* No. 22. Bastora (Goa): Tip. Rangel, 1938.

59. *Sahyadri Khanda (Skhanda Purana)* [marathi]. Translation from Sanskrit by V. D. Gaitonde. Bombay: Katyayani Publications, 1972.

60. Valaulikar, V. V. (Shenoi Goembab). *Goenkaranchi Goeam Bhaili Vosnnuk* [konkani]. Mumbai: Hindi Bhaval Jaldhar, 1928.

61. Moortgat, A. *The Art of Ancient Mesopotamia: The Classical Art of the Near East.* London: Phaidon, 1969.

62. Delaporte, L. *Mesopotamia: The Babylonian and Assyrian Civilizations.* London: Kegan Paul, Trench, Trubner & Company, 1925.

63. Waddell, L. A. *The Makers of Civilization.* New Delhi: S. Chand, 1968.

64. Dikshit, Shankar. *Jyotirvilas athava Ratrichi Don Ghatka Mauj* [marathi]. Pune: R. S. Dikshit, 1890.

65. Lansing, Elizabeth. *The Sumerians: Inventors and Builders.* London: Cassell, 1974.

66. Hawkes, Jacquetta Hopkins. *The First Great Civilizations. Life in Mesopotamia, the Indus Valley and Egypt.* London: Hutchinson, 1973.

67. Radhakrishna, V. "Bali Katha". In *Gomantaka* (marathi newspaper). Panaji (Goa): [n/a], 1972

68. Lopes Mendes, Antonio. *A Índia Portuguesa* (vol. II). Lisboa: Sociedade de Geografia, 1886.

69. Sastri, Sakuntala Rao. *Women in the Vedic Age.* Mumbai: Bharatiya Vidya Bhavan, 1952.

70. Altekar, A. S. *State and Government in Ancient India.* Delhi: Motilal Banarsidas, 1958.

71. Mahajan, Vidya Dhar. *Ancient India.* New Delhi: Chand and Company, 1976.

72. Kosambi, D. D. *An Introduction to the Study of Indian History.* Mumbai: Popular Prakashan, 1975.

73. Garde, D. K. *Prachin Bharatitya Rajya Vichar* [marathi]. Pune: Popular Prakahan, 1979.

74. Kalyanaraman, A. *Aryatarangini* [marathi]. Mumbai: Asia Publishing House, 1969.

75. Shastri Joshi, Mahadev (ed.). *Bharatiya Sanskriti Kosh – Somavansha* [marathi, vol. 10]. Pune: Bharatiya Sanskriti Kosh Mandal, 1979.

375

76. Naik, K. D. *Gomantakachi Sanskritik Ghadan* [marathi]. Margao (Goa): Gomatak Vidya Niketan, 1968.

77. Kosambi, D. D. *Dakshini Saraswat: Purankatha ani Vastavata* [marathi]. Mumbai: H. B. Gokhale, 1962.

78. Ghantkar, Gajanana. *An Introduction to Goan Marathi Records in Halakannada Script.* Panaji (Goa): Srinivas C. B. Caculo, 1973.

79. Dikshit, M. *Bharatavarshache Bhuvarnan.* Mumbai: [n/a].

80. *Sahyadri Khanda (Skhanda Purana)* [marathi]. Translation from Sanskrit by V. D. Gaitonde. Bombay: Katyayani Publications, 1972.

81. Bhargava, M. L. *The Geography of Rigvedic India.* Lucknow: The Upper India Publishing House, 1964.

82. Vaze. K. V. *Hindi Shilashastra.* Pune: D. K. Sathe, 1928.

83. Shastri Joshi, Mahadev (ed.). *Bharatiya Sanskriti Kosh – Satwat Sampradaya* [marathi]. Pune: Bharatiya Sanskriti Kosh Mandal, 1976.

84. Valaulikar, V. V. (Shenoi Goembab). *Kanhi Marathi Lekha* [marathi]. Mumbai: Pungami, 1945.

85. Gokhale, S. *Purabhilekha Vidya* [marathi]. Pune: Continental Prakashan, 1975

86. Mirashi, V. V. *Satavahana ani Pashchimi Kshatrapa: Yancha Itihas ani Koriv Lekha* [marathi]. Mumbai: Maharashtra State Board for Literature and Culture, 1979.

87. Pereira, Gerald A. *An outline of Pre-Portuguese History of Goa.* Vasco da Gama (Goa): G. Pereira, 1973.

88. See P. Pissurlencar's articles. In *O Oriente Português* (No. 6, 18 & 22). Bastora (Goa): Tip. Rangel, 1934.

89. A quarterly publication of Historical Archives, Archaeological Museum, Panaji, Goa, vol. III, nos. 1-4, pp. 42-43. Documents No. 3440 dated 23/11/1782 issued by Official of Ruler of Soundhe to the Portuguese Secretary of State informing that the tobacco brought by the Knot (contractor) Chandra Shenvi Dhumo at Fonda has not been detained.

90. Prabhudesai, P. V. *Adishaktiche Vishwaswarup Arthant Devikosh* [marathi,

Vol. IV]. Pune: S H. Dhupkar, [n/a/].

91. Le May, Reginald. *The Culture of South-East Asia. The Heritage of India*. London: George Allen and Unwin,1954.

92. Altekar, A. S. *State and Government in Ancient India*. Banaras: Motilal Banarsidas, 1955.

93. A quarterly publication of Historical Archives, Archaeological Museum, Panaji, Goa, vol. II, nos. 1-3.

94. Panase, M. G. *Yadavakalin Maharashtra (1000-1350)* [marathi]. Mumbai: V. V. Bhat, 1963.

95. Dikshit, G.S. *Local Self-government in Medieval Karnataka*. Dharwar: Karnatak University, 1964.

96. In *Epigraphia Indica*, Vol. XXI. Delhi: Archaeological Survey of India, 1931.

97. In *Epigraphia Indica*, Vol. XXXI. Delhi: Archaeological Survey of India, 1957.

98. Gune, V. *Ancient Shrines of Goa; a Pictorial Survey*. Panjim (Goa): Publications Unit, Dept. of Information, Govt. of Goa, Daman & Diu, 1965.

99. Shastri Joshi, Mahadev (ed.). *Bharatiya Sanskriti Kosh – Navadi Nalakavya* [marathi, Vol. 4]. Pune: Bharatiya Sanskriti Kosh Mandal, 1967.

100. Wakankar, L. S. *Nagari Lipi: Ugam va Vikas* [marathi]. [n/a/], 1939.

101. Deglurkar, G., M. K. Dhawalikar, and R. N. Gayakwad. *Prachin Bharatiya Itihas ani Sanskriti* [marathi]. Mumbai: Maharahtra Vidyapith Granthanirmiti, 1973.

102. Pereira, Gerald A. *An outline of Pre-Portuguese History of Goa. New India Antiquity* (vol. IV). Vasco da Gama (Goa): G. A. Pereira, 1973.

103. Altekar, A. S. *A History of Village Communities in Western India*. Mumbai: Oxford University Press, 1927.

104. Venkata Ramanappa. M.N. *Outlines of South Indian History*. Delhi: Vikas Publishing House, 1977.

105. Mirashi, V. V. *Silahara Samrajya va Tyamchya Koriv Lekhancha Itihas* [marathi]. Mumbai: Maharashtra State Board for Literature and Culture, 1974.

106. See Benjamin Lewis Rice (ed.). *Epigraphia Carnatica* (12 vols.). Mysore: Director of the Mysore Archaeological Department, 1894-1905.

107. A quarterly publication of Directorate of Archives and Archaeology (Museum). Panaji (Goa), May-June-July, 1977.

108. Moraes, George M. *The Kadamba Kula: a History of Ancient and Medieval Karnataka.* New Delhi: Asian Educational Services, 1931.

109. Xavier, Filipe Nery. *Descrição das Aldeias e Comunidades das Velhas Conquistas.* Curtorim (Goa). [n/a/]

110. Xavier, Filipe Nery. *Leis Peculiares das Novas Conquistas* (vol. II). Nova Goa (Goa): Imprensa Nacional, 1850.

111. Gomes Pereira, R. *Goa Gaunkari: The Old Village Associations.* Panaji (Goa): A. Gomes Pereira, 1981.

112. *Epigraphia Indica,* vol. XXXVII. Delhi: Archaeological Survey of India, 1967–1968.

113. Gosavi, R. *Pancha Upasanapantha* [marathi]. Pune: Prasad Prakashan, 1979.

114. *Guru Paramparamrita* [marathi]. Pune: [n/a/], 1904.

115. Sharma, D.S. *Essence of Hinduism.* Mumbai: Bharatiya Vidya Bhavan, 1971.

116. Diskalkar, D. B. *Maharashtracha Prachin Itihas ani Sanskriti* [marathi]. Pune: Pune University, 1964.

117. Burgess, J. (ed.). *Indian Antiquary* (vol. III). Delhi: Swati Publishers, 1964.

118. Bhide, R. G. *Vijayanagarache Samrajya* [marathi]. Pune: Chihagam Prakashan,1963.

119. Satoskar, B. D. *Gomantak Prakriti va Sanskriti: Samaj Rachana ani Samaj Jivan* [marathi]. Pune: Shubhada Saraswat Publications, 1974.

120. Shastri Joshi, Mahadev (ed.). *Bharatiya Sanskriti Kosh: Havig Brahman.* [marathi, Vol. 10]. Pune: Bharatiya Sanskriti Kosh Mandal, 1979.

121. Kare, G. H. *Madhyayugin Dakshin Bharatachya Itihasache Purave.* Pune: A. V. Patwardhan, [n/a/].

122. Mattos, J. *Vida e Crescimento das Cidades: Introdução ao Urbanismo*. Rio de Janeiro: Globo, 1952.